THE OFFICIAL QUARKXPRESS HANDBOOK
Macintosh 3.1 Edition

The Official QuarkXPress Handbook

Macintosh 3.1 Edition

Diane Burns

Sharyn Venit

BANTAM BOOKS

NEW YORK · TORONTO · LONDON · SYDNEY · AUCKLAND

THE OFFICIAL QUARKXPRESS HANDBOOK
Macintosh 3.1 Edition
A Bantam Book
March 1992

QuarkXPress and QuarkXTension
are registered trademarks of Quark, Inc.

*Throughout the book, the trade names and trademarks of some companies
and products have been used, and no such uses are intended to convey
endorsement of or other affiliations with the book or software.*

Foreword

From the time Quark released the first version of QuarkXPress, our company has been committed to professionalism in the publishing world. A commitment to professionalism in publishing means a commitment to the principle of the free press. Publishing technology is too important to be placed in the hands of a few. Small publishers need as much access to affordable quality tools as large publishers do. Our users include nonprofit organizations helping to make this a better world, educational institutions working with our youth, small businesses concerned with profit margin, and special interest groups with information to share.

At the same time, it is critical that publishing solutions include the full complement of features from layout to design to color separation. The list of professional publishers who use QuarkXPress stands as testimony that QuarkXPress is truly an "industrial-strength" tool: Time, Inc., Tribune Media Services, Mattel Toys, CBS Records, Landor Associates, and many others.

We are very pleased to have been involved in this Bantam book project with two writers I have known and respected for many years. I sought them out years ago as industry experts and experienced users of publishing tools to show them early versions of QuarkXPress, and collect their praises and criticisms. While the publishing world has buzzed about what QuarkXPress can do, can't do, or ought to do, *we have been listening.* In QuarkXPress Version 3.1, basic features have been improved and dozens of new features have been added.

The real value of this book is that it incorporates the practical experiences and knowledge of the authors and other QuarkXPress experts, readily serving as your own "off the shelf" consultants.

—*Fred Ebrahimi, President, Quark, Inc.*

Preface

The *Official QuarkXPress Handbook* is a complete reference designed to answer your questions about all QuarkXPress 3.1 commands, tools, and techniques. The book is an invaluable tool for professionals who use the program every day, and will be useful to anyone seeking professional results. It can also be used as a training manual for beginning QuarkXPress users, or as a reference for professional designers who need to know the capabilities of QuarkXPress 3.1.

The book includes expert advice about all QuarkXPress features, tips about increasing speed and productivity, and specific techniques used to create special effects or solve particular problems. The beginning user will quickly learn how to use QuarkXPress tools and commands. The intermediate user will learn new and valuable techniques for producing complicated documents. The advanced user will receive expert tips on how to use QuarkXPress more effectively, and gain insight into how experienced publishers solve complex problems with QuarkXPress.

How This Book Is Organized

We have organized this book into three parts which follow a brief introductory chapter that describes QuarkXPress and the production process.

Part I: Using QuarkXPress

The first seven chapters provide an overview of the tools, commands, and features available in QuarkXPress 3.1. In Chapter 1 you will find an introduction to basic Macintosh operations and an overview of the screen display in QuarkXPress including the Document window, and the various palettes, including those new to version 3.1. This chapter defines the basic terminology that is particular to the Macintosh and QuarkXPress.

Chapter 2 goes through the preliminary steps in starting a new document and positioning elements on a page. Chapter 3 continues the page layout process in adding pages to a document, creating multiple master pages, editing items on a page, and changing QuarkXPress *defaults*. Chapters 4 and 5 give detailed descriptions of the commands used to handle text. Chapter 6 describes how graphics and imported pictures can be handled. Chapter 7 discusses all of the issues related to printing a document.

Part II: Advanced Techniques

The next seven chapters describe some of the more advanced techniques and procedures that can be used to save time or solve difficult problems. Chapter 8 describes how to set up a template system, with some design tips included. Chapter 9 is full of tips for minimizing the time and trouble involved in laying out pages. Chapter 10 offers more tips specific to handling text created on a mainframe computer or in a database, and Chapter 11 offers tips specific to typography. Chapter 12 includes some special tips on handling graphics, and Chapter 13 covers using QuarkXPress for printing color separations. Chapter 14 offers ideas about project management and file organization methods for large projects or workgroup environments.

Part III: Case Studies

The impact of desktop publishing on designers, professional publishing companies, corporate publications departments, and self-publishing associations and individuals is best seen through the experiences of those who have made the transition from traditional methods to electronic publishing over the past few years. Chapters 15 through 17 of this book offer seven case studies of professional publications that were once produced using traditional methods and are now produced using QuarkXPress. For each example you will find descriptions of how the publisher organized the project and/or handled tricky page elements.

Appendix A lists some of the QuarkXPress shortcuts we use most frequently. Appendix B covers International versions of QuarkXPress and Appendix C describes some of the QuarkXPress Xtension products that are available from other vendors.

Conventions Used in This Book

We have included icons or symbols throughout this book to make it easy to find topics or interpret terms that apply to icons you will see on the screen while working in QuarkXPress. Most of the symbols embedded in the text are self-explanatory in that they look like the element they are intended to represent, such as the ⌘ symbol for the Command key.

Borrowing the convention used in the QuarkXPress manuals, we have used a special arrow symbol (→) as a shorthand method of referencing commands and their menus. Instead of saying "...choose the Cut command from the Edit menu..." we say simply "...choose Edit → Cut..."

We have added three icons in the left margin as reference aids:

The 3.1 icon, shown left, appears next to paragraphs that introduce or describe features that are new or changed in QuarkXPress Version 3.1.

A tip icon appears next to paragraphs that describe the fastest method to accomplish a specific task, or that describe tricks that can make production more efficient.

The alert icon appears next to paragraphs that mention things you should not or cannot do in QuarkXPress, or things that might happen if you change something on a page. In most cases these are simply things you need to be aware of in making decisions.

Acknowledgements

The *Official QuarkXPress Handbook* was made possible thanks to the cooperation and participation of a large number of people, only some of whom could be named here.

We first thank the contributors to Part III of the book for their time and efforts in supplying examples of documents they have created using QuarkXPress. The final list of examples was picked from a longer list of documents that included wonderful examples of design and production expertise, but in the interest of space and time we limited our selections to one from each genre (one magazine, one newsletter, one book, etc.).

For contributions to Part III we acknowledge Gary Ferguson and Wendy Croft at Landor Associates, Bob Clifford, Wade Lapan of Tribune Media Services, Rick Young, Rand Worrel, and Luis Solorzano from Mattel Toys, Barri Klingaman from *MacWEEK*, Tamura Westmark, Christine Homan and Michael Grossman of *Entertainment Weekly*, Diane Croce and Barry DeJaynes from Croce Advertising, Amy Jordan of Rocky Mountain News, Rick Boyde, and all the support staff who helped assemble sample disks and pages.

The people at Quark, Inc., were extremely helpful in supplying names of QuarkXPress users, Beta copies of the software, and early drafts of their manuals for the product—this in the midst of their own heavy production schedule for meeting their own release deadlines. They also took the time to read our first draft, and their comments are responsible for the improvements embodied in this published version of the book. We especially thank Dee Buchanan for her assistance throughout the project; John Cruise, Jeff Gregory, Eric Fife and Paula Budzak for reviewing the manuscript; Johanna McLaverty (IRL QSS Ireland) for providing information on International Versions; and Mark Niemann-Ross for providing information on QuarkXTensions. We especially thank Fred Ebrahimi for his enthusiasm and interest in this project.

We also thank our readers—Dorothy Webster, who read the manuscript as an experienced Macintosh user who has never used QuarkXPress, and David Park Brown, who read the manuscript as an experienced QuarkXPress user. Their comments on the opening chapters lead to significant clarifications for new users and for experienced QuarkXPress users.

The production group at TechArt (San Francisco) was consistently calm and courteous in meeting the last-minute deadlines that always result when the writers keep writing and the editors keep editing up to the last minute. In particular we thank Susan Equitz and Kim Nogay who were responsible for the layout of the book.

Finally, we would like to thank a group that is not often mentioned in book acknowledgements—the people at Bantam Electronic Publishing and their freelance editors, especially Michael Roney who (as the primary editor and project manager) was a great support throughout the project.

We would have liked to include every individual who helped on this book by name, however in some cases the help came anonymously through the companies we contacted, and some companies prefer to be listed by company name only rather than credit individuals who were assigned the task of helping us. If you helped in any way with this book, please know that we are very appreciative.

Contents

THE OFFICIAL QUARKXPRESS HANDBOOK
Macintosh 3.1 Edition

Introduction

QuarkXPress is a page composition application that began as part of the "desktop publishing" revolution. Desktop publishing was kicked off in 1985 with the introduction of the Macintosh and the LaserWriter printer. These combined technologies made it possible to produce type and graphics with an efficiency and convenience never before available. Since then, the combination of capabilities encompassed by the term "desktop publishing" has had a tremendous impact on designers, typesetters, professional publishers, corporate publications departments, and small businesses, as well as those of us who dream of producing our own great novels.

QuarkXPress is a powerful tool that can supplement or replace the traditional tools for handling text, graphics, and page layout. It lets you compose complete documents—including text and graphics—and view full pages on the screen before printing them out to a high-resolution printer or typesetter. You can incorporate text and graphics that were created in other applications, or you can create finished pages using QuarkXPress alone.

QuarkXPress incorporates many commands that perform functions once served by the layout artist's tools and resources: pens, pressure-sensitive tapes, knives, wax, blue-line boards, and acetate overlays. These traditional tools were, and still are, used to lay out typeset galleys of type, photostats of line art, and halftones of photographs.

The ability to merge text and graphics on a screen is not unique to desktop systems. Professional page-composition systems have been doing this for years. *Time* magazine, for example, started composing its pages on a mainframe computer over 20 years ago. Recently, *Time* announced that two years of research had yielded a new publishing system for the magazine. The new system will be Macintosh computers running QuarkXPress.

The primary benefit of using QuarkXPress and the Macintosh computer for publishing is that it affords more control than traditional methods—control over every phase of the process of publishing—at a lower cost, and with greater quality and flexibility than ever before. The benefits are not solely economic. Designers can experiment more freely, editors find that they have more control over content and format, and the time spent preparing documents for printing has been reduced significantly.

This introduction presents an overview of the features of QuarkXPress by first analyzing the anatomy of a page produced using QuarkXPress and then stepping you through production of a typical document. (The steps in the production cycle are keyed to later chapters in this book.)

System Requirements

QuarkXPress runs on a Macintosh computer under System 6.05 (or higher version). The minimum system requirements include 2MB of memory (RAM) and 2.5MB free space on a hard disk drive. In this chapter you will learn why you might want to invest in a more expanded system to run QuarkXPress. You will also learn what other peripherals can be useful in creating and producing documents.

If you are already familiar with QuarkXPress 3.0 or earlier versions, and if you are already using a Macintosh II (or faster model) with at least 2MB of RAM, you can skip this introduction and go to Chapter 1 for more specific descriptions of some of the new interface features added in QuarkXPress 3.1.

Anatomy of a QuarkXPress Document

A QuarkXPress document might be composed of text and graphics created in QuarkXPress as well as text and graphics brought in from other programs. Figure I-1 shows a typical page created using QuarkXPress.

The body copy (text) was typed in a word processing program, then imported into QuarkXPress. The kimono graphic was created in an illustration program, then sized and cropped in QuarkXPress. Some of the short text elements such as the rotated banner across the left side of the page were typed directly into QuarkXPress. Hairline rules and boxes were added using QuarkXPress' graphics tools. Footers and automatic page numbering were set up on the document's *master pages*—special pages that contain elements that will appear on *every* page of the document (master pages are discussed in more detail in Chapter 3).

Banner typed and rotated in QuarkXPress

EPS graphic created in Adobe Illustrator and imported into QuarkXPress.

Article typed in Microsoft Word and imported into QuarkXPress.

Footer text, typed on master pages in QuarkXPress, appears on every page of document.

Figure I-1   Anatomy of a page created using QuarkXPress

In Chapter 2, we present a more detailed description of how a page is created in QuarkXPress.

Desktop vs. Traditional Publishing

Desktop publishing with QuarkXPress merges traditions from four different disciplines—typesetting, graphic design, printing, and computing—each with its own set of technical terms and standards.

Professionals from each of these fields are finding that they need to add a few terms to their vocabulary in order to "speak" desktop publishing. They are gradually discovering that terms like *leading* and *line spacing* mean the same thing and that each area of experience has something to teach the other.

Design Traditions

Designers take a lot of pride in their ability to interpret a client's tastes and ideas and translate them into beautiful finished products. The process of putting design ideas down on paper has been painstaking, time-consuming, and expensive.

QuarkXPress makes it possible to rough out design ideas quickly and deliver what looks like finished work rather than the traditional penciled sketches that are commonly used to present ideas in the preliminary design stages. In many cases, the efforts that go into producing a design idea with a computer are not lost—the same files can be fine-tuned for the final production. Furthermore, the same files can be duplicated and modified for other documents in the same series, or similar documents in another series.

The fact that even amateurs can produce nice-looking designs with a computer program seems a bit frightening to professionals, but good design will always require some of the knowledge and skills that are part and parcel of the trade. You'll learn some of these principles in this book, as well as the production methods that will help you blend the designer's tradition of excellence with the business community's demand for expedience.

Typesetting Traditions

One advantage of QuarkXPress over its competitors is precision in typographic controls. It lets you set the spacing between lines and letters in finer increments than are possible with most other page-composition packages, for instance. Furthermore, with QuarkXPress you can set the width or depth of text precisely—in numbers—rather than using the less precise visual alignment of an on-screen ruler. Traditional typesetters, therefore, need simply to learn how to apply their traditional measures using QuarkXPress commands. Meanwhile, desktop publishers who are already familiar with QuarkXPress can learn something from the traditions of typesetting. You'll learn some of the special terminology and functions related to typesetting as well as some tricks of the typesetter's trade later in this book.

Printing Traditions

Laser printers make it possible to print the entire image of the page—including halftones—directly on whatever color paper you choose. Instead of reproducing your master copy using xerographic or offset printing equipment, you can print out hundreds of "originals" on a laser printer, ready for immediate distribution. The production of hundreds of originals is not desktop publishing's primary benefit, however, since in most cases you will find that xerographic or offset printing equipment is better suited for high print runs, special paper, sizes other than 8.5-by-11-inch finals, and color reproduction.

Whether you use camera-ready mechanicals and an offset printer or a master copy and xerographic equipment, the final result depends on the condition of the original page. Good paste-up artists have the skill of surgeons in meticulously trimming typeset galleys and photostats of line art, painstakingly aligning them (horizontally on the page, vertically with the margins, precise distances from each other), and burnishing down the waxed pieces so they will not fall out of alignment during all the handling on the way to the camera. This, then, is a primary feature and revolutionary contribution of desktop publishing to the history of publishing: the ability to produce clean, camera-ready master pages, including text and graphics, without the marks and hazards of physically pasted-up boards.

Desktop publishing does not always preclude the need for paste-up, nor does it guarantee perfect reproduction under some conditions. You will find—as designers, typesetters, artists, and printers well know—that the camera (used in making plates for offset printing) does not see the image the same way you do. Black text on a gray background might be easy for your eye to read on the laser-printed master, but the camera that produces the negatives might have trouble keeping the gray tone without overexposing the text.

You'll learn how to prepare your QuarkXPress files for output for offset printing, as well as some of the vocabulary you will need to communicate with your printer.

Computer Traditions

The final elements in our "melting pot" derive directly from the computer industry. Pixels and screen fonts, ports and baud rates, icons and menus are all terms that you will quickly become familiar with as you move into the realm of desktop publishing.

You will find throughout this book that we draw clear analogies between the various terms used by different industries to describe the basic concepts underlying desktop publishing: the assembly of finished pages of text and graphics.

Overview of Publishing with QuarkXPress

QuarkXPress can assist in the total publishing process: formulating an idea, creating the document, editing and formatting it, and printing it out. QuarkXPress brings together many functions that were once divided between different people at different locations.

For example, before desktop publishing, a designer would have created comprehensives (samples) with pens and markers, a typist might have typed in the text of a newsletter and sent the file—either on paper or on disk—to the typesetter for formatting and typesetting as per the designer's specifications. Meanwhile, the graphics department used a computer or just pens and ink to create the graphic images, and sent them to an outside service to be photostatted to the size needed. Eventually, the galleys of type and the photostats of the figures landed on a drafting table where the layout artist used X-ACTO knives and wax to trim the paper and paste it down on boards to create final, camera-ready boards.

Now, the same person might type in the text, draw the graphics, and compose the pages directly on the screen using QuarkXPress. The fact that one person is performing the entire sequence of steps does not mean that the steps themselves are much different. The one person responsible for the entire production is likely to be strong in some areas, weak in others. For this reason, many desktop publishing departments still divide the tasks of desktop publishing between different people. Nevertheless, when the production team is small (as is common in desktop environments) there can be weak spots in the production cycle—areas in which no one on the team has experience. This book can help you by providing tips in those areas of expertise that you and your team might lack.

Following is a quick overview of the steps involved in producing a document, from verifying that you have all the necessary disk files, to printing the final copy. Later chapters provide more details and tips on how to execute each step.

The steps of creating a document with QuarkXPress fall into three areas:

1. Designing and planning your document.
2. Constructing the text and graphics with QuarkXPress or other applications.
3. Producing the final page layouts in QuarkXPress.

Once you understand the basic steps in creating a document, you can fit the detailed steps explained in the rest of this book into the overall process.

Whether you are producing a layout from design to final camera-ready mechanicals on your own, or working with a team, an overview of all of the steps involved in a typical production cycle will help you to set up an efficient production schedule. The steps outlined under the next headings do not necessarily occur sequentially or in the order shown. Some steps can take place at the same time, and some projects will call for a slightly different sequence. A typical production schedule showing the relationships between the steps is shown in Figure I-2.

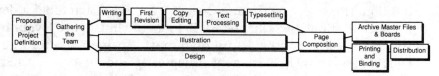

Figure I-2 A typical production schedule.

The following overview of the steps involved in producing a document includes references to other chapters, which discuss each step in more detail.

Design Pages and Typography

Document design really begins with an idea and an outline, but for our purposes we jump into the process at the point where the editor hands the written manuscript (and, hopefully, the text on disk) over to the design department. Here, the designer develops the design specifications, including:

- Typefaces, sizes, and styles for different elements within the text.
- Basic text format. Will the paragraphs have a first-line indent? What will be the space between paragraphs? Will the text be justified? Will headings be flush left or centered?
- Basic page layout or grid, including page size, margins, orientation, number of columns, and positions of other non-printing guides. This is some of the information required before you create a new QuarkXPress document.
- Final (maximum) size of illustrations, as well as typefaces, type sizes, and type styles to be used within the illustrations and in the captions.

- Final page count, or the range of pages expected to be filled. This will help you decide whether and how to divide a long publication into smaller documents or sections, as well as help estimate the printing costs.

Designing has traditionally been performed after the text is written, since the design itself may be affected by the content and structure of the text. If the authors know what the design specifications are before they write the text, however, they can participate in the production by setting tabs and other format requirements as they go along.

Traditionally, design specifications have been handwritten or typed and illustrated as rough pencil sketches with penciled lines indicating text position. However, you can use QuarkXPress as a design tool for developing specifications (see Chapter 8). Before individual page layout begins, the page design can be set up on a master page (Chapter 2) or in a QuarkXPress template document (Chapter 8), and the type specifications can be captured in a QuarkXPress style sheet (Chapter 4).

Collect Text

You can type text in QuarkXPress much the way you type text using your word processor. Although you can build documents from scratch using QuarkXPress alone, often QuarkXPress documents are composed of text that has been typed in other programs.

For instance, most contemporary authors use a computer to write the text, or someone else who has a word processor is paid to type the manuscript. Even if the word processing was not done on a Macintosh computer, any text can be converted or telecommunicated to a Macintosh and then be imported into QuarkXPress.

A design editor usually marks the author's unformatted printed manuscript for formatting according to the design specifications. With QuarkXPress, you can format text using the style sheet feature (Chapter 4). This simplifies the process of formatting text. The designer can describe in detail each different format only once for entry into a QuarkXPress style sheet. The text can then be marked up with simple style names that can be applied using keyboard shortcuts or menu commands in QuarkXPress.

Collect Illustrations

You can draw simple shapes—lines, boxes, polygons, and circles—in QuarkXPress, but you can also import more complicated graphics or other graphic formats (including black-and-white halftone images and color illustrations) that were created using other programs.

Since QuarkXPress lets you import files created with other software programs, you can create the illustrations using the graphics program best suited for each (see Chapter 6):

- PostScript-type drawing packages, like Adobe Illustrator or Aldus FreeHand, are best suited for line art and technical illustrations.
- Scanners can digitize photographs or line drawings that can be traced, creating fine line art using PostScript drawing programs.
- Paint-type programs are best suited for working with digitized images and for "fine art" illustrations, such as Digital Darkroom, ColorStudio, and Photoshop.
- Spreadsheets or charting programs are most efficient for charts that are derived from tables of numbers.
- Some illustrations or graphic elements can be added directly in QuarkXPress.

Build the Pages in QuarkXPress

After the text and graphics have been prepared in other programs, you start QuarkXPress and begin building the document. In this step, you may begin with either a new file or a template file that is already set up with the design specifications (see Chapters 2 and 8).

Define Master Pages

Master pages are nonprinting pages that automatically format document pages. Any item you position on a master page will appear on all other pages in the document associated with that master page. The master pages can include running heads, footers, and any other elements that appear on every page. Master pages also contain the underlying grid—an invisible baseline grid for text plus a matrix of margin guides, column guides, and ruler guides that appear on the screen but are not printed. This grid can be used to align objects consistently on all pages of the document.

Add Text and Pictures

The basic building blocks on any page in QuarkXPress are called *boxes*. You create text boxes to hold text, and picture boxes to hold imported graphics. You use the Get Text and Get Picture commands to import text and graphics files created in other programs. You can add other text and graphic elements using QuarkXPress' tools.

With QuarkXPress you can arrange text in columns and jump text from one page to another, including nonsequential pages. You can use the automatic features to wrap text around graphics or anchor specific graphics frames to captions within the text (see Chapter 3).

Once the text and graphics are in QuarkXPress, you can easily move them around on the page, change their size and shape to fit the space allowed on individual pages, duplicate them, or delete them. QuarkXPress can also rotate text and graphics. In addition, QuarkXPress can adjust the contrast and line screening for grayscale TIFF images (Chapter 6).

Create and Use a Library

Besides importing elements from other applications, you can create libraries of elements collected into QuarkXPress and easily share them among documents through the new Library feature (see Chapter 3).

Edit Text

You can edit the text using all of the normal edit commands such as Copy, Cut, and Paste. QuarkXPress also lets you perform functions normally associated with word processing only, such as Find/Change text (such as global search and replace), Check Spelling, and Add Dictionary Terms to a custom dictionary (Chapter 4). You can also Edit H&J Specifications (the hyphenation and justification specifications) to adjust the appearance of the text.

You can use commands in the Style menu to format text, or create a style sheet to simplify and speed up the process of formatting text (Chapter 4). QuarkXPress offers a wide range of typographic controls that can be applied to text, including customization of kerning and tracking tables (Chapter 5).

Edit Graphics

Besides normal page-layout activities such as positioning, sizing, and cropping pictures, QuarkXPress lets you rotate graphics, adjust the contrast and brightness settings of images, and select from one of several screen patterns for halftone printing (see Chapter 6).

Add Color and Edit Colors

You can create colors and apply them to selected text, lines, or box frames or backgrounds (see Chapter 7), then print color separations for either spot-color printing or process-color printing (Chapter 13).

Print Drafts and Finals

You should expect to print a document many times before you print the final version. Even if you have edited thoroughly the text and graphics before placing them on a page, you still need to print drafts of the QuarkXPress version of the pages to review for format and alignment. QuarkXPress is a WYSIWYG program: "What you see (on the screen) is what you get (on the printed page)." However, there are always minor differences between the screen and the printed page because of the differences in resolution. These discrepancies cannot be seen until you print the document.

After each draft printing, there will be the normal rounds of proofing and then many of the steps outlined above will be repeated as the text and graphics are corrected and massaged until the document is perfect.

Lastly, you will print the final camera-ready masters (including color separations). These might be printed on a laser printer at 300–600 dots per inch resolution, or they can be printed at higher resolutions on an image-setter.

Final Reproduction, Binding, and Distribution

In most cases, the final document will be reproduced from the single final copy printed from QuarkXPress. This master copy might simply be reproduced on a photocopier, or it can be offset printed from camera-ready masters produced by QuarkXPress. You can print QuarkXPress pages out as negatives on film and you can print color separations directly from QuarkXPress, thereby saving steps normally left to the offset print shop. Chapters 7 and 13 describe QuarkXPress' printing capabilities.

When the project is finished, copy all of the files related to that document onto one or more floppy disks or removable hard disks for archiving. Chapter 14 offers more tips on archiving and moving files.

Desktop Publishing Systems

One characteristic of desktop publishing is that it is not a single-product application. QuarkXPress is just one part of a complete system that requires additional software, powerful hardware, new input devices, and high-resolution output devices for a total solution.

QuarkXPress and Other Software

The three key application areas in document production are text processing, artwork (illustrations), and page layout. You can handle all of these elements using only QuarkXPress and a scanner, or you can supplement the capabilities of QuarkXPress by adding other specialized applications to create text and graphics that can be imported into a page in QuarkXPress.

Word Processing

QuarkXPress can import text created by most word processing programs on the Macintosh, including MacWrite, MacWrite II, Microsoft Word, Microsoft Works, Microsoft Write, WordPerfect, and WriteNow. You can also import ASCII files from any word processor (including non-Macintosh applications, after transferring the text to a Macintosh disk), data saved in ASCII format from a spreadsheet or database program, and text that has been telecommunicated from another computer.

QuarkXPress' text formatting features offer a wider range of typographic controls than most word processors, so you will probably want to do most of the formatting using QuarkXPress commands. However, you can format text before importing it into QuarkXPress by using any supported word processor's formatting commands, or you can format text in any word processor by embedding ASCII codes that will be translated into formats when you import the text into QuarkXPress (see Chapters 4 and 10).

Paint and Drawing Applications

Graphic applications offer a wider range of drawing tools and commands than QuarkXPress. By working directly with a drawing or painting program you can access sophisticated features such as curved lines, air-brush effects, and pixel-by-pixel image manipulation. You can also use a paint program to clean up images that have been digitized through a scanner.

The types of graphics programs that can be imported into QuarkXPress include Paint (bitmap) graphics created by programs like MacPaint and SuperPaint; TIFF line art, grayscale, or color images created by scanning applications, and that can be edited in programs like Adobe Photoshop and LetraSet ColorStudio; PICT illustrations from MacDraw II and Cricket Draw; PostScript (EPS) illustrations from Adobe Illustrator and Aldus FreeHand; and EPS formats imported from an IBM PC environment.

The formats listed here are described in more detail in Chapter 6.

Equipment Configurations

Understanding the uses of and differences between the different software applications used in desktop publishing is one half of the process of outfitting a usable desktop publishing system. The other half of the process is to make sure your equipment meets your needs. The root of a QuarkXPress publishing system is a Macintosh computer—an expandable machine that offers access to a range of peripherals that can maximize the capabilities of your system.

Along with QuarkXPress, a full desktop publishing system may include a computer, a laser printer for draft or final printouts, a high-resolution imagesetter for final masters, and a scanning device. Other peripherals, such as video digitizers and color printers, add to the flexibility of a desktop publishing system. The following discussion gives you the background you'll need to make wise hardware decisions for desktop publishing.

Macintosh Models and Memory

QuarkXPress requires at least a 2-megabyte (2MB) RAM system. Some programs that you might be using in your publishing efforts—such as OmniPage for optical character reading—can require 3MB or more of memory in order to run. Adobe's PhotoShop can easily use 8MB of RAM or more to process high-resolution color images. The speed of the processor becomes more important the larger the volume of pages and graphics. If you are working many scanned images, you will appreciate the faster performance of a Macintosh IIci or IIfx system with 4MB or more of memory.

Storage

Besides the temporary storage that is built into any computer (such as RAM), you need to save programs and documents on disks for permanent storage or transportation. Because desktop publishing usually involves the use of several different applications (word processing, graphics, and page composition) and the assembly of files from many sources, it is convenient to store all of your applications and your current document files on a hard disk while you are working, and use removable hard disks, optical drives, tape, or floppy disks for backups.

QuarkXPress requires at least 2.5MB hard disk space if you want to install all of the files that come with the program. Hard disks that are built into the Macintosh usually store 40MB or 80MB of information, and you can get hard disks in many other sizes to use as your primary hard disk or to use in combination with your internal hard disk.

The price of hard disk storage is falling, and you will want to invest in a large hard disk if you are working with high-resolution images. You might want an extra hard disk system just to handle your archived documents. Removable hard disks can be useful for a back-up system, but we do not recommend relying on a removable cartridge system for your active daily work.

Monitors

If you do a lot of publishing, a large-screen monitor can increase your productivity by letting you see a full 8.5-by-11-inch page of work. By eliminating scrolling around the screen, it can boost your productivity by 50 percent. Even larger monitors are available now, which display full views of two facing pages or oversized pages.

A color monitor lets you display high-resolution color images. You can take advantage of QuarkXPress' color capabilities even without a color monitor—using PANTONE colors and mixing your own colors using percentages—but if you intend to work in color we recommend a color monitor and at least an 8-bit video card.

Scanners

A full-service publications department will also want to add a scanning device for digitizing photographs, logos, and line art that already exist on paper. A scanner or digitizer is an input device that converts a printed image into computer-readable dots. Digitized images can be saved in one of the paint-type formats supported by QuarkXPress or in Tag Image File Format (TIFF).

With a scanner you can incorporate halftones or line art of scanned images into your desktop publishing work as final artwork or as position holders for photographic halftones that will be stripped in later at the print shop. Scanners are a good source of graphics if you are not a fine artist and you have a library of logos, line art, and photographs to which you (or your clients) own the rights.

The software that accompanies scanners can offer many of the features of paint programs, with eraser and pen tools for touching up scanned images, and there are a number of packages available for editing high-resolution scanned images (LetraSet's ImageStudio and ColorStudio, Adobe's PhotoShop, and Data Translation's PhotoMac, for example). With the right combination of scanner, page-layout program, and printer, you can produce high-resolution graphics that look like inked line art or halftone photographs. For good results with color photographs, we recommend using high quality scanners. Most "desktop" color scanners, priced for individual use at under $5,000, are not adequate for high-quality results. See Chapter 13 for more information on color scanners.

Most black-and-white flatbed scanners accept 8.5-by-11-inch or larger pages; color scanners can digitize images from a variety of sources, including 35mm slides, transparencies, or flat color artwork. You can also use a video camera to convert printed or three-dimensional images into computer-readable images. Any scanner requires software to set up the specifications for the input image size, the finished image size, the degrees of brightness and contrast, and the resolution of the stored image.

Most scanners let you store the image at 300 dpi or more, and high-resolution images can approach the quality of true halftones when printed on a high-resolution printer. However, a full-page scan can require several megabytes of storage space when saved at high resolutions. You can save scanned images in low-resolution paint formats (usually 72 dpi), but when printed on a 300 dpi (or higher) printer the image will always appear jagged compared with high-resolution scans (unless the image is composed simply of horizontal and vertical lines).

Text-scanning (OCR, or optical character reader) technology has improved over the last few years, becoming faster and more accurate. The breakthrough of most relevance for desktop publishers is that some scanners can interpret typeset text in various sizes (whereas in the past OCRs could read only special characters and typewritten text).

Printers and Other Output Devices

Desktop publishing, by definition, requires a printer that can produce text in a mixture of different sizes and styles merged with graphics on the same page. QuarkXPress documents can be printed on some dot-matrix printers, but the final printer usually is a laser printer or typesetter. The most widely used page description language (PDL) for desktop publishing—and the one supported by QuarkXPress—is PostScript. PostScript has been implemented in dozens of laser printers and at least three phototypesetters.

Besides the PDL built into the printer, the one variable that is directly related to the price of any printer is resolution. *Resolution* is a measure of the sharpness of the edges of printed characters and graphics. It is commonly measured by the number of dots or spots per inch. Laser printers assemble characters and graphics as a pattern of dots, and they use a fine beam of light (a laser beam) to produce the dots in patterns of 300 dpi or more. The laser beam puts electromagnetic charges on a drum which then either picks up powdery charged particles of the toner and lays the toner on paper, or transfers the electromagnetic charges onto photosensitive paper. The resulting text and graphics appear very smooth to the naked eye.

Phototypesetters are available that use the laser technology to set a page image on photosensitive paper or film. Linotype, Varityper, Agfa Compugraphic, and other manufacturers offer PostScript laser typesetters that image at various high resolutions. The resolution can be from 600 to 3,500 dpi, and the output is much crisper, of course, than the output from toner-based laser printers.

Color printers are useful for printing proof copies of color pages, or finished color overhead transparencies or slides.

Modems

Files can be telecommunicated over the phone lines or through a cable from one computer to another. You can also convert files from one application to another type, using communications software that allows you to transfer and translate files. Once the files are transferred, you can edit them using any word processor (if they are ASCII text files), or use the same application that created them to edit them, or import them directly onto a page in QuarkXPress.

Modems can be set to send files at different speeds, measured as baud rates (bits per second). The lowest baud rate is 300; it can take a long time to send a file at this rate, but it ensures a high degree of accuracy in the transmission. A 1,200, 2,400 or 9,600 baud rate is more commonly used to send files over the phone lines. Even higher transmission speeds can be used over direct optical cable connections (rather than over phone lines).

Networks

Desktop publishing in a workgroup allows people to share information. This is especially important in a production setting where one person is responsible for writing copy, another for designing graphics, and still another for laying out the page, for example. Network users can share printers, files, and information.

Apple's System 7 adds several important file sharing capabilities to the operating system, and there are several types of server-based networks available for the Macintosh, including AppleShare, 3-Com, and Novelle. These networks also allow various brands of computers to be used within one workgroup.

Summary

Electronic publishing systems bring together the features and capabilities that were once dispersed among different professional specialties. The rest of this book will help you identify the different tasks associated with a full publishing project, and also update your current designs and production procedures to take advantage of the capabilities of QuarkXPress 3.1. This book will also help you understand the basic vocabulary of desktop publishing applications, distinguish between the different types of programs used in desktop publishing, identify the possible sources of text and graphics in any document produced using QuarkXPress, and determine your own software and hardware needs.

The impact of desktop publishing on designers, professional publishing companies, corporate publications departments, and self-publishing associations and individuals is best seen through the experiences of those who have made the transition from traditional methods to electronic publishing over the past few years. Part III of this book offers several case studies of QuarkXPress users.

P A R T

I

USING
QUARKXPRESS

1 *Basic Concepts and Terminology*

T his chapter will help you understand the basic concepts and terms used in the Macintosh environment and in QuarkXPress procedures. You will learn a few of the basic Macintosh operations that are common to most applications on the Macintosh—operations that we assume you are familiar with in the rest of this book. You will also learn the philosophy and terminology of the page layout process as applied in QuarkXPress.

If you have never used a Macintosh before, you should review this entire chapter carefully. We also recommend that you study the manuals and introductory disk files that come with the Macintosh computer.

If you have used a Macintosh but have never used QuarkXPress before, you may opt to skip the Macintosh Basics sections, but read the sections about QuarkXPress.

 If you have used earlier versions of QuarkXPress, skim this chapter to learn about some new features in QuarkXPress 3.1 flagged with the 3.1 icon shown at left.

Macintosh Basics

QuarkXPress implements the basic "Macintosh interface" features and commands common to most applications on the Macintosh. Throughout this book we assume that you are familiar with Macintosh basics and that you know how to work with the Macintosh Finder, or Desktop. You should also be familiar with common Macintosh terms, such as "click" and "drag." Some of the basic Macintosh procedures are summarized here as they apply to QuarkXPress.

QuarkXPress 3.1 runs under both System 6.0x (System 6.05 or higher) and System 7. Many aspects of these systems are similar, including most aspects of the user interface. Differences between the two systems that affect the operation of QuarkXPress are indicated throughout this book. Beginners may need to refer to the appropriate Apple Computer manuals for the Macintosh System to supplement the information found here.

Using Pull-Down Menus

One of the advantages of the Macintosh is that you are not forced to enter obscure, hard-to-remember commands through the keyboard. Rather, the Macintosh lets you choose commands from a list on pull-down menus. Menu titles appear along the menu bar at the top of the screen. When you position the mouse pointer (▶) over a menu title and hold down the mouse button, the menu drops down to show all commands in that menu (Figure 1-1). Select a command by dragging the pointer down until the desired command is highlighted. Then release the mouse button.

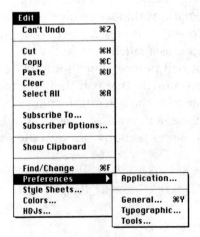

Figure 1-1 A QuarkXPress pull-down menu with a submenu displayed.

A check mark (✓) in front of a command indicates a toggle switch (an on/off option). The feature is on if it is checked; you can turn off the feature by selecting the command. The feature is off if it is not checked; you can activate the feature by selecting the command.

Ellipses (...) following a command indicate that a dialog box asking you for more information will be displayed when you select the command. The dialog box also offers you a chance to cancel the command.

A right-pointing black arrow (▶) on a menu indicates a submenu. When you drag to a command that is followed by a black arrow, a secondary menu will pop out, and you drag the mouse to highlight the desired selection.

Keyboard Shortcuts

Menus make it easy to find a command, but using a menu is usually slower than entering a keyboard command. For this reason, most commonly used commands in QuarkXPress (and other Macintosh applications) have keyboard alternatives, such as holding down the Command key (⌘) while pressing another key. These keyboard shortcuts are shown in the menus, next to the command name. For example, the keyboard alternative to File ➤ New is ⌘-N. You will find that it is easy to remember the keyboard shortcuts for the commands you use most often.

Two symbols are used to indicate shortcuts on the menus: a ⌘ symbol before a letter represents the Command key. To execute the command, hold down the ⌘ key while you type the letter shown. An outlined up arrow (⇧) represents the Shift key. To execute the command, hold down both the Command and Shift keys while you type the letter shown.

Controlling Windows

Windows are another feature of the Macintosh interface that are common to most Macintosh applications (Figure 1-2). You can open a Finder window by selecting an icon and choosing the File ➤ Open command or by double-clicking on a disk or folder icon on the desktop. QuarkXPress documents appear in similar windows.

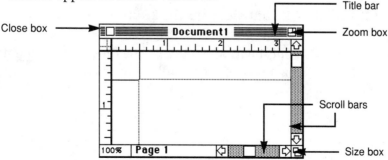

Figure 1-2 Common elements of Macintosh windows.

You can close a window by choosing the File ➤ Close command or by clicking on the Close box at the upper left corner of the window. You can move a window by dragging the title bar. You can adjust the size of most windows by clicking on the Size box in the bottom right corner of the window and dragging the mouse. You can toggle between two window sizes by clicking on the Zoom box at the upper right corner of the window.

Scroll bars can be found in windows and in many dialog boxes that offer lists—whether in QuarkXPress or any other application. To move the view in the window or in the list in small increments, click on an arrow. Click in the gray area of a scroll bar to move the view in the window up or down in larger increments. Drag the scroll box to move any distance. The position of the scroll box on the scroll bar indicates the relative position in a window. For example, if the scroll box is in the center of a scroll bar, you are viewing the center of that window's contents.

Making Entries in a Dialog Box

Many of the commands in QuarkXPress yield dialog boxes, which offer a variety of options (Figure 1-3). These options work the same way as in any other Macintosh application:

- Click on a radio button or its label to make a selection from a list of mutually exclusive options.
- Click on a check box or its label to make one or more selections from a list of options.
- Tab to or click in a field and type a value.
- Click on a name in a scroll list to select the name.
- Hold down the mouse button to display pop-up menus, then drag to highlight the selection you wish to make and release the mouse button.
- Click on the OK button or press the Return key to close the box with changes.
- Click on the Cancel button or click on the Close box (in the title bar) to close a dialog box without recording any changes.

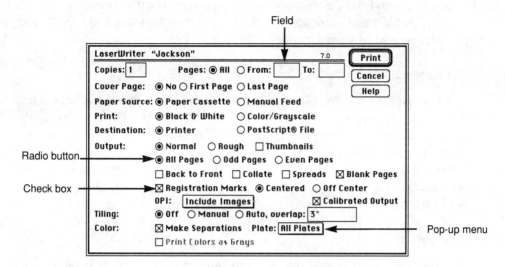

Figure 1-3 The Print dialog box shows examples of a variety of dialog box fields.

The basic techniques for working with all QuarkXPress dialog boxes are the same. Specific dialog box entries and their meanings are described throughout this book.

The Apple Menu

The Apple menu is always displayed at the top left corner of the screen. The Apple menu lists the Macintosh system desk accessories that are available in any program or from the Desktop (Figure 1-4). While the basic functions of desk accessories remain unchanged in System 7, the way items are installed and the way they display differ significantly from System 6.0x. Please refer to Apple Computer's System documentation for the correct procedures to follow to install desk accessory items on the Apple menu.

Figure 1-4 Desk accessories on the System 7 Apple Menu.

While several desk accessory items may appear on this menu, two of direct relevance to QuarkXPress are the Chooser and Key Caps. Both are included as part of your Macintosh System.

The Chooser

The Chooser is used to select devices on a network. For example, if you have more than one printer on your network, use the Chooser to select one. Be sure the correct printer software is installed in your System folder when you start your Macintosh.

The Chooser is also used to select the fileservers or other shared devices on a network. If you are using System 7, you can work with files on another Macintosh for which you have sharing privileges.

Key Caps

The Key Caps accessory is like an electronic reference card. It is handy for viewing the character set available with each installed font, including special symbols such as ™, ¶, •, ®, and ©. Most fonts include these common symbols. The special Symbol font includes a wider range of Greek and mathematical characters, and the Zapf Dingbat font includes a wider variety of symbols such as arrows, boxes, stars, and the like.

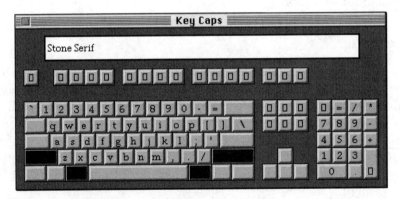

Figure 1-5 The Key Caps window.

View the lowercase character set in the Key Caps window (Figure 1-5). To view the full character set, hold down the Shift key, the Option key, or both the Shift and Option keys. Click on the Close box in the window to exit Key Caps.

Using the Cut, Copy, and Paste Commands

The Edit menu contains basic editing commands that are common to all Macintosh applications, such as Undo, Cut, Copy, Paste, Clear, Select All, and Show Clipboard. They usually have the same keyboard shortcuts across all applications: Cut (⌘-X), Copy (⌘-C), Paste (⌘-V), Select All (⌘-A), and Clear. If you have an extended keyboard, you can also use function keys to invoke these commands in QuarkXPress: F1 = Undo, F2 = Cut, F3 = Copy, F4 = Paste.

Both Edit ➤ Cut (⌘-X) and Edit ➤ Copy (⌘-C) put selected objects in the Clipboard (a temporary storage space in the Macintosh memory). The Cut command removes active objects from a page, while the Copy command leaves the objects on the page and puts a copy in the Clipboard. Edit ➤ Paste (⌘-V) positions whatever is in the Clipboard onto the page in QuarkXPress. Using the Paste command does not change the contents of the Clipboard—you can use the Paste command to paste copies of the same thing from the Clipboard onto the page as many times as you like.

Clipboard Versus Scrapbook

The *Clipboard*—a standard Macintosh feature—is a temporary, memory-resident storage area that is active while you are working. It "saves" a copy of the most recent selection that you cut or copy, and the contents of the Clipboard remain the same until the next time you use the Cut or Copy command (or until you turn your computer off). The same Clipboard is in effect regardless of what applications you are running. If you draw something using MacDraw and make a copy of it, for example, then open a QuarkXPress document, you can use the Paste command to pull that graphic from the Clipboard onto the QuarkXPress page. Rather than using the Clipboard, however, it is usually more convenient to use QuarkXPress's File ➤ Get Picture or File ➤ Get Text command to import graphics or text from other applications into QuarkXPress documents.

The Scrapbook is a more permanent, disk-based storage facility that holds any number of separate items that can be accessed through the Apple menu and copied and pasted into a QuarkXPress document.

QuarkXPress Basics

The next chapters detail specific steps you can follow to build a QuarkXPress document. The rest of this chapter describes the basic QuarkXPress installation, windows, palettes, and menus.

Installing the Program

QuarkXPress is packaged on several diskettes. The program itself is larger than one floppy diskette, and during the installation process, the pieces on these diskettes are assembled into one large program file on your hard disk (along with other files that support QuarkXPress). The manuals that come with QuarkXPress contain complete instructions for installing the program.

Starting QuarkXPress

You can start QuarkXPress the same way you start most applications on the Macintosh:

- Double-click on the program icon or, if you're using System 7, the program's alias on the Macintosh Desktop (Figure 1-6) — the usual shortcut to the alternative of selecting the icon and choosing the File ➤ Open command, or
- Double-click on an icon for a document created in QuarkXPress (Figure 1-6), or

Figure 1-6 To start QuarkXPress, double-click either the program icon, alias icon, or document icon.

- If you are using System 7, drag a document icon over the QuarkXPress program icon or the program's alias icon to open the document (Figure 1-7).

Figure 1-7 System 7 allows you to open a document by dragging its icon over the program icon.

Using the Help Function

QuarkXPress offers two types of on-line help. First, the About QuarkXPress command in the Apple menu (or QuarkXPress Help, under the Help menu in System 7) tells you what version of the program you are using and offers a scroll list of Help topics (if the XPress Help file is in the folder with the QuarkXPress program or in the System folder).

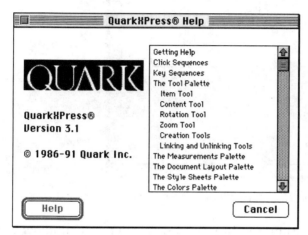

Figure 1-8 The Help topics are listed in the About QuarkXPress dialog box.

The scroll list of topics shows a tiered help system. The first dialog box displays a list of the main topics covered by the Help command (Figure 1-8). When you double-click on one of these topics, you see detailed information on the topic (Figure 1-9). Click on Cancel to return to the document window.

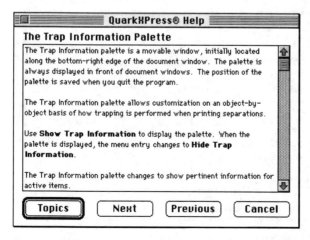

Figure 1-9 Help information.

If you are running QuarkXPress under System 7, you can also use Balloon Help (Figure 1-10). To turn on Balloon Help, choose Show Balloons from the Finder Help menu in the upper right corner of your screen.

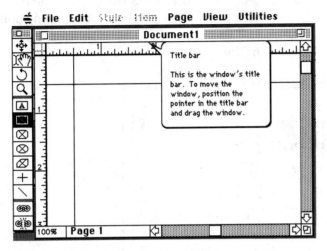

Figure 1-10 Balloon Help is available under System 7.

Knowing the version of your program and your serial number is important if you use Quark's telephone hotline to resolve program problems. This service, available to registered owners, is well worth the subscription fee if you plan to do a great deal of production with QuarkXPress. The serial number, along with other information, can be found in the QuarkXPress Environment window (Figure 1-11). Hold down the Option key and select About QuarkXPress from the Apple menu; on an extended keyboard, hold down the Option key and press the Help key.

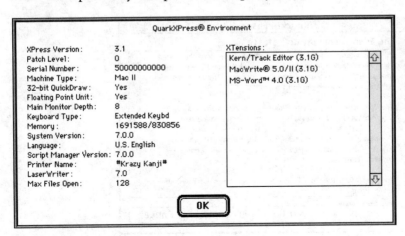

Figure 1-11 The QuarkXPress Environment window.

Examining a QuarkXPress Document

You can learn more about the basic principles and terminology of QuarkXPress by first examining a QuarkXPress document. The next sections describe a document that was briefly profiled in the introduction. Here we introduce some of the new terms used in QuarkXPress manuals and throughout this book. (See also Part III for descriptions of documents created using QuarkXPress.)

QuarkXPress is well suited for designing and producing a wide variety of printed documents, including books, newspapers, magazines, manuals, reports, directories, brochures, packaging—or any printed communication. All of these items can be created using the same basic set of building blocks and tools used in creating the newsletter page described here (Figure 1-12).

Figure 1-12 A newsletter page created in QuarkXPress.

Master Pages and Document Pages

A QuarkXPress document can be composed of up to 2,000 document pages plus up to 127 master pages. Master pages can contain items, both text and graphics, that are repeated on multiple document pages. Both document

NEW
3.1

pages and master pages can contain guides (margin guides, column guides, and ruler guides) that help you position items consistently. Document pages are the ones you'll usually be printing, of course, but QuarkXPress 3.1 allows you to print out master pages as well.

You can apply a master page to any document page; if you do so, then all master page elements will automatically change on that document page. You can also delete master pages from a document.

For example, to create our sample newsletter page, we set up a master page with half-inch margins and with the text of the footer that runs at the bottom of every page to which this master page is applied.

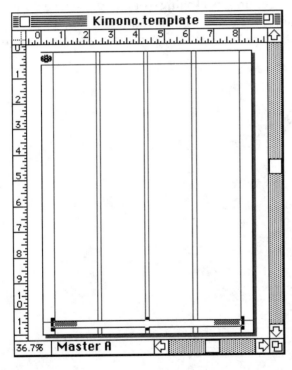

Figure 1-13 Master page elements.

In this example the master page is very simple; however, a master page can contain more guides and other text and graphic elements, as described in the next section.

Lines, Text Boxes, and Picture Boxes

The basic building blocks on any page in QuarkXPress—master pages or document pages—are boxes and lines drawn with QuarkXPress tools, called *items*; the tools that create them are called *item creation tools*. Boxes drawn using QuarkXPress tools can stand alone as graphic elements, or they can contain text or pictures.

Page 1 of our sample newsletter includes one text box and the footer from the master page. The first page also includes items on the document page—one picture box containing the kimono graphic, and three additional text boxes, containing the newsletter banner, the article title, and the article lead-in (Figure 1-12).

The illustration is an EPS (encapsulated PostScript) graphic created in Adobe Illustrator and imported into a picture box. The banner "Kimono West" was typed directly into a text box and rotated 90°. The title text above the illustration is in a one-column text box that is the width of the three-column article. Below the illustration is a one-column text box. The body of the article starts on this page in a three-column text box. The text box containing the article is from the master page, but it has been modified for the first page of the newsletter; you can easily change master page items.

Relationships Between Items

Items (boxes and lines) can stand as separate elements on a page, or they can be associated in several ways: as text chains, as anchored items, or as constrained items. Relationships between items are described briefly here and in more detail in Chapter 3.

The Automatic Text Box and Other Linked Text Chains

Text boxes can be chained to direct the flow of text from one page to another or from one box to another on the same page. This will happen automatically if you set up an *automatic text box* on the master page, or you can use the Linking tool manually to link a series of text boxes and create a chain. The stream of text that flows through a linked chain of text boxes is called a *story*.

Anchored Boxes

Text boxes, picture boxes, and rules can be anchored within a text box. For example, you can create a graphic symbol, import it into a picture box, then paste the picture box into the stream of text. This way, the graphic symbol will move with the flow of text, even if the text before it is edited.

Constrained Items

Text or picture boxes and lines can be constrained within a constraining text or picture box. Constrained items cannot be moved beyond the boundaries of the constraining box, and the entire constrained group can be copied, moved, or deleted.

Guides

You can create *guides* on any page in QuarkXPress—document pages or master pages. Guides are nonprinting lines that appear on the screen and have a snap-to effect: If the optional snap-to effect is turned on (under the View menu), the pointer or the edges of items (boxes and lines) will be pulled into alignment with a guide when you move them close to the guide. In QuarkXPress 3.1, the distance at which objects will "snap" to guides can be set in units of pixels in the General Preferences dialog box (see Chapter 3).

Guides include *margin guides* that are defined on the master page, *column guides* that can be set up on the master page or in any text box, and *ruler guides* that can be dragged onto a page from a ruler. Guides used in our newsletter sample are shown in Figure 1-14.

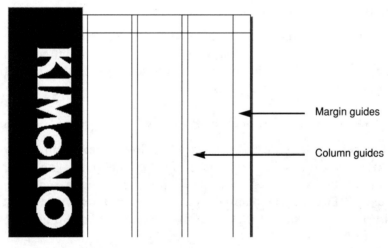

Margin guides

Column guides

Figure 1-14 Guides used in our sample newsletter.

Style Sheets

QuarkXPress offers a wide variety of tools and commands for editing and formatting text. In our newsletter sample, the process of formatting text was simplified through the use of *style sheets*.

A style sheet is simply a shortcut for applying type specifications (character attributes and paragraph formats) used throughout a document. A style sheet lets you define the character attributes, paragraph format, and ruled lines, or rules, for each type of text element in a document, such as major headings, subheadings, captions, and body text.

Instead of using several commands and different dialog boxes to format text, once you set up a style sheet for a document, you can format text by simply using the menu command Style ➤ Style Sheets or keyboard equivalents that you've assigned to a style sheet. QuarkXPress 3.1 lets you apply style sheets using the Style Sheets palette.

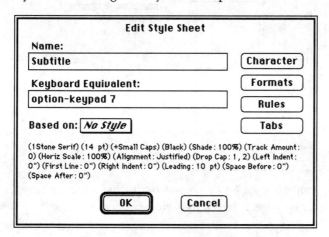

Figure 1-15 A style sheet specification.

Templates and Documents

You can save a QuarkXPress document as a document or as a template. A document is a final product that you print, reproduce, and distribute. A template is a partially complete document, containing common elements that may appear in many documents. For example, the template for this newsletter (Figure 1-16) includes a master page and special items on document pages that appear in every issue, such as the banner on the first page. It also includes style sheets that are used to format the text consistently. Every issue of the newsletter is started from this template; doing so saves having to start from scratch every month.

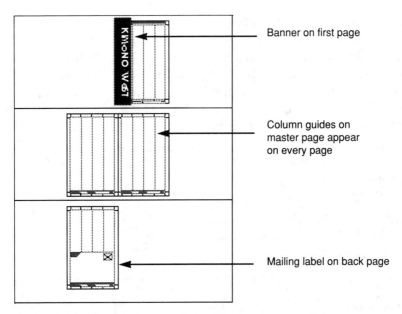

Banner on first page

Column guides on master page appear on every page

Mailing label on back page

Figure 1-16 The template used for this newsletter includes master page elements, the banner on page 1, plus a mailing label area on page 4.

Examining QuarkXPress Windows and Palettes

When you first start QuarkXPress, the screen shows pull-down menu titles on the menu bar, but no document window is open and most of the commands are gray and cannot be selected. The screen might also display any one of six palettes: a Tool palette, a Measurements palette, a Document Layout palette, or, new to version 3.1, a Style Sheets palette, a Colors palette, or a Trap Information palette, depending on how your screen looked when you last quit QuarkXPress.

After you enter the initial specifications in the New dialog box, or when an existing document is open, QuarkXPress displays pages in the document window (Figure 1-17). A quick look at the document *window* and QuarkXPress' palettes gives you an idea of the program's versatility.

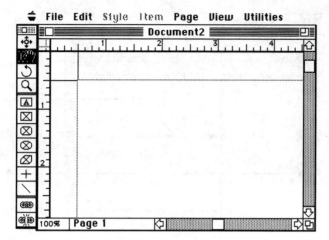

Figure 1-17 A new QuarkXPress file displays the upper left-hand corner of the first page of the document.

A document window can be moved and sized on the screen. You can have more than one document *window* open at a time, but the active document window usually displays on top of any other document windows (unless you have arranged them side by side). If you close a document window, you are closing the document.

A *palette*, on the other hand, displays on top of all document windows and is related to the active document only. You can close any palette without closing the active document. Like windows, palettes can be moved anywhere on the screen, and all palettes, except the tool palette, can be resized.

If you are examining the document window for the first time, choose View → Fit in Window (⌘-0, where 0 is a zero and not the letter O) and follow our descriptions under the next headings.

Examining the Document Window

The document window is a standard Macintosh window. The pointer shows the current position of the mouse and is used for selecting commands and items on the page or pasteboard. The page image shows the outline of the edges of the paper; nonprinting dotted or color lines on the page indicate margins and columns. The surrounding area serves as a pasteboard for storage of text and graphics while you are working. Optionally, rulers can be displayed at the top and right sides of the document window. The bottom left corner of the screen shows the current page view percentage and the page number (Figure 1-18).

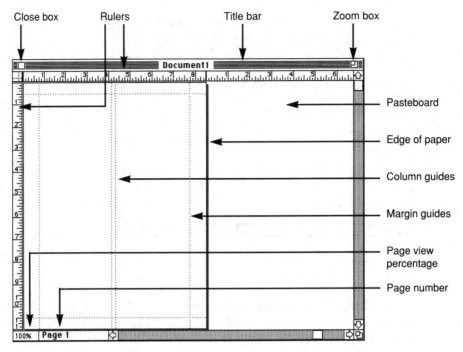

Close box   Rulers   Title bar   Zoom box

Document1

Pasteboard

Edge of paper

Column guides

Margin guides

Page view percentage

Page number

100%   Page 1

Figure 1-18   The document window.

You can view and work on a display of one page at a time, two facing pages at a time, or spreads consisting of two or more pages in documents that might be folded or include fold-out pages. Facing pages can be set up in the New dialog box, or later in the Document Setup dialog box. Facing pages let you set up master pages with different margins, headers, and footers on left and right pages.

Examining the Tool Palette

QuarkXPress' Tool palette is much like a conventional artist's assortment of drawing tools. Here pens, rulers, protractors, and knives are replaced by icons, which you select to perform the artist's work.

The Tool palette is a separate window on the screen (Figure 1-19). You can drag the palette by its title bar to any position on the screen. You can also close the palette by clicking on the Close box or selecting View ➤ Hide Tools. To redisplay the Tool palette after you close the palette, select View ➤ Show Tools.

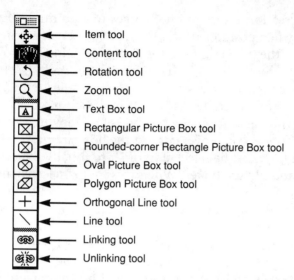

Figure 1-19 The Tool palette.

Selecting a Tool

To select any tool in the Tool palette, click on the tool. Press ⌘-Tab to select the tool immediately below the currently active tool or ⌘-Shift-Tab to select the tool immediately above the currently active tool—or continue pressing ⌘-Tab or ⌘-Shift-Tab until the tool you wish to use is selected. The currently active tool determines the appearance of the pointer on the screen.

Some tools remain active until you deselect them by choosing another tool—the Item tool (✥), Content tool (🖑), and Zoom tool (🔍) fall into this category. All the other tools revert to the Item tool or the Content tool as soon as they are used once. To keep the same tool active for repeated use, hold the Option key as you select it.

Double-clicking on a tool brings up the Tool Preferences dialog box (described in Chapter 3), which enables you to set the default specifications for the Zoom and Item Creation tools (boxes and lines) in the Tool palette.

Editing Tools

The four icons in the first section of the tool palette are for the Item tool, the Content tool, the Rotation tool, and the Zoom tool. Select the **Item tool** to move boxes or lines on a page. When the Item tool is selected, the pointer becomes an arrow (➤). It changes to a four-pointed arrow, or mover pointer (✥), when you position it over a box or line created with one of

QuarkXPress' item creation tools, and it changes to a pointing finger or resizing pointer (☞) when positioned over the handle of an active item.

You need not select the Item tool from the Tool palette in order to move a box or line: With any tool selected, you can hold down the ⌘ key to activate temporarily the Item tool at any time. When you release the ⌘ key, the previously selected tool becomes active. To move a box, click on it to select it and drag. If you pause for half a second before moving a box, you can see the box contents as you move, not just the box outline.

The **Content tool** (☞) must be selected in order to modify the contents of boxes, both text and picture boxes. When this tool is selected and the pointer is positioned in a text box, the pointer changes to an I-beam (I) for inserting and editing text; when positioned in a picture box, the pointer becomes the picture mover pointer (☜).

To select text with the Content tool (☞), position the I-beam beside a character inside an active text box and drag it to the end of the desired selection. Selected text is highlighted or reversed on the screen. Other methods of selecting a range of text are described in Chapter 4.

To select a picture with the Content tool, position the picture mover pointer (☜) inside an active picture box and click once. You can move the picture within the box by dragging the picture mover pointer. To modify the contents of a picture box, including scaling or skewing the picture, you must select the Content tool.

The **Rotation tool** (↻) lets you rotate text boxes, picture boxes, lines, or active groups of boxes and lines, on a page. When this tool is selected, the pointer becomes a target symbol (⊕) at first, and an arrowhead (▸) indicates the direction of the rotation around the target point.

The **Zoom tool** (Q) lets you change the scale in which you are viewing the page. When this tool is selected, the pointer becomes a magnifying glass with a plus sign inside (⊕) for zooming in, or increasing the page view percentage. By holding down the Option key, the tool changes to a magnifying glass with a minus sign inside (⊖) to zoom out, or decrease the page view percentage.

Item Creation Tools

The next seven tools on the tool palette are the item creation tools. They include one text box creation tool, four picture box creation tools, and two line creation tools. When any of these tools is selected, the pointer becomes a crosshair (+), called the Item Creation pointer.

Select the **Text Box tool** (▣) to create boxes on the page that will contain text. Select the **Rectangular Picture Box tool** (⊠), the **Rounded-Corner Rectangle Picture Box tool** (⊠), and the **Oval Picture Box tool** (⊗) to create boxes with square corners, boxes with rounded corners, and circles or ovals, respectively. The boxes created with these tools may contain graphics imported from other sources. Use the **Polygon Picture Box tool** (⊘) to create polygonal boxes that may also contain graphics imported from other sources. Select the **Orthogonal Line tool** (+) to draw horizontal and vertical lines, and the **Line tool** (╲) to draw lines at any angle.

With any of these tools selected, you create an item by dragging the pointer on the page or the pasteboard, as described in Chapter 2.

Linking Tools

The last two tools are called the **Linking tool** (⛶) and the **Unlinking tool** (⛶). Use these to direct the flow of text from one text box to another, as described in Chapter 3.

Examining the Measurements Palette

The Measurements palette (View ➤ Show Measurements) displays information about the currently active item on a page. This information will change dynamically as you move, scale, or otherwise change an active item. You can also change the specifications by making entries directly through the Measurements palette.

The Measurements palette provides a quick method for modifying many item and content attributes that can also be changed through the menus and dialog boxes; the information can be changed in either area. The Measurements palette is by far the fastest way to view or change values. You only need to go into a dialog box when you want to change other variables not shown in the Measurements palette or when the Measurements palette is not displayed.

You can move the Measurements palette anywhere on the screen by clicking and dragging on its title bar. The contents of the palette will vary depending on the type of item selected, as shown in Figure 1-20.

| ▣ X: 5p7 | W: 10p4 | △ 0° | ⬍ 65 pt | ▤ ▤ ▣ Times | ▣ 83 pt |
| Y: 1p7 | H: 39p4 | Cols: 1 | ⬌ 0 | ▤ ▤ ▣ B I O S O U W K K ⬆ ⬇ |

| ▣ X: 1.6" | W: 3" | △ 0° | X%: 60% | ⬌ X+: 0" | △ 0° |
| Y: 1.4" | H: 2.7" | ↗ 0" | Y%: 60% | ⬍ Y+: 0" | ⬔ 0° |

Figure 1-20 Measurements palette when a text box (top) and a picture box (bottom) is active.

When the Measurements palette is displayed, you can jump to its first field by pressing ⌘-Option-M, or you can activate any field by simply clicking on it. Once in this palette, as in any dialog box, you can move through the fields by pressing the Tab key, or press Shift-Tab to tab in reverse order.

Make entries in the Measurements palette by editing the entry as text, using scrolling arrows to select values, or choosing from pop-up menus. To exit the palette and activate all changes, press Return or Enter, or click the mouse in any other window. Changes made to the information on the left side of the palette (related to items, such as boxes and lines) are not reflected on the page until you exit the palette. Changes you make on the right side of the palette (related to the contents of active items) are implemented when you click on an icon in the Measurements palette or exit a field. You can exit the palette without implementing any changes by pressing ⌘-period.

Entering Measurements

QuarkXPress offers unique flexibility in entering measurements. Regardless of the unit of measure that is currently displayed, you can enter a new value in inches, millimeters, centimeters, picas, points, or ciceros. To enter a measure in units other than the current unit of measure, simply indicate the measurement system using the abbreviations listed in Figure 1-21.

Units	Abbreviation	Example
Inches	"	1"
Millimeters	mm	1mm
Centimeters	cm	1cm
Picas	p	1p
		1p3 (one pica, three points)
Points	pt	1pt
Ciceros	c	1c
		1c3 (one cicero, three points)

Figure 1-21 Measurement units and their abbreviations.

You can enter most measurements in increments as fine as .001, and you can enter font sizes from 2 to 720 points. You can change an entry by adding or subtracting from the current value displayed in any field. For example, if the current measure is 4 inches, you can increase it by 1/4 inch by positioning the cursor after the 4 and typing +.25—you need not enter the unit of measure if it is the same as the current default measure. Similarly, you could increase the 4-inch measure by 2 picas and 3 points by typing +2p3 after the 4.

Examining the Document Layout Palette

The Document Layout palette (View → Show Document Layout) shows the master pages and document pages as icons (Figure 1-22). You can move the Document Layout palette around on the screen and enlarge it for a view of more page icons as your document grows.

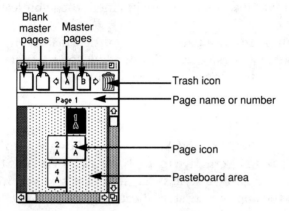

Figure 1-22 The Document Layout palette.

The icons at the top of this palette represent blank pages and master pages. You can have up to 127 master pages. If you have created more than one master page, you can view the icons for various master pages either by enlarging the window or by clicking on the arrows in the palette to scroll through the master page icons. You will learn how to create and use these icons in Chapter 3.

Document page icons are displayed in the lower area of the window. The line down the middle of the document page area indicates the binding edge of a facing-page document. The gray areas to the left and right of the document page icons represent a visual reminder of the 48-inch width, which is the maximum page width or spread width QuarkXPress allows. Each page icon shows the page number and a letter indicating which master is applied to that page. The active page number is shown in outline type on the page icon in the Document Layout palette.

The bar below the master page icons and above the document page icons displays the name of the currently active master page or the number of the currently active document page; this information is also displayed in the lower left corner of the larger document window. The page number you have assigned may be different than the physical page in the file. If, for example, a file called "Chapter 2" started with page number 32, the document palette would display "Page 32" in this bar when you click on the first page icon.

You can double-click on a page icon in the Document Layout palette to display that page in the document window. The Document Layout palette can be used as an alternative to turning to pages by using various commands on the Page menu such as as Previous, Next, or Go To page.

To rearrange pages, drag the page icons in the Document Layout palette to the new position. This can be used as an alternative to rearranging pages in Thumbnails view. Text links will not be maintained when you rearrange pages this way.

Delete a page by dragging the page icon into the Trash icon in the Document Layout palette. QuarkXPress will not allow you to delete pages that contain text links to other pages in the document.

Examining the Style Sheets Palette

 The Style Sheets Palette (View ➤ Show Style Sheets) allows you to apply formats to text easily, as an alternative to applying styles via the Style ➤ Style Sheets command. To apply a style sheet, select the text you wish to format, then click on the appropriate style sheet name in the Style Sheets palette (Figure 1-23). The Style Sheets palette is not active unless the text I-beam pointer (⌶) has been clicked in a text box.

Figure 1-23 The Style Sheets palette.

You may also use the Style Sheets palette to edit style sheet specifications. Hold down the Command key (⌘) and click on a style sheet name in the palette to display quickly the Edit Style Sheet dialog box for that specific style sheet. This is an alternative to selecting the Edit ➤ Style Sheets command, then clicking on the style sheet name to display the Edit Style Sheet dialog box.

Examining the Colors Palette

The Colors palette (View ➤ Show Colors) provides a convenient way of applying color to text, pictures, box backgrounds and frames, and lines (Figure 1-24). Using the Colors palette is the only way to apply a two-color blend to a box background.

Figure 1-24 The Colors palette when a text box is selected.

To apply colors, choose one of the icons across the top of the palette and then choose a color and shade percentage. The icons across the top of the palette will change depending on what type of item is selected. If a text box is selected, for example, the icons across the top are, from left to right, for applying color to the text box frame, the text, or the text box background. An adjacent pop-up menu lets you assign a shade percentage, or you can type in any percentage. The palette lists all the colors created for the document under Edit ➤ Colors.

The Colors palette may also be used to open the Colors dialog box. Hold down the Command key (⌘) and click on the name of a color in the palette to quickly display the Colors dialog box. This is an alternative to selecting the Edit ➤ Colors command.

Examining the Trap Information Palette

The Trap Information palette (View ➤ Show Trap Information) allows you to specify the trapping relationship between adjacent colors on an item-by-item basis (Figure 1-25). Trapping between colors for a document is defined in the Edit Trap dialog box (Edit ➤ Colors), but those relationships may be changed on individual items using the Trap Information palette.

When a box is active, the Trap Information palette shows the trapping values for both the color of the box background and the box contents; if a line is selected, the palette shows the trapping specifications for the color of the line. If a box is framed, trapping may be specified for the way the frame color traps against the background color.

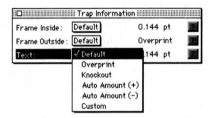

Figure 1-25 The Trap Information palette when a framed text box is selected.

Pop-up menus provide six different options for defining trapping relationships; you can define your own trapping values by choosing Custom and entering a value in the field to the right of the pop-up menu.

Examining the Pasteboard

The area surrounding the master page and document pages, the pasteboard, is a nonprinting area for storing text and graphics. You can also use the pasteboard as a work area. The "pasteboard" is a metaphor for the traditional graphic artist's table: You can put text and graphics on it that you are not using at the moment, or that you want to work on before placing on your page.

The width of the pasteboard is determined by the width of your page. The default setting is for the pasteboard to be 100 percent of the width of your page. The pasteboard is always one-half inch above and below a page or spread. QuarkXPress 3.1 lets you change the width of the pasteboard to less than 100 percent of the page size if desired.

Examining the Menus

QuarkXPress menus function the same way standard Macintosh menus function, described earlier in this chapter. They are divided logically into commands that relate to one another. Further, each menu is sectioned by a gray line, separating groups of commands on each menu.

The File Menu

The File menu includes commands that are common to most Macintosh applications, such as New, Open, Close, Save, Save As, Page Setup, Print, and Quit (Figure 1-26). QuarkXPress adds a Revert to Saved command that lets you cancel any changes you made to the document since you last saved it.

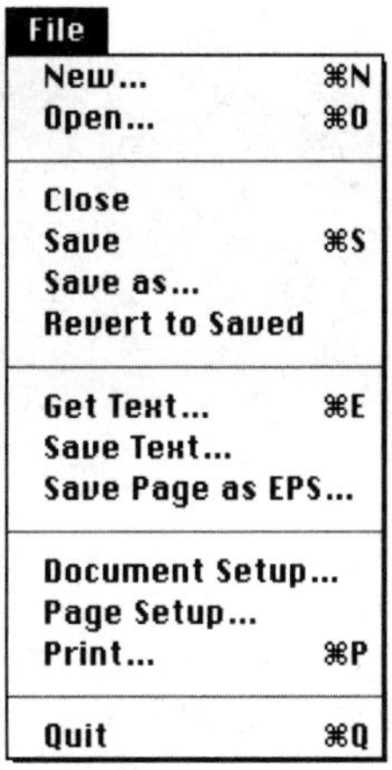

```
 File
   New...           ⌘N
   Open...          ⌘O

   Close
   Save             ⌘S
   Save as...
   Revert to Saved

   Get Text...       ⌘E
   Save Text...
   Save Page as EPS...

   Document Setup...
   Page Setup...
   Print...          ⌘P

   Quit             ⌘Q
```

Figure 1-26 The File menu.

Other commands on this menu let you import text and graphics from other applications, save text to disk, save an entire page as a color or black-and-white Encapsulated PostScript (EPS) file and change the document setup (page size).

The Edit Menu

The Edit menu includes commands common to most Macintosh programs, such as Undo, Cut, Copy, Paste, Clear, Select All, System 7 Subscriber options, and Show Clipboard. QuarkXPress adds commands that let you perform global searches and adjust preferences (default settings). You can also define colors, style sheets, and hyphenation and justification rules.

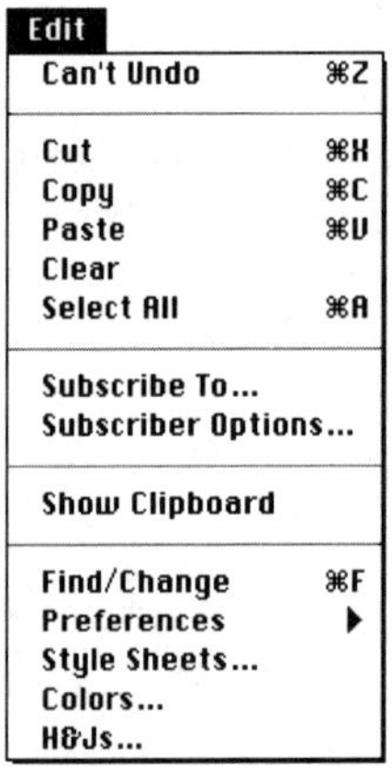

Figure 1-27 The Edit menu.

The Style Menu

The commands listed in the Style menu change depending on what is active when you view the menu. Style menu commands affect the content of boxes and line characteristics.

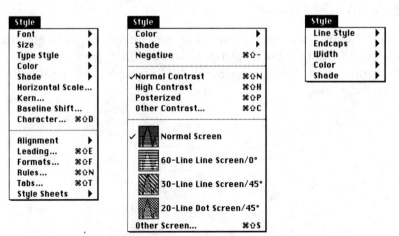

Figure 1-28 Style menu when a text box (left), a picture box with an image (center), and a line (right) is active and the Content tool is selected.

The Item Menu

The Item menu (Figure 1-29) includes commands that let you modify, duplicate, group, and align boxes and lines.

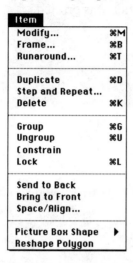

Figure 1-29 The Item menu.

The Page Menu

Commands in the Page menu add, delete, and move pages, set up master guides and page numbers within the document, and change the page view percentage.

Figure 1-30 The Page menu.

The View Menu

The View menu changes the size of the page view in the document window and hides or displays other elements on the screen. None of these commands affects how the document looks when it is printed.

View

Fit in Window	⌘0
50%	
75%	
✓Actual Size	⌘1
200%	
Thumbnails	
Hide Guides	
Show Baseline Grid	
✓Snap to Guides	
Hide Rulers	⌘R
Show Invisibles	⌘I
Hide Tools	
Hide Measurements	
Hide Document Layout	
Show Style Sheets	
Show Colors	
Show Trap Information	

Figure 1-31 The View menu.

The Utilities Menu

The Utilities menu includes commands used in checking spelling and setting up a hyphenation exceptions dictionary. The new Library command lets you set up and easily access collections of commonly used text and graphic elements. Font Usage and Picture Usage commands let you view and edit lists of all the fonts used in a document and all the pictures imported into the document. Through this menu you can also edit or create your own tables used for kerning or tracking the space between letters.

Utilities

Check Spelling	▶
Auxiliary Dictionary...	
Edit Auxiliary...	
Suggested Hyphenation...	⌘H
Hyphenation Exceptions...	
Library...	
Font Usage...	
Picture Usage...	
Tracking Edit...	
Kerning Table Edit...	

Figure 1-32 The Utilities Menu

Summary

You should now be familiar with some of the basic concepts and terminology that you will encounter in learning QuarkXPress. The best way to learn QuarkXPress is to use it. If you have never used QuarkXPress before, go through the tutorial provided with the program to get a quick overview of its features. No matter what your level of experience, you'll find many useful tips throughout this book for using QuarkXPress efficiently.

2 *Creating One Page*

Before you can master QuarkXPress, it's important to understand the basics. In the introduction we summarized the overall sequence of steps involved in creating a QuarkXPress document. In this chapter we isolate the basic steps in the page-layout process and describe them in more detail: starting a new document, defining the page size and margins, and working with items on a page.

In this chapter you will learn how to start a new document or open an existing one. Text boxes and picture boxes, called *items*, are the most basic building blocks of any page in QuarkXPress, and you will learn how to use QuarkXPress' *item creation tools* to create boxes and lines. You'll also learn how to type or import text into a QuarkXPress text box, how to draw simple graphics with QuarkXPress tools, and how to import pictures—graphics that have been created in other applications—into a QuarkXPress picture box. You will learn how to select items and how to resize, rotate, and apply color to them. We'll also take our first look at how to create relationships between items by linking text boxes, anchoring boxes and lines within text, and grouping and constraining items.

This chapter focuses on positioning and determining the appearance of items on a page. Chapter 3 describes commands for adding pages, maneuvering through a document, and changing the page layout. It also describes how to work with master pages and how to use the library feature. Commands for working with the *content* of items—editing text and graphic elements—are described in more detail in Chapters 4 to 6.

We assume that you have already read Chapter 1, which presented an overview of the basic concepts and terminology related to QuarkXPress. If you encounter a term you are unfamiliar with, please refer to the last chapter or to the detailed glossary in the QuarkXPress documentation.

Setting Up a New Document

You can create a new document in QuarkXPress by double-clicking on the QuarkXPress program icon, selecting the File → New (⌘-N) command, and making entries in the New dialog box. If the document you want to create is similar to other documents that you have already created, you may save time by opening the similar document, modifying it, and saving it under a different name. These two options are described later in this section.

Before you begin any project, it's a good idea to plan what you'll be doing. If the document will include text and graphics created in other programs, organize your disk files before you start to build a QuarkXPress document.

Organizing Your Disk Files

Here is a quick summary of our recommendations about file organization:

- Decide on the conventions you will use in naming all new files created during the project.
- Copy all of your source files onto one hard disk.
- Keep a backup version of all files, and back up files regularly.
- Keep all files related to one document in a single folder.

These few steps are worth taking before you begin assembling text and graphics on a page. Taking time with these preliminaries can save you hours over the life of a large project. It's easy to apply these simple steps to small projects as well. Chapter 14 offers more detailed suggestions about organizing large projects.

Creating a New Document

Once you have organized your files, you can create a new QuarkXPress document by double-clicking on the program icon and choosing the New command. When you start QuarkXPress by double-clicking on the program icon, the startup screen displays the QuarkXPress menu titles as well as copyright information and the version number of the program you are using. The screen then changes to display the menu bar. It may also display any one of QuarkXPress' palettes. (QuarkXPress displays only those palettes that were open when you last quit the program.)

When you choose File → New (⌘-N), QuarkXPress displays the New dialog box (Figure 2-1). This is where you specify the page size, column guides, and margin guides.

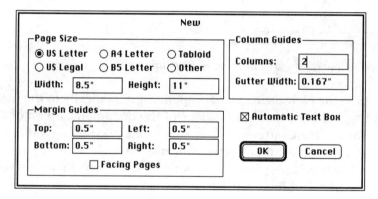

Figure 2-1 The New dialog box.

The values shown when the New dialog box first opens are the same as those specified the last time you started a new document. In other words, the Page Size, Margin Guides, Facing Pages, Column Guides, and Automatic Text Box entries are maintained as new settings each time you use the New command. Once you close the New dialog box, QuarkXPress displays a blank page 1 for a new document. Figure 2-2 shows how the settings in the New dialog box affect a page.

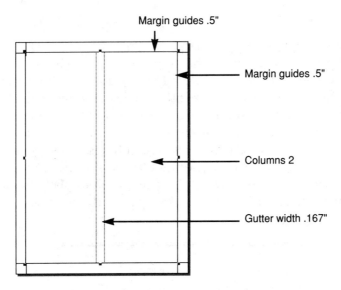

Margin guides .5"

Margin guides .5"

Columns 2

Gutter width .167"

Figure 2-2 How the New dialog box entries affect a page.

Entries in the New dialog box are applied automatically to the first doc-ument page and the first master page of the document. If you decide to change these settings after you have started the document, you can do so using the File ➤ Document Setup command or, if a master page is dis-played, using the Page ➤ Master Guides command. The following sections discuss the effects of these settings.

Page Size

QuarkXPress offers five standard page sizes, or you can enter any size from 1 inch by 1 inch up to 24 inches by 48 inches (if Facing Pages is selected) or 48 inches by 48 inches (for single-sided documents). You can see the five standard page measurements by clicking on each one and viewing the width and height measurements associated with each.

US Letter	8.5 by 11 inches
US Legal	8.5 by 14 inches
Tabloid	11 by 17 inches
A4	210 by 297 millimeters (8.268 by 11.693 inches)
B5	176 by 250 millimeters (6.929 by 9.843 inches)

US Letter and US Legal are standard American paper sizes; A4 Letter and B5 Letter, usually specified in millimeters, are standards in other countries. Tabloid is a small newspaper size.

You can enter values in any unit of measure in the New dialog box or any other dialog box in QuarkXPress, regardless of the unit of measure displayed. You can also change a value by adding or subtracting from the current setting.

The page size you specify in the New dialog box is not necessarily the size of the paper that you will be feeding into a laser printer or imagesetter. The page size determines the measurements of the page defined by the page border on the screen. You may specify Tabloid size, for example, and print the large page out in two pieces on 8.5-by-11-inch sheets of paper, using the Tiling option of the Print command (see Chapter 7).

Or you may specify a page size smaller than the sheets of paper you print on. In that case, you can use the Registration Marks option in the Print command's dialog box to print crop marks that indicate where the pages will be trimmed and registration marks used in aligning color separations (Figure 2-3).

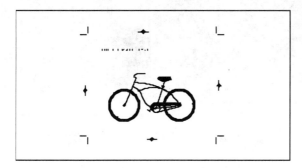

Figure 2-3 Page layouts that are smaller than the paper in the printer can be printed with crop marks and registration marks.

If you decide to change the page size after you have started working on a document, use the File ➤ Document Setup command (Figure 2-4).

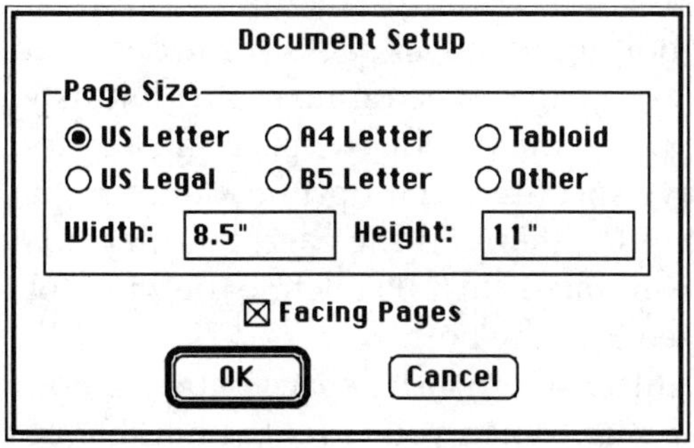

Figure 2-4 The Document Setup dialog box lets you change page size.

If you increase the page size after starting to build a document, all items will retain their position relative to the top left corner—that is, you will have wider white areas to the right and bottom edges of the page. If you decrease the page size to the point where an item no longer fits on the page, the item will extend onto the pasteboard (Figure 2-5).

Figure 2-5 Items are forced onto pasteboard when page size is decreased.

 The automatic text box, described later in this chapter, changes size when you change page size. Changing page size will cause the text to reflow on all pages that use the automatic text box.

Columns

QuarkXPress' default setting is 1 column. The number of columns you specify in the New dialog box applies to all pages of the document, unless you change individual master pages. The number of columns you set in the New dialog box will apply to the first master page and also to the automatic text box, if you have specified that option. Column guides on a page serve as aids in positioning items on the page, but they do not affect text. Column guides in an automatic text box define the width of text that is typed, imported, or pasted into the box.

QuarkXPress' default gutter width—the space between columns—is equal to 1 pica, or 0.167 inches. When you enter the number of columns and the amount of space you want between each column, QuarkXPress divides the page into equal columns between margins (Figure 2-6).

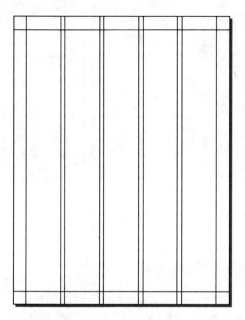

Figure 2-6 QuarkXPress divides a page into columns of equal width.

    QuarkXPress imposes a maximum limit of 30 columns per box, and the
gutter width can be set from a minimum of 3 points up to a maximum of
288 points (or 4 inches). The maximum number of columns allowed on a
particular page is therefore limited by the distance between the margins of
the page and the space between the columns, and not just the 30-column
maximum. In practice, you should rarely exceed this limit.
    On a black-and-white monitor, master column guides are represented as
thin black lines. On a color monitor, they display in the default color,
blue, unless you change their color by selecting Edit ➤ Preferences➤
Application. You can set guides to display in front of or behind boxes on
the page by using the Edit ➤ Preferences ➤ General command (⌘-Y),
described in Chapter 3. Column guides in a text box are displayed as dotted lines within the text box.

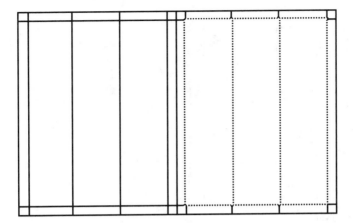

Figure 2-7 Master column guides are displayed as solid lines (left). Text box column guides are displayed as dotted lines (right).

You can change column settings for text boxes using the Item ➤ Modify command or the Measurements palette. You can change the number of columns and gutter width for individual master pages using the Page ➤ Master Guides command, described in Chapter 3.

Margin Guides

Like column guides, the margin guide values entered in the New dialog box apply to all pages of a document, unless they are changed for individual master pages by selecting the Page ➤ Master Guides command.

And, like column guides, on a black-and-white monitor margin guides are represented as thin black lines; on a color monitor they display in the default color, blue, unless you change their color in the dialog box under Edit ➤ Preferences➤ Application.

Margin guides serve as guides only and do not affect the position of text except through their effect on the automatic text box. Margins determine the distance from the edges of the automatic text box to the edges of the page. Headers and footers normally fall outside these margins, and you can position other text or graphics beyond the margins if your design calls for it.

When the Facing Pages option is selected, the inside margin measure is applied to the left margin of odd-numbered pages and to the right margin of even-numbered pages. The inside margin is often wider than the outside margin, to accommodate binding.

Facing Pages

The Facing Pages option lets you create and view pages that will face each other in double-sided printing. Deselect the Facing Pages option if you want to create a single-sided document.

Single-sided documents in QuarkXPress are distinguished by two characteristics:

- They let you create only single-sided master pages.
- They let you specify Left and Right margins. The Left Margin is often set wide enough to accommodate binding.

If you create a new document as a single-sided document, the first master page will be a single-sided master and will remain so even if you change to Facing Pages later through the File ➤ Document Setup command. If you do change to Facing Pages, however, you will be able to create single-sided or facing-page masters later.

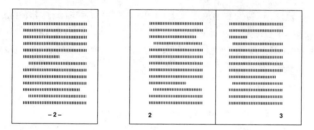

Figure 2-8 Single-sided versus facing-page documents.

Facing-page documents in QuarkXPress are distinguished by the following characteristics:

- They let you view two facing pages at once.
- They offer both single-sided and facing-page master pages. Facing-page master pages provide two page masters each: one for left (even-numbered) pages and one for right (odd-numbered) pages.
- They let you have different headers and footers on left and right pages.
- They let you specify inside and outside margins. The Inside Margin measure applies to the right margin of left pages and the left margin of right pages. Inside margins are usually set wider than outside margins to accommodate binding.

Single-sided and facing-page documents both offer the option of creating spreads—adjacent pages that will face each other across a fold in the final publication. You can *bleed* an illustration across pages in a spread. While facing pages can include elements that bleed from one page to another in a spread, they are usually separated by a bound edge rather than by a fold.

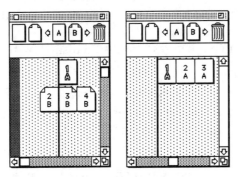

Figure 2-9 Document Layout palette shows a facing-page document with a fold-out page spread (left) and a single-sided, three-fold brochure set up as a three-page spread (right).

You can use the File → Document Setup command to turn Facing Pages on or off, regardless of the option chosen in the New dialog box. However, to turn Facing Pages off, you must first delete all facing-page masters.

Automatic Text Box

Remember that the *box* is the basic building block in QuarkXPress. Text boxes can be linked to direct the flow of text from one page to another or from one box to another on the same page. This will happen automatically if you set up an *automatic text box*, or you can use the Linking tool manually to link a series of text boxes and create a chain.

If Automatic Text Box is checked in the New dialog box, QuarkXPress will automatically create a text box with margins and columns as specified in the New dialog box. This text box will appear on the first master page and on the first page of a new document. When you type or import text into an automatic text box, a new page will be added automatically as needed to accommodate text overflow, unless you set Auto Page Insertion *off* in the General Preferences dialog box.

If Automatic Text Box is not checked, margin and column guides will be displayed on the pages but the text box will not be created automatically. An automatic text box can be added later using techniques described in Chapter 3.

Building a New Document from an Existing Document

At first, you will probably be building all of your documents from scratch, starting with a new blank page. If you are learning QuarkXPress for the first time, however, it may be easier to start with a template or document that someone else has already created.

A template differs from a document. When you use the Save command, a template always displays the Save As dialog box without a document name, so you cannot accidentally overwrite the original. Templates are explained in detail in Chapter 8.

You can open any document or template by double-clicking on the document icon from the Desktop, or you can double-click on the QuarkXPress program icon and use the File ➤ Open command to open an existing QuarkXPress document or template. If you use the File ➤ Open command, a dialog box is displayed that shows the list of QuarkXPress files in the currently open folder on your disk (Figure 2-10). When you click once on a document name to select it, the dialog box will also display the version number of QuarkXPress the document was created in and the latest version number it was saved in.

To open a file, first choose All Types, Documents, or Templates, click on the file name to highlight it, and then click on the Open button. You can also simply double-click on the file name of the document you want to open.

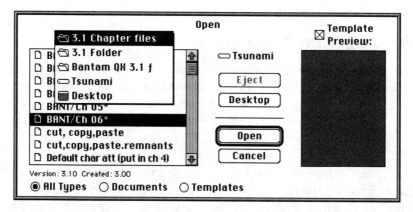

Figure 2-10 The Open dialog box, with pop-down menu listing higher directory levels.

The Open dialog box lets you easily distinguish between templates or documents by choosing to display either one. Chapter 8 lists specific differences between templates and documents.

If you click once on the name of a QuarkXPress template and click on Template Preview in the dialog box, a thumbnail preview of the first page of the template and the page size will display in the dialog box, as shown in Figure 2-11.

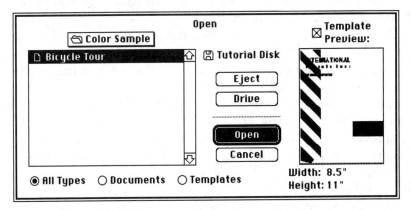

Figure 2-11 Preview of a template in the Open dialog box.

When you open a document or a template, QuarkXPress displays the first page of the document in the view scale in which the document was last saved. Once a document is open, you can modify it using all of the techniques described here and in subsequent chapters.

Viewing Pages on the Screen

When you open a QuarkXPress document, often you can see only part of a page or document in the document window. You can change your view of the page on the screen in several ways. You can use the scroll bars in the document window to scroll up or down on a page or up or down from one page to the next. You can use the View menu commands, the Zoom tool (Q), or input a view percentage directly in the View Percent field in the lower left corner of the screen to jump to enlarged views of a particular area or reduce the page image to a smaller size. The View menu also offers commands for hiding certain elements on the screen or on the page view. These techniques are described below.

Using the View Menu

The first six commands in the View menu change the size of your view of the page—enlarging or reducing your view of the page on the screen. The currently selected view shows a check mark. The two most commonly used views—Fit in Window (⌘-0) and Actual Size (⌘-1)—have their keyboard combination shortcuts shown on the menu.

Fit in Window is a good view for checking and changing the position of objects on the page and for viewing facing pages or multiple-page spreads. Select 50 percent to view the full width of 11-inch-wide formats on a 9-inch screen (or up to 16 inches on a 13-inch screen); 75 percent is ideal for viewing the full width of an 8 1/2-by-11-inch page (without seeing its full length on a normal 9-inch or 13-inch screen). Actual Size is the normal view for editing text and graphics. The 200 percent view is useful for editing small-size text. The Thumbnails view lets you see miniatures of all pages at once, but you cannot edit individual items on a page.

Using the Zoom Tool

The quickest way to change the size of your view of the page is with the Zoom tool (Q). Choose the Zoom tool from the Tool palette, position the pointer over the portion of the page you want to enlarge, and click. To reduce the scale, hold down the Option key as you click the pointer on the page. The Zoom tool pointer shows a plus sign (⊕) when you are enlarging, a minus sign (⊖) when you are reducing, and is empty (Q) when you are already at the maximum enlargement or minimum reduction. The current view percentage is displayed in the lower left corner of the document window. The Zoom tool does not operate in Thumbnails view.

The most efficient way to use the Zoom tool is to switch to it at any time by holding down the Control key. Press the Control key and the pointer will change to the Zoom tool pointer; then click the mouse to enlarge the view. Press Control-Option and click to reduce the view.

You can also drag the Zoom tool to outline a rectangular area on a page; the area you select will enlarge to fill the screen. If you select a very small area on the screen, for example, the view percentage will be high.

The View Scale settings in the Edit ➤ Preferences ➤ Tools dialog box determine the range and increment of the view changes when you click with the Zoom tool selected. See Chapter 3 for information on setting tool preferences.

Using the View Percent Field

The percentage of the view scale is shown in the lower left corner of the document window. This area is called the *View Percent* field (Figure 2-12). This field is interactive: It not only shows what view you are currently in, but you can also type in the view percentage you wish to display.

Double-click on the field, and enter the scale view you prefer. Pressing the return key or clicking in the document window causes the display to change to the scale indicated.

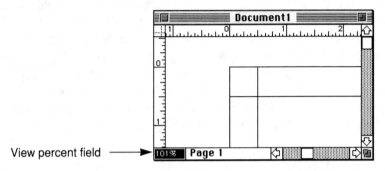

View percent field

Figure 2-12 You can type directly in the View Percent field.

At times, this method may be the fastest way to change the view of a page, and one of the most useful. For example, if you need to see many pages of your document at once, type in a small percentage, such as 15 percent. The display is similar to that shown when you select Thumbnails view, but, as was discussed earlier, you cannot edit items directly in Thumbnails view; by using 15 percent view, you can easily move items from one page to another.

Hiding and Displaying Nonprinting Elements

Four of the next commands in the View menu—Hide Guides, Hide Baseline Grid, Hide Rulers, and Hide Invisibles—let you hide or display nonprinting elements on the screen. These elements include guides (margin guides, column guides, and ruler guides), the baseline grid, rulers, and invisible characters, such as carriage returns and tabs (Figure 2-13).

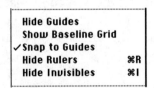

Figure 2-13 View menu commands that affect nonprinting elements on a page.

These commands are toggle commands that change in the menu when selected. In other words, if the guides are currently displayed, the command in the menu is Hide Guides. When you choose Hide Guides, for example, the command in the menu changes to Show Guides; the same is true for the other commands in this section of the View menu. The Snap to Guides command is also a toggle, but it shows a check mark when selected. The snap-to effect is described later in this chapter.

Hide/Show Guides

Guides include margin, column, and ruler guides. To view the page exactly as it will appear when printed, deselect all items by clicking in the margin of the page outside all boxes and choose Hide Guides.

Hide/Show Baseline Grid

The ability to display the Baseline Grid is a feature new to QuarkXPress 3.1. The preset default is that the baseline grid is not displayed. The increments of the baseline grid can be defined by selecting the Edit ➤ Preferences ➤ Typographic command, which is discussed in more detail in Chapter 5.

Hide/Show Rulers

Rulers appear on the left side and top of the document window. The preset default is that rulers are displayed. The increments of the rulers can be defined by selecting the Edit ➤ Preferences ➤ General command, which is discussed in more detail in Chapter 3.

Hide/Show Invisibles

Invisibles are all of the nonprinting characters that can be typed in using the keyboard, such as spaces, carriage returns, and tabs. All of QuarkXPress' invisible characters are discussed in detail in Chapter 4. You may find it useful to display these characters, especially when typing directly in QuarkXPress, because it makes it easier to see exactly what you are typing. For example, accidentally typing in a space after a tab character will cause your text to be misaligned; it is difficult to see the extra space unless invisible characters are displayed. The default setting is that invisible characters are not displayed.

Hiding and Displaying Palettes

 QuarkXPress offers six palettes that provide various aids to efficient production: the Tools palette, the Measurements palette, the Document Layout palette, and, new to version 3.1, the Style Sheets palette, the Colors palette, and the Trap Information palette. The function of each of these palettes is discussed in detail in later chapters.

> **Hide Tools**
> **Hide Measurements**
> **Show Document Layout**
> **Show Style Sheets**
> **Show Colors**
> **Show Trap Information**

Figure 2-14 Commands for displaying or hiding QuarkXPress palettes.

When you first install QuarkXPress, only the Tools palette and the Measurements palettes are displayed. Like the Show/Hide Guides commands, the commands to Show or Hide palettes act as a toggle switch. For example, when the Tools palette is already visible, the command on the menu reads Hide Tools. If the Tool palette is not visible on the screen, the command reads Show Tools.

 You can easily close these palettes by clicking in the Close box on the Title bar for each palette. The menu commands are most efficiently used only to Show the palettes when they are not displayed.

Creating Items

We now describe the basic steps in adding items—text boxes, picture boxes, and lines—to a page, and how to modify them. The techniques described in the following sections are also used to add items to document pages or master pages.

As we have said, the box is the basic building block for all text and pictures in QuarkXPress documents. Before you can add text or a graphic to a page, you must create a box to contain it. Boxes as well as lines can stand alone as graphic elements on the page if you assign a visible background or frame. You can also fill a box with text or an imported picture.

Creating a Box

You can draw two basic kinds of boxes in QuarkXPress: text boxes or picture boxes. For text boxes, you can let QuarkXPress create text boxes automatically on each page. This happens if you select the Automatic Text Box setting in the New dialog box, as described earlier in this chapter. You can also create text boxes using the Text Box creation tool (Ⓐ). After drawing the box, select the Content tool (🖑), and a blinking text cursor appears in the upper left corner of the box. Then you can type text directly into QuarkXPress or import it from a word processing program.

Boxes that can contain graphics are drawn using the Rectangular Picture Box tool (⊠), the Rounded-Corner Rectangle Picture Box tool (⊠), the Oval Picture Box tool (⊗), and the Polygon Picture Box tool (⊠). These tools create boxes with square corners, boxes with rounded corners, circles and ovals, or polygons, respectively, that can contain graphics imported from other sources.

To create a box with any of these tools, select the tool and position the Item Creation pointer (+) on the page. As you drag the pointer on the page, you create a box. The size of a box is displayed in the Measurements palette as you draw, if that palette is open.

The one exception to this technique is the Polygon Picture Box tool [⊠], which is used by clicking on each point of the polygon shape you wish to draw and then double-clicking or clicking on the first point to close the polygon. The size of the polygon does not display in the Measurements palette until it is closed.

 Hold down the Shift key as you draw in order to constrain boxes to square shapes (for text or rectangular graphics boxes) or circles (for oval graphics boxes). When you release the mouse button the box is active, as indicated by its dark border and eight black "handles" (Figure 2-15).

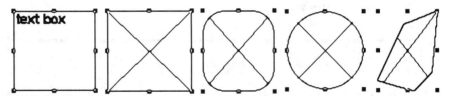

Figure 2-15 Drag the item creation pointer to create a box. When you release the mouse button the box is active, as indicated by its dark border and eight handles.

Creating a Line

Select the Orthogonal Line tool (+) to draw horizontal and vertical lines and the diagonal Line tool (╲) to draw lines at any angle. The Orthogonal Line tool is simply an alternative to the Line tool, since you can constrain any line drawn with the diagonal Line tool to 0-, 45-, or 90-degree angles by holding down the Shift key as you draw. The Shift key also constrains lines to these angles when you resize them by dragging one of their handles.

Selecting Items

While you are creating a document in QuarkXPress, you can use the menu commands, tools from the Tool palette, or keyboard shortcuts to edit text or to work with graphics. Most of these commands will affect only the object or objects that are selected or active at the time the command is invoked; if nothing is active at the time the command is used, then nothing happens! This may seem obvious, yet beginners often mistakenly execute a command without first selecting the object for which it is intended. In this section we describe how to select boxes and lines created with QuarkXPress' item creation tools.

Selecting One Item

To select a single text box, picture box, or line with the Item tool (✥), position the pointer over the box or line and click once to select it. Active boxes show small black handles at the corners and midpoints of edges, and lines have one handle at each end (Figure 2-16). You do not have to select the Item tool from the Tools palette; instead, regardless of what tool is active, hold down the Command key (⌘) to change the pointer to the Item tool pointer temporarily.

Figure 2-16 Handles on an active line.

If an item is hidden by another, QuarkXPress 3.1 allows you to activate the hidden item underneath. With the Content tool selected, hold down the Command key (⌘), the Option key, and the Shift key before clicking where the hidden item is located. If several items are stacked on one another, successive clicks of the mouse will activate items from the top down to the bottom.

Selecting Multiple Items

QuarkXPress version 3.0 introduced the ability to select more than one item at a time. There are five ways to select multiple items; with the Item tool (✥) selected (note that for multiple selection you must select the Item tool from the Tool palette; you cannot use the Command key shortcut temporarily to change the pointer to the Item tool):

- Hold down the Shift key as you click on several different items—one at a time. You can select more than one item at a time this way, and the items need not be adjacent to each other.

- If the items are adjacent to each other, you can position the Item tool pointer (⬉) in an empty area at the top left corner of the area to be selected and drag the pointer to the bottom right corner. A selection rectangle will appear as you drag. Active items will be marked with handles. (Items that are partially encompassed will also be selected.)

- You can use a combination of the preceding two methods: holding down the Shift key and either clicking to select one item at a time or dragging to select groups of items.

- Use Edit → Select All (⌘-A) to select all of the items on the active page or spread, including the pasteboard.

- Use any of the first four methods to select a group of items, then hold down the Shift key and click on an active item to *deselect* it from a group.

The multiple-item select feature enables you to select multiple items and perform actions on all those items at once. For example, when you select multiple items, you can use commands described in this chapter to move, cut, copy, paste, align, duplicate, delete, and lock all items; send all items behind; or bring all items forward. You can also apply the Group command to establish and maintain a group relationship.

The multiple-item select feature works only with the Item tool and only on items within a spread. You cannot select multiple items with the Content tool or select multiple items that are not part of the same spread.

Using the Select All Command

The effect of Edit → Select All (⌘-A) depends on the current tool selection and pointer position on the screen:

- If the Content tool (☜) is selected and the cursor is positioned in a text box (by positioning the I-beam pointer [I] in the text box and clicking once to position the blinking text cursor, then the Select All command will select all of the text in the active box *and the text in all boxes linked to the active box.*

- If the Item tool (✥) is selected, then the Select All command will select all text boxes, picture boxes, and lines on the active spread and on the adjacent pasteboard area. If any of the active items are locked, then the pointer will change to a padlock (🔒) when positioned over *any* item (locked or not), and the active group cannot be moved with the mouse unless you unlock all items in it.

Whenever multiple items are selected, only those commands that are applicable to *all* types of items in the selection will be available. For example, if the selection includes only text boxes and picture boxes, you can use the Item ➤ Frame command to set a common frame (border) for all the active items. If the selection also includes any lines, however, the Frame command will not be available. Commands that are not available will be gray in the menus, or the system will beep when you try to select one inappropriately.

Moving and Resizing Items

QuarkXPress offers different methods for accomplishing the same task. Items often can be modified by using the mouse, keyboard shortcuts, the Measurements palette, the Colors palette, or commands from the Item menu, especially the Item ➤ Modify command. The next sections describe various techniques for moving (repositioning) and resizing items.

Using the Mouse

Once a box is created, you can change the position of a box on the page by selecting the Item tool (✥), clicking on an item, and dragging the item by any part except its handles to move it. As mentioned in the previous section, a good shortcut to use is to hold down the ⌘ key to activate the Item tool temporarily and then move the item. Hold down the shift key to constrain the movement of an item horizontally or vertically as you move it.

If you click on an item and drag it immediately, you will see only an outline of the item. If you pause one-half second before you move an item, you will see the item and its contents as you move.

If you select an item with the Item tool selected (not the Content tool), you can move the item using the arrow keys on the keyboard. Each time you press a key, the item will move in 1-point increments. Hold down the option key and press an arrow key to move in .1-point increments.

With either the Item tool or the Content tool selected, you can change the size of the box by dragging a handle of the box. Drag a corner handle to scale both dimensions at once. Drag a side handle when you want to scale only one dimension. When resizing a box, you can constrain it to a square or circle by holding down the Shift key as you drag a handle.

To change the length of a line using the mouse, drag one of the handles on either end of the line. Hold down the shift key to keep the line straight as you resize it or to constrain it to 45° angles.

Using the Measurements Palette

You can also change the position and size (and other features) of a box or line through the Measurements palette (Figure 2-17) or through the Item ➤ Modify command, described in the next section. The Measurements palette is probably the easiest way to modify items, and we highly recommend you display and use it.

	X: 4.319"	W: 0.917"	⊿ 0°	
	Y: 8.361"	H: 0.486"	Cols: 1	

Figure 2-17 You can view or change the location and size of a box through the Measurements palette.

When a box is active, the fields in the Measurements palette include:

- X—the horizontal position of the origin of the box relative to the current zero point on the rulers.
- Y—the vertical position of the origin of the box relative to the current zero point on the rulers. (Note that the origin is the *original* top left corner of the box, which is not necessarily the apparent top left corner if the box has been rotated.)
- W—the width of the box.
- H—the height of the box.

You can change the position or the size of a box by selecting the appropriate field in the Measurements palette and entering a new value. Press the return key or click on the document window for the new value to take effect. You can also add or subtract values from the current values; QuarkXPress calculates the new value and changes the box accordingly.

The Measurements palette is different when a line is selected, and the values you enter to reposition or resize a line depend on the orientation you have selected: Endpoints, Left Point, Midpoint, or Right Point (Figure 2-18).

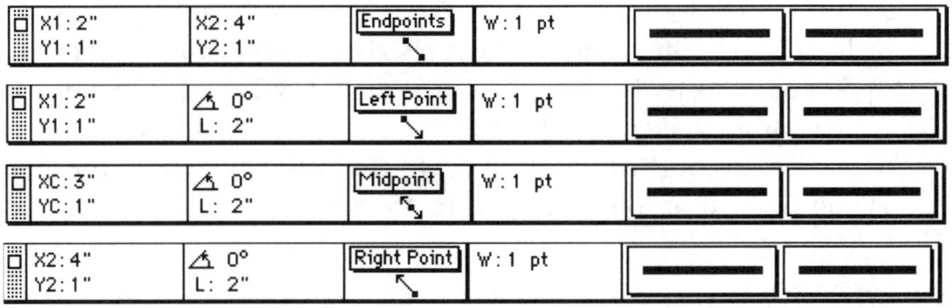

X1 : 2"	X2 : 4"	Endpoints	W : 1 pt	
Y1 : 1"	Y2 : 1"			
X1 : 2"	∠ 0°	Left Point	W : 1 pt	
Y1 : 1"	L : 2"			
XC : 3"	∠ 0°	Midpoint	W : 1 pt	
YC : 1"	L : 2"			
X2 : 4"	∠ 0°	Right Point	W : 1 pt	
Y2 : 1"	L : 2"			

Figure 2-18 The same 2-inch-long line shown by its Endpoints, Left Point, Midpoint, and Right Point.

Besides the position coordinates and size, additional entries in the Measurements palette will vary depending on whether the active item is a text box, an anchored text box, a picture box, an anchored picture box, or a group. These entries are explained in detail in Chapters 3 through 6.

Using the Item ➤ Modify Command

Commands on the Item menu (Figure 2-19), discussed here and throughout the chapter, affect items themselves, as opposed to the *content* of items. Entries for changing the position and size of items, as displayed on the Measurements palette, are duplicated in the dialog boxes displayed by using the Item ➤ Modify command.

Item	
Modify...	⌘M
Frame...	⌘B
Runaround...	⌘T
Duplicate	⌘D
Step and Repeat...	
Delete	⌘K
Group	⌘G
Ungroup	⌘U
Constrain	
Lock	⌘L
Send to Back	
Bring to Front	
Space/Align...	
Picture Box Shape	▶
Reshape Polygon	

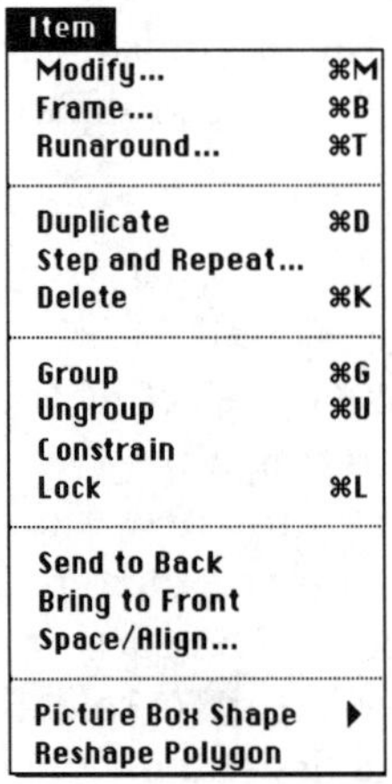

Figure 2-19 The Item menu.

The Item ➤ Modify command is available when a text box, picture box, line, or group is active. You can access this command by choosing it from the menu, using the keyboard shortcut (⌘-M), or simply double-clicking on an item with the Item tool (✛) selected. Depending on which type of item is active, the Modify command displays one of four dialog boxes: Text Box Specifications, Picture Box Specifications, Line Specifications, or Group Specifications.

The values for position and width entered in these dialog boxes (Figure 2-20) are the same as those displayed in the Measurements palette. Remember that in this or any dialog box, you can enter any unit of measure, or you can change a value by adding or subtracting from the current setting.

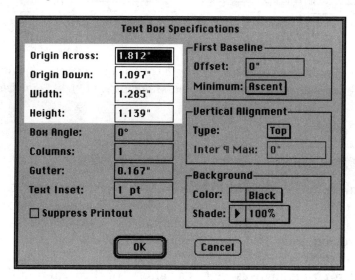

Figure 2-20 All Box Specifications dialog boxes let you enter values for changing the position and size of boxes.

In the Text Box Specifications and Picture Box Specifications dialog boxes, **Origin Across** and **Origin Down** indicate the numerical position of the origin as measured from the zero point on the rulers. (The *origin* is the *original* top left corner of the box, which is not necessarily the apparent top left corner if the box has been rotated.). **Width** and **Height** are the dimensions of the box. By entering these four values numerically, you can specify precise placement of a text box on a page within up to .001 units of any measure.

The minimum text box width and height is 12 points. Text boxes that have no leading (that is, empty ones or ones that contain only one character) can be scaled down to within 10 points (plus the Text Inset value) of the top of the box without causing text to overflow. See Chapter 4 for more information on other modifications that can be made to text boxes and Chapter 6 for more information on picture boxes.

The Line Specifications dialog box also duplicates the position and size values shown in the Measurements palette. And, as in the Measurements palette, values entered for changing the position and length of a line depend on whether Endpoints, Left Point, Midpoint, or Right Point is selected.

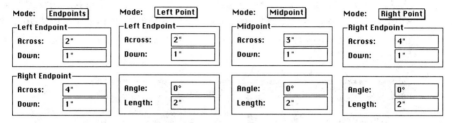

Figure 2-21 The Line Specifications dialog box showing values for the same 2-inch-long line with Endpoints, Left Point, Midpoint, and Right Point selected.

Rotating Items

You can use the Rotation tool (↻) to rotate an item: First, select the item with the Item tool, then select the Rotation tool. Next, click once on or near the item to position the axis of rotation (the point around which the item will rotate), then drag the pointer away from the axis point in a circular motion to rotate the item. You can see the axis point and a line indicating the rotation angle as well as a "ghost" of the item rotate as you move the pointer (Figure 2-22).

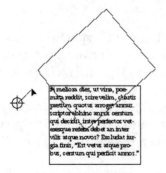

Figure 2-22 In rotating an item with the Rotate tool, you can see the axis point and a line indicating the rotation angle as well as a "ghost" of the item as you move the pointer.

You can enter angles of rotation numerically in either the Measurements palette or by selecting the Item → Modify command. A positive value indicates a counterclockwise rotation, a negative value indicates a clockwise rotation. Boxes are rotated from the center by means of dialog box entries or from first mouse position when rotated with the Rotate tool. If Endpoints is selected lines cannot be rotated using dialog box entries.

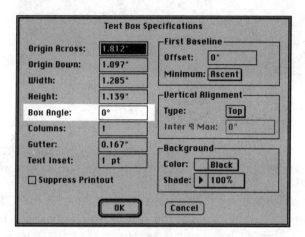

Figure 2-23 Specify the angle of a box numerically in the Measurements palette or in any of the Box Specification dialog boxes (Item → Modify).

Changing the Appearance of Items

There are several ways in which you can modify the appearance of an item, independently of the *content* of the item. For example, you can apply a color to the background of a text box without affecting the text at all. This section looks at the basic steps involved in applying color and shade to an item, and how to add a frame to a box. Reshaping picture boxes is discussed in Chapter 6.

Applying Color and Shade to Items

All boxes drawn in QuarkXPress can have color and shade applied to them, using either the Item → Modify command or, new to version 3.1, the Colors palette (Figure 2-24). The available colors listed include default colors that cannot be deleted, such as black, white, cyan, magenta, and yellow, as well as any colors you have defined with the Edit → Colors command (explained in detail in Chapter 7).

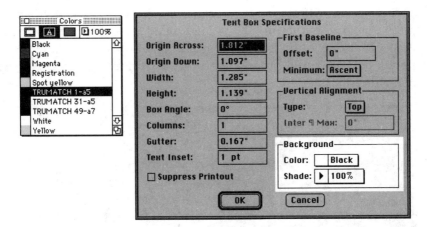

Figure 2-24 Apply a color and shade to the background of a box using the Colors palette or in any of the Box Specification dialog boxes (Item ➤ Modify).

For any box, you can specify a Background of any Color listed in the pop-up menu or on the Colors palette. You can indicate any shade from 0 to 100 percent in .1 percent increments, or choose from the 10 percent increments in the pop-up menu. Specify a background color of None to make a transparent box. The default setting for the background color of a box when it is first drawn is 0 percent black.

Using the Colors palette, you can apply two-color blends to picture or text box backgrounds. See Chapter 7 for more details on how to create blends.

For any line, you can specify a color and shade using the Measurements palette, the Item ➤ Modify command, or the Style menu.

When a text box, even a transparent one (0 percent shade), is made active and the Content tool (☞) is selected, the box is made temporarily opaque (that is, you cannot see through it) and is brought in front of all other boxes and lines to make editing its text easy.

In specifying screen percentages, be sure to take into account the differences between printers that will be used throughout the production cycle and typesetters that will be used for final camera-ready copy. For example, 10 percent gray screen will seem darker when printed on a 300 dpi printer than on a 1200 dpi typesetter, and at 2400 dpi the screen will nearly disappear. Screens that are below 50 percent gray will tend to print lighter on a high-resolution typesetter than on a low-resolution printer; screens that are above 50 percent gray will tend to print darker on a high-resolution typesetter than on a low-resolution printer.

Adding a Frame to a Box

Use Item → Frame (⌘-B) to add a decorative frame or border around an active text box or picture box. Using this command, you can frame boxes that contain text or imported graphics, or you can create framed geometrical items (boxes, ovals, circles) with QuarkXPress' item creation tools.

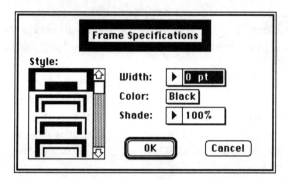

Figure 2-25 Frame Specifications dialog box.

The border around the Frame Specifications title in the dialog box reflects the current frame for the active box, and that frame is highlighted in the list of frame styles. You can select from a variety of styles that come with QuarkXPress and customize to some extent by choosing your own width, color, and shade for a frame. For greater flexibility, you can use the separate Frame Editor program, included in the QuarkXPress package, to create custom frames, as described in Chapter 11.

Style

The Style scroll window shows all of the frames that come with QuarkXPress plus any you have created with the Frame Editor. Bitmap frames—decorative frames provided with QuarkXPress plus any that you create with Frame Editor—can be applied only to *rectangular* boxes. Mathematically generated frames (consisting of continuous solid or dashed lines) can be applied to *any* box, including rounded-corner rectangles and to ovals and circles.

Very large or complex frames might not display accurately in the Style list, but you can preview the frames by applying them to a box on the page.

Width

Simple line frames can be specified to any width from .001 points to 504 points. Most patterned frames will print better in one of the predefined sizes listed in the Width pop-up menu and will look better when printed on a high-resolution printer than they do on the screen. You can use the Frame Editor to define additional sizes of patterned frames.

Remember that in this or any dialog box you can enter any unit of measure, or you can change a value by adding or subtracting from the current setting. See Chapter 1 for details.

When you specify a frame for a text box, the distance between the text and the frame is determined by the Item ➤ Modify ➤ Text Inset setting for that box. When you specify a frame for a picture box, the frame cuts off or crops the picture.

The Edit ➤ Preferences ➤ General command, described in Chapter 3, lets you specify whether new frames will display inside or outside the edges of a box. If the frame is added inside, the dimensions of the box remain the same. If the frame is added outside, the dimensions of the box increase by the frame width. Frame width will be limited under two conditions:

- If there is not enough room between the box edge and the edge of the constraining box in a constrained group or the edge of a pasteboard, and the General Preferences Framing option is set to Outside, and

- If there is not enough room inside the box, and the General Preferences Framing option is set to Inside.

Under these conditions, you can choose a smaller frame or enlarge or move the box. You can remove a frame from a box by choosing 0 as the frame width.

Color and Shade

The Frame Specifications dialog box allows you to select different colors or shades as options. Use the pop-up menu to select any color from a list of colors created using the Edit ➤ Colors command. You can also select any shade (in .1 percent increments) or choose from the 10 percent increments in the pop-up menu.

Importing Text and Pictures

Although you can create text and graphics directly using QuarkXPress' tools, it's common to import text and graphics from other sources into a QuarkXPress document, using the File ➤ Get Text and File ➤ Get Picture commands. Many authors use a dedicated word processing application for their text, for example, then hand their disk files over to a production group for final page layout in QuarkXPress. The author or a graphic artist might also choose a dedicated graphics application to develop complex graphics and manipulate scanned images before importing them into QuarkXPress.

Here we assume that you have already prepared the text and graphics that you intend to import into QuarkXPress. The next sections provide a brief overview of how to import text and graphics. For more detail on importing text, see Chapter 4; more information on importing graphics may be found in Chapter 6.

Importing Text

You can import text into an empty text box or into a text box that already contains text. Imported text will come in at the text insertion point—and this can be within text that is already in the text box—or it will replace text that is selected. With a text box active and the Content tool (🖐) selected, choose File ➤ Get Text to import text.

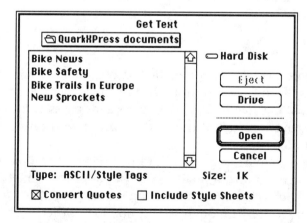

Figure 2-26 The Get Text dialog box.

The Get Text dialog box (Figure 2-26) displays a list of text files in the current disk/file folder. If the Get Text command is dimmed in the menu, be sure that a text box is active and that you have selected the Content tool.

Check Convert Quotes to convert quotation marks that were typed with the inch (") and foot (') symbols to proper opening and closing quotes that are generally preferred by publishers. (You type proper opening and closing quotes in QuarkXPress and in other applications on the Macintosh by pressing Option-[, Shift-Option-[, Option-], and Shift-Option-] to get ", ", ', and ', respectively.)

Check Include Style Sheets if you want QuarkXPress to pick up the styles that were applied in Microsoft Word or as tag codes in ASCII text. Chapter 4 lists the word processing applications that QuarkXPress supports. Chapter 10 describes QuarkXPress Tags that can be typed in ASCII text files.

When you click once on a text file name, the dialog box displays the file format and size. Double-click on a text file name to import it into the active text box. Text following the insertion point will be reflowed to accommodate the imported text, and text overflow will be handled as described next.

Importing Text Within a Stream

To import text into the middle of an existing stream of text, select the Content tool (🖑), click the I-beam to position the cursor at the point in the text where you want the new text inserted, or select a range of text that you want to replace, then choose File ➤ Get Text and follow the procedures just described.

Text Overflow

If you type or import text into an automatic text box, or any chain of two or more boxes, and Auto Page Insertion is on in the General Preferences dialog box (described in Chapter 3), QuarkXPress adds pages at the end of the section for the overflow text if the text file you import cannot fit in the automatic text box.

When you type or import more text than will fit in a text box that is not linked to another text box, a small square (⊠) appears in the bottom right corner of the box (Figure 2-27). You can see the rest of the text by making the box larger or by linking the text box to another, empty text box. The procedures for linking text from one box to another are described later in this chapter.

Figure 2-27 Symbol in lower right corner indicates text overflow (left) unless text box is enlarged (middle) or linked to another text box (right).

If you find that there is overflow text (as indicated by a ⊠ in the lower right corner of the last text box in a chain) but new pages are not added automatically when you import the text into the first box, then one of three conditions exists: The Auto Page Insertion is disabled in the General Preferences dialog box), the master page specified in Auto Page Insertion has a broken chain icon (⊕) in the upper left corner, or the overflow is from a single text box that is not defined on the master page as the automatic text box.

Importing Pictures

To import a graphic, draw or select the picture box that will contain the graphic, select the Content tool (☞), then choose File ➤ Get Picture. The Get Picture dialog box (Figure 2-28) displays a list of graphic-format files in the current disk or file folder.

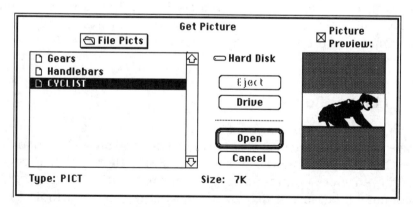

Figure 2-28 Get Picture dialog box with thumbnail preview.

When you click once on a file name, the dialog box displays the file format and size. If you check the Picture Preview option in the dialog box, a thumbnail preview of the picture displays in the dialog box (Figure 2-28) when you click once on the file name. To import a file into the active picture box, double-click on a file name.

QuarkXPress can import any of these formats: Paint (bitmap), TIFF and RIFF line art, TIFF and RIFF grayscale, TIFF color, PICT, black-and-white Encapsulated PostScript (EPS), and color Encapsulated PostScript (EPS). If you are not familiar with these terms, you can learn more about them in Chapter 6.

The entire unscaled picture that you import is placed in the active picture box, replacing any previous contents of the box. You may need to scale the picture to make it fit the box. You can scale a picture using a combination of keyboard and mouse techniques, described in Chapter 6.

Deleting Items

Four alternatives are available for deleting items from a page: choosing Edit ➤ Cut, choosing Edit ➤ Clear, pressing the Delete or Backspace key, or choosing Item ➤ Delete (⌘-K). The effects of these commands depend on what *tool* as well as what *items* are selected, as described under the next headings.

Regardless of what tool or element is selected, the Edit ➤ Clear command, the Item ➤ Delete command, and the Delete or Backspace key do *not* put the selection into the Clipboard, as the Edit ➤ Cut command does. The selection cannot be retrieved using the Paste command. The only way to retrieve objects after using the Clear command, the Delete command, or the Delete or Backspace key is to use the Undo command *immediately*.

Deleting Lines or Boxes

You can delete an *un-Anchored* line or box (including all box contents) by selecting it with the Item tool (✛) and choosing Edit ➤ Cut, choosing Edit ➤ Clear, pressing the Delete key, or choosing Item ➤ Delete (⌘-K). The Item ➤ Delete command is a useful alternative to using the Cut command, because it deletes items whether the Item tool (✛) or the Content tool (☞) is selected.

If a deleted text box is linked to any other text boxes, the links are reconnected around the deleted box and the text is reflowed to the other boxes in the chain. If deletion of a linked text box causes text to overflow in the linked chain, one or more new pages will be inserted automatically to handle the overflow if Auto Page Insertion and automatic linking on the master page are both enabled. You can prevent this by using Edit ➤ Preferences ➤ General to turn Auto Page Insertion off before deleting linked text boxes.

Deleting Text or Graphics from Within a Box

To delete text or graphics from within a box without deleting the box itself, you must select the text or picture with the Content tool (🖑) and then choose Edit ➤ Cut, Edit ➤ Clear, or press the Delete or Back-space key.

The Content tool automatically activates the entire contents of a picture box that contains an imported graphic. In deleting text from a text box, you can select all of the text or only part of it, using text selection methods described in Chapter 4.

If you select contents of a box and choose Item ➤ Delete (⌘-K), QuarkXPress will delete the entire box. If you use the Item tool (✤) to select a box, Item ➤ Delete (⌘-K), Edit ➤ Cut, Edit ➤ Clear, or the Delete or Backspace key deletes the entire box.

Undoing Your Most Recent Action

The Edit ➤ Undo (⌘-Z) reverses the action taken immediately before the command was invoked. For this reason, work cautiously when you are making major changes to a document—such as changing the type specifications or formatting a whole block of text or a whole story. Check the results of each action as you go along. You can reverse your last action if you use the Undo command *immediately* after making a mistake or changing your mind.

When you use the Undo command, the menu changes to Redo until you perform the next action. This command allows you to perform an action and then Undo and Redo as many times as you like, so long as you do not go on to any other actions. The command is handy for reversing mistakes or changing your mind, and you can use this command to compare two ideas while designing a page.

Some actions cannot be reversed by the Undo command. QuarkXPress usually displays a dialog box warning you that the action you are about to perform cannot be undone and gives you a chance to cancel the action.

Using Rulers to Position Items on a Page

Use View ➤ Show/Hide Rulers (⌘-R) to display or hide the horizontal and vertical rulers at the top and left edges of the document window. You can use these rulers to help position ruler guides, text, and graphics on the page, to measure distances, or to draw or scale graphics to fit an area.

To display rulers on the screen, select View ➤ Show Rulers (⌘-R). This is a toggle command—the menu displays Show Rulers if they are hidden and Hide Rulers if they are displayed.

The position of boxes or lines on the screen is indicated by a dotted marker on each ruler when you initially create the item or when you click, drag, or scale the item with the Mover pointer (✥) (Figure 2-29). This marker can be especially helpful in positioning items visually on the screen. (You can specify an item's position precisely in numerical terms through the Measurements palette or the Item ➤ Modify command.)

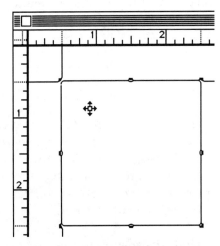

Figure 2-29 Markers on the rulers show the position of items as they are being moved or scaled.

The ruler origin is the intersection of the zero points of the two rulers. Normally, the origin is set at the top left corner of the page or spread (depending on the Item Coordinates setting in the General Preferences dialog box), but you can move the zero points by positioning the pointer in the small box where the rulers intersect and dragging the zero point to a new position. Crossed lines appear as you drag the zero point, to help you see where the new location will be when you release the mouse.

You can position the zero point anywhere on a page. To restore the zero point to the upper left corner of the page, click on the box where the rulers intersect. (One instance in which you change the zero point is when you print with the Manual Tiling option, described in Chapter 7.)

The rulers must be displayed in order to create nonprinting guides on the page, described below.

Choosing the Unit of Measure

Use Edit ➤ Preferences ➤ General (⌘-Y) to set the unit of measure displayed on the rulers. You can change the unit of measure at any time without affecting the document itself—only the rulers and other displays that show measurements will change. You may choose to work with one unit of measure throughout the production, or with different measures (using picas for margins and columns, and inches for scaling figures, for example).

The number of increments displayed along the rulers will vary depending on the size in which you are currently viewing the page. Rulers show finer increments of measure in enlarged views, such as 200 percent, than in reduced views.

Ruler Guides

In addition to the margin and column guides, up to 100 vertical and 100 horizontal ruler guides can be dragged from the rulers. You can use ruler guides on any page to help align items horizontally and vertically, as described here. You can also create ruler guides on a master page as a grid for positioning items consistently on document pages, as described in Chapters 3 and 8.

To create a ruler guide on any page, first choose View ➤ Show Rulers to display the rulers at the top and left edges of the document window, then hold down the mouse pointer on the vertical or horizontal ruler and drag a vertical or horizontal guide onto the page. The current position shows as a dotted line on the ruler as you drag and in the Measurements palette. Release the mouse to position the guide. You can reposition the guide at any time by dragging it, or you can delete it by dragging it back to the ruler. You can delete all ruler guides at once by holding the Option key and clicking on each ruler.

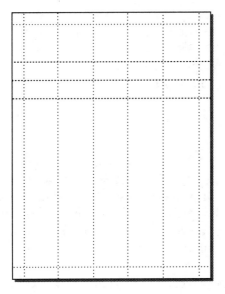

Figure 2-30 Ruler guides are displayed as green lines on color monitors and dotted gray lines on monochrome monitors.

Note that in order to move a ruler guide, you should click on it in the margins of the page or some place where it is not positioned on top of anything else on the page. Otherwise, you might move the item instead of the guide.

Ruler guides are useful for positioning items on a page, but they do not directly affect the width of text (as column guides do). Ruler guides that you create on a master page show on all pages created from that master; ruler guides created on a document page show on that page only.

Using the Snap-to Effect

Guides—margin guides, column guides, and ruler guides—have a snap-to effect: They pull the pointer or the edges of a line, a text box, or a picture box into position when you bring the item to within 3 points of the guide. The snap-to effect is extremely useful when you want to align items quickly and precisely, especially when you are working in reduced views such as Fit in Window.

Sometimes you may prefer to work with the snap-to effect turned off—as when you are forcing something into a position outside of the basic grid structure. You can do this by choosing View ➤ Snap to Guides. This is a toggle switch—it is checked in the menu when the effect is on, and it is not checked when the effect is off. Turning snap-to on and off has no effect on text and graphics that have already been positioned on the page.

The margin and column guides that have a snap-to effect are those on the master pages—created by entries in the New dialog box when you first start a document, or by the Page ➤ Master Guides command. Margins and columns within text boxes *do not* have a snap-to effect except in two instances: The margin guides in the automatic text box also have a snap-to effect, and the margins of a constraining box (created with the Item ➤ Constrain command, described later in this chapter) have a snap-to effect on constrained elements within the box.

Controlling Text Runaround

Text *runaround* is text that is forced to flow around a box or a line that falls within the text column. In versions before QuarkXPress 3.0, runaround was forced by any box background, frame, or line assigned a shade greater than zero. In QuarkXPress 3.0, runaround is controlled entirely by the Item ➤ Runaround command, and not by the shade of the line, box background, or frame.

Use Item ➤ Runaround (⌘-T) to set the Runaround specifications for an active box (Figure 2-31). You can set Mode to None, Item, Auto Image, or Manual Image. Runaround settings of None or Item can be applied to text or picture box; Auto Image or Manual Image runaround apply to picture boxes only.

Selecting a Mode of None allows text to flow behind the active item. You can force text to flow around any item—including a transparent box or line—by setting Mode to Item.

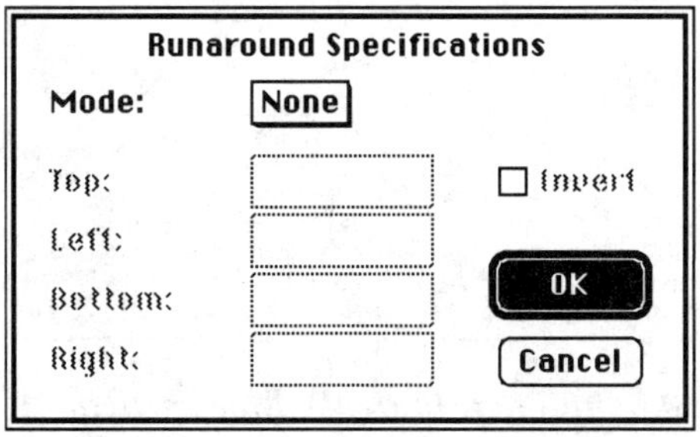

Figure 2-31 Runaround Specifications dialog box.

Item

If the active item is a text box or picture box and you have selected Item mode, you can specify the distance between the runaround text and the top, left, bottom, and right edges of the box. However, when you flow a single column of text around an item, the text will flow only on the side with the widest text area (between the item and the column edges). To flow text around both sides, you must set up two or more columns.

Auto Image

If the active item is a picture box, you can have text automatically flow around the picture edges by setting Mode to Auto Image. Text will be positioned to follow the contour around the picture edges—whatever the shape—at the distance specified as the Text Outset in the Text Box Specifications dialog box. The shape created by the Auto Image option cannot be edited.

Manual Image

Set Mode to Manual Image and QuarkXPress creates an editable runaround polygon (a many-sided object) around the picture in the active picture box. You can modify a runaround polygon by adding, removing, or repositioning handles and by repositioning segments, as described in Chapter 6. You can specify the Text Outset for Manual Image mode just as you can for Auto Image mode.

When you specify Manual Image for an empty picture box or for a picture box whose picture is out of view, QuarkXPress creates a runaround polygon along the inside edge of the box.

You can also select Invert to run the text inside a picture's manual image polygon. After setting up the polygon, you can delete the picture and the polygon will remain.

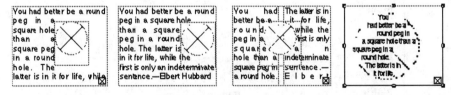

Figure 2-32 Examples of text runaround (left to right): Mode = Item, Mode = Auto Image, Mode = Auto Image with text set in two columns, Mode = Manual Image with Invert option.

Duplicating Items

You can make copies of boxes and lines in QuarkXPress using the Macintosh Copy and Paste commands, but QuarkXPress also offers two commands—Duplicate and Step and Repeat—that provide more control over the positioning of the duplicated elements.

The difference between these two commands is that Step and Repeat lets you make one or more duplicates at a time and specify new offsets (horizontal and vertical distances that determine where the copies will be positioned relative to the original) through the dialog box, whereas Duplicate makes one duplicate at a time using the previously specified offsets.

Using the Duplicate Command

Use Item → Duplicate (⌘-D) to make an exact copy of any active box or line, as an alternative to using the Copy and Paste commands from the Edit menu. When you copy and paste, the pasted item is positioned in the center of the view of the active page in the document window. When you use Duplicate, the new copy is positioned relative to the original at the offset distances specified in the Step and Repeat dialog box, described next. If you duplicate again, the next duplicate will appear in the same relative position.

A linked text box or a box containing a linked constrained box cannot be duplicated. The Duplicate command will not position a copy of an item outside its constraining box if it is part of a constrained group; the message "Can't make the duplicate using these offsets" will display if you try to do so.

Using the Step and Repeat Command

Use Item → Step and Repeat (or the keyboard shortcut, ⌘-Option-D) to specify the offset distance used by the Duplicate command (just described) or as an alternative to the Duplicate command. Step and Repeat lets you make one or more duplicates at a time and specify new offsets through the Step and Repeat dialog box (Figure 2-33).

```
┌─────────────────────────────────┐
│ ╔═════════════════════════════╗ │
│ ║        Step and Repeat       ║ │
│ ║                              ║ │
│ ║ Repeat Count:    [2       ]  ║ │
│ ║ Horizontal Offset: [0.25" ]  ║ │
│ ║ Uertical Offset:  [1"     ]  ║ │
│ ║                              ║ │
│ ║  ( OK )      ( Cancel )      ║ │
│ ╚═════════════════════════════╝ │
└─────────────────────────────────┘
```

Figure 2-33 Step and Repeat dialog box.

Repeat Count is the number of duplicate copies to be made. Horizontal and Vertical Offset determine where the copies will be positioned relative to the original. Positive entries are to the right or below the original, negative entries are to the left or above the original. You can enter measurements in any unit of measure, and (like other dialog boxes) you can change a value by adding or subtracting from the current setting.

A quick alternative to using the Step and Repeat command to make multiple duplicates is to use the keyboard shortcut for the Duplicate command—⌘-D—as many times as needed.

By the way, the Duplicate and Step and Repeat commands do not affect the contents of the Clipboard. Part II provides more tips on using Duplicate and Step and Repeat for forms and other common uses.

Arranging Items in Layers

One feature of QuarkXPress that is characteristic of drawing applications, and that distinguishes it from any word processing program, is that items can be arranged on top of each other in *layers*. Normally, the first item you position on a page establishes the bottom layer, and each item added occupies another layer on top of the last.

You can click through to items hidden underneath others, or you can use the Send to Back/Send Backward and Bring to Front/Bring Forward commands to change the order of layered items.

Clicking Through Layers

Any time an item is hidden under another, you can select the hidden item easily by holding the Shift-Option-⌘ keys and clicking on the location of the hidden item. This feature is useful when multiple layers are stacked on top of one another. But this feature also can be useful when an item that is normally visible is hidden by a text box, since text boxes become opaque when you edit them, even if they are set to have a transparent background. Clicking through layers is a feature that is important to become familiar with and use frequently.

Using the Send to Back/Bring to Front Command

Normally, if you draw one item on top of another, the most recently drawn item will fall on a layer above the items created earlier. The Send to Back command, available only if the active item is layered above another item on the page, sends the active item to the bottom layer in a series. The Bring to Front command, available only if the active item is behind another item, brings an item to the "top" of a stack of items.

In QuarkXPress 3.1, if you hold down the Option key before selecting either Send to Back or Bring to Front, the menu changes to Send Backward or Bring Forward, and moves items by one layer only, instead of placing them at the very front or back layer of layered items.

If the active item is a constraining box, then it and all of its constrained items will be sent to the lowest layer. If the active item is a constrained item, it will be layered behind other constrained items within the same constraining box, but not behind the constraining box.

Aligning Items

Use Item → Space/Align to control the position of active items relative to one another. First select two or more items on a page, using any of the multiple-select methods described earlier in this chapter. Then choose Item → Space Align to display the Space/Align Items dialog box (Figure 2-34).

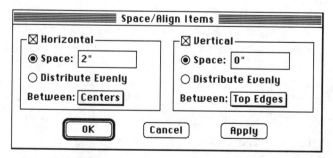

Figure 2-34 The Space/Align Items dialog box.

Check Horizontal to align the active items horizontally, check Vertical to align the active items vertically, or check both to align the active items along both axes at once. In each case, you can specify the amount of space you want between items. If three or more items are active, you can let QuarkXPress determine the space between items by selecting Distribute Evenly.

You can specify that QuarkXPress measure the horizontal space between items, left edges, centers, or right edges, and measure the vertical space between items, top edges, centers, or bottom edges. See Part II for more tips on how to use this command.

Creating Relationships between Items

There are several ways to create a relationship between items on a page.

- Text boxes can be *linked* in a chain so that the text flow from text box to text box is automatically readjusted in all linked boxes when text is edited.

- Text boxes, picture boxes, or lines can be *anchored* within text, so that the anchored box or line automatically moves whenever the text shifts due to edits.

- Multiple items can be *grouped* so that whenever you select one of the items with the Item tool (✦), you automatically select them all. Individual items within a group can still be moved or edited with the Content tool (☜).

- A group can also be *constrained* so items within it cannot be moved beyond the borders of the constraining box.

Each of these options is described under the next headings.

Linking Text Boxes

You control the flow of text through a document by linking text boxes. In QuarkXPress terminology, any series of linked text boxes is called a *chain*, and the text in a chain is called a *story*. Normally, the primary text chain is linked automatically in any QuarkXPress document. When you import more text than will fit in a text box, QuarkXPress automatically adds pages for the text overflow *if all of the following conditions are true*:

- Auto Page Insertion is enabled (see Chapter 3), *and*

- The master page specified in Auto Page Insertion has an automatic text chain (as indicated by the intact chain icon (⛓) in the upper left corner of the master page), *and*

- The overflow is from the automatic text box.

Automatically inserted pages will be added at the location specified in the Auto Page Insertion pop-up menu in the General Preferences dialog box. Options include End of Section, End of Story, or End of Document, as described in Chapter 3.

You can use the last two tools in the Tool palette—the Linking (⬛) and Unlinking (⬛) tools—manually to direct the flow of text from one text box to another or to sever existing links. Manual linking is useful for creating independent text chains within the document—separate from the automatic text chains (described next).

You can also use these manual linking tools to insert and link a new text box into a chain of linked text boxes. You can link text boxes in any order, and you can link boxes that are separated by many intervening pages (as is common in newspapers and magazines). You can link or unlink boxes in any view except Thumbnails, but the Fit in Window view makes the process easiest.

The Automatic Text Chains

The automatic text box, described earlier in this chapter, creates a chain of linked text boxes as needed for text overflow. A master page can have only one automatic text box. A text box on a master page, however, can result in more than one *chain* in a document. Let's say you flow a story into an automatic text box on page 1, for example, and two additional pages are added automatically. The first three pages, then, are one chain or one story. If you insert a new page 4 based on the same master page that has the automatic text box, text you type or import to page 4 will start a new chain or a new story (Figure 2-35). There is no linkage between the text on page 3 and the text on page 4.

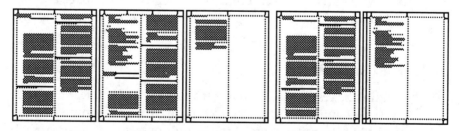

Figure 2-35 First three pages contain one story, linked in an automatic text chain. A new story—and a new automatic text chain—starts on page 4 and continues to page 5.

You can add or remove boxes in these linked chains manually as described under the next headings as well as create additional chains of text boxes—not connected to the automatic text chain.

Creating a New Chain of Linked Text Boxes

To create a new chain of linked text boxes, first, draw the text boxes. Either leave all boxes empty or fill only one with text (you cannot link two boxes that both have text). Then select the Linking tool (⊟), and click on the first text box in the chain. The box will be surrounded by a marquee (moving dotted line) to indicate that it has been activated by the Linking tool. Then click on the box you want to link to the first, and continue clicking sequentially through all of the text boxes in the order you want them to be linked.

Adding Text to Empty Linked Boxes

To add text to newly linked boxes, select the first empty box in the chain, then type the new text, or choose File ➤ Get Text, or use the Edit ➤ Copy and Edit ➤ Paste commands to copy text from another source. If any box in the newly linked chain already contains text that cannot fit in that box, the overflow text will automatically flow into the next linked text box.

Linking Boxes that Already Contain Text

You can link a box that contains text to subsequent empty text boxes, but you cannot link two boxes that contain text. To link boxes that already contain text, first, select and Edit ➤ Cut (⌘-X) the text from the *second* box. Then select the Linking tool and link the two boxes. Finally, use Edit ➤ Paste (⌘-V) to insert the cut text at the end of the linked text.

Viewing the Links Between Boxes

To view the links between boxes, select a box on the page and then select the Linking or the Unlinking tool. The page will display existing links as arrows.

Unlinking Boxes

To unlink boxes, first select a box from the chain you want to unlink, then select the Unlinking tool (⊟) to display the link arrows. Click on either the head or the tailfeathers of the arrow you want to delete, thereby severing the link. The unlinking tool must be completely within the box. When you unlink two boxes in a chain, the last box before the break in the chain will contain all of the overflow text, and subsequent boxes in the broken chain will appear empty.

Inserting a New Box in the Middle of a Linked Chain

To insert a new box in the middle of a linked chain (and make it part of the chain), first use the Text Box tool (Ⓐ) to create the new box. Next select the Linking tool (⊕), and click on the last box in the chain preceding the new box(es), then click on the new, empty box(es). The text will automatically flow through the original chain.

Inserting New Pages Within a Linked Chain

To insert a new page within a linked chain (and make it part of the chain), first select either the Item tool (✛) or the Content tool (☝) and activate any text box in the chain. Then choose Page → Insert Pages and, in the Insert Pages dialog box, check Link to current text chain. This option is available only if the master page applied to the last page before the insert shows an intact chain in the upper left corner.

Note that the text will flow into the new pages from the *end* of the story, even if the pages are inserted in the middle of the chain.

Anchoring Text and Graphics

You can anchor a text box or a picture box to text so that the anchored box moves when editing causes the text to reflow. This feature is useful for anchoring figures to captions, anchoring graphic drop caps to paragraphs, including graphic symbols in the text, and many other functions. You can also anchor rules to text using QuarkXPress's paragraph formatting specifications (rather than creating and anchoring lines as separate graphic elements).

Anchoring Boxes and Rules to Text

To anchor a box or a line to text, select the Item tool (✛) and activate the box or line you want to anchor, then choose Edit → Cut (⌘-X) or Edit → Copy (⌘-C). Next select the Content tool (☝), position the text insertion point in the text where you want the box anchored, and choose Edit → Paste (⌘-V).

If the Item tool (✛) is selected when you paste, the item will be pasted onto the active page but not anchored to the text.

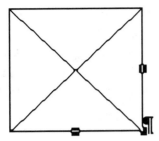

Figure 2-36 An active anchored box displays three handles that you can use to resize the box.

Once anchored, you can select the item and the text around it using the Content tool (☞) and normal text selection techniques. You can cut or copy selected text and paste it elsewhere, along with the anchored item. You can resize an active item by dragging one of the handles.

You can apply Style ➤ Baseline Shift to raise or lower the anchored item, and use paragraph alignment commands to align the item (if it is on a line of its own). In addition, you can use Item ➤ Modify to make entries in the Anchored Text Specifications (Figure 2-37) and Anchored Picture Specifications (Figure 2-38) dialog boxes, or to make entries in the Measurements palette (Figure 2-39), to position an anchored item with its bottom edge aligned with its associated text baseline or with its top edge aligned with the top of the text.

```
┌─────────────────────────────────────────────────────┐
│              Anchored Text Box Specifications          │
│ ┌─Align with Text─────────┐ ┌─First Baseline─────────┐ │
│ │ ○ Ascent    ⦿ Baseline  │ │ Offset:    [0"      ]  │ │
│ │                         │ │ Minimum: [Ascent]      │ │
│ │ Width:    [0.819"]      │ └────────────────────────┘ │
│ │ Height:   [0.667"]      │ ┌─Vertical Alignment─────┐ │
│ │                         │ │ Type:         [Top]     │ │
│ │ Columns:  [1]           │ │ Inter ¶ Max: [0"     ] │ │
│ │ Gutter:   [0.167"]      │ └────────────────────────┘ │
│ │ Text Inset: [1 pt]      │ ┌─Background──────────────┐ │
│ │                         │ │ Color: [Black]          │ │
│ │ ☐ Suppress Printout     │ │ Shade: [▶|0%    ]       │ │
│ │                         │ └─────────────────────────┘ │
│          ( OK )             ( Cancel )                  │
└─────────────────────────────────────────────────────┘
```

Figure 2-37 Anchored Text Specifications dialog box.

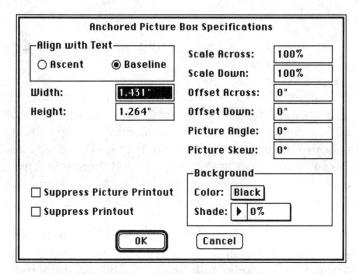

Figure 2-38 Anchored Picture Specifications dialog box.

In the Measurements palette, click on ▣ to align the anchored item with the text ascent, or on ▣ to align the anchored item with the text baseline.

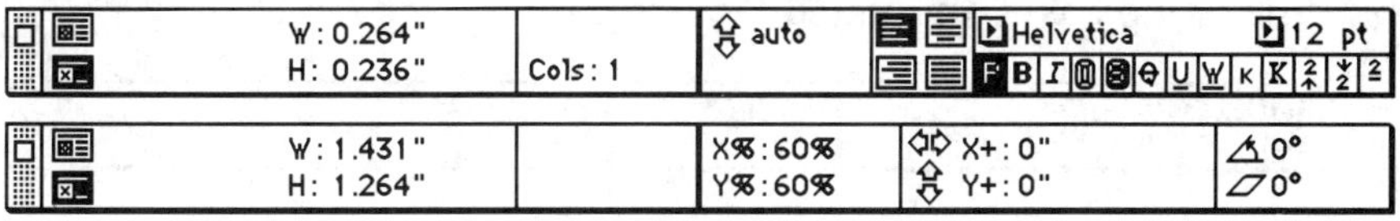

	W: 0.264"			⇕ auto		Helvetica	12 pt
	H: 0.236"	Cols : 1				F B I ⦿ ⦿ ⦿ U W K K	

	W: 1.431"		X% : 60%	⇔ X+ : 0"	⊿ 0°
	H: 1.264"		Y% : 60%	⇕ Y+ : 0"	⊿ 0°

Figure 2-39 Anchored Text Measurements palette (top), and Anchored Picture Measurements palette (bottom).

To move an anchored item from its current text location, use the Content tool (☝) to select the item and then use the Cut and Paste commands—you cannot move an anchored item by dragging it with the Item tool (✥).

Note that you cannot anchor an item to text that is within an anchored box. See Part II for more ideas on using anchored boxes in text.

Deleting Anchored Items

To delete a box or line that is *anchored within* a text box, you must select the box by dragging over it with the I-beam pointer (I), then choose Edit � Cut, Edit ➤ Clear, or press the Delete or Backspace key. You can also position the text insertion point immediately after the anchored box and press the Delete or Backspace key.

Grouping Items

You can select multiple items using the techniques described earlier in this chapter. If you want a group of items always to be associated (and selectable) as a group, you can select them all and choose Item → Group (⌘-G).

Items within a group are still separate entities that can be selected, edited, scaled, or repositioned individually. Any item can be selected with the Content tool (🖑) and edited normally or scaled by dragging a handle. To move an item or to use any of the commands that call for selection with the Item tool (✛), first select the Content tool and then hold down the ⌘ key as you click on the item and drag. Holding the ⌘ key temporarily activates the Item tool, and you can select individual items instead of the whole group with the ✛ pointer.

You will notice that whenever you have selected multiple items on a page—whether they are grouped or not—the Measurements palette (Figure 2-40) changes to display only three variables: X (horizontal position of the origin of the group's boundary or bounding box relative to the current zero point), Y (vertical position of the origin of the group's boundary relative to the current zero point), and rotation angle of the group, if it was rotated as a group. (Remember that the origin is the *original* top left corner of the group, which is not necessarily the apparent top left corner if the group has been rotated.)

X: 3.875" Y: 3.319"	△ 0°	

Figure 2-40 Measurements palette when a group is selected.

These are the only variables from the Measurements palette that can be changed for the group as a whole. You cannot resize a group, for instance, but you can rotate the group as a whole.

Similarly, when multiple items are selected—whether or not they are grouped—the available menu commands and dialog box entries will be limited to only those that can be applied to the group as a whole, and this will depend on the composition of the group. Also, you cannot cut or copy a group that contains a text box that is part of a chain.

Group Specifications

When a group of items is selected, the fields in the Specifications dialog box and in the Measurements palette change to allow only those entries that are appropriate for *all* items in the group. For example, if the entire group is composed of text boxes, the Item → Modify command will display a full Text Box Specifications dialog box with all fields as described earlier for text boxes. If the group contains both text boxes and picture boxes and lines, the Item ➤ Modify command will display a Group Specifications dialog box with only those fields that are common to all types of items: Origin Across, Origin Down, Angle, Color, Shade, and Suppress Printout.

Deleting Items from a Group

To delete a box or line that is part of a group (created using the Item ➤ Group command), you must select the item with the Content tool (☞) and then choose Item ➤ Delete (⌘-K). Edit ➤ Cut, Edit ➤ Clear, or the Delete or Backspace key is not available when an item within a group is selected—whether or not the group is also constrained.

If you select an item within a group and choose Item ➤ Delete (⌘-K), QuarkXPress will display a warning that "This will delete an item from a group and cannot be undone. OK to continue?" If you click on OK in the warning box, you will delete the item *and there is no way to reverse that action*.

If you use the Item tool (✥) to try to select an item within a group, you will be selecting the whole group. Item ➤ Delete (⌘-K), Edit ➤ Cut, Edit ➤ Clear, or the Delete or Backspace key will delete the entire group.

Constraining Items Within a Box

Normally, you can move items anywhere on a page, regardless of their relationship to other items on a page, because the normal default for the Auto Constrain option in the General Preferences dialog box is off. If you turn this option *on*, any items you create within a box are constrained by that box.

The ability to set Auto Constrain on or off is a new feature in QuarkXPress 3.0. In earlier versions, any item positioned on top of a box was automatically constrained by that box; this was called a "parent/child" relationship. In QuarkXPress 3.0, a box that contains other constrained boxes or lines is called a *constraining* box, and any lines or boxes within another box are *constrained* by the box in which they are drawn. You cannot position a constrained item beyond the constraining box's boundaries or scale them to be larger than the constraining box.

In place of Auto Constrain, you can use Item ➤ Constrain to constrain a group of items to within one box or use the Unconstrain command to reverse a constraint. Item ➤ Constrain can override the Auto Constrain setting for active items. You can also use Constrain to associate a group of boxes that were not originally set up that way.

Constraining a Box or Line

To constrain a box or line when the Auto Constrain setting is On in the General Preferences dialog box, first draw and select the box that you want to be the constraining box. Then choose the appropriate tool and, starting within the constraining box, draw the box or line that you want to be constrained.

Constraining a Group of Items

To Constrain a group of items, first create the items, including one box that surrounds all of the items and falls on the lowest layer of the group—this box will become the constraining box. Select all of the items and choose Item ➤ Group, then choose Item ➤ Constrain. When a group is constrained, items within the bounding box can be moved or changed individually, but they cannot be resized or moved beyond the edges of the constraining box. If you delete the constraining box, all associated constrained items are also deleted.

Removing the Constraint Attribute

To remove the constraint attribute, select the constrained group and then choose Item ➤ Unconstrain. (The command in the menu changes from Constrain to Unconstrain when a constrained group is active.) The Unconstrained set is still grouped until you choose the Ungroup command.

See Part II for ideas on how constrained groups can be useful.

Locking Items

Use Item ➤ Lock (⌘-L) to lock an active box, line, or a group on the page so you cannot inadvertently move or scale it. Locked boxes can still be moved or scaled through the Measurements palette or the Item ➤ Modify command, but they cannot be moved or scaled with the mouse. Locked lines must be unlocked in order to be moved or scaled. Most menu commands can be applied to locked items, including Delete.

The Lock command is a toggle switch: If you select an unlocked item, the command displays as Lock in the Item menu; if you select a locked item, the command displays as Unlock in the Item menu. In either case, the keyboard shortcut is ⌘-L. When you position the Mover pointer over a locked item, the pointer changes to a padlock (🔒).

Saving Your Work

While you are working on a document, the work you do is being stored in the computer's memory (RAM)—a temporary work area that is "erased" whenever the computer is turned off or when you quit an application. If the power fails or something else forces you to restart the computer, anything in the computer's memory is erased; but whatever you have saved on the disk is preserved. For this reason, save your document often while you are working. QuarkXPress handles this function like most other Macintosh applications—with the added advantage of a Revert to Saved command, as described under the next headings.

Saving a Document or Template

Use File → Save (⌘-S) to save your work onto a disk. Each time you use the Save command to save the document, the version that is in memory is copied to the disk.

The first time you use the Save command on a new document, a dialog box is displayed in which you can specify the name of the document and the disk or folder where you want to store it (Figure 2-41). This dialog box is common to most Macintosh applications.

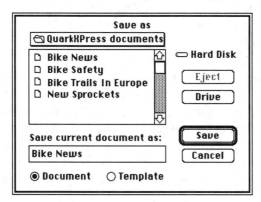

Figure 2-41 The Save dialog box.

You should get accustomed to saving your work at regular intervals—not just at the end of a work session. The keyboard shortcut (⌘-S) makes saving your document easy.

When to Save a Document

- When you finish a page—before turning to another page.
- When you finish placing a long text file.
- When you finish placing, sizing, and cropping a graphic.
- As you are working, every five minutes or so.
- Before you print.
- Before you globally change type specs or format.
- After you make any changes to the master pages.
- Before leaving your computer, using the phone, or pausing.
- OFTEN!

You can save a QuarkXPress template to use as the basis for starting other documents. Click on the template button in the Save dialog box. The next time you open the file and save it, QuarkXPress will display the Save dialog box so that you rename the template file as a document.

Saving with a Changed Name, Format, or Disk Location

Use the File ➤ Save As command to save an existing document under a different name. This feature is useful when you want to create a new document based on one that you have previously created. For example, you could start the February newsletter by opening the file for the January newsletter (called Vol. 1 No. 1, for instance) and saving it under a new name (such as Vol. 1 No. 2). See Chapter 8 for suggestions about creating templates instead of copying complete documents.

You can also use the Save As command to put the document into a different folder or onto a different disk. This ability is useful when you want to make an updated version of a document without changing the name or modified date (recorded by the System) of the original version, thereby creating a backup version. For example, you could start the second revision of a heavily edited report by opening the file for the first version (stored on a file server, for instance) and saving it on a different disk (your own local hard disk).

You can also use the Save As command to save the document in a different format (template versus document). For example, after finishing the first newsletter in a series, you can save the newsletter as a *document* (to store as an archive) and then use Save As to create a *template* (for use in starting subsequent issues).

The Save As dialog box is the same as the Save dialog box (Figure 2-41) and is common to most Macintosh applications.

Reverting to the Most Recently Saved Version

The Revert to Saved command in the File menu can be used to eliminate all of the edits or changes made since the last time the document was saved. This command is simply a convenient shortcut to an alternative that is available with almost any application: Close the active document without saving changes, then reopen the saved version of the document.

Closing a Document Window

As mentioned earlier, choosing Close from the File menu has the same effect as clicking on the Close Box in the active document window. When you close a document that has never been saved or that has been changed since it was last saved, QuarkXPress displays a dialog box asking if you want to save the changes.

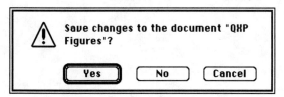

Figure 2-42 A warning dialog box is displayed when you close a document without saving changes.

Click Yes or press Return to save the changed document or to display the Save As dialog box; click No to ignore the changes; or click on Cancel to cancel the Close command and keep the document open. Or you can use the keyboard shortcuts, ⌘-N for No and ⌘-C for cancel.

Quitting QuarkXPress

Use the File ➛ Quit command when you want to exit QuarkXPress. If you use this command when a document window is open and the document has not been saved since the last change, QuarkXPress will prompt you to save the document. You'll see the same warning dialog box as is displayed when you close a document window without first saving the changed document (Figure 2-42).

Summary

This chapter presents an overview of how to create a new QuarkXPress document and how to add items to document pages. This chapter also describes how you can modify text and picture boxes in QuarkXPress and create relationships between them. We provide an overview of how to change the position or appearance of boxes and lines created using QuarkXPress' tools (except the Picture Box Shape and Reshape Polygon commands, which are covered in Chapter 6). Some of the other commands from the Item menu are also reviewed in Chapters 4 to 6, where you learn how to edit *lines* and change the *contents* of boxes (text and graphics).

The next chapter continues the page layout process by adding, moving, or deleting pages, including master pages. You also learn how to change the *defaults*, or assumed settings, for QuarkXPress.

3 *Expanding the Document*

Understanding how to work with items, the basic building blocks of QuarkXPress documents, is essential; but unless you're creating only the simplest of documents, you'll need to understand how to work with multiple pages. It's also important to know how to change QuarkXPress' default Preferences settings, because these settings affect many aspects of how the program operates.

In Chapter 2, you learned how to start a new document, position items on a document page, and create relationships between items. This chapter covers additional aspects of the page layout process, including creating master pages, sectioning a document, and adding, moving, or deleting pages. You also learn how to create and use a QuarkXPress library. Finally, you learn how to change the *defaults,* or assumed settings, for the program using the Edit ➤ Preferences command.

Working with Master Pages

Whenever you start a new document, QuarkXPress displays a blank page. You can begin building a document as described in Chapter 2, by immediately creating boxes on each page and using File ➤ Get Text and File ➤ Get Picture commands to bring in text and graphics that you have prepared in other programs, or by using QuarkXPress' built-in graphics and text tools.

However, if you are creating a document that is more than one or two pages in length, you need to think about setting up master pages. Using master pages, you fit each page layout to an overall "grid". These master pages establish basic components of the document, and can save you a lot of time. Any text, graphics, or guides on the master page appear on every page based on that master page. Text, graphics, or guides added to a document page appear on that page only.

Figure 3-1 shows items that are normally included on master pages. These include column guides, running headers and footers, and nonprinting guides that define the basic grid of the document's design.

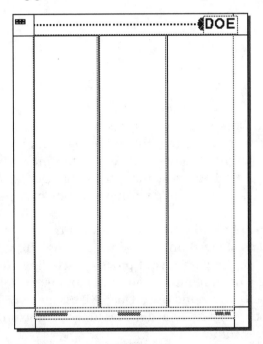

Figure 3-1 Master page elements include column guides, running header and footer, ruler guides, and other text or graphic elements that repeat on every page based on this master.

Every document starts with at least one master page, with the margin guides, column guides, and (optional) automatic text box as specified in the New dialog box, described in Chapter 2. This master page serves as the basis of all document pages, unless you choose to create document pages based on *no* master (described later in this chapter) or to create additional master pages (described next). Settings made on master pages can be changed on individual document pages as needed; you can move or delete master items on document pages.

Creating a New Master Page

When you open a new document, the document contains one master page, labeled "Master A". To create a new master page, display the Document Layout palette by selecting View ➤ Show Document Layout. Click on one of the blank page icons at the top of the Document Layout palette and drag the blank page icon to position a new master page icon between the scroll arrows (Figure 3-2). QuarkXPress assigns a letter to each master page you create, but you can add additional text in the label field just below the master page icons, described later in this section. You can create up to 127 master pages for a single document or delete all master pages.

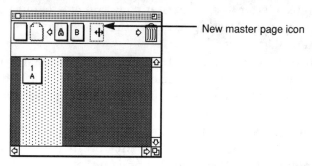

Figure 3-2 Drag a blank page icon to the right to create a new master page.

In the Document Layout palette, the blank page icon on the left represents a single-sided master (□); the second blank page icon (◻), with two turned-down corners, represents a facing-page master page, with both a left and right master page. If you have selected the Facing Pages options in the New or Document Setup command's dialog box, you will be able to work on both single-sided and facing-page master pages. If you do not have Facing Pages selected, you will be able to create only single-sided master pages.

Single-sided master page elements—such as guides, text boxes, and graphics—will appear on every page to which the master page is applied, whether the final document is single-sided or a facing-page document.

Those elements that are set up on the right page of a facing-page master page will appear only on odd-numbered pages of facing-page documents. Elements that are set up on the left master page will appear on even-numbered pages of facing-page documents.

You can position a new master after any existing master page icon, or rearrange the order of the master page icons by dragging them to new positions in the Document Layout palette, but the letter assigned to each master will always be based on the sequence in which the master was *created* rather than the sequence in which the masters are *arranged*.

You can replace or overwrite an existing master page by dragging another existing master page icon or a new blank master page icon over the icon to be replaced and releasing the mouse button. QuarkXPress always displays a warning box asking you to confirm that you want to overwrite a master.

Naming a Master Page

QuarkXPress assigns a letter to each master page you create, but you can give a master page a more descriptive name, such as "Chapter Opening Master" or "Contents List Master."

To name a master page, click on the icon for that master in the Document Layout window. When you select a master page icon, the field below the icons displays the current name of the master page. You can change that name by selecting and retyping the text in the field. A name can be up to 70 characters long, though the icons will still be labeled A, B, C, and so on. To turn to that page, double-click on its icon (or use the Page ➤ Display command to select from a submenu that lists master pages by name).

When a master page is displayed, QuarkXPress displays the page name in the lower left corner of the document window, along with an R or L for right and left pages of a facing-page master page.

Editing a Master Page

To activate or turn to a master page, choose Page ➤ Display and select the master page you want to edit. Another way of turning to a master page is to double-click on the appropriate master page icon in the Document Layout palette (Figure 3-3).

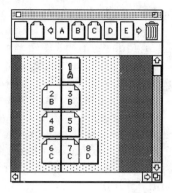

Figure 3-3 Turn to a master page by double-clicking on the appropriate master page icon at the top of the Document Layout palette.

Changing Master Page Margins and Column Guides

A new master page takes on the margin and column settings that you initially specified in the New dialog box when you first started the document. You can change those settings for any master page through the Master Guides dialog box that is displayed when you use the Page ➤ Master Guides command (Figure 3-4). This command is available only when the active document window displays a master page.

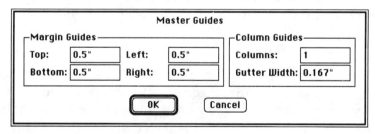

Figure 3-4 Master Guides dialog box.

Once you define the margins and column guides for a master page, those settings will apply automatically to any page in the document based on that master page. The master guides serve two functions: On the master page that includes the automatic text box (defined in Chapter 2 and in this chapter), column guides define the number of columns in the automatic text box. On pages that do not have an automatic text box, master guides serve as aids in positioning items on the page, but they do not affect text—the width of text is determined by the columns set up for each text box (as described in Chapter 2).

If you later change the margin settings for a master page, or if you select a different master page for a document page that you have already started, QuarkXPress automatically resizes the automatic text box on the page (if one has been specified) and resizes any other text box whose four sides exactly meet the margin guides.

QuarkXPress automatically divides the automatic text box on each document page based on that master page if the text box has not been moved or changed on individual document pages. All other page items remain unchanged when you redefine margins and columns on a master page.

Remember that you can enter any unit of measure, or you can change a value by adding or subtracting from the current setting in this or any dialog box and in the Measurements palette. See Chapter 1 for details. Refer to the description of the New dialog box, in Chapter 2, for more information.

Adding Text and Graphic Elements to a Master Page

You can add text and graphic elements to a master page the same way you add text or graphics to any page in the document, as described in Chapter 2. The next sections describe elements that are commonly used on master pages: the automatic text box, text boxes for headers and footers, and other elements that you want to appear repeatedly on document pages.

The Automatic Text Box

If the Automatic Text Box option is selected in the New dialog box, the first master page (and the first document page) of that document includes an empty text box that has margins and columns you set up in the New dialog box. The master page shows an intact chain icon (⬚) in the top left corner when the automatic text box is in effect (Figure 3-5).

You can change the margin and column settings through the Page ➤ Master Guides command; changes made to these settings will affect the size and number of columns in the automatic text box. You can also use the Item ➤ Modify and Item ➤ Frame commands (described in Chapter 2) and commands under the Style menu (described in Chapter 5) to change the automatic text box specifications.

Any text formatting that you apply to this text box—character attributes or paragraph formatting—will become the default format when you type text in this box on document pages. (You cannot type text in an automatic text box on a master page.)

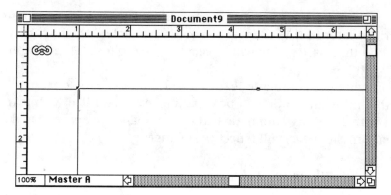

Figure 3-5 Master page with automatic text box shows an intact chain icon in the top left corner.

When you type or import text into an automatic text box on a document page, additional pages are automatically added as needed for text overflow, unless you turn Auto Page Insertion *off* in the General Preferences dialog box, described later in this chapter.

Removing the Automatic Text Box

You may want to deactivate the automatic text box on one master page so you can activate an automatic text box on a different master page. To turn the automatic text chain off on a master page, select the Unlinking tool (⊕ᵽ) and click on the intact chain icon in the top left corner on the master page. A text box will remain on the master page, but text overflow will not add new pages in the document.

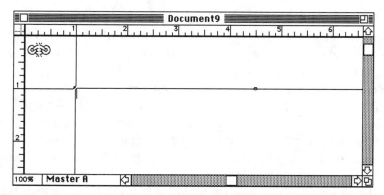

Figure 3-6 A master page without an automatic text box shows a broken chain icon in the top left corner of a master page.

You can delete this box using the Cut or Clear or Delete commands described later in this chapter. If you do not delete the box, new pages based on this master page will have a text box, but it will not be an automatic text box.

Removing the automatic text box will not affect any document pages on which the automatic text box has already been filled with text. Only pages with an empty automatic text box, and any new pages based on the changed master page, will reflect the change.

Creating an Automatic Text Box

Documents that were started with the Automatic Text Box option turned *off* in the New dialog box, or in which the automatic text box is later turned off as described in the last section, have no automatic text box. Pages will not be added automatically for overflow text, even if the Auto Page Insertion option is turned *on* in the General Preferences dialog box (described later in this chapter).

To create an automatic text box in a document that does not have one, first display the master page that you want to hold the box. Select the Text Box creation tool (Ⓐ) and add a text box to that master page (if it does not have one already). Select the Linking tool (☜) and click on the broken chain icon (⛓) in the upper left corner on a master page. The broken chain icon will be surrounded by a marquee. Treat this marquee as the *previous text box*, and click on the text box(es) that you wish to become the automatic text chain. Use this same technique to link text boxes on other master pages to the automatic text box.

Headers, Footers, and Page Numbers

Additional text elements that are most commonly added to the master page(s) include a header and/or footer, showing the page number and any other text that you want to appear on every page.

To create a header or footer, you first choose the Text Box creation tool (Ⓐ) and draw a text box at the top or bottom of the page—usually beyond the top or bottom margin defined for the automatic text box (unless that box defines the entire printing area of the page). Then type and format the text that you want to appear on every page. (Chapters 4 and 5 describe how to format text.)

In the position where you want the page number to appear, type ⌘-3 (Figure 3-7). On the master page(s) the page number appears as the characters <#> (angled brackets around the uppercase value of 3 on the keyboard—the pound sign or number sign). On document pages the page number will appear as assigned through the Page ➤ Section command, described later in this chapter.

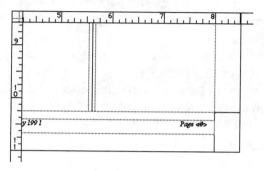

Figure 3-7 Type ⌘-3 to position the page number in a text box in the header or footer on the master page.

Other Text and Graphics Elements

You can add other text boxes, picture boxes, and lines to the master page using techniques described in Chapter 2 and the rest of this chapter, including:

- Arranging boxes on the page.
- Using QuarkXPress' tools to type text and draw graphic elements.
- Importing text and graphics.
- Copying elements from other QuarkXPress documents.
- Linking text boxes.
- Anchoring text and graphics.
- Editing boxes and lines.

You can add blank text boxes to master pages. Any text formatting that you apply to these boxes will become the default formats when you type text in these boxes on document pages. Similarly, you can format a picture box with predefined settings for background, frame, or contrast, for example. Those settings will be the default in that box on every document page based on that master.

Any elements that you add to a master page automatically appear on all pages based on that master—pages that have already been created as well as new pages based on that master. You can revise, move, or delete individual master page elements on any document page, but these changed elements will not be affected if you later change the master page.

See Chapter 8 for tips on how the master pages can be part of a template document to increase productivity.

Applying a Master Page to a Document Page

You can start a new page by applying a master page to it; in that way you start the new document page with all of the guides plus any printing items that are set up for that master.

To create a *new* page based on a master page, drag a master page icon into the document page area of the Document Layout palette and position it *next to* (that is, above, below, or beside) an existing document page icon. To apply a master page to an *existing* document page, click on the appropriate master page icon in the Document Layout palette and drag it *onto* an existing document page icon (Figure 3-8).

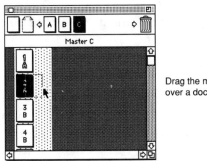

Drag the master page icon
over a document page icon

Figure 3-8 Applying a new master page to a document page.

You can use the procedures described in Chapter 2 and the rest of this chapter to add or change any of the elements on a document page—including changing or deleting elements that are derived from the master page on which a particular document page is based.

If you change elements on the master page later, those changes will be reflected in the document pages based on that master, *except* that the master page–based elements you *changed* on the document pages will not be changed. In other words, when you modify master page items, the modifications are *not* applied to the corresponding items on document pages that you have moved or changed in any way.

When you drag a master page icon onto an existing document page, QuarkXPress deletes all previous *unmodified* master page elements from that page and applies the new master page's elements. Figures 3-9 and 3-10 show how master page changes affect a document page when no elements have been modified on the document page. In these examples note that the text box on Master B had been linked to the automatic text box as described earlier under "Creating an Automatic Text Box." If the text box on Master B had not been linked to the automatic text box, a page would be inserted with no text in the text box.

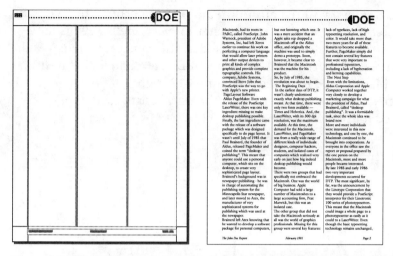

Figure 3-9 Master page A (left) and a document page based on Master A (right).

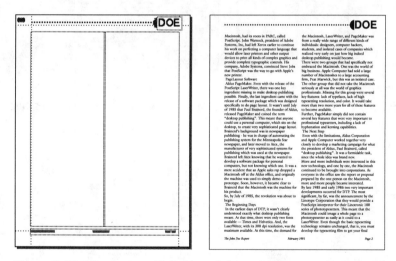

Figure 3-10 Master page B (left) and the same document page with Master B applied (right).

Keep Changes Versus Delete Changes

Modified items might be kept or deleted when the new master page is applied, depending on the setting for Master Page Items in the General Preferences dialog box (described later in this chapter).

Modifications include *moving* a master page element on a document page. If you position a logo in the upper right corner of the master page, for example, and then move it to the upper left corner on page 1 (Figure 3-

11), the logo will remain in the upper left corner when you change the master page or apply a new master to page one if Keep Changes is specified in the Master Page Items field of the General Preferences dialog box (Figure 3-12, left). It will be deleted if Delete Changes has been specified in the Master Page Items field (Figure 3-12, right). If you change this setting after working on a document, the new setting will apply only to pages added to the document.

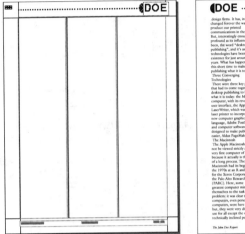

Figure 3-11 Master page A (left) and a document page based on Master A (right), with logo position modified.

Figure 3-12 The same document page with Master A reapplied when Delete Changes (left) or Keep Changes (right) is specified in the General Preferences dialog box.

Adding, Deleting, and Moving Pages

QuarkXPress offers several methods for adding, deleting, or moving pages in a document. When you insert, delete, or move pages, QuarkXPress automatically updates the page numbers on each page throughout the document (if they have been set up using automatic page number characters, as described later in this chapter). See Chapter 9 for special considerations in adding, deleting, or moving pages in a facing-page document.

Adding Pages

As described in Chapter 2, QuarkXPress automatically adds pages for text overflow that occurs when you type or import more text than a text box can display. It performs this function only under the following conditions:

- Auto Page Insertion is enabled (via Edit ➤ Preferences ➤ General); *and*

- the master page specified in Auto Page Insertion has an automatic text chain (as indicated by the intact chain icon [⬚] in the upper left corner of the master page); *and*

- the overflow is from the text box defined on the master page as the Automatic Text Box, or from a chain of at least two text boxes.

You can add a new page based on a particular master page by selecting the appropriate master page icon in the Document Layout palette and dragging it into the desired position next to a document page in the palette. You can also add a new blank page *not* based on a master page by dragging one of the blank page icons (from the upper left area of the palette) into position.

While you are dragging, the pointer changes to indicate how the page will be inserted.

- A single-sided page icon (□) indicates that the added page will not affect the spread placement of existing document pages (that is, their position relative to the spine of the document).

- A right page icon (a page icon with the right corner dog-eared—◰) indicates that the added page will become a right-facing page (that is, right of the spine in a facing-page document) and will not affect the spread placement of existing document pages.

- A left page icon (a page icon with the left corner dog-eared—◳) indicates that the added page will become a left-facing page (that is, left of the spine in a facing-page document) and will not affect the spread placement of existing document pages.

- A left- (⊣) or right-pointing (⊢) arrow indicates that the page will become part of a spread, forcing one or more pages out from the spine.
- A down-pointing arrow (⊤) indicates that the page will force all subsequent pages down one position but will not affect the spread placement of previous document pages.

To view the new page, double-click on its icon.

Insert Pages Dialog Box

If you want to insert more than one page at a time, hold the Option key while clicking and dragging a blank page or a master page icon into the document page area. When you release the mouse button, QuarkXPress displays the Insert Pages dialog box. If you prefer to work with the Document Layout palette closed, you can use the Insert command from the Page menu to display the Insert Pages dialog box and add blank pages or pages based on master pages.

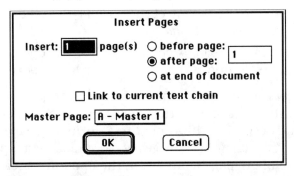

Figure 3-13 Insert Pages dialog box.

The Insert Pages dialog box (Figure 3-13) lets you insert up to 99 pages in the active document. This is the limit *per insertion*—not the limit for the document. You can specify whether the pages are to be inserted before or after the active page (or whatever page number you specify), or at the end of the document.

You can enter an actual page number, or you can enter the *absolute* location within the active document by preceding the number with a plus sign. For example, if the active document includes 10 pages beginning with a user-defined page number 11 and you want to insert a new page 13, you can insert after page 12, or you can insert after page +2 (that is, after the second page in the document). (An *absolute page sequence* number represents a page's sequential location in a document, regardless of the automatic page numbers.)

In specifying a page number, you must include any prefix that has been assigned as part of the page number through the Page ➤ Section command (described later in this chapter).

Choose the master page you want to apply to the inserted pages from the Master Page pop-up menu, which lists all of the master pages that have been set up in the active document.

If the automatic text box on a document page is active when you insert pages, you can check Link to Current Text Chain to link the inserted pages automatically to the automatic text chain. The active text box or chain can be anywhere in the document. This option is available only if the intact chain icon (⧉) is in the upper left corner of the master page and the automatic text box or chain is active on a document page.

When you add an odd number of pages to a facing-pages document, subsequent pages are automatically updated to contain the appropriate left- or right-facing master page items.

Deleting Pages

You can delete a page by dragging the page icon into the trash icon in the Document Layout palette, as described in Chapter 1, or you can use the Delete command from the Page menu.

The Page ➤ Delete command displays the Delete Pages dialog box (Figure 3-14), through which you can delete any number of pages by user-specified page number or by absolute page sequence (which you can enter with a plus sign as described above for inserting pages). In specifying a section page number, you must include any prefix that has been assigned as part of the page number through the Page ➤ Section command.

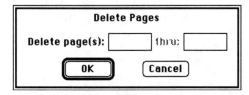

Figure 3-14 The Delete Pages dialog box.

If the deleted pages contain text that is linked to text boxes on remaining pages, the text is reflowed and anchored items are retained. QuarkXPress automatically replaces the deleted pages with newly inserted pages, using the master page format of the page preceding the first automatically inserted page. It does this if the remaining pages cannot fit all the text from the deleted pages, Auto Page Insertion is enabled (through the Edit ➤ Preferences ➤ General command), and the master page to be used has the intact chain icon () in the upper left corner.

    If you delete a master page, document pages will lose all items that were derived from that master page if they have not been modified (depending on the setting of Master Page Items in the General Preferences dialog box). These document pages will no longer be based on any master. You cannot delete the only page in a one-page document.

Moving Pages

You can rearrange pages within a document by dragging the page icons in the Document Layout palette or by dragging the thumbnail icons in the document window (when set to View ➤ Thumbnails). In either window, you can select multiple pages by holding the Shift key as you click on different pages. Otherwise, use the Move command from the Page menu to rearrange pages, described below.

Moving Pages in the Document Layout Palette

To move a page in the Document Layout palette, choose View ➤ Show Document Layout, then drag any page icon into the desired position and release the mouse button.

Moving Pages in Thumbnails View

To move a page in Thumbnails view, choose View ➤ Thumbnails, then drag the thumbnail page image from one position to another and release the mouse button.

While you are dragging pages in either Thumbnails view or in the Document Layout palette, the pointer changes to indicate how the page will be inserted (see the pointer descriptions under "Adding Pages", earlier in this chapter).

Moving Pages Using the Move Command

You can also use the Page ➤ Move command to get the Move Pages dialog box. The Move Pages dialog box lets you move any number of pages by user-defined page number or by absolute page sequence number, which you can enter with a plus sign as described above for inserting pages. You can specify whether the pages are to be moved before or after the active page (or whatever page number you specify) or at the end of the document.

In specifying a page number, you must include any prefix that has been assigned as part of the page number through the Page ➤ Section command.

Regardless of which method you use when you move pages, QuarkXPress does not change the links—the order in which text flows between text boxes. For example, if a story starts on page 2 and continues on page 3, and if you move page 2 to follow page 3, then the story will still start on the *moved* page and flow backward (Figure 3-15).

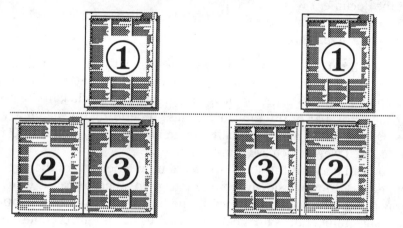

Figure 3-15 Moving Pages does not change the order in which text is linked.

Copying Pages from One Document to Another

To move entire pages from one document to another, open both documents (using File ➤ Open) and select View ➤ Thumbnails for both documents, then drag pages back and forth between the document windows. You can select and move multiple sequential pages by shift-clicking on two or more pages and then dragging the multiple-selected pages. Use ⌘-Click to select multiple, nonsequential pages. The pointer changes as described above, under "Adding Pages".

Links between text boxes on moved pages are preserved, and the entire story (all of the text in the linked chain) is brought in from the source document. In the target document, copied pages display text from the beginning of the story, even if the story did not start on the copied pages in the source document.

Moving a page from one document to another brings in the associated master pages from the source document as well. You cannot move pages based on a facing-page master page into a single-sided document.

Turning Pages

You can turn pages by using the scroll bars to scroll up or down within the document; by using special keys on an extended keyboard; by double-clicking on the icon for a page in the Document Layout palette; or by using the Go To, Previous, Next, First, and Last commands from the Page menu.

The page number of the active page is displayed in the lower left corner of the document window.

Using the Scroll Bars

The scroll bars in the document window also let you scroll vertically and horizontally—this is a standard Macintosh operation, described in Chapter 1. The distance the image moves when you click in the gray part of the scroll bar or on an arrow varies, depending on the view you are using. The increments are smaller in enlarged views (such as 200%) than in reduced views (such as Fit in Window).

You can click on the scroll arrows to move the view of the page in the window or to move slowly from one page to adjacent pages. Click in the gray area of the scroll bar to scroll one full window per click. Notice that the page number does not change until the page is entirely out of the document window.

To move more quickly through the document, you can drag the vertical scroll box. As you do this, the page view does not change immediately, but the page number in the lower left corner of the document window indicates the page that would be displayed if you released the mouse button.

 If you hold the Option key as you drag the scroll box, you can obtain a "live scroll" in which the page view changes more quickly as you are scrolling.

Using Keys on an Extended Keyboard

If you have an extended keyboard, you can use the following keys to move through a document:

- The Home key displays the top of the first page of a document.
- The Page Up key scrolls up one document window.
- The Page Up key with the Shift key scrolls to the top of the active page.
- The Page Down key scrolls down one document window.
- The Page Down key with the Shift key scrolls to the top of the next page.

- The End key scrolls to the bottom of the last page of the document.
- The End key with the Shift key scrolls to the top of the last page.

Using the Go To Command

You can use Page ➤ Go to (⌘-J) to jump quickly to any page in the document. In the Go To Page dialog box, you can enter the user-defined page number or the absolute page sequence, which you can enter with a plus sign as described earlier in this chapter for inserting pages.

In entering the user-defined page number, you must include any prefix you assigned using the Section command along with the page number. If two pages in a document have the same section and/or page numbers, including prefix, QuarkXPress goes to the first occurrence of that page number.

Using the Display Command

You can use the Page ➤ Display command to change from views of the document pages to views of any master page. The Display command shows a submenu that lists all of the master pages plus Document (for returning to views of the most recently viewed document page).

Remember that you can also turn to any master page by double-clicking on the page icon for that master page in the Document Layout window, as described earlier in this chapter.

Numbering Pages and Sectioning a Document

You can set up page numbers to print on every page by setting up a text box for the page number on the master page(s), as described earlier in this chapter. Here we describe how to divide a document into sections and assign the starting page number for a document or section, as well as how to create page number references within a document.

Assigning Page Numbers

Normally, QuarkXPress starts a document with page number 1. You can change the starting page number of a document by turning to its first page and using the Page ➤ Section command to specify a starting page number (described under the next heading). The lower left corner of the document window displays the active page number, and page numbers that start a new section are followed by an asterisk (*).

Dividing a Document into Sections

You can divide a large publication into sections by creating a separate QuarkXPress document for each part of the publication. For example, you could create a separate QuarkXPress document for each chapter in a book. Chapter 12 gives some good reasons for dividing a document into parts this way.

You can also use the Section command to divide a single QuarkXPress document into any number of sections. A section is a group of sequentially numbered pages within a document. Individual sections within a document can have their own page number format and sequence. This can be useful if you are creating a document that includes a front page (with no page number), a preface (with roman page numbers i, ii, iii), and a body (with page numbers 1, 2, 3). You can also create sections with compound page numbers, such as 1-1, 1-2, 1-3, followed by 2-1, 2-2, 2-3, and so on.

To start a new section, first make sure that the page number showing in the bottom left corner of the document window is the page on which you wish the new section to start. (See also "Turning Pages" earlier in this chapter.) Next choose the Page → Section command to display the Section dialog box (Figure 3-16).

You can access the Section dialog box for the active page quickly by clicking on the page number field in the Document Layout palette, if that palette is open on the screen.

Figure 3-16 The Section dialog box.

In the Section dialog box, check Section Start. You can enter up to four characters in the Prefix box. This number of characters is useful if your document renumbers pages starting at number 1 for each section, such as 1-1, 1-2, 1-3, followed by 2-1, 2-2, 2-3, or APX-1, APX-2, APX-3.

Whenever you use commands that prompt you to enter a page number—such as Page → Go to, Page → Insert, Page → Delete, and Page → Move—you must enter the prefix assigned in the Section dialog box along with the page number.

You can enter any starting page number in the Page Number box. Page numbers must be entered in Arabic numerals (1, 2, 3) regardless of the format you select. The Format pop-up menu lists QuarkXPress's five page number format options: Numeric (1, 2, 3), Uppercase Roman (I, II, III), Lowercase Roman (i, ii, iii), Uppercase Alphabetic (A, B, C), and Lowercase Alphabetic (a, b, c).

If you choose Page → Section when the active page is already set up as the start of a section, the Section Start box will already be checked and the assigned starting page number and format will show in the Prefix, Page Number, and Format boxes. You can change any of these values, or you can merge the current section with the previous section of the document, by unchecking Section Start. QuarkXPress updates the page numbers to follow the preceding section's format and sequence.

Remember that in order for page numbers to display on printed pages, you must set them up using the automatic page number characters (described under the next heading).

Referencing Page Numbers

QuarkXPress automatically numbers pages in a document and displays them in the document window and in the Document Layout palette, but in order to *print* the page number, you must type ⌘-2, ⌘-3, or ⌘-4 as part of a text box entry. The following table shows the meaning of each of these entries.

Keyboard Entry	Page Number
⌘-2	Previous Text Box Page Number
⌘-3	Current Text Box Page Number
⌘-4	Next Text Box Page Number

Figure 3-17 Keyboard entries for referencing page numbers.

It should be easy to remember that ⌘-3 is the entry for current page number: The uppercase value of 3 on the keyboard is the pound sign or number sign (#), and this is the page number symbol displayed on the master pages. You make the ⌘-3 entry on a master page so that the page numbers will be positioned automatically on all document pages.

Wherever you type ⌘-2 in a text box, QuarkXPress displays the page number of the previous box in a linked chain. Similarly, wherever you type ⌘-4 in a text box, QuarkXPress displays the page number of the next box in a linked chain. If the text box containing the ⌘-2 or ⌘-4 character is not linked to any other box, the page number will reflect the links of the box immediately behind or below it.

Use ⌘-2 in references such as "Continued from page..." that appear at the top of text that jumps text from several pages earlier in the document. Use ⌘-4 with references such as "Continued on page..." that appear at the bottom of text that jumps to several pages later in the document.

It's a good idea to put jump-to text such as "Continued from page..." or "Continued on page..." in a separate, unlinked text box at the top or bottom of the linked text box that contains the story. This way, the jump-to lines will not reflow when the story is edited.

QuarkXPress automatically renumbers pages and updates all page number references within the text whenever you add, delete, or move pages within a document.

Using the QuarkXPress Library

Perhaps one of the most useful features new to QuarkXPress 3.0 is the library. A QuarkXPress library is a file, created by selecting Utilities ➤ Library, that can store any page element you can create or import into QuarkXPress. An entry can be a line, a box, a group of items, or multiple-selected items. Once items are stored in a library, they can be dragged to any document page. You can store up to 2,000 items in a library.

To store items in a library, you must first create or open a library file by selecting Utilities ➤ Library. This command lets you type in a new file name or select from a list of files. When you open a library, the library appears as a palette on your screen (Figure 3-18). You can drag-copy an item onto the Library palette, and when the cursor changes from the Mover pointer (✥) to Library pointer (6ᕽ), release the mouse; the item will display as a thumbnail in the Library palette.

To bring items from the library onto a document page, drag the thumbnail image onto the page. When you release the mouse button, the items will appear full size on the screen. A full-size shadow image appears first that will help you position the elements.

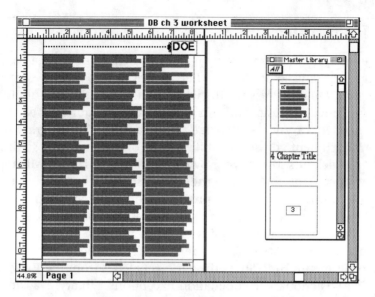

Figure 3-18 Select Utilities ➤ Library to open a library.

Library Labels

Any item that is stored in a library can have a "label" attached to it that allows you to display selectively only those items you want to see. To give an item in a library a label, double-click on the item to display the Library Entry dialog box (Figure 3-19). To select which entries will display, choose a label from the pop-up menu at the top of the palette, or type in the label of the item you wish to display.

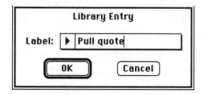

Figure 3-19 The Library Entry dialog box.

Libraries can be extremely useful for storing commonly used document elements. Using a library is far more convenient than using the Macintosh Scrapbook.

Changing Preferences

You have many options for setting up a document—choosing a page size, setting margins, and so on. Rather than forcing you to specify every detail from scratch, QuarkXPress begins with certain assumptions about your document, called defaults. You can change these defaults for each document as needed, or you can change the defaults *for the program* so that every new document you start will have your own customized settings.

To change defaults so that your own custom specifications will apply to every new document you start in the future, start the application by double-clicking on the QuarkXPress program icon. *Before* you open a document or start a new one, commands that affect the program defaults are shown in black in the menus.The commands that can be changed before you open a document include Preferences, Style Sheets, Colors, and H&J from the Edit menu; Hide/Show the various palettes from the View menu; and Auxiliary Dictionary, Hyphenation Exceptions, Library, Tracking Edit, and Kerning Edit from the Utilities menu.

 The Preferences command displays a submenu of four categories of preferences: Application, new to version 3.1, General, Typographic, and Tools.Application preferences, no matter when you change them, affect the program and all files that you open. If you use the other preferences commands—General, Typographic, and Tools—with no documents open, the changes you make will be applied to all subsequently created documents. If you use these commands with a document open, your selections apply to that document only (or whatever document is active, if you have two or more documents open at once).

The Preferences command is described next. The other commands and their functions are explained in detail elsewhere in this book, but we mention them here to highlight the usefulness of customizing your defaults. For example, if you frequently use a particular color for your corporate logo color that is not part of QuarkXPress's original default palette of colors, you can add it to the default palette using Edit ➤ Colors *before* you open a document.

Setting Application Preferences

Unlike the other preference settings, changes made in the Application Preferences dialog box (Figure 3-20) affect all documents, including previously created documents, currently active documents, and any new documents. If you have used the QuarkFreebies 3.0 XTension, you will recognize many of the options in this dialog box. Do not use the 3.0 Freebies Xtension with QuarkXPress 3.1.

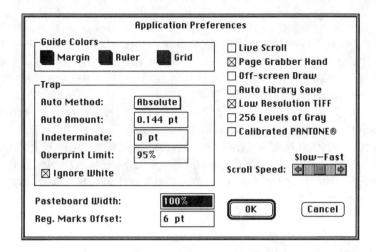

Figure 3-20 The Applications Preferences dialog box.

Guide Colors

If you are using a color monitor, you can change the colors in which margin guides, ruler guides, and the baseline grid display. If you are using a grayscale monitor, you can change the levels of gray. Click on the color box in front of the appropriate guides you want to change; a dialog box with the standard Macintosh color wheel is displayed (Figure 3-21). When desired color is displayed, click OK.

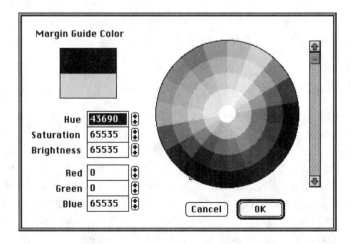

Figure 3-21 Guide Colors can be changed using a variation of the Apple color wheel.

Trap

Trap controls the way QuarkXPress applies trapping between two colors when printing color separations. Trap values for specific colors are specified in the Trap Specifications dialog box (Edit ➤ Colors) or by using the Show Trap Information palette.

When the Trap value is set to Automatic, the default setting is that the trapping relationship between colors is determined by an **Absolute** value, that is, one specified in the **Auto Amount** field. If the object color is darker, it will be choked by the background color; if the object color is lighter, it will spread by the Auto Amount. **Proportional** will trap automatically using a fraction of the value in the Auto Amount field, based on the luminance of the object color and background color.

Figure 3-22 You can specify that QuarkXPress apply trapping values by an Absolute amount, or as a Proportional value, based on luminance of the colors.

When an object color is in front of several different colors, QuarkXPress traps to the value specified in **Indeterminate**. The **OverPrint Limit** allows you to specify the shade at or above which an object color will overprint its background color. Check **Ignore White** to specify that an object color in front of several different colors does not take white into account when trapping. When **Process Trap** is checked, QuarkXPress traps process separation plates individually when a page contains process colors that touch each other. When Process Trap is unchecked, all process colors are trapped equally. See Part II for more detailed information on how QuarkXPress handles trapping for color separations.

Pasteboard Width

The Pasteboard Width option lets you control the width of the pasteboard, the nonprinting area to the left and right of each page or spread where you can work with or store items. The default setting is that the pasteboard is 100 percent of the page size. So, for example, if your page is letter size (81/2 × 11 inches), the pasteboard will be 8 1/2 inches wide to the left and right of the page. You can set the pasteboard width value from 0 percent to 100 percent, but the width of pages and pasteboard combined cannot exceed 48 inches. The pasteboard is always 1/2 inch above and below a page or spread, and at least 1/2 inch of the pasteboard will surround document pages, even if you set a width percentage that would be less than 1/2 inch.

Registration Marks Offset

 When the Registration Marks option is checked in the Print dialog box (File → Print), you can specify the distance from the edge of the page at which registration marks will print. When the Registration Marks option is checked, QuarkXPress prints registration marks and crop marks. The default distance from the edge of a page at which registration marks print is 6 points, but you can use this option to change that value from 0 to 30 points in .001-point increments.

Live Scroll

 When you scroll through a document using the scroll box on the scroll bars, QuarkXPress updates the screen display as you scroll if the Live Scroll option is checked. If Live Scroll is unchecked (the default setting), the screen is updated only after you finish scrolling and release the mouse.

If Live Scroll is unchecked, you can achieve a Live Scroll by holding down the Option key as you drag a scroll box. If Live Scroll is checked, holding down the Option key as you scroll temporarily disables a live scroll.

Page Grabber Hand

 If you want to scroll in any direction by holding down the Option key and using the page grabber hand (✍), check the Page Grabber Hand option. If the option is not checked, you cannot scroll using the page grabber hand. The preset default is that Page Grabber hand is checked.

If this option is checked, you must have Caps Lock on to use the Option-click and Option-⌘-click methods of changing document views.

Off-Screen Draw

 Normally, when you scroll by using the scroll bar arrows or by clicking on the scroll bars, the screen is actually updated in successive pieces. The redraw begins the moment you scroll, but it may take a few seconds for the entire screen to display, especially if you have complicated graphics on the page. If you check Off-screen draw, the screen updates at once as you scroll. There is a momentary pause before screen redraw occurs, but then the entire screen is redrawn at once. Checking this option does not actually decrease the time it takes the screen to redraw; it merely changes the method by which the redraw occurs.

Auto Library Save

 Normally, QuarkXPress saves library additions and changes only when you close a library or quit the program. If you want all changes to a library saved as they are made, check Auto Library Save. The preset default is that it is unchecked.

Low Resolution TIFF

 With Low Resolution TIFF checked (the preset default), imported TIFF and RIFF images are displayed at 36 dpi. If this option is unchecked, they are displayed at 72 dpi. This option has no effect on the way images print.

   If this option is checked and you want an imported image to display at 72 dpi, hold down the Shift key when you click OK in the Get Picture dialog box. If this option is unchecked so that images display at 72 dpi, but you want an imported image to display at 36 dpi, hold down the Shift key when you click OK in the Get Picture dialog box.

256 Levels of Gray

 If you want grayscale pictures to display in 256 levels of gray, check this option. If the option is unchecked, the preset default, images display in 16 levels of gray, and the screen redraw is faster. If you check this option, you must be using a monitor capable of displaying 256 levels of gray, and the image must have been scanned at 256 levels of gray.

Calibrated PANTONE

 Calibrated PANTONE is available only if you have the Professional Color Toolkit Control Panel device, available from Radius, Inc., installed in your System. If the option is checked, it updates the display of PANTONE colors to display accurately as they are in the PANTONE selector.

Scroll Speed

 Use the Scroll Speed to set the speed at which a document scrolls when scrolling through a document using the scroll bar arrows. The faster the speed is set, the greater the distance the document moves with one click of a scroll arrow.

Setting General Preferences

Unlike Application preferences, settings in the General Preferences dialog box affect only currently active documents or newly created ones. The settings do not affect documents created previously. You can display the General Preferences dialog box (Figure 3-23) by choosing Edit → Preferences → General or by typing the keyboard shortcut: ⌘-Y.

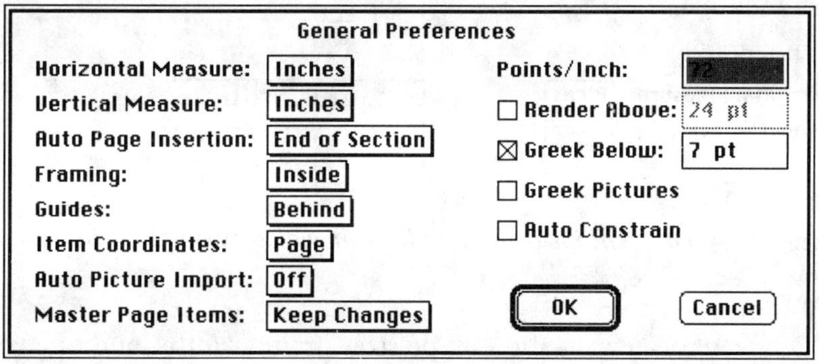

Figure 3-23 The General Preferences dialog box.

Horizontal and Vertical Measure

You can set the rulers on the screen to display inches (8 units per inch), inches decimal (10 units per inch), picas, points, millimeters, centimeters, or ciceros. You can set the two rulers separately, so that the horizontal ruler displays picas, for instance, while the vertical ruler displays inches (common in traditional newspaper production).

Inches, picas, and points are common measurements used in the United States and other English-speaking countries. There are 12 points in a pica and 6 picas in an inch—or approximately 72 points in an inch. (The actual measure is 72.051 points per inch, and you can adjust this as described under the heading Points/Inch which follows.) Ciceros are a French measure, with 1 cicero equivalent to approximately 4.552 millimeters.

Horizontal Measure:	Inches
Vertical Measure:	Inches

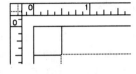

Horizontal Measure:	Inches Decimal
Vertical Measure:	Inches Decimal

Horizontal Measure:	Picas
Vertical Measure:	Picas

Figure 3-24 Different measures and how they display on rulers in actual-size view.

QuarkXPress always shows type sizes, frame widths, and line widths in points in the Measurements palette and dialog boxes related to these elements, regardless of your selection for the ruler displays. Similarly, page width and height are usually measured in inches, the measurement QuarkXPress displays in the dialog boxes related to page size, regardless of your selection for the ruler displays.

Auto Page Insertion

When you import more text into a text box than it can display, QuarkXPress automatically adds pages for the text overflow *if* all of the following are true:

- Auto Page Insertion is enabled (not set to *Off*) in the General Preferences dialog box;
- the master page specified via Auto Page Insertion has an automatic text box (indicated by the intact chain icon [⌘] in the upper left corner of the master page); *and*
- the overflow is from the automatic text box or from a chain of at least two text boxes.

Normally, when there is overflow text QuarkXPress adds pages at the end of the section. A *section* is a group of pages—one chapter of a book, for example—with sequential page numbering defined by the Page ➤ Section command.

You can change the default for automatic page insertion in the General Preferences dialog box by choosing *Off* (to prevent QuarkXPress from adding pages automatically), or End of Story (to add new pages immediately after the last text box in the chain that overflows), or End of Document.

You can *prevent* pages from being added automatically by setting Auto Page Insert to *Off*, or by adding text to a text box that is not the automatic text box and that is not linked to any other box.

Framing

The Framing option in the General Preferences dialog box lets you specify that frame widths be added either Inside or Outside the box edge. If the frame is added inside, the dimensions of the box remain the same. If the frame is added outside, the dimensions of the box *increase* by the frame width. This setting determines the immediate effect of using the Item ➤ Frame command—*existing* frames in the document do not change when you change the Framing preference.

For example, if you draw a 12-pica square box and add a 1-pica wide frame using the Item ➤ Frame command, the effective size of the box will remain 12 picas square if the Framing option is set to Inside, or will increase to 14 picas square if the Framing option is set to Outside.

Guides

Nonprinting guides—margin guides, column guides, and ruler guides—can be set to display behind all items on the page (the preset default) or in front of them.

Item Coordinates

Normally, the horizontal ruler shows a 0 at the top left corner of each page. On facing pages or multiple-page spreads, the measurements begin again at 0 at the top left corner of each new page. The pop-up menu for Item Coordinates lets you change this so that the measurements along the ruler are continuous across the spread.

Auto Picture Import

If Auto Picture Import is on, when you open a document QuarkXPress automatically updates all imported pictures that have been modified using another program (one, outside of QuarkXPress) since you last saved the document. If it cannot locate a picture, it displays the Missing/ Modified Picture dialog box (described in Chapter 6) through which you can locate the moved or renamed file. If you set this value to On (verify), and open a file that contains modified or missing pictures, QuarkXPress will display an alert (Figure 3-25) asking if you want to list missing or modified pictures; if you click OK, the Missing/Modified Picture dialog box listing each missing or modified picture file is displayed.

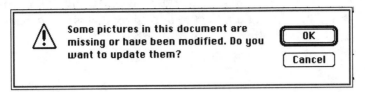

Figure 3-25 The option Auto Picture Import On (verify) causes an alert each time you open a file containing missing or modified pictures.

If Auto Picture Import is Off, you can selectively update pictures through the Utilities ➤ Picture Usage command, or QuarkXPress will ask you if you want to update modified pictures when you use the File ➤ Print command.

If you use Edit ➤ Preferences ➤ General to change the Auto Picture Import preference On (or Off), modified pictures will be updated (or not updated) *when you next open* the active document; no changes take place immediately.

Master Page Items

As discussed earlier in this chapter, QuarkXPress 3.0 introduces the option of having changes made to master pages apply automatically to all document pages that have already been created based on that master page *unless you have modified those items on the document page.* The Master Page Items option in the General Preferences dialog box lets you control how applying a new master page affects document pages.

If you choose Keep Changes, when you apply a new master page, *unmodified* master page items are deleted from the document page and replaced with elements from the new master page. Master page elements that have been *modified* on the document page will remain unchanged.

If you choose Delete Changes, when you apply a new master page, both *unmodified* and *modified* master page items are deleted from the document page and replaced with the elements from the new master page.

Points/Inch

Normally, QuarkXPress converts points to inches (and vice versa) using 72 points per inch. You can change this by entering a value between 72 and 73 in .01-point increments. The true measure is 72.051 points per inch.

Ciceros/cm

QuarkXPress converts ciceros to centimeters using 2.1967 ciceros per centimeter. To change the value of ciceros to centimeters, enter any value between 2 and 3 in .0001-cicero increments.

Snap Distance

As discussed in Chapter 2, items will "snap-to" guides if Snap to Guides is checked in the View menu. The preset default is that items snap when they are moved within 6 pixels of a guide. You can change the distance at which items will snap by entering a value from 0 to 100 (pixels).

Render Above

QuarkXPress can optimize the display of *nonencrypted* (Type 3) fonts on the screen via font rendering, which eliminates the jagged edges sometimes associated with screen fonts. Fonts from Bitstream, Compugraphic, Casady, The Font Company, ImageClub, and other sources can be optimized, so long as the printer fonts are in the System folder or one level deep in a folder within the System folder. QuarkXPress cannot render encrypted (Type 1) fonts, such as those from Adobe Systems, Inc., but you can use Adobe Type Manager to accomplish the same thing (as described in Chapter 5).

Only fonts that are 24 points or larger will be rendered. You can increase this value (up to 720 points) to speed the time required for screen redraw.

Greek Below

QuarkXPress accelerates the speed of screen redraw by *greeking* text below a certain point size—displaying the text as a gray bar on the screen (Figure 3-26). The preset value is 7 points, but you can set this to any value from 2 to 720 points.

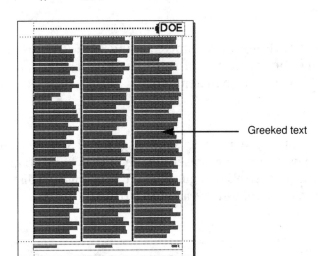

Greeked text

Figure 3-26 Greeked text.

The value you enter here determines the size below which text is greeked in Actual Size view. The value is adjusted automatically for other magnifications. For example, if you set type to be greeked below 7 points in Actual Size, then it will be greeked below 3.5 points in 200 percent view or below 14 points in 50 percent view.

Greeking increases the speed at which pages are displayed on your screen, but it does not affect printing.

Greek Pictures

QuarkXPress displays inactive, imported pictures as gray boxes if Greek Pictures is checked. This is a great way to speed up screen redraw while editing a document with a lot of imported pictures. Picture greeking does not affect printing.

Accurate Blends

The Accurate Blends option affects how blends will display on the screen of 8-bit monitors. The preset default is that Accurate Blends is checked, so that blends display without banding. To display blends more quickly, uncheck this option. Monitors with 24-bit video displays always show blends as accurate blends, whether the option is checked or not. This option does not affect how blends print.

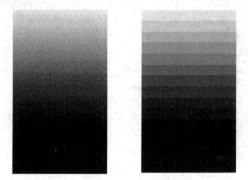

Figure 3-27 Screen display when Accurate Blends is checked (left) and unchecked (right).

Auto Constrain

You can move items anywhere on a page regardless of their relationship to other items on the page. In earlier versions of QuarkXPress, items created within the borders of any box were always constrained in a "parent/child" relationship, and you could not position a child beyond the parent's boundaries.

If Auto Constrain is checked, items that you create within a box are constrained by that box. You cannot move constrained items out of their constraining box or scale them to be larger than the constraining box. Changes in Auto Constrain affect items that you add to the document but will not affect items previously positioned on pages.

Setting Typographic Preferences

You can display the Typographic Preferences dialog box (Figure 3-28) by choosing Edit → Preferences → Typographic or by typing the keyboard shortcut: ⌘-Option-Y. Unlike the General Preferences settings, Typographic Preferences *do* affect how the page—specifically the type—will appear when printed.

Although you can change your Preferences settings at any time, it is a good idea to set preferences that affect the way a document will print before you build the document. Otherwise, changing these preferences can result in text reflow and change the appearance of pages you have already laid out. Preference settings that can affect the appearance of the text include Superscript, Subscript, Small Caps, Superior, Baseline Grid, Auto Leading, Auto Kern, Character Widths, and Leading Mode from the Typographic Preferences dialog box.

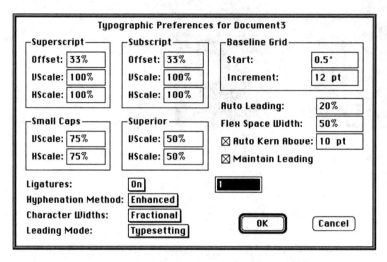

Figure 3-28 The Typographic Preferences dialog box.

Entries in the Typographic Preferences dialog box are described in Chapter 5.

Setting Tool Preferences

You can display the Tool Preferences dialog box (Figure 3-29) by choosing Edit ➤ Preferences ➤ Tools or by double-clicking on a tool in the Tool palette. The Tool Preferences dialog box lets you modify defaults for the Zoom tool and the item creation tools.

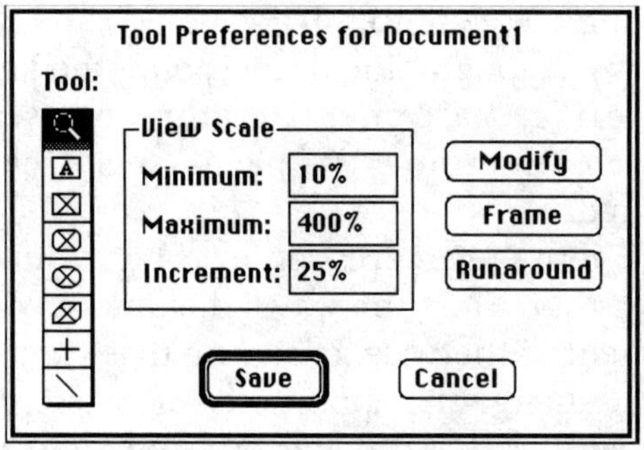

Figure 3-29 The Tool Preferences dialog box.

View Scale

The View Scale determines the range and increment of the view changes when you click on the document window with the Zoom tool (🔍) selected. You can set the Minimum to 10 percent view or higher, the Maximum to 400 percent or lower, and the Increment to any value from 10 percent to 400 percent.

Modify, Frame, and Runaround

The Modify, Frame, and Runaround options are available when one of the item creation tools is selected in the abbreviated Tool palette displayed inside the Tools Preferences dialog box.

The Modify button displays the Text Box Specifications dialog box if the Text Box tool (Ⓐ) is selected; it displays the Picture Box Specifications dialog box if one of the picture box creation tools is selected (⊠, ⊗, ⊗, or ⊘); or it displays the Line Specifications dialog box if one of the line tools (+ or ╲) is selected.

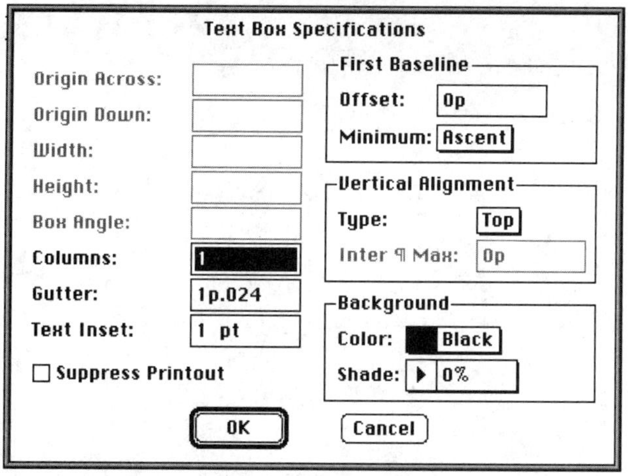

```
┌───────────────────────────────────────────────────┐
│              Text Box Specifications                │
│                                                     │
│  Origin Across:  [        ]  ┌First Baseline──────┐ │
│                              │ Offset:   [0p    ]  │ │
│  Origin Down:    [        ]  │                     │ │
│  Width:          [        ]  │ Minimum: [Ascent]   │ │
│                              └─────────────────────┘ │
│  Height:         [        ]  ┌Vertical Alignment──┐ │
│  Box Angle:      [        ]  │ Type:      [Top]    │ │
│  Columns:        [1       ]  │ Inter ¶ Max:  0p    │ │
│  Gutter:         [1p.024  ]  └─────────────────────┘ │
│  Text Inset:     [1  pt   ]  ┌Background───────────┐ │
│                              │ Color:  ■ [Black]   │ │
│  ☐ Suppress Printout         │ Shade:  ▶ [0%   ]   │ │
│                              └─────────────────────┘ │
│              (   OK   )    ( Cancel )                 │
└───────────────────────────────────────────────────┘
```

Figure 3-30 Text box specifications that can be modified in the Tool Preferences dialog box.

The Frame and Runaround buttons display the Frame Specifications and Runaround Specifications dialog boxes (respectively). You can change the defaults for items created with the selected tool.

Summary

In Chapter 2 you learned how to start a new QuarkXPress document and begin adding elements to a page. In this chapter you went on to learn how to create and apply multiple master pages; add, move, and delete pages; add page numbers; and divide a document into sections. You also learned how to set QuarkXPress preferences.

Up to this point we have focused on creating and editing boxes created using QuarkXPress' item creation tools. The next chapters describe how to edit lines and the *contents* of boxes (text and imported pictures) in QuarkXPress.

4 *Word Processing*

QuarkXPress has many of the same capabilities as a dedicated word processing program, and many people input text, even long documents directly into QuarkXPress without using a word processor. You can, however, input text using a word processing program, then import the text into QuarkXPress. In so doing you can preserve not only the text, of course, but much of the formatting as well, such as type specifications, tabs, and paragraph alignment. This chapter presents an overview of the process of getting text onto a page—by typing, copying, or importing—and describes some of QuarkXPress' basic formatting commands and word processing capabilities, including global search, global replace, and spell checking.

It's important to understand how text that has been formatted in a word processing program is interpreted when it is imported into QuarkXPress. By seeing what you can do in QuarkXPress and knowing what you can do using your word processor, you'll be able to make decisions about how to prepare text and whether to put more time into formatting from the beginning—during the word processing step—or later, in QuarkXPress.

Chapter 3 explained how to position text boxes on a page and link boxes on the same page or link boxes from one page to the next. In this chapter you learn how to get text onto a page, how to edit the *content* of the text, and how to apply basic formatting. Chapter 5 covers issues that pertain to typography, including leading, spacing, and special effects, such as drop caps.

Setting Up a Text Box

As mentioned in earlier chapters, before you type in text or import text typed in a word processing program, you must first draw a text box using QuarkXPress' Text Box tool. In Chapter 2, you learned how to move, resize, and apply color to boxes. You need to understand how to adjust three other specifications, unique to text boxes: setting the number of columns in a text box, setting gutter width, and adjusting the text inset value.

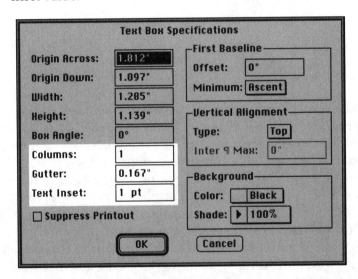

Figure 4-1 Basic text box specifications include setting the number of columns, gutter width, and text inset.

The number of columns may be set using the Measurements palette or the Text Box Specifications dialog box (Item → Modify), but gutter width and text inset can be specified only in the Text Box Specifications dialog box. The preset defaults for all three may be changed by modifying the Text Box tool preferences (Edit → Preferences → Tools), as described in Chapter 3.

Setting Columns

QuarkXPress divides the number of columns in a text box evenly. You cannot have columns of two different widths within the same text box (unless a text inset value is specified; see below). The preset default is 1 column. The maximum number of columns in a text box is 30 columns.

Gutter Width

Gutter width is the space between columns. The preset default is .167 inches, or 1 pica. You can specify a gutter width from 3 points to 24 points in .001-point increments.

Text Inset

Text inset is the distance that text will be spaced from the four edges of a text box. The preset default is 1 point.

 If you specify a text inset in a text box with three or more columns, the rightmost and leftmost columns will be 1 point narrower than all other columns in the text box, since text inset is calculated from the edges of the box, not from the columns within a text box. We highly recommend that you set the text inset to zero by changing the preferences for the text box tool (Edit ➤ Preferences ➤ Tools).

Sources of Text

There are several ways of entering text on a page in QuarkXPress: You can type text directly using QuarkXPress; you can select the File ➤ Get Text command to bring in text that has been typed using a word processing program (or other programs that can save data as text); you can copy text from a QuarkXPress library; or you can select the Paste command to copy the contents of the Clipboard. You'll see the pros and cons of each of these methods under the following headings

Typing Text

Most QuarkXPress documents that are longer than one page—and many one-page documents—are composed of text that has been typed in a word processing program and *imported* into QuarkXPress, as described under "Importing Text" later in this chapter. In this section you will see how to input text directly using QuarkXPress.

To type text on a page in QuarkXPress, first create a text box (or activate the automatic text box, as described in Chapter 2), then select the Content tool (🖑) in the Tools palette. When the Content tool is selected, the blinking text insertion bar appears at the top of an empty text box or, in a text box that already contains text, wherever the insertion bar was last positioned. When the Content tool is positioned inside an active text box, the mouse pointer changes to an I-beam pointer. You can click the I-beam pointer in the text box to set the insertion point and start typing.

Step 1   Create or activate a text box.

Step 2   Select the Content tool in the tool palette.

Step 3   The text insertion point blinks in the text box. (If the box already contains text, you can click anywhere in the text to reposition the text insertion point.)

Step 4   Type text in through the keyboard.

The format and position of the typed text will vary depending on where you click the I-beam to position the text insertion point. If you click the I-beam in existing text, the typed text will be inserted within the text block and will appear in the same format as the text immediately left of the insertion point.

If you click the I-beam in an empty text box, the typed text will be in the default character format or the format set up for the active text box. The default settings that are initially set up for text when you first install QuarkXPress are listed in Figure 4-2.

Font:	Helvetica 12-point
Alignment:	Left
Leading:	Auto
Tabs:	Set every half inch
Hyphenation:	Auto Hyphenation is off
Auto kerning:	Above 10 points
Spacing between paragraphs:	Zero

Figure 4-2 QuarkXPress' default settings for text.

Text typed directly into QuarkXPress will take on these default characteristics unless you specify otherwise. If you want to change the format for the next text you will type, first click the I-beam to position the text insertion point, then select the commands under the Style menu (as described later in this chapter) to format the text, then type the text. In this case, you will be setting new specifications for the current insertion point only.

To change the default settings for text, select the Edit ➤ Style Sheet command (as described later in this chapter) and change the specifications for the Normal type style sheet. The default character format is defined by the Normal style sheet.

Typing Symbols and Other Special Characters

Most fonts have a variety of special characters available, including ™, ®, and ©. You can access these symbols by pressing the Option key before pressing a key on the keyboard. To find out what keys need to be pressed for certain characters, use the Key Caps accessory on the Apple menu.

Certain fonts are composed of symbols and special characters, such as the Symbol font and Zapf Dingbats, both of which are built into Apple's LaserWriter printers. QuarkXPress offers a handy shortcut for accessing these characters (assuming the font is installed in your system, as described in Chapter 5): To input one character in the Symbol font, type ⌘-Shift-Q; the next character you type will be in the Symbol font, then the following character returns to the previous font. To input one character in Zapf Dingbats, type ⌘-Shift-Z; the next character you type will be in Dingbats, then the font returns to the previous font.

Typing Invisible Characters

Besides typing the normal characters you associate with text, you can insert special characters by typing the entries shown in Figure 4-3. These special characters are normally invisible on the screen and on the printed pages. You may find it useful to display the invisible characters while you are typing in QuarkXPress; these characters can be displayed by choosing View ➤ Show Invisibles.

Special Character	*Typed Entry*	*Onscreen display*
Space	Space bar	.
Tab	Tab	→
New Paragraph	Return	¶
New Line	Shift-Return	↵
Discretionary Line Break	⌘-Return	no display
Indent Here	⌘-\	¦
New Column	Enter	↓
New Box	Shift-Enter	⤋

Figure 4-3 Typing Special Characters

The New Line, Discretionary Line Break, Indent Here, New Column, and New Box characters are described later in this chapter, under "Paragraph Formatting."

Importing Text

You can select File ➤ Get Text (⌘-E) to import text that has been typed in a word processor or to import data that has been saved as text from a spreadsheet or database program.

To import text into QuarkXPress, first create or activate a text box. Next select the Content tool; a blinking text cursor will appear automatically in a new text box, or you can position the cursor within an existing block of text. Select the File ➤ Get Text command, then find the file name from the list displayed in the Get Text dialog box. Double-click on the file name to select it, or click once and click the Open button. These steps are illustrated in Figures 4-4, 4-5, 4-6, and 4-7.

Notice that you can change directories and disks through the Get Text dialog box (File ➤ Get Text) using the same techniques you learned in Chapter 2 for the Open dialog box (File ➤ Open). The one difference is that only QuarkXPress documents are listed in the dialog box when you select the Open command, and only text files in formats for which the corresponding import/export filter is available are listed when you select the File ➤ Get Text command.

Step 1   Create or activate a text box and select the Content tool, or position the cursor within an existing block of text with the Content tool.

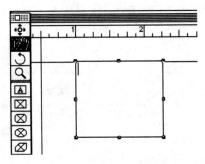

Figure 4-4 Active text box.

Step 2 Select the File → Get Text command.

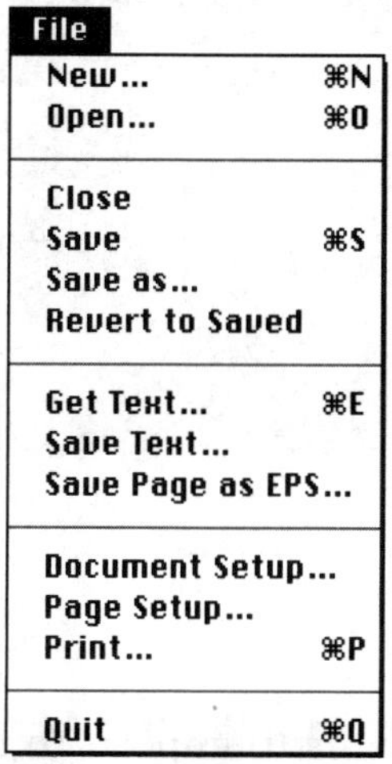

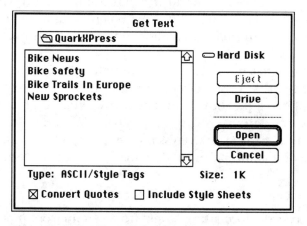

Figure 4-5 Get Text command.

Step 3 Find the name of the text file you want to import in the Get Text dialog box.

Figure 4-6 Get Text dialog box.

When you click once on a file name, QuarkXPress displays the file Type and Size. Check **Convert Quotes** if you want inch and foot marks (",') converted to open and close quotes and apostrophes (",",',') and double hyphens (--) converted to em dashes (—). Click on **Include Style Sheets** if you want the style sheet names and formats imported with the text from Microsoft Word, or if you want to convert XPress Tags to format text.

Step 4 **Select the name by double-clicking on it. (This is a shortcut for the more obvious method: Click on the file name to select it, then click on Open.)**

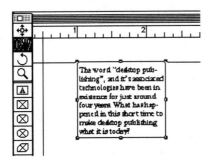

The word "desktop pub-
lishing", and it's associated
technologies have been in
existence for just around
four years. What has hap-
pened in this short time to
make desktop publishing
what it is today?

Figure 4-7 Imported text.

Long files or complex formats can take awhile to import. To take the worry out of waiting, the lower left corner of the Document window displays the percentage of the file that has been imported during the import process.

Imported text will be inserted at the text insertion point or will replace text that was selected when the Get Text command is chosen. The text will take on the width of the column in which it is imported. It will stop flowing when it reaches the bottom of the text box (if links have not been established) or flow into linked boxes and/or add new pages as needed for overflow text (as described in Chapter 2).

If the imported text has not already been formatted in a word processing program, or if QuarkXPress does not support the word processor and therefore cannot preserve the formatting, the text will take on the default format and type specifications. If the text has been formatted in a word processing program that the QuarkXPress program supports, QuarkXPress will preserve some of that formatting as described under the next heading.

Formatted Text

QuarkXPress preserves the formatting of text from certain word processing programs, including MacWrite, MacWrite II, Microsoft Word, Microsoft Works, Microsoft Write, Word Perfect, and Write Now. You can format text using any supported word processor's formatting commands, or you can format text in any word processor by embedding QuarkXPress codes that will be translated into formats when you import the text into QuarkXPress. See Chapter 10 for the procedure and codes for creating XPress Tags.

In order for the formatting from any of these applications to be preserved when imported into QuarkXPress, the correct filter must be available. Filters you selected during the installation procedure are always available; other filters were stored in folder called "Other XTensions". To make a filter available to the program, simply move it out of the Other XTensions folder and into the folder on the same level as the QuarkXPress program. When you restart QuarkXPress, the filter will be available.

Formatting characteristics that are usually preserved include:

- Left margin
- Left and right indents
- First-line indent
- Carriage returns
- Tabs
- Character formats (font size, style)
- Style sheets from Microsoft Word only, and only if Include Style Sheets was checked

The right margin is changed to match QuarkXPress' column width, with right margin indents preserved from some word processors. QuarkXPress ignores specialized formatting commands such as headers and footers or footnotes.

Tables created using Microsoft Word's Insert Table command are imported as text, with each cell separated by a tab and each row separated by a carriage return. If you want to maintain the graphic borders of a table, first convert it to a graphic in Microsoft Word by selecting the table, then copy it into the Clipboard as a graphic by pressing Option-Command (⌘)-D. You can then paste the table back into your Word document. The table will be imported into QuarkXPress as an anchored graphic.

If the fonts specified through the word processor are not loaded in your system when you import the text into QuarkXPress, a warning message appears (Figure 4-8).

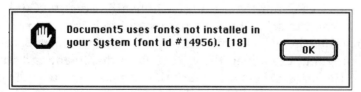

Document5 uses fonts not installed in your System (font id #14956). [18]

OK

Figure 4-8 QuarkXPress issues a warning when you import a word processing file that was created with fonts not currently loaded in your system.

Unformatted Text

Although it is usually preferable to do as much formatting as possible in the word processing program, you can also import unformatted text to QuarkXPress and format it with QuarkXPress' features. There are three common sources of unformatted text: ASCII files from any word processor, data saved in ASCII format from a spreadsheet or database program, and text that has been telecommunicated through the type of electronic mailbox or bulletin board that forces you to use ASCII text.

Initially, unformatted text will take on the default type specifications and format, or whatever format is specified for the current location of the text insertion point. It's a good idea to set up the text specifications at the insertion point before you select the Get Text command to import ASCII text. Choose specifications appropriate to the largest percentage of the imported text (not necessarily the first line of imported text: if it is a heading, for example).

See Chapter 5 for a description of how to change text formats, and see Chapter 10 for tips on handling imported data files (from a database or spreadsheet) or telecommunicated text files.

Text from a Library

You can drag text from a QuarkXPress library as described in Chapter 2. Text dragged from a library will retain all of its formatting. If a style sheet was used to format the text in the library, the style sheet names will be added to the document's style sheet list when the text is dragged from the library. If the library text uses the same style sheet names as in the target document, the text will use the style sheet specification of the target document, though the library text will retain its original formatting and the style sheet will need to be reapplied.

Pasting Text from the Clipboard

If you have already put text into the Clipboard using the Cut or Copy command, you can select the Paste command to bring in text from the Clipboard. You can put text into the Clipboard while you are working in another program, then open the QuarkXPress document and paste the text onto the page. You can also use the Clipboard to paste from one QuarkXPress document to another, or from one part of a document to another.

A pasted text *box* will appear in the center of the screen. If you have clicked an insertion point in existing text, the box will paste at the insertion point as an anchored box and move instream with the text.

Selecting and Editing Text

Once text is on a page (or on the Pasteboard), you can use QuarkXPress' rich and flexible assortment of commands and tools to edit it, including the commands from the Edit menu and the Style menu, plus global search, global replace, and spell checking features. The first step in changing any text is to position the text insertion point or select a range of text. To select portions of text within a block of text or to establish the text insertion point before typing new text, be sure the Content tool (☞) is active.

The basic methods of selecting text in QuarkXPress are similar to selecting text in any Macintosh application, although QuarkXPress adds additional shortcuts (Figure 4-9).

Basic Macintosh Techniques

Certain selection techniques are common to all Macintosh programs, including QuarkXPress:

- Position the I-beam in a text box and click once to position the text insertion point for typing or importing new text.
- Position the I-beam beside a character, and drag the I-beam to the end of the desired selection. You can drag the I-beam in any direction—you need not follow along one line of text.
- Double-click on a word to select it.

QuarkXPress Techniques

QuarkXPress adds its own shortcuts for selecting text:

- Triple-click anywhere in a line of text to select it.
- Click four times anywhere in a paragraph to select it.
- Click five times anywhere in a story to select the text in the active box and the text in all boxes linked to the active box.
- If the Content tool is selected and the cursor is positioned in a text box (by positioning the I-beam pointer [I] in the text box and clicking once to position the blinking text cursor [(I)]), then the Select All command will select all of a story.

- Arrow keys move the text insertion point. Holding the Shift key as you press the arrow key will highlight (that is, select) the text as the insertion point moves:
    - Arrow keys alone move the insertion point one character (left or right) or one line (up or down) at a time.
    - Arrow keys with the ⌘ key move the insertion point one word (left or right) or one paragraph (up or down) at a time.
    - Arrow keys with the ⌘ and Option keys move the insertion point to the beginning or end of the line (left or right) or to the beginning or end of the story (up or down).

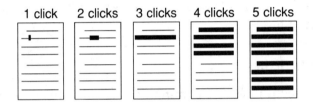

Figure 4-9 Methods of selecting text in QuarkXPress.

Highlighted text will be replaced when you begin typing from the keyboard—you need not delete it first before inserting new text.

Character Formatting

You learned in Chapter 2 how to control the position and size of text boxes, how to set up the number of columns in a box, and how to link text from one box to another. You also learned earlier in this chapter that typed and imported, unformatted text take on the default text specifications, or QuarkXPress retains the text formatting that was set up in the word processing program used to prepare the imported text. In the next sections you will learn how to change the attributes of individual characters and the format of paragraphs once text is on a page.

From one perspective, there are two ways of changing the format of text in QuarkXPress. One way—the obvious way—is to select text and then select the commands described next to change the appearance of the selected text. The second method is to apply a Style Sheet, as described later in this chapter.

QuarkXPress lets you apply Character attributes using any one of three different methods: through commands under the Style menu, using keyboard shortcuts, or through the Measurements palette. In this section we discuss the basic character attributes: Font, Size, Type Style, Color, and Shade. Other Character attributes listed on the Style menu are discussed in the next chapter, which covers typography.

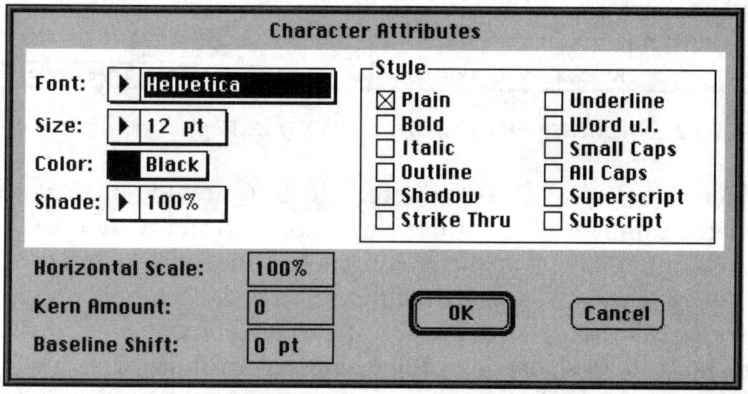

Figure 4-10 QuarkXPress lets you apply the same character attributes found in many word processing programs.

The Style menu lets you apply attributes that are also included in the Character Attributes dialog box (⌘-⇧-C). If you need to apply several different attributes, you may find it's faster to open the Character Attributes dialog box rather than to select several commands from the menu.

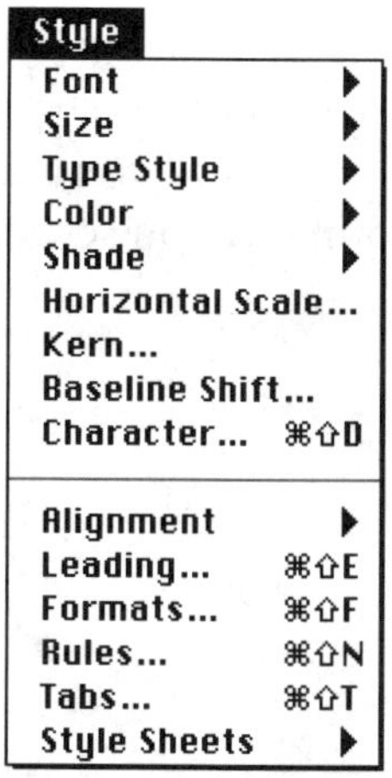

Figure 4-11 The Style menu when a text box is active.

Keyboard shortcuts are available for most character attributes. These shortcuts are listed under individual headings later in this section. Appendix A contains a complete list of keyboard shortcuts.

The Measurements palette (View ➤ Measurements) can also be used to apply character attributes when a text box is selected. The right half of the palette displays various icons and pop-up menus that affect selected text (Figure 4-12).

X: 5p7 Y: 1p7	W: 10p4 H: 39p4	◿ 0° Cols: 1	⇕ 65 pt ◇◇ 0	Times 83 pt F B I ...

Figure 4-12 The Measurements palette when a text box is active.

When you display the Character Attributes dialog box or any of the associated submenus, the options that apply to the current selection are checked or displayed. If the current selection includes more than one attribute of the same type—two different sizes or both bold and italic text, for example—then none of the options will be checked or displayed. Check boxes for Type Style in the Character Attributes dialog will display in gray when more than two styles exist in selected text.

The units of measure shown in the Character Attributes dialog box reflect the current settings of the Edit ➤ Preferences ➤ General command. Remember that you can enter in any unit of measure in any dialog box and in the Measurements palette, or you can change a value by adding or subtracting from the current setting.

Font

Fonts are displayed in the submenu of the Style ➤ Font command (Figure 4-13), in the pop-up menu in the Measurements palette, or in a pop-up menu in the Character Attributes dialog box. Only fonts available to your system are shown. See Chapter 5 for information on setting global conditions that relate to fonts.

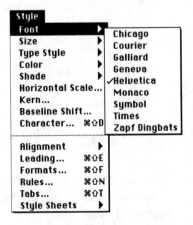

Figure 4-13 The Font list under the Style menu.

To select a font, position the pointer over one of the menus and hold down the mouse button to view the list, then drag the pointer to highlight the desired font name.

As a shortcut, you can type the font name in the Measurements palette or the Character Attributes dialog box, or type the first character(s) of a font name. For example, you can choose Zapf Chancery by simply typing "z" in the font name area *if* that is only font name beginning with the letter z. Otherwise, QuarkXPress displays the *first* font name that it finds—scrolling either forward or backward—that matches or follows the characters typed.

Size

Font sizes are displayed in the submenu of the Style ➤ Size command, in the pop-up menu or field in the Measurements palette, and in a pop-up menu or field in the Character Attributes dialog box. Sizes shown in outline type in the lists are installed screen font sizes. Other sizes listed are commonly used ones that are not installed in the system. You are not limited to the sizes listed on the submenu or in the pop-up menus; you can enter any size from 2 to 720 points in .001-point increments.

To select a size, position the pointer over one of the three menus and hold down the mouse button to view the list, then drag the pointer to highlight the desired font size, or type the new size in the entry field in the Measurements palette, in the Character Attributes dialog box (⌘-Shift-D), or in the Font Size dialog box (⌘-Shift-\) as shown in Figure 4-14.

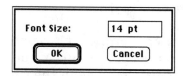

Figure 4-14 Press ⌘-Shift-\ to display the Font Size dialog box.

You can also change the size of selected type using keyboard shortcuts: ⌘-Shift-> increases the size of the selected type, ⌘-Shift-< decreases the size. These shortcuts change the size in the following preset sequence of sizes: 7, 9, 10, 12, 14, 18, 24, 36, 48, 60, 72, 96, 120, 144, 168, and 192 points. To change the size in 1-point increments between 2 points and 720 points, press ⌘-Option-Shift-> or ⌘-Option-Shift-<. You can use ⌘-Shift-\ to check the resulting size quickly.

Style Menu Command	Measurements Palette	Keyboard Shortcut
Size	Yes	⌘-Shift-\ to specify a size
		⌘-Shift-> to enlarge selected type
		⌘-Option-Shift-> to enlarge selected type in 1-point increments
		⌘-Shift-< to reduce selected type
		⌘-Option-Shift-< to reduce selected type in 1-point increments

Figure 4-15 Keyboard shortcuts for changing the size of text.

Type Style

The 13 styles listed in the Type Style submenu are repeated in the Measurements palette (Figure 4-16) and in the Character Attributes dialog box (⌘-Shift-D). They all have keyboard equivalents.

Figure 4-16 Symbols in the Measurements palette are set in the font style they represent: �P *= Plain,* ⒝ *= Bold,* ⒤ *= Italic,* ⓞ *= Outline,* ⓢ *= Shadow,* ⓢ *= Strikeout,* ⓤ *= Underline,* ⓦ *= Word Underline,* ⓚ *= Small Caps,* ⓚ *= All Caps,* ② *= Superscript,* ② *= Subscript,* ② *= Superior.*

To select a style, position the pointer over the style name on the Style ➤ Type Style submenu, click on the appropriate symbol in the Measurements palette, or click on the style name in the Character Attributes dialog box.

You can apply more than one style to selected text, but some styles are mutually exclusive, such as SMALL CAPS and ALL CAPS. With SMALL CAPS, lowercase characters are set as caps that are 75 percent smaller than normal for the font size. (You can change this default through Edit ➤ Preferences ➤ Typographic, as described in Chapter 5.) ALL CAPS sets all characters as normal capitalized letters, whether they were typed as caps or as lowercase letters. Other mutual exclusives include Underline and Word Underline, and Superscript and Subscript.

This text is upper and lowercase Stone Serif
THIS TEXT IS SMALL CAPS STONE SERIF
THIS TEXT IS ALL CAPS STONE SERIF

The Underline style underlines words and spaces between words
Word underline only underlines words, not the spaces between them

Figure 4-17 Mutually exclusive styles include Small Caps and All Caps (top), Underline and Word Underline (bottom).

The difference between Superscript and Superior characters is that Superior characters are roughly half the size of normal characters in the font size, and they are set above the baseline but never rise above cap height for the font. Superscript characters are usually set in normal size and can rise above the top of the ascent line; they also can run into text on the line above (depending on the leading and your settings through Edit → Preferences → Typographic).

Each style can be applied with its keyboards shortcut, listed in (Figure 4-18). The shortcuts are usually obtained by pressing down the ⌘-key and the Shift key, then pressing one other key.

Style Menu Command	Measurements Palette	Keyboard Shortcut
Type Style	Yes	various:
		⌘-Shift-B = Bold
		⌘-Shift-H = Small Caps
		⌘-Shift-I = Italic
		⌘-Shift-K = All Caps
		⌘-Shift-O = Outline
		⌘-Shift-P = Plain
		⌘-Shift-S = Shadow
		⌘-Shift-U = Underline
		⌘-Shift-W = Word Underline
		⌘-Shift-+ = Superscript
		⌘-Shift-Hyphen = Subscript
		⌘-Shift-/ = Strike Through
		⌘-Shift-V = Superior

Figure 4-18 Keyboard shortcuts for applying styles to text.

Color

Color can be applied to text by choosing from the Style ➤ Color submenu, from the pop-up menu in the Character Attributes dialog box, or by using the Colors palette. The colors listed are those created through the Edit ➤ Colors command. Chapter 7 describes the basics of setting up new colors; advanced issues relating to printing color separations are discussed in Chapter 13.

To apply a color to selected text, position the pointer over the Colors submenu on the Style menu or in the Character Attributes dialog box, and select from the list of colors.

To use the Colors palette to apply a color to selected text, click on the icon for text at the top of the palette, then click on a color name in the list.

Figure 4-19 To apply color to text using the Colors palette, click on the text icon and choose a color from the list.

Shade

You can set selected type in a shade (sometimes called "screen" or "tint" in other programs) of gray or a shade of color by choosing from the Style ➤ Shade submenu, from the pop-up menu in the Character Attributes dialog box, or, in QuarkXPress 3.1, by using the Colors palette.

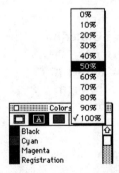

Figure 4-20 To apply a shade to text using the Colors palette, input a percentage or choose a percentage from the list.

To indicate selected text be shaded, position the pointer over the Shade submenu on the Style menu or in the Character Attributes dialog box, and input a percentage in increments up to .001 percent or select from the list of percentages, which lists shades in 10 percent increments.

To use the Colors palette to apply a shade percentage to selected text, select the icon for text at the top of the palette then choose the percentage field and input a value or choose from the list.

Paragraph Formatting

A "paragraph" in QuarkXPress includes all of the text between two hard carriage returns. A hard carriage return occurs wherever you press the Return key while entering text. You can force text onto a new line without marking it as a new paragraph by typing the special character for a new line: Shift-Return. This and other special formatting characters are described under the heading "Special Characters" later in this section.

When you select one of the commands that affect whole paragraphs, the options you choose will apply to all of the text between hard carriage returns, regardless of how much text is actually highlighted. In other words, you need not select every word in a paragraph in order for these commands to apply the whole paragraph in which the text insertion/selection point is positioned.

You can format paragraphs using any one of three different methods: through commands under the Style menu, using keyboard shortcuts, or through the Measurements palette. In this section we discuss those paragraph formats that QuarkXpress shares in common with many word processing programs: alignment, indents, space before or after, and tabs.

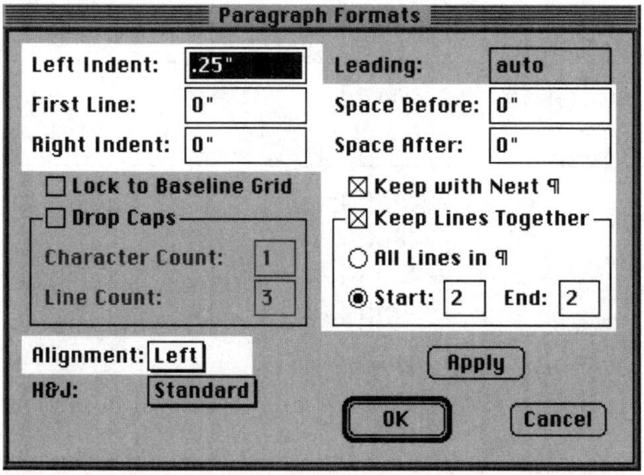

```
┌──────────────── Paragraph Formats ────────────────┐
│                                                    │
│  Left Indent:   │.25"│     Leading:      │auto│    │
│                                                    │
│  First Line:    │0"│       Space Before: │0"│      │
│                                                    │
│  Right Indent:  │0"│       Space After:  │0"│      │
│                                                    │
│  ☐ Lock to Baseline Grid   ☒ Keep with Next ¶      │
│  ┌☐ Drop Caps─────────┐  ┌☒ Keep Lines Together┐   │
│  │                    │  │ ○ All Lines in ¶     │   │
│  │ Character Count: 1 │  │ ● Start: │2│ End: │2││   │
│  │ Line Count:      3 │  │                      │   │
│  └────────────────────┘  └──────────────────────┘  │
│                                                    │
│  Alignment: │Left│              ┌─ Apply ─┐        │
│  H&J:     │Standard│                                │
│                            ┌─ OK ─┐  ┌─ Cancel ─┐  │
└────────────────────────────────────────────────────┘
```

Figure 4-21 QuarkXPress lets you apply many of the paragraph formatting commands found in word processing programs.

When you display the Paragraph formats dialog box, the Alignment submenu, or any of the dialog boxes associated with tabs, the options that apply to the current selection are checked or displayed. If the current selection includes more than one format, then none of the options is checked or displayed.

Besides using the commands described under the next headings to format a paragraph, you can also format paragraphs using a style sheet (as described later in this chapter), or you can copy the format of one paragraph to others in the same text chain. To copy the paragraph format from one paragraph to another, first select the paragraph you want to change, then hold down the Option and Shift keys and click in the paragraph containing the format you want to copy.

Alignment

You can specify the alignment of a paragraph by selecting from a pop-up menu in the Paragraph Formats dialog box (⌘-Shift-F), from the Alignment submenu, by clicking on icons in the Measurements palette (Figure 4-22), or by using keyboard shortcuts.

X: 5p7	W: 10p4	◿ 0°	⬍ 65 pt		Times	▶ 83 pt
Y: 1p7	H: 39p4	Cols: 1	◇ 0		B I ⓘ ⑤ Q U W K K	

Figure 4-22　The Alignment icons in the Measurements palette.

The keyboard shortcuts for alignment are shown in Figure 4-23.

Style Menu Command	Measurements Palette	Keyboard Shortcut
Alignment	Yes	⌘-Shift-L for Left
		⌘-Shift-C for Centered
		⌘-Shift-R for Right
		⌘-Shift-J for Justified

Figure 4-23　Keyboard shortcuts for aligning text.

You may be accustomed to using typographical terms to describe the four alignments listed in QuarkXPress' menus:

- Left = left aligned, flush left, ragged right.
- Centered = ragged left and right.
- Right = right aligned, flush right, ragged left.
- Justified = flush left and right.

The spacing between words and characters for Left aligned, Centered, or Right aligned text is determined by the Edit ➤ Preferences ➤ Typographic settings for Auto Kern Above and Character Widths, and Style ➤ Kerning settings. Spacing between characters also is determined by entries made through the Edit ➤ H&Js command.

Indents

You can select Style ➤ Formats (⌘-Shift-F) to display the Paragraph Formats dialog box to set paragraph indentation as well as leading, spacing between paragraphs, and other formats. When the Paragraph Formats dialog box is displayed, a text ruler for the selected paragraph appears at the top of the text box (Figure 4-24). You may need to move the dialog box to see the ruler.

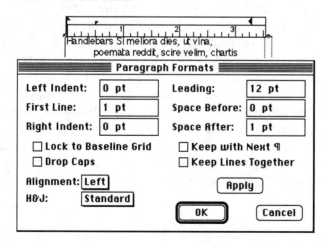

Figure 4-24 Paragraph Formats dialog box and ruler (⌘-Shift-F).

You can make all entries through the dialog box, or you can make changes by positioning or moving icons on the ruler. Icons that can be positioned and moved on the ruler include:

- First Line

- Left Indent

- Right Indent

You can also set left tabs by clicking on the ruler when the Paragraph Formats dialog box is open, but you must set other tabs and tab fill characters through Style → Tabs (⌘-Shift-T), discussed later in this section. If you cannot see both ends of the ruler on the screen, click on the ruler to create a tab marker and drag the marker to the left or right to make the ruler scroll in the window. Once you have the ruler view you want, you can delete the "transport" tab by dragging it off the ruler.

The appearance of the text on the page does not change immediately as you make changes to the ruler or dialog box entries. Click on Apply to view the effects on the page, then click on OK to keep the settings or Cancel to close the dialog box without recording any of your changes.

If you find you must click on the Apply button repeatedly as you try to make adjustments, hold the Option key and click on Apply to view the effects of changes dynamically as you make them. When the indents are adjusted correctly, you can then click OK to keep the settings.

There are three different indention settings for any paragraph: Left Indent, First Line Indent, and Right Indent. The Left and Right Indents are measured from the left and right side of a text box, less the text inset, described earlier in this chapter. The First Line Indent is measured relative to the Left Indent. To create a hanging indent, for example, you would enter some positive value for the Left Indent and then enter a negative value for the First Line Indent. Values that would force text beyond the margins or column guides are not valid entries and will result in a warning message. Figure 4-25 shows how different indention settings affect the text, and what those settings look like in the dialog box and on the text ruler.

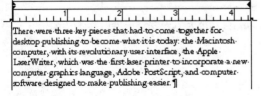

- *Flush-left paragraph with no indent.*

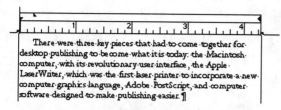

- *Normal paragraph with first-line indent.*

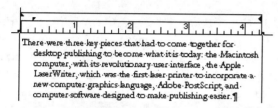

- *Hanging indent format positions first-line indent left of the other lines.*

Figure 4-25 Paragraph indentation settings.

Space Before/Space After Paragraphs

The amount entered in the Space Before and/or Space After boxes is added to the normal spacing between lines (leading) wherever there is a new paragraph. More precisely, the value you enter for spacing between paragraphs is added wherever there is a hard carriage return in the text.

This method of defining breaks between paragraphs is more flexible than using extra carriage returns (empty lines) to add space between paragraphs. Where there are two or more hard carriage returns in a row, the spacing value will be added twice or more. If you are accustomed to double-spacing between paragraphs, you might want to play with the spacing setting on small documents before you decide globally to strip out all double carriage returns in your text.

Space Before does not add space before paragraphs at the top of a text box or when the paragraph begins after an opaque box or line, and Space After is not added when a paragraph falls at the bottom of a text box or when it ends at an opaque box or line. Select Item → Modify to set the First Baseline to adjust the white space at the top of a text box.

Keep with Next Paragraph

If you check Keep with Next ¶, the selected paragraph will not be split from the next paragraph by a page break, column break, or text box border. This command can be used to prevent headings from appearing at the end of a page or column, for example, or to keep lines of a table or list together.

Keep Lines Together

Check Keep Lines Together to control widows and orphans, the line(s) of text that are separated from the rest of the paragraph by a page break, column break, or text box border. You can specify that the entire paragraph should be kept together by checking All Lines in ¶, or you can specify the number of lines at the Start and at the End of the paragraph that must be kept together.

QuarkXPress ignores the settings for Keep with Next ¶ and Keep Lines Together if by following the rules a box in a chain would be left empty. If you apply both All Lines in ¶ and Keep with Next ¶ to a range of paragraphs and QuarkXPress cannot do both, the program will keep all lines together and ignore the Keep with Next ¶ setting.

Tabs

You can select Style ➛ Tabs (⌘-Shift-T) to display the Paragraph Tabs dialog box. When the Tabs dialog box is displayed, a text ruler for the selected paragraph appears at the top of the text box; you might need to move the dialog box to see the ruler. Select the dialog box and ruler to set or change tabs and indentation settings for selected paragraphs. QuarkXPress sets default tabs every half inch on the ruler for Normal text. If you set tabs in a word processing program, then QuarkXPress' rulers will change to reflect those settings when you import the text.

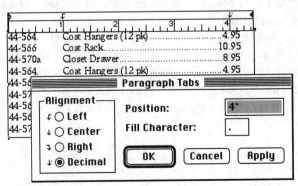

Figure 4-26 Paragraph Tabs dialog box (⌘-Shift-F) and text ruler.

You can make all entries through the dialog box, or you can make changes by positioning or moving icons on the text ruler. Up to 20 tabs may be set. Tab character icons that can be positioned and moved on the text ruler include:

   ↓   Left
   ↧   Right
   ↓   Center
   ↓⋅   Decimal
   ↓ʹ   Comma
   ↓ˣ Align On

plus paragraph indent markers (described earlier):

   ˋ   First Line
   ʳ   Left Indent
   ◀   Right Indent

To set a tab, first choose the appropriate tab character from the pop-up menu, then either click on the ruler to position and move the tab, or enter a value in the Position field in the dialog box. The position can be entered in any measure using the abbreviations described in Chapter 1. The measure always starts with 0 at the left edge of the ruler (as defined by text inset and left indent).

Left, Right, and Center tab characters align text flush left, flush right, or centered, respectively, relative to the location of the tab character. Decimal tabs align text on a decimal point, and are used most often for aligning financial data.

Comma tabs and the Align On tab characters are new to QuarkXPress 3.1. Comma tabs work like decimal tabs, except text is aligned on commas, which are used in place of decimal points in many countries. Align On lets you specify the character you want QuarkXPress to use for alignment.

When there is no decimal, comma, or other character in text set with the Decimal, Comma, or Align On tab characters, a numeral that precedes a nonnumeric character will be aligned with the tab. This enables correct alignment of columns text that may include numbers with parentheses or that may not contain a decimal or comma.

> $4,259.50⇥   100%⇥ $0.19↵
>   ($987.90)⇥   96%⇥ $45↵
>   12,000⇥   1%⇥   ($10.70)

Figure 4-27 Tabs align on a numeral preceding a nonnumeric character, or on the final numeral in text that does not contain a decimal.

You can specify any Fill Character for a selected tab. The most common fill characters (other than blank spaces) include periods (for dotted lines) and hyphens (for dashed lines), but any character can be a fill character. The fill character will be repeated from the end of the text where the tab key is pressed up to the tab mark to which the fill character is applied (Figure 4-28). To adjust the spacing between fill characters, use the Tracking command.

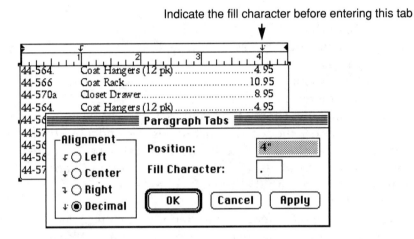

Figure 4-28 How fill characters are applied.

You can change the alignment setting for a tab by clicking on it in the ruler and then clicking on an alignment setting in the dialog box. You can move a tab by dragging it on the ruler or by clicking on it to select it and then changing the Position value. The dialog box for any selected tab shows the current position and fill character.

To delete individual tabs, simply click on the tab marker and hold down the mouse button as you drag the tab off the top or bottom of the ruler. To clear all tabs from a ruler, hold the Option key and click on the ruler.

You can adjust the indent markers as well as the tabs when the Tab dialog box is open. If you cannot see both ends of the ruler (due to screen limitations), click on the ruler to create a tab marker and drag it to the left or right to make the ruler scroll in the window. Once you have the ruler view you want, you can delete the "transport" tab by dragging it off the ruler.

To copy the paragraph format, including tab settings, from one paragraph to another, first select the paragraph(s) you want to format, then position the I-beam pointer over the paragraph whose tabs you wish to copy and press Option-Shift-click.

The appearance of the text on the page does not change immediately as you make changes to the ruler or Paragraph Tabs dialog box entries. Click on Apply to view the effects on the page, then click on OK to keep the settings or Cancel to close the dialog box without recording any of your changes.

If you must click on the Apply button repeatedly as you try to make adjustments, hold the Option key and click on Apply to view the effects of changes dynamically, as you make them. When the indents are adjusted correctly, you can then click OK to keep the settings.

Once tab stops are set on the ruler, text that already has tab characters will fall into place below each tab stop. You can add tabs within the text by positioning the I-beam as appropriate for text insertion and pressing the Tab key. Remember that you can view the tab characters on the page (⇥) by choosing View ➤ Show Invisibles, as described in Chapter 2.

QuarkXPress 3.1 adds a new tab character, the Right Indent tab, that lets you align characters flush with the right indent. To obtain this character, press the Option-Tab keys. Unlike other tab characters, this character must be set individually in each line; it cannot be preset on the tab ruler before typing. The Right Indent tab is useful for setting up headers or footers, where text appears on a left indent and a page number symbol needs to be flush with the right indent.

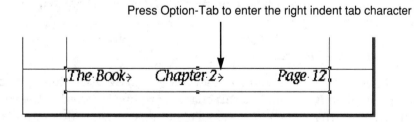

Figure 4-29 The Right Indent tab can be useful for setting up footers.

Special Characters

As mentioned earlier, you can insert special characters by typing the entries shown in Figure 4-30.

Special Character	Typed Entry	Onscreen display
New Paragraph	Return	¶
New Line	Shift-Return	↵
Discretionary Line Break	⌘-Return	no display
Indent Here	⌘-\	¦
New Column	Enter	↓
New Box	Shift-Enter	↡

Figure 4-30 Typing special characters.

Pressing the Return key signals a new paragraph. All of the formatting described under the next headings applies to whole paragraphs; you cannot apply different formatting to lines within a paragraph.

New Line Character

The New Line character forces a line break without signaling a new paragraph. This is useful when you are using a style sheet to format whole paragraphs that might add space before or after a hard carriage return. Space will not be added before or after the New Line character, which acts as a "soft" carriage return.

Discretionary Line Break

The Discretionary Line Break character acts like a discretionary hyphen, but no hyphen is shown. Use this character to break a word at the end of a line without inserting a hyphen. This character does not signal a new paragraph.

Indent Here

The Indent Here character causes the current line of text and all subsequent lines to be indented at the location of the character (Figure 4-31).

Use this special character to create hanging initial caps and for other special paragraph indent effects.

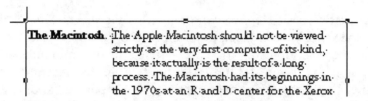

Figure 4-31 Effect of the Indent Here Character.

To delete the Indent Here character, position the insertion point behind it and press the Delete or Backspace key.

New Column/New Box

You can force text to jump to the next column or the next text box in a linked chain by inserting the New Column or New Box characters. These characters are useful in front of headings that you always want to start at the top of a column or a page.

Working with Style Sheets

One of the most powerful yet underutilized features of desktop publishing applications (word processing *and* page layout) is the electronic style sheet. A style sheet is simply a collection of shortcuts for applying type specifications (character attributes and paragraph formats) used throughout a document. A style sheet system lets you define the character attributes and paragraph format for each type of text element in a document, such as major headings, subheadings, captions, and body text. Once you set up a style sheet for a document, you can format the text using short keystroke commands or menu selections instead of using several commands to format each paragraph. Style sheets are applied to paragraphs, not to individual characters within a paragraph.

Character-specific formats that can be applied using style sheets include all attributes that are applied using the Font, Size, Type Style, Color, Shade, Horizontal Scale, Tracking, and Baseline Shift commands from the Style menu. Paragraph-specific formatting includes all settings that are applied using the Alignment, Leading, Formats, Rules, and Tabs commands from the Style menu. Document-wide formatting, such as setting margin guides and column widths, is handled outside of the style sheet functions.

There are two basic steps in working with style sheets: First, you must create a style sheet; second, you must apply it to the appropriate text. New style sheets are set up using the Edit ➤ Style Sheets command. The Style Sheets dialog box (Figure 4-32) lists all the styles in the current document. You can click on any style sheet name to view a partial list of specifications for that style sheet, displayed in the lower half of the dialog box.

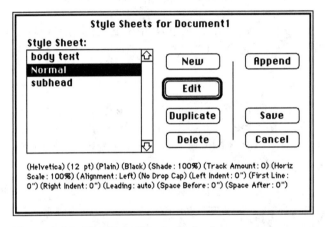

Figure 4-32 The Style Sheets dialog box.

Choose New to add a new style sheet name, Edit to modify the specifications for a selected style sheet name, Duplicate to create a new style sheet based on an existing style sheet name, Delete to remove a style sheet name, or Append to import the style sheet specifications from another QuarkXPress or Microsoft Word document. Style sheets can be applied using any one of several techniques, described later in this section.

The process of formatting characters and paragraphs with a style sheet can take place in either QuarkXPress or in Microsoft Word. Style sheets created in Microsoft Word can be imported along with the text into QuarkXPress by clicking Include Style Sheets in the Import Text dialog box. The proper filter must be in the folder with the QuarkXPress program.

Creating and Editing Style Sheets

In setting up a style sheet in QuarkXPress, the first step is to create a style sheet name—one for each different paragraph format in your document. To set up a style sheet, select Edit ➤ Style Sheets to display the Style Sheets dialog box (Figure 4-32) and click on the New button. When you choose New, QuarkXPress displays the Edit Style Sheet dialog box (Figure 4-33). This dialog box is used for creating new style sheets or editing existing ones.

The Edit Style Sheet dialog box allows you to assign or change a style sheet name, assign or change the keyboard equivalent for applying the style sheet, select a style on which this style sheet will be based, and change the character attributes, paragraph format, rules, or tabs.

The Style Sheets palette allows you to access the Edit Style Sheet dialog box quickly. Hold down the Command key (⌘) as you click on a style sheet name, and the Edit Style Sheet for that name will be displayed.

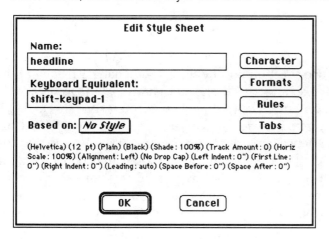

Figure 4-33 The Edit Style Sheet dialog box.

Name

You can enter a style sheet Name up to 64 characters long. This name will be displayed in the Style ➤ Style Sheets submenu and the Style Sheets palette. A single document can include up to 127 different style sheet names. You must name every new style sheet; the OK button does not become active until text is entered in the Name field.

Keyboard Equivalent

You can assign a Keyboard Equivalent that you can later use to apply the style sheet instead of going through the Style ➤ Style Sheets submenu or Style Sheets palette. When the cursor is in the Keyboard Equivalent field, press any keys on the numeric keypad or any of the Function keys on an extended keyboard (except keys F1 to F4, which are reserved for other uses), plus ⌘, Option, Control, and/or Shift. Whatever keys you press when the cursor is in the Keyboard Equivalent field will be those you press to assign the style sheet. If you make Keypad 5, for example, a keyboard shortcut, you cannot use it as the numeral 5 any more; it's a good idea, then, to use ⌘, Option, Control, and/or Shift in combination with the keypad numbers.

The Macintosh assigns the common commands Undo, Cut, Copy, and Paste to function keys F1 to F4. If you assign one of these keys as a keyboard shortcut for a style sheet, you will replace the original Macintosh function. You can, however, assign these keys in combination with the Option/Shift/⌘ keys without upsetting the installed functions.

Based On

The Based On entry is a pop-up menu of all the current style sheet names. If you base a style sheet on another one, then changes made to the other style sheet will also affect style sheets that are Based On it except those attributes that were specifically altered for the new style sheet.

For example, if you create a new style sheet Based On Normal, and the only difference between Normal and the new style sheet is that the new style sheet is indented 1 inch from the left, then any changes you make to the character specifications, rules, or tabs for the Normal style sheet will also be applied to the new style sheet. But if you change the left indent for Normal style sheet, the new style sheet's left indent will not be changed.

Defining the Style Sheet

Click on Character, Formats, Rules, or Tabs to display the Character Attributes dialog box, the Paragraph Formats dialog box, the Paragraph Rules dialog box, or the Paragraph Tabs dialog box, respectively. When any of these dialog boxes is first displayed, it shows the settings of the currently selected text if you have chosen New in the Style Sheets dialog box; if you have chosen Edit, it shows the settings that apply to the selected style sheet name.

To save your entries, you must click on OK (or press Return) to close all dialog boxes up to the Style Sheet dialog box, and then click on Save. Changes made to any style sheet are applied automatically throughout the document to all paragraphs to which that style is applied. Paragraphs that use style sheets that are Based On the changed style sheet are changed.

The Edit ➤ Style Sheets command is always available; if you create a style sheet when no documents are open, the style sheet will be included with all subsequently created new documents. Style sheets created with a document open are saved as part of that document only.

Applying Style Sheets

 To apply a format that has been defined as a style sheet, select the text to be formatted and then use any one of three techniques to apply a style sheet: press the keyboard equivalent; select Style ➤ Style Sheets to choose from a list of style sheet names; or, with version 3.1, select a style sheet name from the Style Sheets palette (View ➤ Show Style Sheets). Both the Style Sheets submenu and the Style Sheets palette list the names of all the style sheets you have defined. If you have assigned keyboard equivalents, those will show next to the style sheet name.

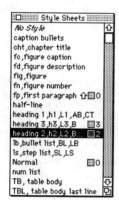

Figure 4-34 The Style Sheets palette.

Remember, style sheets apply to whole paragraphs; they cannot be assigned to individual characters within a paragraph. You need not select an entire paragraph to which you want to apply a style; just click once so that the text insertion point is within the paragraph.

To see what style sheet has been applied to a paragraph, position the cursor in the paragraph. The applied style sheet name will be checked in the Style ➤ Style Sheets submenu or will be selected in the Style Sheets palette. If you select a range of paragraphs that share the same style sheet, that style sheet will be checked in the Style Sheets submenu or selected in the Style Sheets palette. If the selection includes mixed style sheets, no style sheet name will be indicated.

While style sheets cannot be applied to individual characters, you can, of course, still apply "local" formatting; that is, you can format individual characters within text that has been formatted using a style sheet. For example, you can italicize a single word within text that has been formatted using a style sheet called "heading 1".

 If you apply a new style sheet to a paragraph that contains local formatting, the text in the paragraph will change according to the specifications of the new style sheet, *except* for the local formatting. To change all the text in the paragraph, you must first apply No Style from the Style Sheets submenu or the Style Sheets palette, then apply the new style sheet. When using the Style Sheets palette, you can apply No Style before applying a style sheet by holding down the Option key as you click on the style sheet name.

Deleting Style Sheets

To delete a style sheet, click on the style sheet name in the list displayed in the Style Sheets dialog box (Edit → Style Sheets), then click the Delete button. You cannot delete the Normal style sheet; it is the default format for all newly typed text and for imported ASCII text. You can change the specifications for the Normal style sheet by selecting Normal and choosing Edit in the Style Sheets dialog box.

If you delete any other style sheet name, all text that is currently formatted based on that style sheet name will retain its formatting but will be assigned a No Style identification. To change those paragraphs to another style sheet, you need to go through the document, select those paragraphs, and assign another style sheet.

Duplicating Style Sheet Specifications

Sometimes you may want to create a style sheet using several specifications from another one. In that case, the fastest way is to select the Duplicate command in the Style Sheets dialog box. Click on the style sheet name you want to duplicate, then click the Duplicate button; the Edit Style Sheets dialog box appears with "Copy of *<style sheet name>*" in the name field (Figure 4-35). You can then use the dialog box to change any of the specifications for the new style sheet.

```
                    Edit Style Sheet
  Name:
 ┌──────────────────────────────────┐    ┌───────────┐
 │ Copy of Normal                   │    │ Character │
 └──────────────────────────────────┘    └───────────┘
  Keyboard Equivalent:                    ┌───────────┐
 ┌──────────────────────────────────┐    │  Formats  │
 │                                  │    └───────────┘
 └──────────────────────────────────┘    ┌───────────┐
                                          │   Rules   │
  Based on: │ No Style │                  └───────────┘
                                          ┌───────────┐
                                          │   Tabs    │
                                          └───────────┘
 (1Stone Serif) (10  pt) (Plain) (Black) (Shade : 100%) (Track Amount : 0)
 (Horiz Scale : 100%) (Alignment : Justified) (No Drop Cap) (Left Indent : 3p)
 (First Line : 1p) (Right Indent : 0p) (Leading : 13  pt) (Space Before : 0p) (Space
 After : 0p)

          ┌──────────┐      ┌──────────┐
          │    OK    │      │  Cancel  │
          └──────────┘      └──────────┘
```

Figure 4-35 Duplicating a style sheet.

Appending Style Sheets from Other Documents

Style sheets are a great way to ensure consistency among various documents, and you may find you want to reuse style sheets created in another document. The Append command allows you to add style sheets from another document to your active document.

If you choose Append in the Style Sheets dialog box, QuarkXPress displays the Append Style Sheets dialog box (Figure 4-36). The list in the dialog box shows QuarkXPress document and template names and Microsoft Word document names; when you select one and choose Open (or simply double-click on a document name), all of the style sheets used in that document are added to the list in the active document's style sheet list.

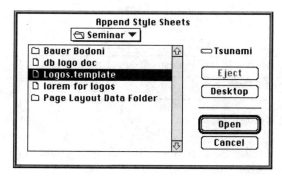

Figure 4-36 The Append Style Sheets dialog box.

If any of the appended style sheet names match names that are already in the current style sheet, the format for the style sheet in the active document is retained—the different format is not appended. If an appended style sheet uses the same keyboard equivalent as already applied in the current style sheet, the appended style sheet is brought in without a keyboard equivalent.

If the appended style sheets call for a font that is not currently loaded in your system, you get an error message that indicates the font that is missing, for example, "(-2, Bodoni Bold)."

Finding and Changing Text

The Edit ➤ Find/Change command (⌘-F) finds and changes specific words or characters or specific text attributes in text. You can search through part of a story, a whole story, or a whole document at once. Remember, from Chapter 2, that a story is all of the text in a chain of linked text boxes.

To find or change text in a story or all the stories in a document, first select the Content tool and position the text cursor in a block of text, then select Edit → Find/Change (⌘-F) to display the Find/Change dialog box (Figure 4-37). Type in the text or select character attributes you want to find, then click the Find Next button. QuarkXPress begins the search at the text insertion point and proceeds through to the end of the text block.

If you want to begin the search from the beginning of the document, you can type ⌘-Option-↑ to jump quickly to the beginning of a story. Alternatively, you can use a new feature of version 3.1: Hold down the Option key and the Find Next button changes to Find First.

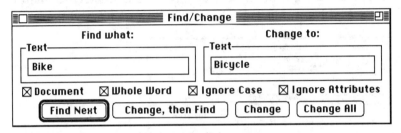

Figure 4-37 Find/Change dialog box.

In the Find/Change dialog box (Edit → Find/Change), you type text in the Find What field, specify changes, if any, in the Change To field, and select the type of search you want:

- If **Document** is checked *and no text boxes are active when you begin the search*, QuarkXPress searches the entire document. If a text box is active, QuarkXPress searches the entire document, but only from the current text insertion point to the end of the story; text before the insertion point is not checked, unless you hold down the Option key and click Find First.

- If **Whole Word** is checked, QuarkXPress searches for the Find What text followed by a space or punctuation mark. Otherwise, QuarkXPress finds all character strings that match the Find What entry, even when they are part of a longer word.

- If **Ignore Case** is checked, QuarkXPress finds the Find What text in all forms—with and without any capital letters. If it finds text in all lowercase, it replaces it with the all-lowercase version of the text you typed in the Change To area. If it finds text in all uppercase, it replaces it with the all-uppercase version of the text in the Change To area. If it finds initial-cap text, it replaces it with the initial-cap version of the text in the Change To area. If it finds mixed upper and lowercase characters (other than initial cap only), it replaces the found word with the Change To text exactly as you typed it.

- If the **Ignore Case** option is not checked, then QuarkXPress finds only those instances of text that match the capitalization exactly as you typed it in the Find What area, and it changes that text to the text exactly as typed in the Change To area.

- If **Ignore Attributes** is checked, QuarkXPress finds the Find What text in all type styles and replaces it with the text you typed in the Change To area formatted exactly the same as the found text. For example, if it finds one version of the Find What text in 10-point Times, it replaces it with the Change To text in 10-point Times. If it finds the next instance of the Find What text in 12-point Helvetica, it replaces it with the Change To text in 12-point Helvetica.

- If the **Ignore Attributes** option is not checked, then the expanded Find/Change dialog box is displayed (as described under the next heads). QuarkXPress finds only those instances of the word that match the character attributes exactly as specified and changes them to the Change To text formatted exactly as specified.

Once you have typed the Find What and (optional) Change To text and selected the search options, you can click on **Find Next**, or hold down the Option key and click on **Find First**. After the first instance is found, you can choose **Change, then Find** to change the word and keep searching to the next occurrence, or **Change** to change the word and pause the search. If you don't want to make a change on a particular occurrence of the text, click Find Next. QuarkXPress will move on to the next occurrence without making any changes.

If you choose **Change All**, QuarkXPress will change all found instances of the Find What text. When the search is finished, it will display a dialog box with a count of the total number of instances changed. If no instances are found, the Macintosh will beep to signal the end of the search.

If no instances are found but you know one should have been found, make sure that you started the search at the beginning by holding down the Option key and clicking on Find First or that you positioned the text insertion point at the beginning of the story (⌘-Option-↑). Also, be sure that you have spelled the Find What text correctly and not entered any extra spaces before or after it.

If the edits cannot be handled by global changes but can be found by a global search, you can also select Find Next simply to find occurrences of text or text attributes. When an instance is found, you can click in the document window and edit the text manually, then select Find/Change (⌘-F) again to resume the search. For example, you might type "see page xx" throughout the draft versions of a document, and then search for "xx" and manually type in the final page number after the pages have been laid out.

It is a good idea to move the Find/Change dialog box to the bottom of the screen to maximize your view of the document window during a search. You can also make the dialog box smaller—reducing it to the search buttons only—by clicking in the zoom box at the top right corner of the dialog box title bar (Figure 4-38).

Figure 4-38 Use the zoom box at the top right corner of the window to toggle from full size to a reduced version of the Find/Change dialog box.

Find or Change Text

You can type up to 80 characters in the Find What and the Change To areas of the Find/Change dialog box. If you don't type anything in the Change To area, then the text typed in the Find What area will be deleted when found in the story or document.

You can include spaces in the Find What and Change To fields by using the space bar, but other "invisible" characters, such as a Tab or Return, require special entry. (Otherwise, the Tab key alone jumps you to the next field in the dialog box, and the Return or Enter key starts the search.) You can search for special characters and invisible characters by holding the Command key and typing the key that you would normally use to insert the special character in the text, as shown in Figure 4-39.

Special Character	Find/Change Entry	Dialog Box Display
Tab	⌘-Tab	\t
New Paragraph	⌘-Return	\p
New Line	⌘-Shift-Return	\n
Discretionary Line Break	(cannot search for this character)	
Indent Here	(cannot search for this character)	
New Column	⌘-Enter	\c
New Box	⌘-Shift-Enter	\b
Previous Box Page #	⌘-2	\2
Active Box Page #	⌘-3	\3
Next Box Page #	⌘-4	\4
Wild Card	⌘-?	\?
Back Slash	⌘-\	\\

Figure 4-39 Searching for special characters.

When searching for special characters, it is usually best to uncheck Whole Word since special characters are usually bounded by other letters or numbers. To view invisible characters on the screen, choose View ➤ Show Invisibles.

You can type the wild card character (⌘-?) in the Change From field to find words with similar but different spellings. For example, a search for "gr?y" will find both "gray" and "grey."

You cannot use wild cards in the Change To text field. You can find or change spaces by typing a space in either field (using the space bar), but if the space falls at the end of the entry the program will ignore instances where the word or phrase is followed by punctuation. If you type a space on either side of the Find What entry, however, be sure to type a space in the Change To field as well (unless you want the replacement to eliminate the space).

Find or Change Character Attributes

You can find or change attributes such as font, size, and type style. This feature is especially handy for globally changing words that have been given special attributes within paragraphs. For example, if you are working on a review of a book titled *Never Tomorrow* and the title was set as underscored (except in some cases where the author of the review forgot to apply the underscores), you can globally change all cases to italics. You can also select Find/Change globally to change the formats of headings or captions or other standard elements within the text; however these changes are handled more efficiently through a style sheet.

To find or change attributes, uncheck Ignore Attributes to display the expanded Find/Change dialog box (Figure 4-40). The initial display shows the attributes of the active text selection (or shows grayed options if more than one attribute is represented). You can search for specific text as entered in the Text area under Find What, or uncheck Text if you want to search for attributes only.

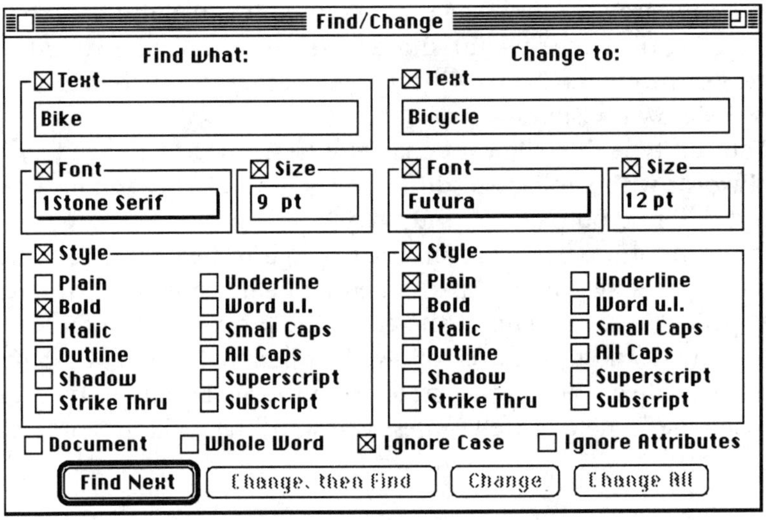

```
┌──────────────────────────── Find/Change ────────────────────────────┐
│       Find what:                           Change to:                 │
│ ┌⊠ Text ─────────────────┐   ┌⊠ Text ─────────────────┐              │
│ │ Bike                    │   │ Bicycle                 │             │
│ └─────────────────────────┘   └─────────────────────────┘            │
│ ┌⊠ Font ───────┐┌⊠ Size ─┐   ┌⊠ Font ───────┐┌⊠ Size ─┐             │
│ │ 1Stone Serif ││ 9 pt   │   │ Futura       ││ 12 pt  │             │
│ └───────────────┘└─────────┘  └───────────────┘└─────────┘            │
│ ┌⊠ Style ──────────────────┐ ┌⊠ Style ──────────────────┐           │
│ │ ☐ Plain      ☐ Underline │ │ ⊠ Plain      ☐ Underline │           │
│ │ ⊠ Bold       ☐ Word u.l. │ │ ☐ Bold       ☐ Word u.l. │           │
│ │ ☐ Italic     ☐ Small Caps│ │ ☐ Italic     ☐ Small Caps│           │
│ │ ☐ Outline    ☐ All Caps  │ │ ☐ Outline    ☐ All Caps  │           │
│ │ ☐ Shadow     ☐ Superscript│ │ ☐ Shadow     ☐ Superscript│         │
│ │ ☐ Strike Thru ☐ Subscript│ │ ☐ Strike Thru ☐ Subscript│           │
│ └───────────────────────────┘ └───────────────────────────┘          │
│ ☐ Document   ☐ Whole Word   ⊠ Ignore Case   ☐ Ignore Attributes     │
│ ┌ Find Next ┐  ( Change, then Find )  ( Change )  ( Change All )     │
└──────────────────────────────────────────────────────────────────────┘
```

Figure 4-40 Expanded Find/Change dialog box.

You can check Font, Size, and/or Style to include these categories of attributes as part of the search, or uncheck them if you want to search for other characteristics only. The Font list is a pop-up menu. Any Style option can be checked (so *only* text with that style will be found), unchecked (so *no* text with that style will be found), or grayed (so text *with and without* that style will be found). Simply click on each style option until the desired setting is shown.

Similarly, under Change To you can check Font, Size, and/or Style to include these categories of attributes as part of the replacement, or uncheck them if you want to replace other characteristics only. Any Style option can be checked (so all text found will be changed to that style), unchecked (so all text found will be changed to not have that style), or grayed (so found text will retain its style in that category).

The expanded Find/Change dialog box is similar to the Font Usage dialog box (Utilities ➤ Font Usage). In fact, if you want to change character attributes only and not change any text, you can use the Font Usage dialog box (Figure 4-41).

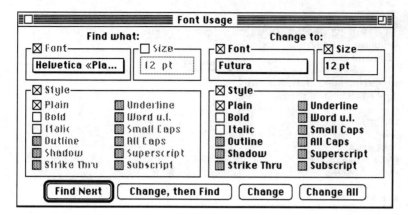

Figure 4-41 Font Usage dialog box.

The fonts shown in both the expanded Find/Change dialog box and the Font Usage dialog box include only those actually used in the document. The Change To font list includes all fonts currently loaded in the system.

Checking Spelling

QuarkXPress 3.1 offers a spelling check feature that compares the words in your text against a 120,000-word dictionary called *XPress Dictionary* (versus a 90,000-word dictionary used in version 3.0). This file is included in the same folder as the QuarkXPress program when you first install QuarkXPress, if you follow normal installation procedures, or you can copy it into the System folder. Note that it must be in one of these two places in order for the Check Spelling command to work. You can also create auxiliary dictionaries to add your own terms for use in spelling checks. The Utilities ➤ Check Spelling command lets you check the spelling of a highlighted word, all the words in a story, or all the words in a document.

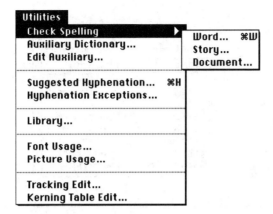

Figure 4-42 The Utilities ► Check Spelling pop-up menu.

To check spelling for any **word**, first select the word or position the insertion bar to the left of or anywhere within the word, then select Utilities ► Check Spelling ► Word (⌘-W) to check the spelling of the selected word only. If more than one word is selected, QuarkXPress checks the spelling of only the first word or partial word selected.

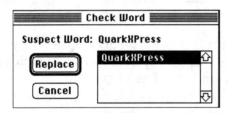

Figure 4-43 Check Word dialog box for a word search.

QuarkXPress checks the dictionary and displays the Check Word dialog box, showing close or exact matches from the dictionary in the scrolling window, or displaying the message "No similar words found." You can choose a replacement word by double-clicking on the word in the list (or clicking on the word once to select it and then click on Replace) to replace the word with a found match, or Cancel the process and leave the word unchanged.

To check spelling for any **story**, first activate a text box and select the Content tool, then select Utilities ► Check Spelling ► Story (⌘-Option-W) to check the spelling in the selected story. (Remember from Chapter 2 that a story is all of the text in a chain of linked text boxes.)

After QuarkXPress checks spelling, a **Word Count** dialog box (Figure 4-44) shows how many **Total** words are in the story or document, how many **Unique** words were found (how many different words), and how many **Suspect** words are identified (words not found in the dictionary).

Figure 4-44 Word Count dialog box.

To close the dialog box, click on OK. If no suspect words were found, then the spelling check process is complete for the story. If suspect words were found, then the Check Story dialog box (Figure 4-45) is displayed when you close the Word Count dialog box.

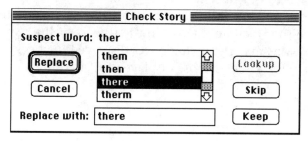

Figure 4-45 Check Story dialog box.

The Check Story dialog box displays the first suspect word found in the text and shows how many instances of the same word were found, if more than one occurred. If you click on Lookup, QuarkXPress offers suggested alternatives (if any close matches are found in the dictionary) or displays the message "No similar words found." You can click on one of the suggested alternatives, or type the correct word in the Replace with area of the dialog box, then click on Replace (or simply press Return) to replace the suspect word. To let the suspect word remain unchanged and go on to the next found suspect word, click on Skip. To let the suspect word remain unchanged, add it to the open auxiliary dictionary (see next heading), and go on to the next suspect word found, click on Keep. To end the spelling check process, click on Cancel.

To check spelling for a whole document, select Utilities ➤ Check Spelling ➤ Document. QuarkXPress starts on the first page of the currently open document and goes through all of the stories in it. The first dialog box displayed is the Word Count dialog box, showing the Total words in the document, how many Unique words were found (how many different words), and how many Suspect words are identified (words not found in the dictionary). If any Suspect words are found, click on OK to display the Check Document dialog box (Figure 4-46).

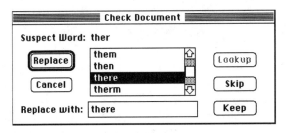

Figure 4-46 Check Document dialog box.

The Check Document dialog box is handled exactly the same as the Check Story dialog box, described above.

You can check the spelling on Master Pages by turning to a master page in the document—the Document entry in the Check Spelling submenu changes to display **Masters**. The dialog boxes displayed to check spelling on Master Pages are the same as those displayed for checking a story or a document.

Customizing Your Own Dictionaries

You cannot change the XPress Dictionary that comes with the package, but you can add your own terms to auxiliary dictionaries. To create a new auxiliary dictionary, choose Utilities ➤ Auxiliary Dictionary and then choose New in the dialog box. When you do so, QuarkXPress asks you to name the new dictionary. To open an existing auxiliary dictionary, choose Utilities ➤ Auxiliary Dictionary, locate the appropriate file, and select it from the dialog box.

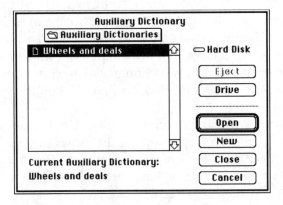

Figure 4-47 Auxiliary Dictionary dialog box.

If you choose Utilities ➤ Auxiliary Dictionary when no document is open, the new or existing dictionary you open will be applied automatically to all new documents that you create (until you change the setting later when no document is open). If you choose the Auxiliary Dictionary command when any document is open, the new or existing dictionary you open will be applied automatically to that document whenever you open it (until you change the setting later when the document is open).

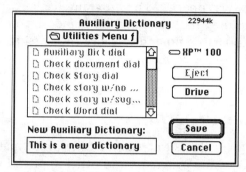

Figure 4-48 New Auxiliary Dictionary dialog box.

You can add terms to the open auxiliary dictionary by going through the spelling check process and using the Keep option in the dialog box, as described above. (An auxiliary dictionary *must* be open during the spelling check process in order for the Keep option to be available in the Check Story, Check Document, or Check Masters dialog box.) You can also add or delete terms in an open auxiliary dictionary by using the Utilities ➤ Edit Auxiliary command.

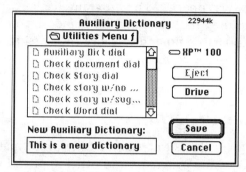

Figure 4-49 Edit Auxiliary Dictionary dialog box.

Terms in a dictionary are all stored in lowercase form—you cannot type uppercase characters in the entries. Only one auxiliary dictionary can be open at a time during a spelling check. You can select the Auxiliary Dictionary command to Close the currently open auxiliary dictionary and Open a different one.

QuarkXPress will be unable to locate a dictionary if either the dictionary or the document has been moved to a different disk or folder since the first time the dictionary was opened. The program displays an alert message whenever you select the Check Spelling command, so you can go through the Auxiliary Dictionary command to Close the missing dictionary or find and Use the relocated dictionary.

Exporting Text to Other Programs

You can export text from QuarkXPress to create text files in formats that can be opened by word processing programs and other applications, or imported to other QuarkXPress documents. Remember that you can also copy text from one QuarkXPress document to another by dragging the text box from one open Document window to another, or through the Library feature, as well as through the Edit menu's Copy and Paste or Cut and Paste commands.

To export text, first activate a text box with the Content tool selected, or highlight a range of text to be exported. Then select File ➜ Save Text to display the Save Text dialog box (Figure 4-50).

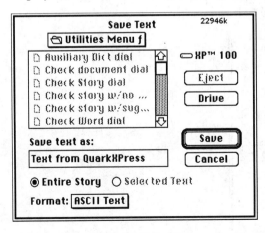

Figure 4-50 Save Text dialog box.

Type the name of the exported text file in the Save Text As area. If you activate a text box without selecting any text within it, you must save the

Entire Story (the text in the currently active box plus all linked text boxes). Otherwise, you have the option of saving the Entire Story or the **Selected Text** only. You can export only one story at a time.

The **Format** pop-up menu lets you choose the format in which to save the exported text, including ASCII Text plus any other formats for which the import/export filter is stored in the System folder or in the same folder as the QuarkXPress program before you launch the program. Formatting is retained in all formats except ASCII Text. (See notes under "Importing Formatted Text," earlier in this chapter, about import/export filters, and see Chapter 12 for tips on efficient file organization.)

If you save in ASCII Text format, all formatting is lost. If you save text as XPress Tags format, then the formatted text from QuarkXPress is exported as ASCII Text with embedded XPress Tags for formatting. See Chapter 10 for a description of ASCII formatting tags.

Summary

In this chapter you learned that the process of importing text in QuarkXPress is relatively simple—select a text box with the Content tool and use the File ➤ Get Text command to bring in text files created in a word processing program. Select the Paste command to bring in text that was Cut or Copied from another part of the document. Select the Item tool to move text boxes from another QuarkXPress document or library. Select the Content tool to type text directly in a text box.

Build a test file using your own word processor to see how QuarkXPress handles the text when you import it on a page. Try placing the same test file under each of the options—Convert Quotes and Include Style Sheets—to see how they differ.

Once you are familiar with how QuarkXPress handles your files, you may want to do as much preparation as you can in the word processing program before importing the text in QuarkXPress, or you may use QuarkXPress only for word processing. Once the text is in QuarkXPress, you can format it directly or use style sheets. You can also find and change text or character attributes, and spell check your document. Text from QuarkXPress can be exported to disk where it can be opened by word processing programs. The next chapter describes QuarkXPress' rich assortment of typographical features.

5 *Typography*

Typography, the study and application of the aesthetics of letterforms, is an integral part of design. Designers and typographers have a unique way of describing characteristics of text in a document, expressed in terms not only of fonts but also of leading, kerning, intercharacter spacing, and other words that may be somewhat foreign to the typical user of word processing programs. Typographic control from the desktop is one of QuarkXPress' strong points.

In this chapter you will learn how to work with QuarkXPress' typographical features, including inputting special typographic characters; working with leading, hyphenation, and justification; and kerning and tracking characters.

Whether you—as the designer or typographer—are writing out the design specifications for a document or actually using QuarkXPress to set up a template, knowing how QuarkXPress works before you make your design specifications will help you.

Setting Global Conditions

Before you start working with the typographic specifications for a document, it's a good idea to set up the global conditions that will affect how type looks in a document or how type prints. The first condition that affects your typographic choices is the set of installed fonts. The fonts you want to use should be available to your Macintosh System before you create a new QuarkXPress document.

A second source of settings that can globally change the type in a document is the set of typographic preferences set up through the Edit → Preferences → Typographic command. It is a good idea to set these preferences before you start formatting text in a document, since changes to these settings can change the way text fits on lines throughout the document.

Loading Screen Fonts

The word "font" is derived from the French word *fondre*, which means to melt or cast. It once referred to the trays of cast metal characters that printers used to compose a document. Each tray or font included all letters of the alphabet (plus special characters) for a specific typeface/style/size combination. For example, one tray held only 10-point Times italic characters, another tray held only 10-point Times bold, and so on. A font, then, was a particular typeface, style, and size combination.

More recently, however, font has been taken more loosely to mean simply the name of the typeface, such as Times or Helvetica. This is the meaning of the word in QuarkXPress' Style menu and Character Attributes dialog box, for instance. This definition is appropriate for the new computer fonts that are based on formulas, such as PostScript fonts. Each letter of the alphabet is "cast" or designed only once, to define the shape of the letter. This information is then stored as a complex curve-fitting equation. A printer that uses a programming language—such as PostScript—to create text can produce any size typeface once the shape of each character is provided.

PostScript fonts available for the Macintosh have two versions of each font—a screen font and a printer font. The screen font is necessary to display the fonts on the screen, and the printer fonts contain the information needed by the output device, whether it's a laser printer or a high-resolution imagesetter, to create and print the font on a page.

Most PostScript laser printers come with a basic set of fonts. The fonts that are built in to the LaserWriter Plus and LaserWriter II series printers include Avant Garde, Courier, Times, Helvetica, Bookman, New Century Schoolbook, Symbol, Palatino, and Zapf Dingbats, along with a set of screen fonts for each. (Some other fonts that come with the Macintosh—primarily those with city names, such as New York, Geneva, Chicago, and the like—are not true typographic fonts and are not commonly used in typeset documents.) In addition, various vendors, including Adobe Systems, Bitstream, and Monotype, among others, sell fonts.

True Type fonts became available with the advent of Apple's System 7. Unlike PostScript fonts, they do not require a separate screen and printer font; essentially they derive the screen image of a font from its printer font outlines, which must be present in the system file.

To display a font name in the QuarkXPress menus, the font must be available to your system. There are a number of different ways to load fonts, depending on what type of fonts and which version of the Macintosh System you are using. The method you use also depends on your personal preference.

Loading Fonts Into the System

If you are using Apple's System 7, you can load fonts simply by dragging the font file, in the case of TrueType fonts, or the suitcase file containing the screen fonts, in the case of PostScript fonts, into your System file. If you are using System 6.07 or earlier, you must use Font/DA Mover, a utility that comes with the Macintosh System, to load fonts and desk accessories into the System file. In either case, you must Quit QuarkXPress before you can load fonts using this technique. Once fonts are loaded into your Macintosh System and you start QuarkXPress, font menus will be updated to display all the fonts in your system.

Screen fonts of varying sizes can be loaded into the System, but only one size is needed for the software to use the font at any size specified and for a printer to be able to print the font. You can load only 10-point Times into the System, for instance, and still be able to use any size of Times in QuarkXPress. However, screen font sizes that are not loaded into the System might be hard to read on the screen, because the software application is actually scaling up (or down) the closest size of that font available in your System.

Using Suitcase II

For many situations, particularly where a number of different fonts are used, it is not practical to load all the fonts used into the System file. Thousands of fonts are available for the Macintosh, and a design studio or service bureau, for example, may use many different ones for different jobs. It then becomes practical to use any one of several desk accessories available to easily open and close screen font files as they are needed.

One of the most popular desk accessories is Suitcase II (use Suitcase II version 1.2.11 or higher), a software product available from most Macintosh software suppliers. It can be used to load PostScript screen fonts selectively. Suitcase II also lets you store fonts anywhere on your hard disk; they do not have to be stored in the System folder.

When you load a new screen font with Suitcase II, you must close all active QuarkXPress 3.1 documents but you need not exit the program, as was required using earlier versions of QuarkXPress.

On-Screen Font Rendering

Regardless of the sizes of the screen fonts that are loaded through the Font/DA Mover into the System, QuarkXPress can render Type 3 (unencrypted) screen fonts with optimal resolution for more accurate screen display. To activate screen font rendering, select the Edit ➤ Preferences ➤ General to set up the Render Above type size, as described in Chapter 2.

To take advantage of the Font Rendering feature, copies of the Type 3 printer fonts must be stored in the System folder. Type 3 fonts include those from Bitstream, Compugraphic, Casady, The Font Company, ImageClub, and other sources—but not fonts from Adobe. (You can use Adobe Type Manager to accomplish the same thing, as described under the next heading.)

Using Adobe Type Manager

One of the advantages of TrueType fonts is that the characters do not appear jagged on the screen. The on-screen font rendering feature of QuarkXPress does not work with Type 1 PostScript fonts, which are by far the most widely used fonts. But Adobe Type Manager (ATM), a software product available from most Macintosh software suppliers, provides a way of getting a clear screen display of PostScript fonts in all sizes—not just those loaded in the System.

In order for Adobe Type Manager to work, you must store the printer fonts in the System folder. If you are using Suitcase II, the printer fonts need only be in the same folder with the screen fonts for ATM to work; they do not have to be in the System folder.

Typographic Preferences

The Edit ➤ Preferences command lets you set specifications for a document globally. Two preferences that affect the appearance of the type on the *screen*—Render Above and Greek Below—are in the General Preferences dialog box and were described in Chapter 3. These two settings do not affect how type looks when it is printed. The preferences that affect how type looks on the screen *and* prints are set through Edit ➤ Preferences ➤ Typographic (⌘-Option-Y), in the Typographic Preferences dialog box (Figure 5-1).

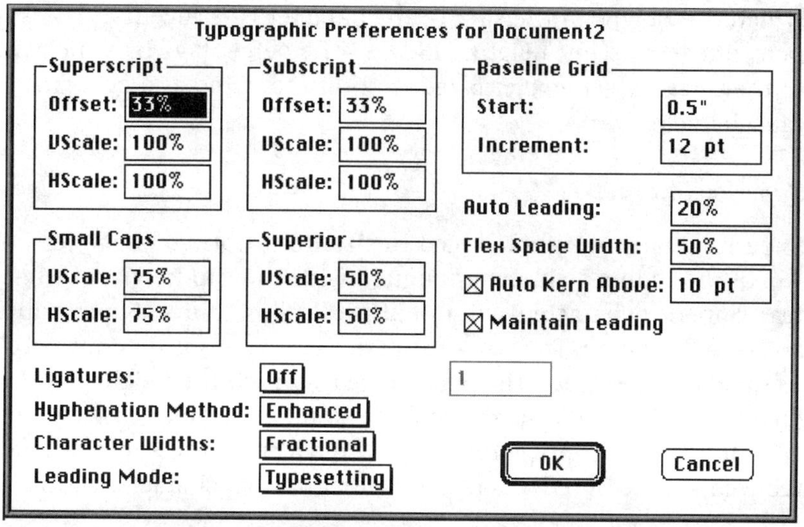

```
┌─────────────────────────────────────────────────────────────┐
│           Typographic Preferences for Document2              │
│ ┌Superscript─┐ ┌Subscript──┐ ┌Baseline Grid──────┐          │
│  Offset: [33%]   Offset: [33%]   Start:    [0.5"]            │
│  VScale:[100%]   VScale:[100%]   Increment:[12 pt]          │
│  HScale:[100%]   HScale:[100%]                               │
│                                 Auto Leading:    [20%]      │
│ ┌Small Caps─┐ ┌Superior───┐    Flex Space Width: [50%]      │
│  VScale:[75%]   VScale:[50%]   ⊠ Auto Kern Above:[10 pt]    │
│  HScale:[75%]   HScale:[50%]   ⊠ Maintain Leading           │
│                                                              │
│ Ligatures:          [Off]        [1        ]                 │
│ Hyphenation Method: [Enhanced]                               │
│ Character Widths:   [Fractional]   ( OK )    [Cancel]        │
│ Leading Mode:       [Typesetting]                            │
└─────────────────────────────────────────────────────────────┘
```

Figure 5-1 The Typographic Preferences dialog box.

When you specify Typographic Preferences with no document open, your specifications apply to all subsequently created documents but not to previously created ones. When you specify Typographic Preferences for an active document, your specifications apply only to that document; changes made while the document is active will change the document retroactively.

Superscript and Subscript

The **Offset** value determines how high above (or below) the normal baseline QuarkXPress places the baseline of a superscript (or subscript) character, expressed as a percentage of the *ascent height* (the height of the capital letters in the current font). **VScale**—the percentage by which the height of the superscript or subscript is reduced—is also measured as a percentage of ascent height. **HScale**—the percentage by which the width of the superscript or subscript is reduced—is measured as a percentage of normal character width (one of the internal font specifications that cannot be changed).

Small Caps

The Small Caps style (Style → Type Style → Small Caps) changes all non-capital letters in selected text to small capital letters. The proportion of small capitals to regular-size capital letters is determined by setting similar to the Superscript and Subscript preferences. **VScale**—the percentage by which the height of the small-cap character is reduced—is measured as a percentage of ascent height. **HScale**—the percentage by which the width of the small-cap character is reduced—is measured as a percentage of normal character width.

Superior Characters

Superior characters are reduced in size from normal characters, with the top of the reduced character aligned with the cap height of the adjacent text. Superior characters will not affect leading, unlike Superscripted characters, which may. The size of superior characters is determined similarly to small caps: **VScale**—the percentage by which the height of the superior character is reduced—is measured as a percentage of ascent height, and **HScale**—the percentage by which the width of the superior character is reduced—is measured as a percentage of normal character width.

Baseline Grid

You can lock the baselines of text to the nonprinting baseline grid of a document. This is useful if you are producing a multicolumn document and you want the baselines of the text to align across columns—a common practice in most newspapers and magazines. To define the baseline grid, enter the **Start** value, which determines how far from the top of the page the first line of the grid is placed, and the **Increment** value, which determines the distance between the grid lines.

To lock text to the baseline grid, check Lock to Baseline Grid in the Paragraph Formats dialog box (Style ➤ Formats). To display the baseline grid, select the View ➤ Show Baseline Grid command.

Auto Leading

Normally, when you select Auto Leading for selected text, QuarkXPress sets the leading (the space between lines of text) to 120 percent of the point size of the largest font in the line. In other words, auto leading for 10-point type will be 12 points, or 10/12 specifications. (You can change the leading for selected text to a specific value other than auto by using various methods described later in this chapter.)

You can change the Auto Leading value to a different percentage, or you can enter a signed incremental value, from –1080 to 1080 points. For example, a value of +1.005 will add 1.005 points of leading above the largest point size on the line. You can enter measurements in any unit of measure, but you must add the abbreviated code for measurements other than points.

If you change the Auto Leading value in the Typographic Preferences dialog box, QuarkXPress automatically adjusts all of the text in the document that has been set to Auto Leading. Since this change can affect the entire document, it is a good idea to change the Auto Leading setting before you lay out each page with text and graphics.

Flex Space Width

The width of a flexible space, a user-modifiable space based on an en space, can be changed. Flexible width space is defined as a percentage of the normal flexible space width for any given font. The default flexible space width is 50 percent, and can be changed from 0 percent to 400 percent in .1 percent increments.

Auto Kern Above

Check Auto Kern Above to specify that QuarkXPress use kerning tables built into fonts to control intercharacter spacing, and specify the size above which fonts will be kerned—from 2 to 720 points. Under the kerning option, QuarkXPress removes spaces between certain character pairs using the kerning tables built in to individual fonts. Since this adds time to screen redraw and during printing, some people prefer to kern only large font sizes. If you are going to use this feature, set your preferences *before* manually kerning individual letter pairs. If this option is not checked, QuarkXPress will not use any custom kerning tables, and any modifications made to tracking curves are not implemented. "Tracking and Kerning Text," later in this chapter, includes a more detailed description of the kerning customization option.

Maintain Leading

Maintain Leading affects how text is leaded following a box or line with a runaround (Figure 5-2). If Maintain Leading is turned off, the ascenders of text that follows an item with a runaround butt against the item. If Maintain Leading is turned on, the default setting, QuarkXPress adds the currently specified leading between the bottom of the item and the baseline of the line of text following.

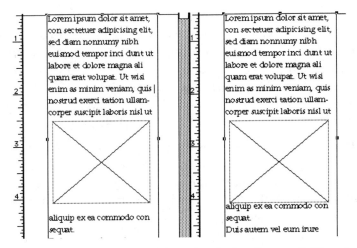

Figure 5-2 A document with Maintain Leading on (left) and off (right).

Ligatures

Most fonts have ligatures built in. Ligatures are the combinations of letters "f" and "i", and "f" and "l" that are pulled close together and printed as one character. QuarkXPress 3.1 lets you specify that the ligatures in a given font are substituted when these letters are typed. If you do not want QuarkXPress to use ligatures, choose Off, the default setting. If you want QuarkXPress to substitute ligatures for all occurrences of "f", "i" and "f", "l", choose On. If you want QuarkXPress to substitute ligatures, but not where two consecutive "f" characters are followed by "i" or "l", choose On (not ffi or ffl).

In the field to the right of the ligatures pop-up, you can specify a kerning or tracking value above which QuarkXPress will not substitute ligatures. For example, a headline would probably not contain ligatures.

On the screen, ligatures produced using the Ligatures option are actually two characters that appear close together. When the page is printed, however, the single ligature character is substituted. This allows the characters to be spell-checked correctly. You can input single-character ligatures from the keyboard using Shift-Option-5 for fi and Shift-Option-6 for fl, but it's probably better to use QuarkXPress' ligatures.

Hyphenation Method

The hyphenation algorithm used in QuarkXPress 3.1 has been improved over that used in version 3.0. All new 3.1 documents use enhanced hyphenation. Documents created using version 3.0 open in version 3.1 with Standard hyphenation, the method used by 3.0.

Figure 5-3 Standard hyphenation was used in QuarkXPress 3.0; Enhanced hyphenation, available in version 3.1, offers an improved hyphenation algorithm.

Character Widths

The Character Widths setting is a pop-up menu that lets you determine how characters are spaced, both on screen and when printing. To print to a PostScript printer, choose Fractional. To print to a dot matrix printer, choose Integral. The normal default is Fractional, and you should leave it that way while building your documents. Changing the setting can result in automatic text reflow.

Leading Mode

Normally, with the Leading mode set to Typesetting, QuarkXPress measures leading upward from the baseline of one line of text to the baseline of the line of text above it. If you change this to Word Processing mode, QuarkXPress will measure leading downward from the top of the font height on one line of text to the top of the font on the line below.

The space above the first line in a text box is determined by the text inset plus the height of the ascender of the largest font in the line for both modes. You can change the distance of the first line of text, regardless of which mode you use, by changing the First Baseline setting under Item ➤ Modify. In Typesetting mode, when Absolute Leading is specified, baselines will line up across columns when different font sizes are used; text baselines will *not* line up in Word Processing mode if different type sizes are present.

Special Typographic Characters

Typesetters have special characters that are often not available, or often not used, in word processors. Some of these characters include the use of true opening and closing quotes (",") rather than inch marks ("), an apostrophe (') rather than a foot mark ('), and an em dash (—) rather than a hyphen (-).

In Figure 5-4, the first five typographic characters are built into the Macintosh, and may be found using Key Caps (⌘ ➤ Key Caps); the others are unique to QuarkXPress. This table is not exhaustive; rather it lists those characters used most frequently.

Character description	Printed Character (where applicable)	Keyboard Entry
Opening double quote	"	Option-[
Closing double quote	"	Shift-Option-[
Opening single quote	'	Option-]
Closing single quote	'	Shift-Option-]
Virgule (fraction slash)	/	Shift-Option-1
Standard hyphen	-	Hyphen
Nonbreaking standard hyphen	-	⌘-=
Discretionary hyphen	-	⌘-Hyphen
Nonbreaking en dash	-	Option-Hyphen
Em dash	—	Option-Shift-Hyphen
Nonbreaking em dash	—	⌘-Option-Hyphen
Nonbreaking standard space		⌘-Space
En space		Option-Space
Nonbreaking en space		⌘-Option-Space
Half en space		Option-Shift-Space

Figure 5-4 Special typographic characters that can be used in QuarkXPress.

It's a good idea to familiarize yourself with these basic characters that typesetters have been using for years.

Working with Leading

Leading is a measure of the distance from the base of one line of text to the base of the next line. The term "leading" rhymes with "bedding." It originally referred to thin strips of lead that typesetters used to adjust the space between lines of metal type—the precursor of electronic or phototypesetting methods. Usually, leading is measured from baseline to baseline (unless you change the Leading mode as described earlier in this chapter).

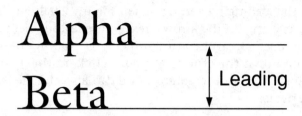

Figure 5-5 Leading is the distance from the base of one line to the base of the next.

Three different leading methods can be used in QuarkXPress: auto, absolute, and incremental. The default setting, auto, is set at 120 percent of the point size—to the nearest .001 point. Ten-point type would have 12-point leading, for example. You can specify a different default value for Auto Leading through Edit ➤ Preferences ➤ Typographic, described earlier in this chapter.

Absolute leading is achieved by entering an unsigned numeric value. The value entered will be applied no matter how you change the point size. If you enter a leading value of 14 for 12-point type, for instance, the leading will remain 14 when you change the type size to 10. If you enter an absolute value for leading, when you change the point size you may need to change the leading as well.

Incremental leading can be specified by entering a value preceded by a + or - sign. Incremental leading is based on the largest type size in a line plus or minus the value as indicated.

You can specify leading through the Paragraph Formats dialog box (⌘-Shift-F), the Leading dialog box (⌘-Shift-E), the Measurements palette, or keyboard shortcuts. Enter an absolute or incremental value, up to .001-point increments, in the leading field in the Paragraph Formats dialog box or Measurements palette, or enter a value in the Leading dialog box.

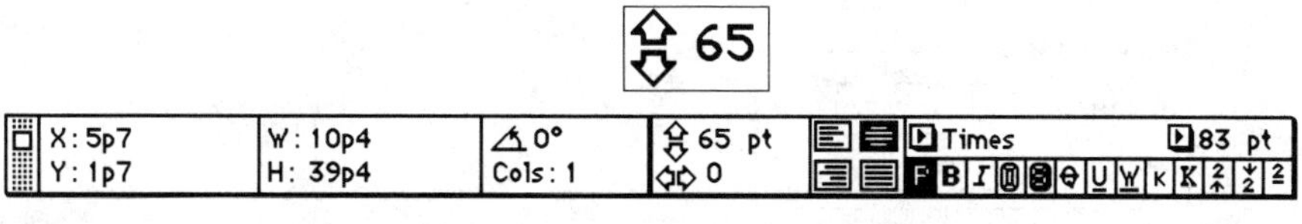

⇧ 65

| X: 5p7 | W: 10p4 | △ 0° | ⇧ 65 pt | Times | 83 pt |
| Y: 1p7 | H: 39p4 | Cols: 1 | ◇◇ 0 | F B I ⓪ ⑧ ⊕ U W K K ↑ ↓ ² | |

Figure 5-6 Using the Measurements palette, you can type in a leading value or use the scroll arrows to change the leading.

You can change the leading by adding or subtracting a value from the current entry or by clicking on the arrows next to the leading field in the Measurements palette. Click on the arrows to change leading in 1-point increments, or hold down the Option key and click on the arrows to change the leading in .1-point increments. You can also change leading using keyboard shortcuts:

- ⌘-Shift-" to increase leading 1 point.
- ⌘-Shift-: to decrease leading 1 point.
- ⌘-Option-Shift-" to increase leading 0.1 point.
- ⌘-Option-Shift-: to decrease leading 0.1 point.

    With QuarkXPress 3.1, both the Measurements palette and the keyboard shortcuts can be used to adjust auto leading as well as absolute and incremental leading. When the leading is set to auto and you click on a leading arrow in the Measurements palette or use the keyboard shortcuts to change leading, the automatic value is changed to its absolute value; values are then added to or subtracted from the absolute equivalent.

Changing the leading is one way of fitting copy to a defined space. You can make fine adjustments to the leading in order to squeeze text onto a tight page, to expand text to fill an area, or to force two columns to be the same length. Even though leading can be adjusted in .001-point increments, you may not be able to detect fine changes on low-resolution printers.

Setting the First Baseline

The baseline of the first line of text in a text box can be adjusted in the Text Box Specifications dialog box (Item → Modify). Enter a value in the Offset field to add more space at the top of the box than allowed by the Text Inset alone.

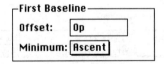

Figure 5-7 The first baseline of text in a box is set in the Text Specifications dialog box.

The Minimum pop-up menu displays three choices for determining the position of the first baseline:

- Cap Height positions the first baseline based on the size of capital letters.
- Cap + Accent positions the first baseline based on the size of capital letters plus the size of accents.
- Ascent positions the first baseline based on the height of ascenders (portions of lowercase letters such as "b" and "d" that rise above letters without ascenders such as "a" and "c").

The position of the first baseline is determined by whichever is larger, the Offset value or the selection in the Minimum pop-up menu (Figure 5-8).

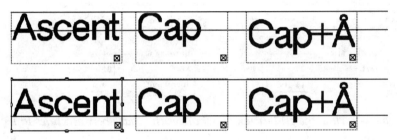

Figure 5-8 First baseline determined by Ascent, Cap Height, and Cap + Accent (left to right, top row) when Offset is small (.25 inches). Minimum values are overridden by large (.5-inch) Offset in bottom row.

Lock to Baseline Grid

Check Lock to Baseline Grid to lock the baselines in the selected paragraph to the baseline grid specified in the Typographic Preferences dialog box (Edit ➤ Preferences ➤ Typographic).

To lock text to the grid, first select the paragraph or range of paragraphs, then choose Style ➤ Paragraph Formats to get the Paragraph Formats dialog box, and check the Lock to Baseline Grid option. Lines in a paragraph locked to the baseline grid are spaced in multiples of the grid's Increment value. The Increment value of the baseline grid should be a multiple of the leading of the text you plan to lock to the grid. For example, if the body copy throughout the document has 12-point leading, the grid Increment should be 12 points.

If the leading for the locked paragraph is *less* than the baseline grid increment, the lines will be spaced wider apart than the leading specification in order to match the grid. If the leading for the locked paragraph is *more* than the baseline grid increment, the lines will be spaced two grid lines apart. If you later change the Baseline Grid, lines in paragraphs that are locked to it will be respaced throughout the document as shown in Figure 5-9.

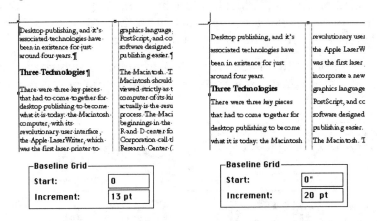

Figure 5-9 How the grid increment changes the space between lines in locked paragraphs.

 In QuarkXPress 3.1, you can display the baseline grid by selecting the View ➤ Show Baseline Grid command.

Vertical Alignment

The space between the last line of text and the bottom of the text box is determined by the Vertical Alignment specifications in the Text Box Specifications dialog box (Item ➤ Modify); choose Top, Centered, Bottom, or Justify. If you choose Justify, then small increments of space (up to the Inter ¶ Max) will be added between the lines and paragraphs of text to make the text fill the box (Figure 5-10).

Figure 5-10 Vertical alignment set Top (left), Centered (middle), and Justify (right).

Baseline Shift

You can shift the position of selected characters relative to the baseline by using the Style ➤ Baseline Shift command to get the Baseline Shift dialog box (Figure 5-11), or by using Styles ➤ Character (⌘-Shift-D) to get the Character Attributes dialog box. In either case, enter a positive value to shift the baseline up, or enter a negative value to shift the baseline down.

You can also select two keyboard shortcuts: ⌘-Option-Shift-hyphen to shift down in 1-point increments, ⌘-Option-Shift-+ to shift up in 1-point increments. Notice that if you do these operations *without* the Option key, these keystrokes become the shortcuts for applying Superscript (⌘-Shift-hyphen) or Subscript (⌘-Shift-+).

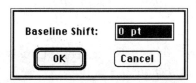

Figure 5-11 The Baseline Shift dialog box.

You can enter a positive or negative Baseline Shift value up to three times the font size of the selected text. For example, 10-point type can be shifted up to 30 points above or below the baseline. If you change the size of characters that have been shifted, the baseline shift is automatically adjusted proportionately.

Hyphenation and Justification

Hyphenation and justification are so interrelated that professional type-setters usually refer to them simultaneously as "H&J." Both hyphenation and justification function, each in its own way, to make text appear as even as possible—a common aesthetic goal in typesetting—and they both affect how many characters or words will fit on a line. For example, in left-aligned paragraphs, the right margin is less ragged and QuarkXPress can fit more words on a line when hyphenation is allowed than when it is not allowed.

The default setting is that hyphenation is turned off, but you can change the Standard H&J specification to Auto Hyphenation On. You can turn hyphenation on or off for selected paragraphs and make other adjustments, including how long a word must be before it is hyphenated and how many hyphens are allowed in a row. You can specify how wide the spaces between words and characters will be in justified text, and you can also build your own list of hyphenation exceptions. All of these adjustments are described later in this section.

There were three key pieces that had to come together for desktop publishing to become what it is today: the Macintosh computer, with its revolutionary user interface, the Apple LaserWriter, which was the first laser printer to incorporate a new computer graphics language, Adobe PostScript, and computer	There were three key pieces that had to come together for desktop publishing to become what it is today: the Macintosh computer, with its revolutionary user interface, the Apple Laser-Writer, which was the first laser printer to incorporate a new computer graphics language, Adobe Post-Script, and computer software designed to make	There were three key pieces that had to come together for desktop publishing to become what it is today: the Macintosh computer, with its revolutionary user interface, the Apple LaserWriter, which was the first laser printer to incorporate a new computer graphics language, Adobe PostScript, and computer

Figure 5-12 How text changes with hyphenation and justification.
1. *Paragraph with no hyphenation shows extremely ragged right margin.*
2. *Same paragraph shows less ragged right margin when hyphenated.*
3. *Same paragraph shows wide "rivers" of white space between words and characters when justified but not hyphenated.*

Hyphenating text is a two-step process in QuarkXPress: First you must define hyphenation and justification "rules," then you must apply those rules to paragraphs in the Paragraph Formats dialog box (Style ➤ Formats). New H&J specifications are set up using the Edit ➤ H&Js command. The H&Js dialog box (Figure 5-13), listing all the H&Js that have been defined in the current document, is similar to the Style Sheets dialog box.

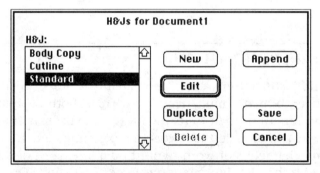

Figure 5-13 The H&Js list and dialog box.

Choose New to add a new H&J specification, Edit to modify the specifications for an existing H&J, Duplicate to create an H&J based on an existing one, Delete to remove an H&J, or Append to import H&J specifications from another QuarkXPress document.

If you select the H&J command when no documents are open, you can create or edit the sets of rules that will be applied to all subsequently created documents. If you select this command with a document open, you can edit the sets of rules that apply to that document only.

 QuarkXPress uses an algorithm to hyphenate text and also looks to hyphenation exceptions that you've defined. In version 3.1, the basic hyphenation algorithm has been improved; thus there is less incorrect hyphenation than in previous versions. Documents created in version 3.0 will open with Standard hyphenation set in the Typographic Preferences dialog box.

 Version 3.1 has eliminated the *XPress Hyphenation* file. Hyphenation formulas are now contained within the program itself and do not reference an external file.

Creating and Editing H&Js

You can create and apply more than one set of H&J rules within a document—you need not use the same rules throughout one document. For example, you could apply one set of rules to all Normal body copy and apply a different set of rules to all headings. Different named sets of rules can be applied to selected paragraphs through the Style → Formats command, as described later in this section.

When you choose New or Edit, QuarkXPress displays the Edit Hyphenation & Justification dialog box (Figure 5-14). This dialog box lets you set up all the specifications for how QuarkXPress will hyphenate text and how it will space justified text.

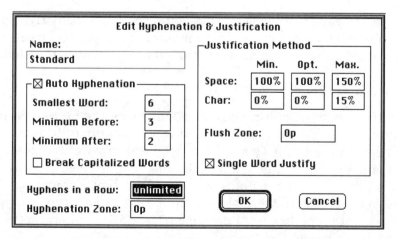

Figure 5-14 The Edit Hyphenation & Justification dialog box.

Name

The first field in the Edit Hyphenation & Justification dialog box lets you enter the name of a new H&J set or change the name of the set you are currently editing or duplicating. You must name new H&J specifications.

Auto Hyphenation

QuarkXPress will hyphenate if Auto Hyphenation is checked; uncheck this field to turn hyphenation off. The Auto Hyphenation area lets you specify the **Smallest Word** that will be hyphenated. For example, the word "area" might be hyphenated (a-re-a) if you allow four-letter words to be hyphenated, but it will never be hyphenated if you specify that only words of five letters or more will be hyphenated.

You can also specify the **Minimum** number of characters you want on a line **Before** a hyphen, and the **Minimum** number of characters you want on a line **After** a hyphen. For example, even if you allow four-letter words to be hyphenated, word "area" will never be hyphenated if you specify that there must be at least two letters before and two letters after a hyphen (since ar-ea is not a valid form).

You can also specify whether you want to **Break Capitalized Words**. If you want to allow the first word of a sentence to be hyphenated, you will need to check this field. If at the same time you do not want proper nouns hyphenated, you will have select Utilities ➤ Hyphenation Exceptions to list them individually in the Hyphenation Exceptions dictionary.

Hyphens in a Row

The next area of the dialog box lets you specify how many Hyphens in a Row will be allowed. You can enter a number (including 0) or type the word "unlimited." Entering the value of zero is the same as typing "unlimited".

Hyphenation Zone

The Hyphenation Zone can be entered in any unit of measure (using the abbreviations listed in Chapter 1) and applies to nonjustified text only. If you enter a value of 0, QuarkXPress will break any words that start on a line and would cross the right margin if not hyphenated. You can enter a value higher than 0 to set how far in from the right margin QuarkXPress will go to hyphenate a word—the word must have an acceptable hyphenation point that falls within the zone (Figure 5-15), otherwise the entire word will be brought to the next line.

Hyphenation Zone: | 0" | **Hyphenation Zone:** | .5" |

Desktop pub-
lishing, and it's
associated tech-
nologies have
been in exis-
tence for just
around four
years.

Desktop
publishing, and
it's associated
technologies
have been in
existence for
just around four
years.

Figure 5-15 How the hyphenation zone works.
1. Hyphenation zone specification allows hyphenation.
2. Hyphenation zone specification prevents hyphenation.

Justification Method

Most of the entries under the Justification Method area apply to justified text only—except Optimum values, which is applied to nonjustified text as well. You can enter the Minimum (down to 0 percent between words, or –50 percent between characters), Optimum, and Maximum (up to 500 percent between words, or 100 percent between characters) Word Spacing (space between words) and Character Spacing (space between characters) that QuarkXPress will apply in adjusting horizontal space in order to justify a line of text. Values are normally entered as percentages of the manufacturer's normal interword space for the font and size currently in use. QuarkXPress will never go below the Minimum space specified, but it will exceed the Maximum if there is no other alternative.

Flush Zone

The Flush Zone determines whether the last line of a justified paragraph will be justified. A value of zero indicates that the last line will never be justified. Otherwise, the last line of a paragraph *will* be justified if the last word falls within the Flush Zone as measured from the right indent.

Single Word Justify

If Single Word Justify is checked, any single word that falls on its own line will be justified from the left to right indent. If Single Word Justify is not checked, the word will be flush to the left margin (Figure 5-16). This option does not apply to the last line in a paragraph; the last line is controlled by the Flush Zone option.

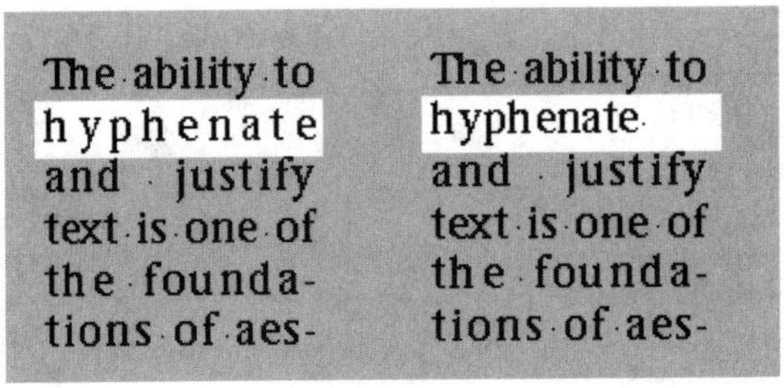

> The ability to
> **hyphenate**
> and justify
> text is one of
> the founda-
> tions of aes-

> The ability to
> hyphenate
> and justify
> text is one of
> the founda-
> tions of aes-

Figure 5-16 Single Word Justify checked on (left) and unchecked (right).

Applying H&Js to Text

Once you have defined a set of rules for hyphenation and justification, you can apply those rules to selected paragraphs using Style ➤ Formats (⌘-Shift-F). The Paragraph Formats dialog box (Figure 5-17) includes a pop-up menu of the H&J rule sets that you have prepared for the active document. Normally, the Standard H&J set is applied automatically to all Normal text unless you change the H&J associated with Normal through the Edit ➤ Style Sheets command.

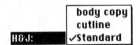

Figure 5-17 The H&J pop-up menu in the Paragraph Formats dialog box.

The H&J selection can be applied as part of the style sheet specification, described in Chapter 4.

Deleting H&Js

To delete an H&J specification, click on the H&J name in the list displayed in the H&J dialog box (Edit ➤ H&Js), then click the Delete button. When you delete an H&J specification, QuarkXPress displays an alert asking if you want to delete it (Figure 5-18). All paragraphs to which this specification has been applied will take on the specifications listed in the Standard H&J.

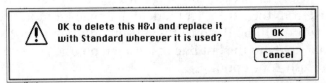

Figure 5-18 Deleting an H&J specification causes an alert.

Since a different H&J will apply to the text, deleting an H&J specification may cause text reflow.

Duplicating H&J Specifications

Sometimes you may wish to duplicate an H&J specification using another H&J. The fastest way is to click on an H&J you want to use as the basis for a new one, and click Duplicate. The Edit Hyphenation & Justification dialog box will appear with "Copy of *<H&J name>*" in the name field. You can then use the dialog box to change any of the specification.

Appending H&Js from Other Documents

If you want to use H&Js set up in another document, click on the Append button in the Edit H&Js dialog box. The Append H&Js dialog box (Figure 5-19) displays a list of the QuarkXPress documents and templates—you can change drives or folders as you would in other dialog boxes. Choose a document by double-clicking on the name. You cannot append the H&J specifications from an open document. QuarkXPress imports all of the H&J specifications from the selected document except those that have the same names as the H&J specifications already in the list.

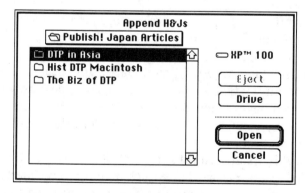

Figure 5-19 The Append H&Js dialog box.

Suggested Hyphenation

You can see how QuarkXPress would hyphenate a selected word (or the first word to the left of the insertion bar or the first word in a selected range of text) by using Utilities ➤ Suggested Hyphenation (⌘-H). This is handy as a precheck before you enter a word in the Hyphenation

Exceptions dictionary, or if you want manually to hyphenate a word in a paragraph that is formatted with Auto Hyphenation turned off. The Suggested Hyphenation dialog box (Figure 5-20) shows the hyphenated word.

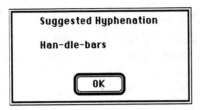

Figure 5-20 Suggested Hyphenation dialog box.

To access this feature, the Content tool must be selected and the insertion point must be positioned within a word. You cannot make changes to the suggested syllable breaks, and this command and dialog box do not make any changes to the text itself. If you want to change the way QuarkXPress hyphenates a word, you can insert your own discretionary hyphens or select Utilities ➤ Hyphenation Exceptions, described under the next headings.

Discretionary Hyphens

You can insert discretionary hyphens within words manually by typing ⌘-hyphen. These discretionary hyphens can be inserted using some word processing programs, before the text is imported in QuarkXPress, or after the text is imported in QuarkXPress. Discretionary hyphens behave exactly the same way that automatic hyphens behave: They appear only on the screen and the printed pages when they fall at the end of a line. To prevent a word from being hyphenated, enter the word in the Hyphenation Exceptions (see next section).

Discretionary hyphens are useful for quick fixes or one-time-only exceptions, but if you want permanently to change the way QuarkXPress hyphenates a word, or turn hyphenation off entirely for selected words, you can build a dictionary of Hyphenation Exceptions, as described next.

Hyphenation Exceptions

Select Utilities ➤ Hyphenation Exceptions to display the Hyphenation Exceptions dialog box (Figure 5-21) and control the way QuarkXPress breaks a word. This command is always available. Any exceptions will be included with all subsequently created new documents.

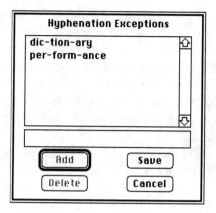

Figure 5-21 Hyphenation Exceptions dialog box

In the Hyphenation Exceptions dialog box, type a word in the field with hyphens positioned where you want QuarkXPress to break the word—or without hyphens if you never want the word hyphenated—then click on **Add**. You must enter every variant of the word (plural, gerund, and so on) separately. If you click on an entry in the list of exceptions, the word appears in the entry field where you can make changes, and the Add button changes to **Replace**. Use the **Delete** button to remove a selected word from the list. When you are finished making changes to the exceptions list, click on **Save** to keep all your changes, or click on **Cancel** to ignore all changes.

By the way, any changes you make to the hyphenation exceptions affect all documents when you next open them—whether they are new documents or ones that existed before you changed the hyphenation exceptions.

Hyphenation exceptions are no longer stored in the XPress Data file (which no longer exists in version 3.1). Hyphenation Exceptions are stored within a document; if they were created when no document was open, they are stored in XPress Preferences. See Part II for more details on how Hyphenation Exceptions are stored.

Kerning and Tracking Text

Kerning and tracking characters are other methods of aesthetically improving the spacing of text. *Kerning* refers to the spacing between two specific letters; *tracking* refers to the adjustment of white space between multiple characters and words.

When the text insertion point is positioned between two characters of text, the Style ➤ Kern command lets you adjust the space between the characters numerically; or you can make the same adjustment in the Measurements palette, the Character Attributes dialog box, or using the keyboard shortcuts. The command changes to Style ➤ Track when a range of text is selected; as with kerning, you can make the same adjustment in the Measurements palette, the Character Attributes dialog box, or using the keyboard shortcuts.

Values entered in these fields must be from –100 to 100, and each unit represents 1/200th (0.005) of an em space. (An em space is the equivalent of two zeros, 00, in any given font.) You can enter values in .001 increments, which means you can kern or track in increments as fine as 1/200,000th of an em.

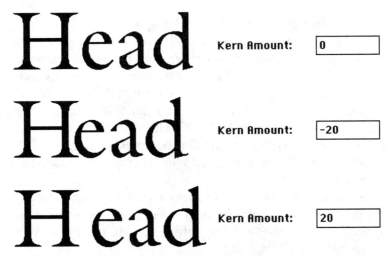

Figure 5-22 *Examples of various kern settings between the H and the e.*

Entering a positive value increases the space between characters; entering a negative value tightens it. In the Measurements palette, you can also click on the arrows adjacent to the entry field to increase or decrease the value in 1-unit increments. Hold down the Option key and click to make changes in .1-unit increments.

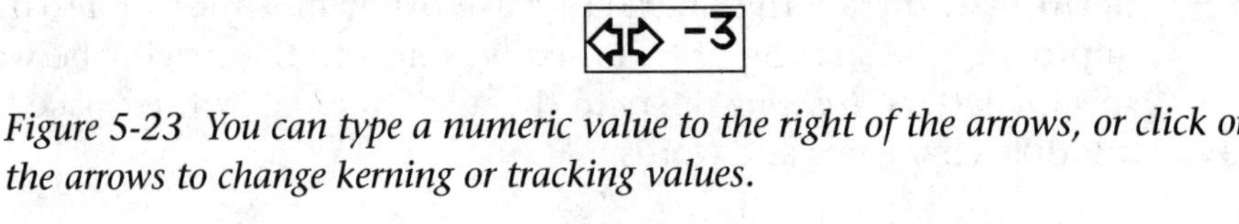

Figure 5-23 *You can type a numeric value to the right of the arrows, or click on the arrows to change kerning or tracking values.*

You can use keyboard shortcuts for kerning or tracking:

- ⌘-Shift-{ decreases the kerning or tracking space by 1/20th of an em.
- ⌘-Shift-} increases the kerning or tracking space by 1/20th of an em.
- ⌘-Option-Shift-{ decreases the kerning or tracking space by 1/200th (0.005) of an em.
- ⌘-Option-Shift-} increases the kerning or tracking space by 1/200th (0.005) of an em.

Tracking values affect both word and character spacing, and can be useful for copy-fitting. Tracking values, unlike kerning values, can be applied as part of a style sheet.

There were three key pieces that had to come together for desktop publishing to become what it is today.	Track Amount: `0`
There were three key pieces that had to come together for desktop publishing to become what it is today.	Track Amount: `-5`
There were three key pieces that had to come together for desktop publishing to become what it is today.	Track Amount: `20`

Figure 5-24 Examples of various track settings.

The results of entries in the Kern, Track, or Character Attributes dialog boxes are not reflected on the screen display until you close the dialog box, but entries made in the Measurements palette or using the keyboard shortcuts are reflected immediately. For this reason, it is a good idea to perform all manual kerning through the Measurements palette or with the keyboard shortcuts, unless you are applying a specific numeric value consistently.

Since kerning and tracking adjustments are a percentage of an em of any given font, rather than a fixed size, the actual space between letters will be scaled proportionally if you change the font size of the kerned or tracked characters. For example, if you kern by 1 unit two letters that are 10 points in size, then scale them to 20 points in size, the unit they are kerned will still be 1; however, the em of a 20-point font, of which the unit is a percentage, is larger, and the unit represents a correspondingly larger space. QuarkXPress does *not* offer any way to set an absolute distance between characters, a feature common to many typesetting systems.

Global Kerning Adjustments

Usually, text above 10 points in size is automatically kerned using the built-in kerning tables for the font—unless you change this setting through the Edit ➤ Preferences ➤ Typographic dialog box as described earlier in this chapter. When kerning, the spacing between characters is adjusted slightly in accordance with the values stored in a table of "kerning pairs." For example, the space between the characters *AV* should be tighter than the space between the characters *AX*. In fact, if the spacing between the different pairs is not adjusted, then it will appear to the eye that the *A* and *V* are farther apart than the *A* and *X* are. For this reason, kerned text generally looks better than text that is not kerned—especially in larger point sizes.

You can select Edit ➤ Preferences ➤ Typographic to change the point size above which kerning is enabled, or turn kerning off entirely for a whole document. (Your pages will redraw and print more quickly if kerning is turned off for small point sizes.)

You can customize a font's kerning table using Utilities ➤ Kerning Table Edit. In order for this command to be available, the *Kern/Track Editor* extension must be in the same folder as the QuarkXPress program when you launch the program. The first dialog box displayed when you use this command is the Kerning Table Edit dialog box (Figure 5-25), which shows a list of all the installed fonts.

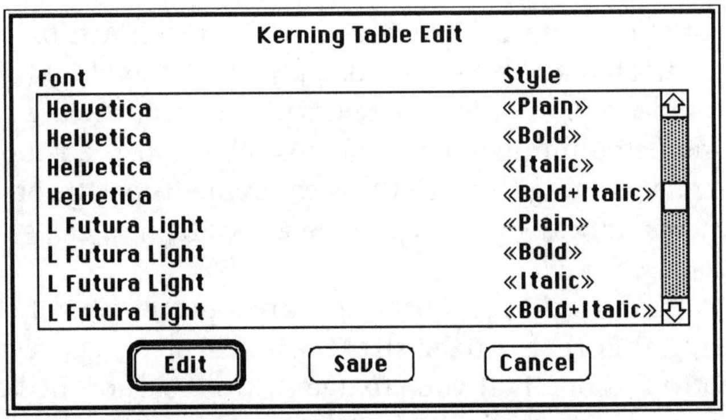

Figure 5-25 The Kerning Table Edit dialog box.

To Edit a font's kerning table, double-click on the font name/style in the list. (You must edit the kerning tables for plain, bold, italic, and bold-italic styles separately.) QuarkXPress displays the Kerning Values for the selected font (Figure 5-26). If the selected font has a kerning table, the values are displayed and you can edit them as described next. If no values are displayed in the dialog box, then no kerning table exists for that font. You can create one by entering values in the dialog box.

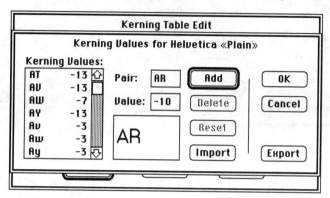

Figure 5-26 Kerning Values dialog box.

The Kerning Values scroll list shows all of the pairs that have assigned kerning values. Pairs *not* on the list have an assumed kerning value of zero. To edit a value, first click on a pair in the list to select it or simply type the pair in the Pair text box. The Value field shows the currently assigned kerning value or remains blank if you typed a new pair that is not on the list. The window below the Value field shows how the pair would be spaced with the current Value setting; the display changes as you enter different numbers in the Value field. Values are entered in 200ths (0.005) of an em space, and can be between –100 and 100. A value of –20, for example, will reduce the space between letters by 1/10 of an em space.

If you have typed a new pair in the Pair field, you must click on **Add** to add it to the list. If you have selected an existing pair, the Add button changes to **Replace**. You must click on Replace in order to update the table, or you can click on **Delete** to remove a pair from the table (and thereby set the kerning value to 0). The **Reset** button restores the original kerning table set up by the font manufacturer. If Reset is grayed, you know that the original table has not been modified.

Click on Export to create an ASCII text file version of the table. This displays a directory dialog box that lets you name an exported table and specify where to store it (Figure 5-27). Click on Import to replace the entire table with values from a table that was generated using a text editor or by the Export command. The Import command displays a list of all ASCII files, but it displays a warning and does not import any files that are not in the proper format for kerning tables.

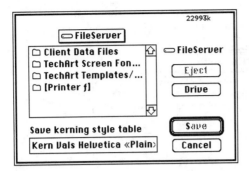

Figure 5-27 The Export dialog box.

When you click on OK, the new kerning table for that font is stored *temporarily*, QuarkXPress displays the Kerning Table Edit dialog box, and you can Edit another font's kerning table. To end the process, click on Save in the Kerning Table Edit dialog box—or click on Cancel to reverse all changes made to the kerning tables.

Changes you make to the kerning table are stored as part of the document and in the XPress Preferences file. If you export text to a word processing format (File → Save Text), kerning adjustments are lost.

Editing Tracking Values

Global intercharacter spacing (tracking) values are built in to QuarkXPress. You can select Utilities → Tracking Edit to change the global setting for a specific font. The Utilities → Tracking Edit command is available only if the Kern/Track Editor extension is in the same folder as the QuarkXPress program when you launch the program.

The first dialog box displayed when you select the Utilities → Tracking Edit command lists all of the installed fonts (Figure 5-28).

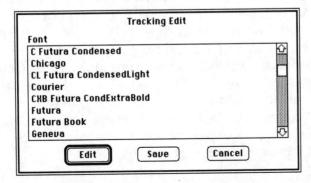

Figure 5-28 The Tracking Edit dialog box.

To Edit a font's tracking values, double-click on the font name. QuarkXPress displays the Tracking Values chart for the selected font (Figure 5-29). Normally tracking is set to zero for all sizes—indicated by a horizontal line across the center of the chart.

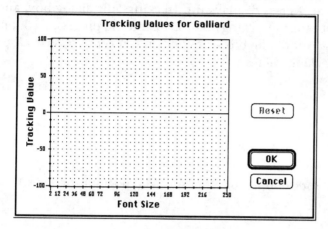

Figure 5-29 Normal Tracking Values chart.

You can specify tracking values from –100/200ths to 100/200ths of an em space for font sizes from 2 to 250 points by clicking on the line in the chart area to create new handles. Each click positions a handle and changes the direction of the line. When you click on a handle, the font size and tracking table value are shown in the upper right corner of the dialog box (Figure 5-30). You can move a handle by dragging it. You can position up to four handles in a chart.

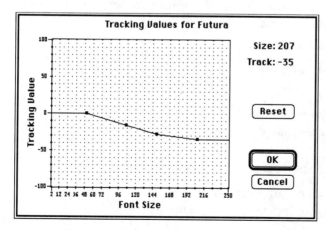

Figure 5-30 Custom Tracking Values chart.

Hold the Option key and click on a handle to remove it. Click on Reset to revert to normal tracking (0 for all sizes), or click on Cancel to reverse any changes you have made to the current font.

When you click on OK, the new tracking values for that font are stored *temporarily*, QuarkXPress displays the Tracking Edit dialog box, and you can Edit another font's tracking values. To end the process, click on Save in the Tracking Edit dialog box—or click on Cancel to reverse all entries made to the Tracking Values.

Special Effects

You can create many special typographic effects, such as custom-scaled type, drop caps, and rules attached to text, which are discussed in this section. See Part II for examples of other special typographic effects.

Horizontal Scale

QuarkXPress allows you to make expanded or condensed versions of a font's normal character widths by adjusting the width of characters numerically. You can select the Style ➤ Horizontal Scale command (Figure 5-31), input a value in the Horizontal Scale entry in the Character Attributes dialog box or the Measurements palette, or use keyboard shortcuts to scale characters horizontally. Values entered in these fields represent percentages of the font's normal character widths: entries above 100 percent (up to 400 percent) make the characters wider than normal; values below 100 percent (down to the minimum 25 percent) make the characters narrower than normal.

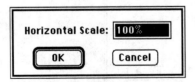

Figure 5-31 The Horizontal Scale dialog box.

The keyboard shortcuts for changing scale are:

- ⌘-[to condense in 5 percent increments.
- ⌘-] to expand in 5 percent increments.

Because horizontal scaling distorts a font in only one direction, over-scaling can result in some character strokes being relatively thin compared to other strokes.

This is Galliard at normal width

This is Galliard EXPANDED
to 140% of original width

This is Galliard CONDENSED to 75% of original width

Figure 5-32 Examples of expanded and condensed characters.

Drop Caps

A drop cap is a large initial character, or characters, in a paragraph with two or more lines of text beside it. To create a drop cap, click on Drop Caps in the Paragraph Formats dialog box (Style ➤ Formats). In Character Count, specify the number of characters that you want to make drop caps (the first characters in the paragraph), and in Line Count give the number of lines of text that you want to fall next to the drop cap.

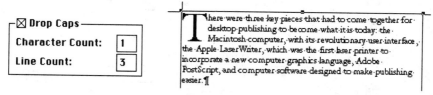

Figure 5-33 The Drop Cap area of the Paragraph Formats dialog box and the resulting drop cap.

QuarkXPress automatically scales the first letters of the paragraph to the size needed to match the number of lines you specified as being beside the drop cap. To enlarge or reduce the size of drop caps, highlight the drop cap characters; then choose Size from the Style menu. Enter a size value or a percentage value between 10 percent and 400 percent in .1 percent increments in the Font Size dialog box. If you enter a percentage, the drop cap characters will be scaled as a percentage of the number of lines deep you specified the characters to be.

You can change the space between the drop cap and the adjacent lines by clicking in between the drop cap and the adjacent first line of text, then applying kerning values using any one of the several methods described earlier in this chapter. All lines indented by the drop cap will move at once, based on the kerning values used.

You can specify alignment (left, right, centered, justified) in this dialog box, as described earlier. You can select a set of H&J rules as described earlier, and you can specify Leading (space between lines) in this dialog box, also as described earlier. Drop caps can also be specified as part of a style sheet.

Applying Rules to Text

QuarkXPress lets you specify rules—ruled lines—as part of the paragraph formatting. Thus you can create rules above and/or below a selected paragraph through numerical specifications (instead of using one of QuarkXPress' drawing tools). Those rules will move automatically with the text when the text is reflowed due to editing changes; you don't have to use the anchoring feature.

Select Style → Rules (⌘-Shift-N) to display the Paragraph Rules dialog box (Figure 5-34) and set rules above and/or below a paragraph. Check Rule Above and/or Rule Below to expand the initial dialog box.

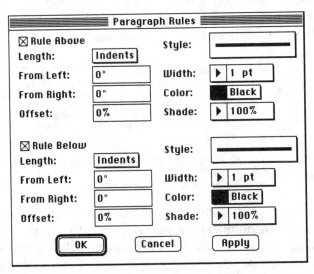

Figure 5-34 Paragraph Rules dialog box (⌘-Shift-N).

A rule can be assigned a Style, Width, Color, and Shade just as in the Line Specifications dialog box, used to define lines drawn with QuarkXPress' line drawing tools.

Length

For text rules, you can also specify Length to match the line of **Text** to which the rule is attached or to match the **Indents** set up for the paragraph through the Style ➤ Formats command. You can further adjust the length by specifying distances in the From Left and/or From Right fields, determining how the rule will be shortened (by a positive value entry) or extended (by a negative value entry) relative to the Text or Indents as specified in the Length setting.

Offset

The Offset distance specified is added between the rule and the baseline of the text below (for rules above text) or between the rule and the baseline of the text above (for rules below text). The Offset value can be an absolute measure or a percentage of the total space between paragraphs (as determined by the values entered for Space Above and Space Below in the Paragraph Formats dialog box).

If you enter an absolute offset value, the rule will be placed from the bottom of the rule to the baseline of the first line of text for rules above. For rules below, an absolute value will determine the space from the top of the rule to the baseline of the last line of text.

Values entered as percentages are determined as a percentage of the total space between paragraphs. For example, if you enter an Offset value of 20 percent, QuarkXPress will divide the total space between paragraphs so that 20 percent of the space falls between the rule and the ascent height of the tallest character in the text below (for rules above text) or between the descent of the largest character in the text above (for rules below text); 80 percent of the space will fall between the rule and the following paragraph. When the Offset is a percentage, rules are displayed between paragraphs but not above the first paragraph or below the last paragraph in a text box.

> Desktop publishing, and it's associated technologies have been in existence for just around four years.
>
> **Key Technologies**
>
> There were three key pieces that had to come together for desktop publishing to become what it is today: the Macintosh computer, with its revolutionary user interface, the Apple LaserWriter, which was the first laser printer to incorporate a new computer graphics language, Adobe PostScript, and computer software designed to make publishing easier.

Figure 5-35 Example of a rule attached to text.

Summary

Now that you know the alternatives available for formatting text in QuarkXPress, you can create design specifications that take advantage of QuarkXPress' extensive typographic capabilities, and you can decide which method of applying the specifications will be most efficient.

The next chapter describes the basics of how to work with graphics that have been created in other programs and imported into QuarkXPress.

6 *Graphics*

Text and typography represent just one aspect of design and printed communication. Images play an important role, and one of the key characteristics of QuarkXPress is its ability to incorporate complex graphics with text on a page. QuarkXPress offers some graphic tools of its own, but you can also import graphics that were created in other programs, such as MacDraw, Adobe Illustrator, Aldus FreeHand, and Adobe Photoshop, to name a few.

Chapter 2 presented an overview of the basic steps for working with boxes and lines created using QuarkXPress. In this chapter you learn how to further manipulate graphics that have been created using QuarkXPress, and how to work with graphics that have been imported from other programs.

Before you start, it's a good idea to set up the global conditions that will affect all the graphics in a document. These include options in the the Edit ➤ Preferences ➤ General and the Edit ➤ Preferences ➤ Tools commands, described in Chapter 3. You may also want to begin building your color palette before you begin working, using the Edit ➤ Colors command, described in Chapter 7.

Broadly, there are ways to bring graphics onto a QuarkXPress page:

- Use the Paste command to bring in a graphic from the Clipboard.

- Drag elements from another QuarkXPress document or library, which essentially copies them.

- Use QuarkXPress' own built-in graphic tools with the File ➤ Get Picture command to bring in graphics that were created in other programs.

- If you are running under System 7, You can use the Edit ➤ Subscribe To command to subscribe to an edition created in another program.

The Paste command is common to most applications on the Macintosh and was described in Chapter 1. Methods of copying elements from another QuarkXPress document or library were described in Chapter 2. In this chapter we first take a closer look at how to use QuarkXPress' built-in graphic tools, then we look at how to work with graphics created in other programs using the File ➤ Get Picture command and the Edit ➤ Subscribe To command.

Working with QuarkXPress Drawing Tools

As you learned in Chapters 1 and 2, QuarkXPress' built-in graphics tools are shown as icons in the tool palette (Figure 6-1).

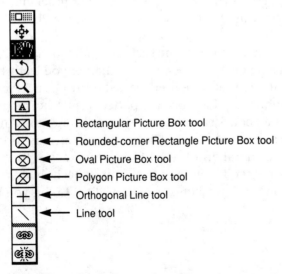

Figure 6-1 The drawing tools in the tool palette.

You can select the Rectangular Picture Box tool, the Rounded-corner Rectangle Picture Box tool, the Oval Picture Box tool, or the Polygon Picture Box tool to create boxes with square corners, boxes with rounded corners, circles and ovals, or polygons, respectively. You can select the Orthogonal Line tool to draw horizontal and vertical lines, and the Line tool to draw lines at any angle. Each of these items may be used as a stand-alone graphic; or the picture box items may contain graphics created in other programs.

Modifying Picture Boxes

Chapter 2 covered the basic techniques for drawing, moving, resizing, and rotating boxes as well applying color to the background of a box and adding a frame to a box.

You can make most basic modifications to a box with one of three methods: with the mouse and keyboard, through the Measurements or Colors palettes, or by making entries in the Picture Box Specifications dialog box (Item → Modify).

The Measurements palette can be one of the fastest and most precise ways to modify picture boxes. Note that the entries on the left side of the Measurements palette affect the selected picture box itself, not the content. The content—that is, a graphic—is modified through entries in the right side of the Measurements palette, discussed later in this chapter.

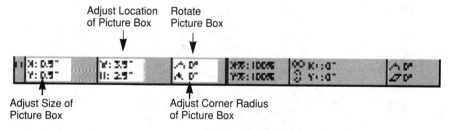

Figure 6-2 The left side of the Measurements palette contains entries that affect the picture box, not its content.

The Colors palette is the fastest way to apply color to box backgrounds. The palette displays a list of all colors created using the Edit → Colors command. The Colors palette is the only way to apply two-color blends to box backgrounds. See Chapter 7 for more detail on applying color to box backgrounds.

Figure 6-3 The Colors palette allows you to apply color to a picture box background quickly.

The Picture Box Specifications dialog box contains the same entries as those found in the Measurements palette, but it also contains an option to Suppress Printout of the picture box (and its content). The Picture Box Specifications dialog box also gives you options similar to the Colors palette. You can a color and shade to the background of the picture box, but you cannot apply a blend to the box background in the Picture Box Specifications dialog box.

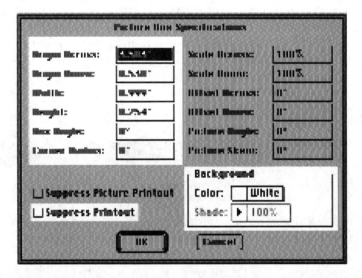

Figure 6-4 Entries in the Picture Box Specifications dialog box that affect a picture box without affecting the content.

Any of the objects created using QuarkXPress' built-in tools can be defined further by selecting line widths, styles, and colors. Picture box items can be framed and filled with colors and shades. Drawn objects initially have the default settings for line widths, styles, colors, and shades.

The program starts with default values set to 1-point black lines for the line creation tools and no frame and a white background for picture boxes. You can change the defaults by changing these settings before you draw the item, or you can change the settings after you draw the item. You'll see how to change these settings later in this chapter.

Changing the Shape of Picture Boxes

No matter what drawing tool you used to draw a picture box, you can change its shape instantly using Item ➤ Picture Box Shape. With this command you can change a rectangular box, oval, or polygon to any of six basic shapes: a rectangle with square corners, a rectangle with rounded corners, 2 concave-cornered rectangles, an oval, or a polygon.

To use this command, first select the box(es) you want to change, then choose a shape from the Picture Box Shape submenu (Figure 6-5). See Part II for examples of how unusual shapes, such as cartoon balloons, can be created by converting ovals to polygons and dragging a handle.

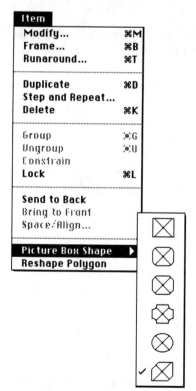

Figure 6-5 The Picture Box Shape submenu.

Reshaping Polygons

Once you have drawn a polygon, you can resize it by changing the size of its bounding box or reshape it by moving, adding, and deleting box handles and by moving line segments. You can follow these procedures using either the Item tool (✥) or the Content tool (🖑).

When a polygon is active and Reshape Polygon is *not* checked in the Style menu, you can adjust the size of the polygon by moving any of the eight handles displayed on the bounding box (Figure 6-6). Hold down the Shift key while you resize if you want to maintain the same proportions.

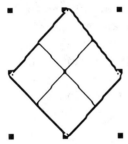

Figure 6-6 Adjusting a Polygon's bounding box. The bounding box is displayed when Reshape Polygon is not *checked in the Style menu.*

When a polygon is active and Reshape Polygon *is* checked in the Item menu, you can adjust the shape of the polygon by moving any of the handles displayed at the vertices of the polygon or by moving a line segment (Figure 6-7). You can add new handles by holding the ⌘ key as you click the pointer anywhere on a line segment. You can move any handle or line segment by positioning the pointer over it and dragging the mouse. You can constrain the movement of a handle or a line segment to 45° lines (0°, 45°, or 90°) by holding the Shift key as you drag.

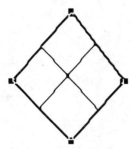

Figure 6-7 Adjusting a Polygon's shape. The corner handles are displayed when Reshape Polygon is checked in the Style menu.

You can delete a handle by positioning the pointer over it and holding the ⌘ key as you click. A new line segment will automatically join the two vertices that were adjacent to the deleted handle. You cannot delete a handle from a three-sided polygon.

Modifying Lines

You can select the Orthogonal Line tool to draw horizontal and vertical lines, and the diagonal Line tool to draw lines at any angle. You need never select the Orthogonal Line tool, since you can constrain any line drawn with the diagonal Line tool to 0°, 45°, or 90° angles by holding down the Shift key as you draw. The Shift key also constrains lines to these angles when you resize them by dragging one of the handles.

The same option is available when changing the length or angle of any line with the mouse. If you hold down the Shift key as you drag one of these handles, you will force the line to follow an angle that is a multiple of 45°; if you do not hold down the Shift key while dragging, you can stretch the line in any direction.

For precise positioning of lines against other objects (text or graphics), you can position them numerically using Item ➤ Modify, the Measurements palette, or use nonprinting guides, or work in magnified views, such as 200 percent view. When drawing lines, the line itself will be centered at the crosshair, regardless of the line's thickness.

Normally, the tool that was selected before you select a line creation tool is automatically reselected as soon as you draw a line. If you want to draw more than one line, hold down the Option key when you select the line tool.

Lines drawn with the Line tool or Orthogonal Line tool show small black squares as handles at each end when they are first drawn, or when they are later made active with the Item tool. Change the length and/or angle of a line by dragging one of these corner handles. Move a line to another position by dragging anywhere on the line *except* on a handle. Change the line style of an active line or group of lines by making a different selection from the Style menu (described later in this chapter).

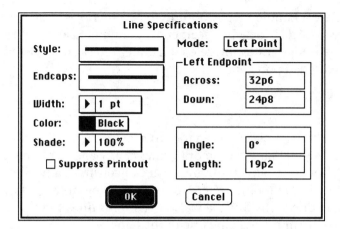

Figure 6-8 Line Specifications dialog box.

When a line is active, the commands under the Style menu (Figure 6-9) list the types of changes you can apply to lines that have been drawn using one of QuarkXPress' two line tools: the Orthogonal Line tool or the Line tool. (These commands *do not* apply to lines that are part of imported artwork.)

Figure 6-9 Style Menu when a line is active.

These attributes can also be assigned through the Item ➤ Modify command or through the Measurements palette.

The size, position, and angle of a line is adjusted differently in the Measurements palette (and in the Line Specifications dialog box, shown under the next heading) depending on the Mode selected. Choose **Endpoints** to describe a line by specifying the position of the endpoints. Choose **Left Endpoint** to describe a line by specifying the position of its left endpoint, its length, and its angle. Choose **Midpoint** to describe a line by specifying the position of its midpoint, its length, and its angle. Choose **Right Endpoint** to describe a line by specifying the position of its right endpoint, its length, and its angle (Figure 6-10).

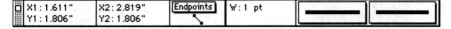

Figure 6-10 Measurements palette when lines are active.

The Measurements palette for lines changes depending on the Mode selected. A pop-up menu lets you select the Mode for the line and the display changes depending on the Mode chosen:

- When Endpoints is chosen, X1 and Y1 show the locations of the left end of the line, and X2 and Y2 show the location of the right end of the line.
- When Left Point is chosen, X1 and Y1 show the position of the left point; $\angle$ shows the rotated angle of the line; and L shows the length of the line.
- When Midpoint is chosen, XC and YC show the location of the midpoint of the line; $\angle$ shows the rotated angle of the line; and L shows the length of the line.
- When Right Point is chosen, X2 and Y2 show the position of the right point; $\angle$ shows the rotated angle of the line; and L shows the length of the line.

Regardless of the Mode selected, some of the entries in the Measurements palette represent the line consistently:

- W shows the width of the line.
- A pop-up menu lets you select the Style for the line.
- A pop-up menu lets you select the Endcaps for the line.

In entering angles of rotation, a positive value indicates a counterclockwise rotation, a negative value is measured clockwise.

Line Style

The Line Style submenu (Figure 6-11) lists 11 basic line styles that are built in to QuarkXPress, including solid lines, dashed and dotted lines, and double and triple lines. You can also set line style in the Line Specifications dialog box or by choosing from the first pop-up line menu in the Measurements palette.

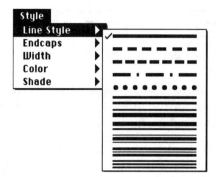

Figure 6-11 Line Style submenu.

Width

The Width submenu (Figure 6-12) lists seven common widths that you can choose from the menu, or you can choose Other (⌘-Shift-\) to display the Width dialog box. You can also adjust the line width in the Line Specifications dialog box or by entering a value in the Width field in the Measurements palette.

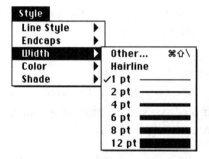

Figure 6-12 Width submenu.

You can specify any line width from 0 to 504 points. The printed width of a hairline depends is .25 points. You can also use the following keyboard shortcuts to change the width of an active line:

- ⌘-Shift-< decreases line width by 1 unit at increments that follow the menu list: hairline, 1, 2, 4, 6, 8, 12 points.

- ⌘-Shift-> increases line width by 1 unit at the increments that follow the menu list.

- ⌘-Option-Shift-< decreases line width by 1 point (from 0 to 504 points).

- ⌘-Option-Shift-> increases line width by 1 point (from 0 to 504 points).

Endcaps

The Endcaps submenu (Figure 6–13) lists six variations of endcaps that you can specify for lines, including arrows at one or both ends or arrows and tailfeathers. You can also set endcaps in the Line Specifications dialog box or by choosing from the second pop-up line menu in the Measurements palette.

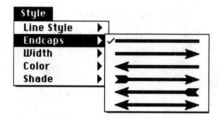

Figure 6-13 Endcaps submenu.

Color and Shade

You can make a line any Color and Shade, or specify a color of None to make a transparent line. Normally, the line color is set to 100 percent Black. If the line is transparent, there is no displacement of the text behind the line and you can "see through" the line to the contents of the box below. You can force text to runaround a transparent line by using the Item ➤ Runaround command (described in Chapter 2). You can also specify that a line not print, and still have it affect text runaround. See Part II for examples of using transparent or nonprinting lines to force text runaround, such as slanted margins.

The Color submenu (Figure 6-14) lists the colors that you have set up for the active palette through the Edit ➤ Colors command. You can also specify color in the Colors palette or in the Line Specifications dialog box.

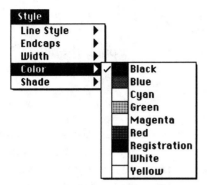

Figure 6-14 Color submenu.

The **Shade** submenu (Figure 6-15) lists shades from 0 percent to 100 percent in 10 percent increments. You can also specify shade in the Colors palette or in the Line Specifications dialog box.

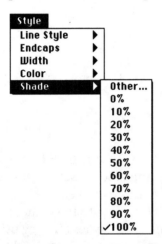

Figure 6-15 Shade submenu.

In this or any dialog box that offers colors or shades as options, you can select any color in the menu or create your own custom colors, and you can select any shade (in .1 percent increments) or choose from the 10 percent increments in the pop-up menu. Chapter 7 provides a detailed discussion of applying color.

Importing Graphics from Other Sources

As you learned in Chapter 2, you can bring graphics created in other programs on to a page by drawing a picture box and selecting the File ➤ Get Picture command. You can import a graphic into any box created with QuarkXPress' four picture box tools: the Rectangular Picture Box tool, the Rounded-corner Rectangle Picture Box tool, the Oval Picture Box tool, and the Polygon Picture Box tool. The types of graphics that can be imported into QuarkXPress and some of the programs that can be used to create them are listed in Figure 6-16.

File Formats	Sources
Paint (bitmap)	MacPaint, SuperPaint, FullPaint, and scanning applications
TIFF line art, grayscale, or color image	scanning applications
RIFF	ImageStudio
PICT	MacDraw, MacDraft, Claris CAD, Canvas, and some scanning applications
Encapsulated PostScript	Adobe Illustrator, FreeHand

Figure 6-16 Sources of graphics that can be used in QuarkXPress.

Some programs, such as Adobe Photoshop, can save graphics files in any of these formats.

Types of Graphics

One of the factors that has contributed to the success of the Macintosh in the publishing industry is the consistency of graphic file formats across applications. Almost every graphics application on the Macintosh supports at least one of the above-listed formats (except for RIFF, a format used exclusively by Letraset products). All graphics formats are listed in the Picture Usage dialog box when you select Utilities ➤ Picture Usage, and can be previewed there.

Paint-type Bitmaps

Bitmapped graphics are composed of a pattern of dots or pixels rather than stored as mathematical formulas. This type of graphic comes from a paint-type program, such as MacPaint. Scanned images are also bitmapped images, and they can usually be saved in MacPaint format, but they can also be stored at higher resolutions than allowed by most paint-type programs. (See "TIFF and RIFF Files," later in this section.)

Figure 6-17 Bitmapped images drawn using MacPaint.

PICT Graphics

PICT graphics are object-oriented graphics that are created by some drafting programs, draw-type programs, and spreadsheet graphics. Programs that produce object-oriented graphics that can be imported in QuarkXPress include MacDraw, MacDraft, Cricket Draw, Cricket Graph, SuperPaint, FreeHand, Canvas, Mac3D, MiniCAD, Pro3D, and scanning applications. Some scanning software will allow you to save files in the PICT format, which creates a bitmap associated with the data. PICT graphics are called object-oriented graphics because the lines and patterns that you see are actually stored as mathematical formulas of the objects that compose the image.

Because object-oriented graphics are defined mathematically, they are smooth, and create crisp line art and precise fill patterns. Object-oriented graphics are considered better quality images for line art, therefore, than bitmapped graphics.

Figure 6-18 A PICT graphic created in MacDraw.

EPS Graphics

Encapsulated PostScript files are PostScript files that have a screen preview, so they can be viewed. EPS files can be created using some drawing programs, such as Adobe Illustrator (Figure 6-19) or Aldus FreeHand. EPS files can also be created using QuarkXPress by selecting the File → Save Page as EPS command.

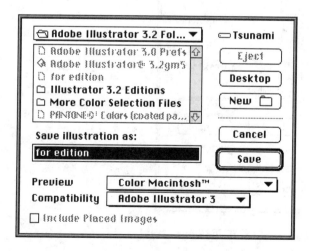

Figure 6-19 The Save As dialog box from Adobe Illustrator—graphics must be saved as Encapsulated PostScript (EPS).

You can use certain programs on the IBM PC or other platforms to create graphics and save them in Encapsulated PostScript format, then telecommunicate that EPS file to the Macintosh to import it in QuarkXPress.

Because EPS images can be quite large, QuarkXPress stores and displays the images in a low-resolution PICT format rather than incorporating them in the document. The EPS file is linked to the document, however; when you print the document, QuarkXPress looks for the original EPS file on the disk in order to print at high resolution. You can select Item ➤ Modify to Suppress Printout of very large graphics to save time in printing drafts.

Save Page as EPS

To save a page as an EPS picture, choose Save Page as EPS from the File menu. In the dialog box (Figure 6–20), enter the page number you want to save and a name for the picture. You can save the page as a color or black-and-white EPS picture, and you can specify the scale of the picture from 10 percent to 100 percent. You can also choose to include OPI comments or not. See Chapter 7 for more information on OPI comments.

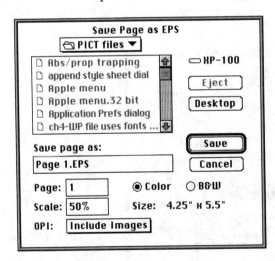

Figure 6-20 Save Page as EPS dialog box.

Figure 6-21 EPS version of a page.

You can also create a PostScript version of the document, so that all of the printing information will be stored as a disk file instead of being sent to the printer.

TIFF and RIFF Files

Tag Image File Format (TIFF) and Raster Image File Format (RIFF) are picture file formats designed for use with scanners and printing programs. They are used to store information about continuous-tone images. When these images are printed on a high-resolution typesetter, such as a Linotronic 330, most of the levels of gray found in the original image will appear on the page printed through QuarkXPress. When printed on a relatively low-resolution printer, such as a LaserWriter, some of the levels of gray stored in the TIFF or RIFF format will be compressed out (not printed). True grayscale viewing is available on Macintosh II models with color or grayscale monitors.

Because TIFF and RIFF images are usually stored at 300 dpi resolution or higher, image files can be quite large—often larger than 800K. Rather than incorporating such large images in the document, QuarkXPress stores and displays the images in a low-resolution PICT format. The TIFF or RIFF file is linked to the document, however; when you print the document, QuarkXPress looks for the original scan file on the disk in order to print at high resolution.

For this reason, it is a good idea to store the TIFF or RIFF file in the same folder as your document. If you copy the document to another disk, copy the TIFF or RIFF image too. Without that file, the image will be printed at low resolution, even on high-resolution printers. If QuarkXPress cannot find the TIFF or RIFF file when you print, it prompts you to locate the file.

You can convert a TIFF picture format as you import it by using various keyboard commands:

- Holding the Command key when importing a TIFF grayscale picture converts it to TIFF line art.
- Holding the Option key when importing TIFF line art converts to TIFF grayscale.
- Holding the Command key when importing TIFF color converts it to TIFF grayscale.

Normally, an imported TIFF or RIFF image is displayed at 36 dpi on screen. You can increase the on-screen display resolution to 72 dpi by holding the Shift key as you import the image, or you can choose to display 256 levels of gray by setting that option in the Application Preferences dialog box (Edit ➤ Preferences ➤ Application).

Scanned Images

Graphics can also be created when images are digitized through a scanning device (Figure 6-22). These images can usually be saved in PICT format (usually for line art), in MacPaint format, or in Tag Image File Format (TIFF) for halftones.

Figure 6-22 A scanned image.

Scanning is a good method for capturing grayscale images, such as photographs and watercolor paintings, for placement in a QuarkXPress document.

Importing Graphics

To import graphics, first select one of QuarkXPress' Picture box creation tools (⊠ ⊠ ⊗ ⊘) to create or activate the picture box into which you wish to import the graphic. Next select the Content tool (☞) and select the File ➤ Get Picture to display the Get Picture dialog box (Figure 6-23). Find the name of the graphics file you want to import in the dialog box. Use the scroll bars to scroll through the list names, and click the drive identification to view the graphics files on other disks if you don't see the file you want.

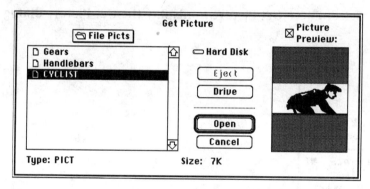

Figure 6-23 The Get Picture dialog box—click once on a file name to preview the size, type, and thumbnail of the graphic you are importing.

When you click once on a graphics file name, the dialog box displays the file format and size. If you check the Picture Preview option in the dialog box, a thumbnail preview of the picture will be displayed in the dialog box when you click once on the file name, as shown in Figure 6-24. Double-click a file name to import it into the active picture box. With Quark XPress 3.1, all picture types, including TIFF and RIFF files, will preview.

Step 1   First create or select the picture box into which you want to import the graphic.

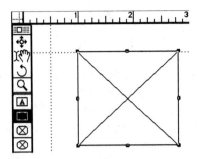

Figure 6-24 Active picture box.

Step 2   Select File → Get Picture to display the Get Picture dialog box.

File	
New...	⌘N
Open...	⌘O
Close	
Save	⌘S
Save as...	
Revert to Saved	
Get Picture...	⌘E
Save Text...	
Save Page as EPS...	
Document Setup...	
Page Setup...	
Print...	⌘P
Quit	⌘Q

Figure 6-25 The Get Picture command in the File menu.

Step 3   Next find the name of the graphics file you want to import in
the dialog box. Use the scroll bars to scroll through the list
names, and click the drive identification to view the graphics
files on other disks if you don't see the file you want.

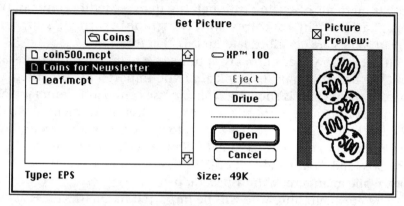

Figure 6-26 The Get Picture dialog box.

Step 4   Once you have found the name of the file you want to
import, click once to view the file format and size, or double-
click to import the graphic.

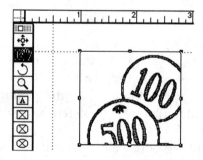

Figure 6-27 An imported graphic.

The entire, unscaled picture that you import is placed in the active picture box, replacing any previous contents of the box. You may need to scale the picture to make it fit the box. You can scale a picture using the techniques described in Chapter 2 (under "Arranging Boxes on the Page"). Other methods of scaling (through the Item ➤ Modify command), cropping, and editing pictures, and the graphic formats supported by QuarkXPress are described later in this chapter.

 If the large *X* that normally appears in a blank picture box disappears but the box still appears blank after you import a picture, then a blank part of the picture is showing. You can use command Command-Shift-M to center the image in the picture box, or select the Content tool (with the Picture Mover pointer displayed (☝)) to move the picture around (usually up and left) in the box. Command-Shift-F scales the picture to fit within the box, and Command-Option-Shift-F scales the picture to fit within the box while maintaining the aspect ratio.

The entire graphics file will be imported in QuarkXPress as a single graphic object, regardless of how large the graphic or how many different objects were in the original source file. If the graphic includes text, QuarkXPress retains the font settings made in the graphics program. You cannot change individual parts of the graphic, such as the line styles or the colors of individual elements.

Using the Subscribe to Command

If you are running QuarkXPress under Apple's System 7, you can Subscribe to files created in programs that offer System 7's publisher feature. The Subscribe to and Subscriber Options commands on the Edit menu are available only if you have published an edition with another application. If you are using System 7 and are unfamiliar with these terms, please refer to Apple's System 7 documentation.

To use the Subscribe to command, first draw a picture box with one of QuarkXPress' picture box tools. Select the Edit ➤ Subscribe to command. The Subscribe to dialog box appears. Find the file you want to Subscribe to and and click the Subscribe button.

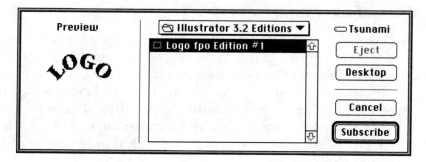

Figure 6-28 The Subscribe to dialog box.

QuarkXPress can Subscribe to files only in the PICT format. Once you have subscribed to a graphic, you can select the Edit → Subscriber Options command. Use this command to set the graphic to be updated automatically every time the edition is changed, or to prompt you to update the edition manually.

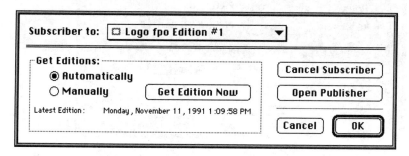

Figure 6-29 The Subscriber Options dialog box.

Manipulating Imported Graphics

Up to this point, most of the commands described affect items created in QuarkXPress—lines and boxes—but they do not change the appearance of pictures that have been imported into QuarkXPress. The next headings describe commands and features that can be used to change the position and appearance of imported graphics within the picture box.

Scaling Imported Graphics

In Chapter 2 you learned how to move, scale, or rotate a box, without affecting the content of the box. Here you learn how to move, scale, or rotate the *content* of a box—an imported picture. Most of these procedures can be accomplished using the Content tool or keyboard commands described under the next headings, but they also can be accomplished by making entries in the Measurements palette or through the Picture Box Specifications dialog box that is displayed by the Item ➤ Modify command.

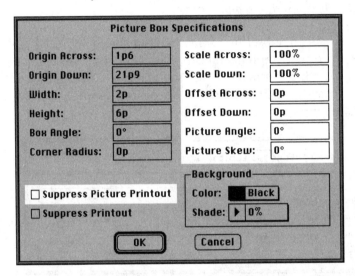

Figure 6-30 Entries that affect the content of a box in the Picture Box Specifications dialog box.

As you learned in Chapter 2, you can resize a box without affecting the content and apply these special keyboard shortcuts:

- Shift-click and drag to constrain boxes to square shapes (for text or rectangular graphics boxes) or circles (for oval graphics boxes).
- Option-Shift-click and drag to force the box to maintain its same aspect ratio.

You can also scale the picture box and the picture inside it using the following keyboard/mouse combinations:

- ⌘-Shift-click and drag to constrain boxes to square shapes (for text or rectangular graphics boxes) or circles (for oval graphics boxes) and scale the picture.

- ⌘-Option-Shift-click and drag to force the box to maintain the same aspect ratio for the box and scale the picture.

- ⌘-click and drag to resize box and the picture within it without maintaining proportions.

Four more keyboard commands scale the picture without scaling the box:

- ⌘-Shift-F scales the picture to fit within the box without changing the box size; this may change the aspect ratio of the picture.

- ⌘-Option-Shift-F scales the picture to fit within the box without changing the box size while maintaining the aspect ratio.

- ⌘-Option-Shift-< scales the picture down by 5 percent.

- ⌘-Option-Shift-> scales the picture up by 5 percent.

You can also select Item ➤ Modify to display the Picture Box Specifications dialog box and scale a picture numerically by entering percentage values in the **Scale Across** and **Scale Down** fields, or by entering percentage values in the **X percent** and **Y percent** fields of the Measurements palette. If you have previously scaled the picture, the amount by which the picture has been scaled will show in these areas. You can enter values from 10 percent up to 1000 percent. Unless the values in the two fields are equal, the picture will be distorted.

Moving a Picture Within a Box

The simplest way to move an imported picture within a picture box (without moving the box itself) is first to select the Content Tool (☞). When you position the pointer over an imported picture, the pointer changes to a hand (☜) . Hold down the mouse button and drag the hand to move the picture within the box. ⌘-Shift-M centers a picture in a box.

As described in Chapter 2, you can also select Item ➤ Modify to display the Picture Box Specifications dialog box and specify the distance from the edge of the box by which the picture will be Offset Across and Offset Down from the left and top edges of the box. You can also move a picture by entering values in the ↕ and ↔ fields of the Measurements palette. These fields appear in the palette only when the Content Tool (☞) is active. You can also move a picture by pressing the arrow keys when the Content Tool is selected. Enter negative values to offset the picture to the left or upward from the top left corner of the box.

Rotating a Picture Within a Box

You can rotate a picture box using the Rotation tool, but to rotate the picture within the box at a different angle you must select the Item ➤ Modify command or the Measurements palette. You can rotate a picture numerically without rotating the picture box that contains it by entering an angle value (from –360 to 360 degrees) in the Picture Rotate field, or you can enter an angle value in the second ∠ field of the Measurements palette. (The first ↻ field is used to rotate the picture box.) If you have previously rotated the picture, the amount by which the picture has been rotated will show in these areas.

In entering angles of rotation in either the Picture Box Specifications dialog box or the Measurements palette, a positive value indicates a counterclockwise rotation, a negative value rotates the picture clockwise.

Skewing a Picture Within a Box

Skewing a picture within a box changes the angle of its vertical axis. Skew a picture by entering degree values (from 0 to 75) in the ⃟ field of the Measurements palette. In entering skew angles, a positive value skews the top of the picture toward the right, a negative value skews the top of the picture toward the left.

You can also select Item ➤ Modify to display the Picture Box Specifications dialog box and skew a picture numerically by entering percentage value in the Picture Skew field. If you have previously skewed the picture, the amount by which the picture has been skewed will show in this dialog box.

Applying Color and Contrast to Pictures

Color and shade can be applied to picture box frames and backgrounds as described in Chapter 2. But you can also apply color to certain kinds of pictures. The commands listed under the Style menu change depending on what type of picture is active when you view the menu. When a picture box that contains an imported black-and-white TIFF, RIFF, or bitmap (including PICT bitmaps) picture is active and the Content tool (☞) is active, the Style menu (Figure 6-31) shows commands that let you adjust a picture's color and shade (separate from the *picture box's* background color and shade), as well as contrast and line screen (for grayscale images or halftones). The Style menu commands cannot be applied to object-oriented PICT or EPS format pictures. You can also apply color to pictures using the Colors palette.

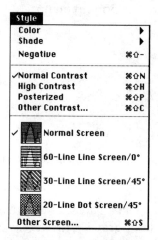

Figure 6-31 Style Menu when a picture is active.

To apply a color, first select the picture box that contains the image, then choose a color from the Color submenu (Figure 6-32) under the Style menu. This list includes the QuarkXPress default colors plus any that you have added using the Edit → Colors command.

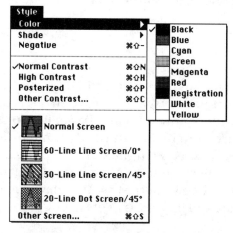

Figure 6-32 The Color submenu.

To apply a shade, first select the picture box that contains the image, then choose a shade from the Shade submenu under the Style menu. The submenu lists shades in 10 percent increments, or you can enter any shade by choosing Other and entering a value in the Shade dialog box.

To apply color to a picture using the Colors palette (Figure 6-33), click on the icon for the picture box content and click on a color from the list. You can input a shade value or choose from the pop-up menu.

Figure 6-33 You can apply color to certain types of pictures using the Colors palette.

The color and shade that you apply will affect all areas of the image that would otherwise print as black or a shade of gray—white areas are not affected. If you specified a Color and Shade for the box background using the Item ➤ Modify command or the Colors palette (described in Chapter 2), then the box background will appear in the white areas of the bitmap or TIFF or RIFF image. Background color does not show through color TIFF images.

As mentioned earlier, you cannot use Style menu commands to change the colors or shades of an imported color image or of object-oriented PICT or EPS formats.

Contrast

Contrast is a term used to describe the relationship between the light and dark areas of an imported grayscale picture in TIFF or RIFF format—color or black and white. Contrast cannot be applied to line art. Normal contrast is the picture's original contrast when imported into QuarkXPress (the contrast that was set up in the scanning process or in a photo retouching application). High-contrast settings make the light areas lighter and the dark areas darker. Low-contrast settings have the reverse effect, making light areas darker and dark areas lighter.

Applying Predefined Contrast Settings

In QuarkXPress you can select commands under the Style menu to choose from three predefined contrast settings (Figure 6-34) or to set your own custom contrast. Choose Style ➤ High Contrast (⌘-Shift-H) to convert the picture to two shades of gray: solid black and white. This setting in effect converts a grayscale image to line art. Choose Style ➤ Posterized

(⌘-Shift-P) to convert the picture to six levels of gray (including black and white as two of the gray levels). Choose Style ➤ Other Contrast (⌘-Shift-C) to display the Picture Contrast Specifications dialog box and set custom contrast, as described below.

The contrast setting affects only the way QuarkXPress displays and prints the image, not the way the image is stored or saved. You can change contrast settings or convert to normal contrast at any time. Choose Style ➤ Normal Contrast (⌘-Shift-N) to reset the picture to the original contrast at which it was imported.

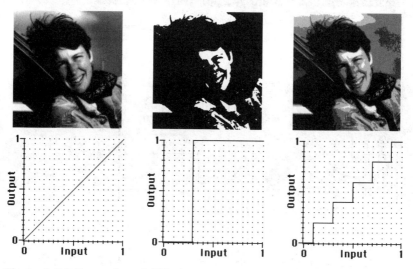

Figure 6-34 Examples of different contrast settings and their curves for one image.

1. *Normal contrast shows as a 45°-line in the Picture Contrast Specifications dialog box.*
2. *High contrast shows as a two-stepped line in the Picture Contrast Specifications dialog box. Shades of less than 30 percent black display and print as white (0 percent black), and shades greater than 30 percent black display and print as 100 percent black.*
3. *Posterized contrast shows as a six-stepped line in the Picture Contrast Specifications dialog box.*

Creating Negative Images

Choose Style ➤ Negative (⌘-Shift-hyphen) to create a negative of the image based on the *Normal curve* settings. This selection reverses any changes made to the contrast curves (described under the next sections) and is the same as checking the Negative field in the Contrast dialog box.

Applying Custom Contrast

Choose Style → Other Contrast (⌘-Shift-C) to display the Picture Contrast Specifications dialog box (Figure 6-35). The chart in this dialog box maps the darkness percentages of the input (the original image as imported) to darkness upon output (on the screen and when printed). The best way to see how the chart works is to study how it changes under the three predefined contrast settings.

The Picture Contrast Specifications dialog box provides nine tools on the left of the box to help you adjust the contrast.

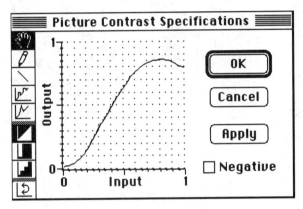

Figure 6-35 The Picture Contrast Specifications dialog box.

- Click on the **Hand** tool (☝) and use the hand to drag the entire curve around on the chart. Hold down the Shift key to constrain the movement to horizontal or vertical.

- Click on the **Pencil** tool (𝒫) and click anywhere on the chart to create spikes or drag any point on the chart to reshape the curve in any path.

- Click on the **Line** tool (╲) and drag any point on the chart to reshape the curve in straight lines. Hold down the Shift key to constrain the lines to 45° angles: 0°, 45°, or 90°.

- Click on the **Posterizer** tool (🖉) to create handles *in between* the 10 percent incremental marks on the curve. Click on the **Spike** tool (🖊) to create handles *on* the 10 percent incremental marks on the curve. You can then move each handle in any direction.

- Click on the **Normal Contrast** tool (◤) to set the picture back to its original contrast. This is the same as choosing Style → Normal Contrast.

- Click on the **High Contrast** tool (▆) to set the picture to high contrast. This is the same as choosing Style ➤ High Contrast.

- Click on the **Posterized Contrast** tool (▙) to set the picture to posterized contrast. This is the same as choosing Style ➤ Posterized.

- Click on the **Inversion** tool (🔁) to rotate the curve around an imaginary line that is parallel to the X-axis and bisects the curve, thereby creating a negative of the image by changing the *current curve* settings.

- Check the **Negative** box to create a negative of the image based on the *Normal curve* settings. This is the same as choosing Style ➤ Negative.

Normally, the changes you make in the dialog box will not be reflected on the page display until you click Apply or use the keyboard shortcut ⌘-A (to view the effects and still have a chance to change or cancel them) or OK (to apply the changes). If you hold the Option key and click Apply or use the keyboard shortcut ⌘-Option-A, you can see the effects of the changes as you make them, but this might be a slow process if the image is very large. Click ⌘-Z while the dialog box is open to reverse the most recent change.

Adjusting Contrast for Color Images

When you choose Style ➤ Other Contrast with a color TIFF or RIFF image active, the Picture Contrast Specifications dialog box changes to let you adjust contrast for each component of the color image (Figure 6-36). The component list changes depending on which color model you choose: HSB (Hue-Saturation-Brightness), RGB (Red-Green-Blue), CMY (Cyan-Magenta-Yellow), or CMYK (Cyan-Magenta-Yellow-Black).

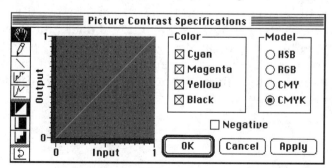

Figure 6-36 The Picture Contrast Specifications dialog box when a color image is active and CMYK is active.

You can select each model, and the dialog box will let you adjust the curves for each of the applicable components. You can click more than one component at a time to adjust several at once. All other tools and buttons in the dialog box operate as described earlier.

Adjusting color is easy to do in QuarkXPress, but adjusting color effectively requires considerable skill and experience—or extensive trial and error. See Chapter 13 for details on working with color separations.

Defining Halftone Screens

In QuarkXPress you can import *line art* that is composed of solid black-and-white areas or *grayscale* images that are continuous-tone images (like photographs) incorporating shades of gray as well as black and white. In traditional publishing, a photograph that has been prepared for printing is called a *halftone* rather than a grayscale image. With traditional methods, a halftone is created by photographing the artwork through a *screen*. The term "screening" has therefore carried over to the electronic process applied through QuarkXPress. The fineness of a screen is defined in terms of lines per inch (lpi) and is as important as setting resolution when printing a high-resolution continuous tone image.

The halftone settings in QuarkXPress let you specify the line screen (lines per inch), screen angle, and dot shape that will define the pattern of dots in the halftone that you print of grayscale TIFF and RIFF images.

Applying Predefined Screen Settings

The Style menu offers four predefined settings, or you can set your own custom screen angle and line frequency. Choose 60-Line Line Screen/0° (Figure 6–37), 30-Line Line Screen/45° (Figure 6–38), or 20-Line Dot Screen/45° (Figure 6–39) to print the active image at one of the three most common lines per inch and angle settings. Choose Style ➤ Other Screen (⌘-Shift-S) to display the Picture Screening Specifications dialog box (Figure 6-40) and set custom line frequency and angle, as described under the next heading.

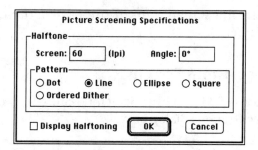

Figure 6-37 60-Line Line Screen/0°. "Screen" lines are spaced 60 lines per inch, 0° (horizontal).

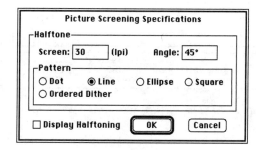

Figure 6-38 30-Line Line Screen/45°. "Screen" lines are spaced 30 lines per inch, at 45° angle.

Figure 6-39 20-Line Dot Screen/45°. "Screen" dots are spaced 20 lines per inch, at 45° angle.

The halftone screen setting affects only the way QuarkXPress prints the image, not the way the image is displayed, stored, or saved. You can change screen settings or convert to normal screen at any time. Choose Style ➤ Normal Screen to reset the picture to the normal setting of a 45° angle, with the line frequency determined by the value entered in the

Halftone Screen field in the Page Setup dialog box (as described in Chapter 7).

Applying Custom Screens

Choose Style ➤ Other Screen (⌘-Shift-S) to display the Picture Screening Specifications dialog box.

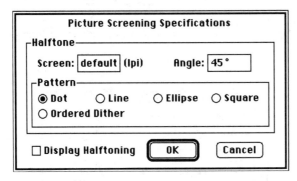

Figure 6-40 The Picture Screening Specifications dialog box.

Screen

You can enter any value from 15 to 400 lines per inch in the Screen field. If you leave the Screen field blank, the default frequency defined in the Halftone Screen field in the Page Setup dialog box will be used in printing. The normal default—60 lpi—is the most common setting for printing halftone pictures in newspapers. A 300 dpi printer cannot accurately reproduce screens finer than 75 lpi. Higher line frequencies will not display accurately on most monitors and will work best when printed on high-resolution printers and on glossy paper stocks or film.

Divide twice the number of *lines per inch* in the screen into the *dots per inch* resolution of the output device to get an idea of how many dots *wide* each line will be. On a 300 dpi printer, for example, a 60-line line screen will print with only five dots per black line/white line pair, leaving only two to three dots for the line width. Finer screens would be imperceptible to the human eye when printed on a 300 dpi printer. When printed at 1270 dpi, however, the same screen will print with up to 10 dots per line; you could specify up to a 130-line line screen and still get good results at 1270 dpi. (All of the images in preceding figures were printed at 1270 dpi on a Linotronic typesetter.)

Screen Angle

You can enter any angle between 0 and 360 in the Angle field, but the most common settings are in 15° increments. In entering angles of rotation, a positive value indicates a counterclockwise rotation, a negative value is measured clockwise.

Screen Pattern

Select Pattern to choose from five different halftone screens: Dot, Line, Ellipse, Square (Figure 6-41), or Ordered Dither. The Ordered Dithered screen pattern is designed for printing grayscale images on a low-resolution laser printer, such as a LaserWriter, and should not be used when your output will be reproduced using offset lithography.

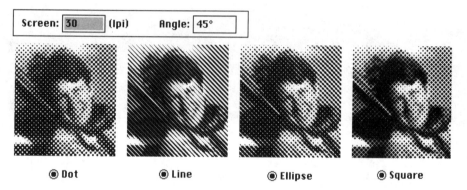

Figure 6-41 Examples of different halftone screen patterns.

Click Display Halftoning to preview the effects of the settings you have chosen. Once you have previewed the image, it is a good idea to turn this option off, since it slows down the screen display. Note that you can specify line frequencies and angles for active imported images only—shaded lines, box frames, and box backgrounds specified in QuarkXPress are always printed using the Halftone Screen field in the Page Setup dialog box.

Summary

Now that you know the alternatives available for adding graphics to a page, you can decide whether to use QuarkXPress or another program to create various graphics, and which other applications to use. Part II offers tips on advanced graphic techniques. Chapter 7 describes printing procedures.

7 Printing

The ultimate goal of the production process with QuarkXPress is to print the document on a high-resolution printer. Sometimes this output becomes the distribution copy or copies. More often this output will become the "camera-ready pages" from which the document is reproduced using xerographic or offset printing equipment. In this chapter you learn about how to to select the printer for a document (if you are using more than one printer) and how to print a document.

You also learn about the basic techniques involved in creating and editing colors and how to apply color to the elements on a page; Chapter 13 contains more detailed information on printing spot color and process color separations. Finally, you learn how to handle special problems related to printing, including font limitations, linking large pictures, printing oversize pages, and printing a document from another system (other than the one on which it was created) or through a service bureau.

Differences Between Printers

Publications that have been created using QuarkXPress can be printed on certain dot-matrix printers, laser printers, and typesetters that are supported by the Apple Macintosh environment, including (among others):

- Apple LaserWriter series and other PostScript laser printers
- PostScript imagesetters, such as those manufactured by Linotype, Agfa, and Varityper
- PostScript color printers

It's a good idea to become familiar with the capabilities of your particular printer before designing pages for QuarkXPress. You will generally want to design with the capabilities and limitations of your final printer in mind.

Resolution

One of the key differences between printers is the resolution at which they print. Resolution is a measure of the density in which text and graphics are printed, and it is usually expressed in dots per inch (dpi). Laser printers such as the LaserWriter print at 300 dpi. But laser printers produce higher resolutions (400 dpi and 600 dpi). While this is considered high resolution compared to dot matrix printers, which print at 120 dots per inch, it is low resolution compared to typesetting equipment, or imagesetters, that print at 1,200, 2,400, or 3,600 dpi (Figure 7-1). Some printers have a range of settings for resolution.

Printer	Resolution Settings—dpi
ImageWriter	72
ImageWriter II	120
LaserWriter	300
Linotronic 100	1270, 900, or 600
Linotronic 300	2540, 1270, or 600

Figure 7-1 Some QuarkXPress-compatible printers and their resolutions.

The higher the resolution, the smoother the appearance of the edges of text and graphics; the lower the resolution, the greater the jaggedness of the edges. The average reader may not notice jaggedness in text printed at 300 dpi, but professional designers, typesetters, and lithographers can readily see the difference between low (300 dpi) and high (1,200 dpi or more) resolution.

Some of the adjustments you can make through QuarkXPress commands have no discernible effect when printed on a low-resolution printer. For example, leading can be adjusted in .001 point increments, but low-resolution printers do not print leading adjustments in such fine

5.08

Packaging   Colour coding

When similar products need to be both related and differentiated at the same time, follow these guidelines:

• use the same layout on the main panel of all packages to help relate them

• use different colours on each package to help differentiate them.

As shown in the examples, the colour coding may appear at the bottom of the format. Or, not shown, the different colours may appear in the graphic band with the signature reversed in white or overprinted in black.

For more information, see the following pages in the Basic standards section:

Signatures	2.03
Colour in signatures reverse use	2.18
Graphic bands	2.21
Supporting typography	2.23
Alignment	2.27

Identity standards manual for CSR Limited designed by Landor Associates. Original Size 21 cm x 29½ cm. See Chapter 16.

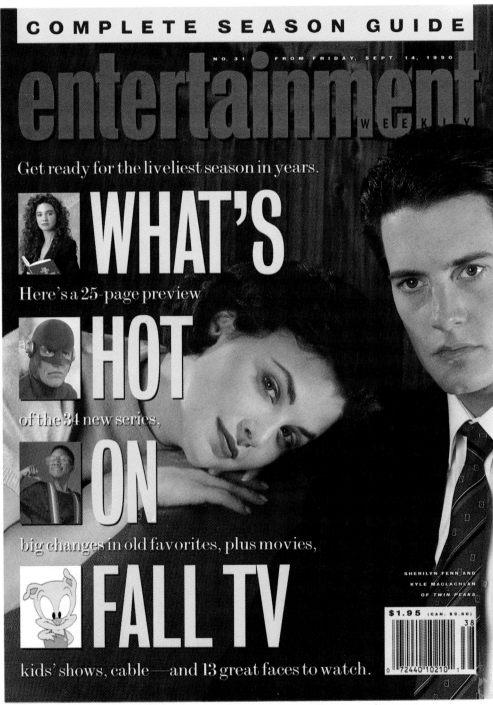

Cover (above) and facing-page spread (facing page) from Entertainment Weekly. All photos were scanned and separated through Visionary on a Scitex system. Original size of cover 8" x 10¾"; orignial size of spread 16" x 10¾". See Chapter 15.

NEWS & NOTES

BETWEEN IRAQ AND A HARD PLACE

RECENT EVENTS IN THE PERSIAN GULF have prompted one prime-time TV show with a lot of a problem: What should *CBS* comedy series *Bagdad Cafe* do about its newly touchy name? "We discussed the situation," co-executive producer Paul Mundani told ENTERTAINMENT WEEKLY. "But as we decided to keep the title the same, that show has nothing to do with the Bagdad in Iraq. [It takes place in the] California desert.] The matter's just an understandable conclusion. The decision could still change. Says Mundani: "If the war escalates, and there's massive loss of life, then we'll have to discuss it."

Gritty Woman

FOR MOVIE GOERS who didn't buy Julia Roberts as Ivory Soap call girl routine, get ready for *Whore*. British filmmaker Ken Russell singlehandedly version of life as a prostitution in L.A.'s mean streets. Based on a play by former London cabdriver David Hines, the story—about a hooker fleeing from her bloodthirsty pimp—has been Americanized to fit the new Sunset Boulevard setting. **Theresa Russell** above, last seen as a streetwalking undercover cop in Sandra Locke's *Impulse*, has the role. With sex she doesn't rule off into the sunset in a white limo.

COMING ATTRACTIONS

Vega-ly Familiar

SUZANNE VEGA has a hit single, but not exactly in the way she or her record company planned. Her current album, *Days of Open Hand*, is no higher than No. 140 on the Billboard album chart. But in England, Vega has a top 5 pop hit: a technoremix of the stream-of-conscience a cappella song *Tom's Diner* from her previous effort, 1987's *Solitude Standing*. The revised single, on which a sparsely electronic instrumental track was added

SINEAD'S CHILE RECEPTION

Sinead O'Connor above, **Sting, Jackson Browne, Ruben Blades,** and **Wynton Marsalis** have been confirmed for two Chilean benefit concerts for Amnesty International at the National Stadium in Santiago, Chile, on Oct. 12 and 13. The country was passed over on Amnesty's 1988 Human Rights Now! tour, but the fall of dictator Augusto Pinochet means that the "For Chile — An Embrace of Hope" concerts can now be held there — in the same stadium where dissenters of the Pinochet regime were once imprisoned and tortured. For those who will go to any lengths to hear "Fortunate" or "Running on Empty," tickets will be available soon in the New York and Washington offices of Amnesty International. Promoters expect 75,000 people to attend the concerts.

Diane on the Beach

Diane Keaton — landing on *China Beach* the actress-turned-auteur will soon be directing an episode of ABC's Vietnam series according to the show's producer, Carol Flint. It's called "Fever" and it'll focus on Dana Delany's first days back in Kansas after the war, says Flint. "I'm not sure why she decided to do it — I guess she just likes the show." Keaton has done TV before — last January she directed a CBS Schoolbreak Special called *The Girl with the Crazy Brother* — but as a director she's best known for her 1987 after-life documentary *Heaven*. Expect to see her *China Beach* episode sometime in late October.

ROLE CALL

Japanese Turn

After **Richard Gere** is preparing for his first role since playing the corporate raider with a heart of gold in *Pretty Woman*, but don't expect another Hollywood blockbuster. Gere is learning his lines for *kiiru*, Kurosawa's 26th film. *Rhapsody in August* he will be learning them in Japanese. Gere plays the half Japanese son of an aging pineapple grower in the contemporary drama scheduled for release next year. While on location near Tokyo, the American actor attended a news conference where he discovered just how popular his director is. "I expected there to be

Toy packaging from Mattel, Inc., designed by Luis Solorzano. Original size 6" x 8⅝". See Chapter 16.

MacWEEK

09.25.90 Vol. 4 No. 32 — W O R K S T A T I O N   N E W S

GA 100

The top 100 graphic arts & communication sites in North America

See Page 41

Jobs makes his NeXT move

'040 models offer color, lower cost

NeXT's lower-cost, 68040-based machines may attract corporate customers looking for workstation power with a Jobsian flair.

By Daniel Farber

San Francisco — Steve Jobs took center stage last week to unveil a series of new NeXT machines that he said would "exceed customer expectations," and that analysts said would prevent the company from falling into obscurity.

The NeXT founder and CEO told the crowd of 2,000 at the rollout here that the new machines address customer complaints about the original NeXT cube. Despite the excitement that model generated when it was unveiled in October 1988, many potential buyers found it too slow, too expensive, lacking color and bereft of applications.

The models introduced last week include two new compact, lower-cost NeXTstations and two cubes.

See NeXT, Page 8

Denise Caruso interviews Steve Jobs. See BusinessWatch, Page 28.

Networking still sore subject

Users seek stronger Apple commitment

By Margie Wylie

Cupertino, Calif. — Jim Groff is in the hot seat. Groff, who earlier this month became Apple's director of product marketing and public relations for networking and communications, must answer lots of questions.

What is Apple doing about connections to non-Apple networks? Where are all the announced products that will give the Mac the support that companies with large and complex networks need? And how will AppleShare fit into the much-delayed System 7.0?

Perhaps the biggest challenge facing Groff, who is helping to fill the months-old vacuum left by former Networking Vice President Don Casey, may be convincing users, integrators and developers that Apple has not abandoned the cross-platform commitments it made more than a year ago.

See Networking, Page 8

With the uncertain state of Mac networking, Jim Groff, Apple's new director of marketing for networking, has his work cut out for him.

Rivals agree on DTP link

SERIF format to allow exchange across apps, platforms

By Carolyn Said

San Jose, Calif. — A broad-based coalition of computer companies next week will announce a new document interexchange standard that allows for exchange of page-layout files between programs and platforms.

To be announced and demonstrated at the Seybold Computer Publishing Conference & Exposition here, the standard, called SERIF (Standard Entity Rendering Interchange Format), defines the exchange of page geometry within a frame-based architecture.

It will let users create a desktop publishing document in one application and open and edit it in another. For example, a user could rough out a document with Aldus PageMaker on the IBM PC and paginate and polish it in QuarkXPress on the Mac.

"This would mean interoperability across the spectrum," said Craig Cline, associate editor of Seybold Reports on Desktop Publishing in Malibu, Calif. "Most people work in mixed environments. There's been a strong desire among users to exchange geometry between

See Seybold, Page 9

It's official: System 7.0 ship slips to '91

By Raines Cohen

Cupertino, Calif. — Apple last week admitted what many in the Mac market already knew: System 7.0 will not hit the streets until next year (see MacWEEK, Sept. 18).

Announcing that end users will have to wait until sometime "in the first half of calendar 1991" for the long-awaited new release of the Mac operating system, Apple said the latest delay was necessary to meet the company's "exacting quality standards."

"Apple's internal standards for software testing are extremely rigorous," said Roger Heinen, vice president of software engineering, in a prepared statement. "With the additional feedback from our developers, we are confident that System 7.0 will shatter traditional notions of what personal computers can do."

See System 7.0, Page 8

System 7: Project management, Cupertino style

Spring '89	Summer '89	Fall '89	Winter '89	Spring '90	Summer '90	Fall '90	Winter '90	Spring '91	Summer '91

May '89: "While it's still too early ... to announce a customer availability plan or introduction date, we will begin seeding developers with code in the fall."

Dec. '89: "We anticipate shipping it to customers in the summer 1990 time frame."

May '90: "Our goal is to ship to end users by the end of the year or bust."

Sept. '90: "[We] have revised estimates for customer shipments of System 7.0 ... to the first half of calendar 1991."

—Roger Heinen, Apple VP of software

Apple, Claris split HyperCard 2.0; bundled version to lack scripting

By Connie Guglielmo

Cupertino, Calif. — Two is an appropriate number to describe the new version of HyperCard, which Apple last week moved to its Claris subsidiary.

Two versions of HyperCard 2.0 will be made available in November. Claris Corp. said it will distribute, market and support "a complete HyperCard 2.0 authoring system" under its label. The official release now is due in November, three months behind schedule.

Meanwhile, Apple said it will bundle free with each Macintosh a version of HyperCard 2.0 that will run existing HyperCard stacks and new HyperCard 2.0 stacks.

The bundled version, however, won't give users access to the scripting features in HyperCard's user Level 5, which means users won't be able to reprogram stacks, according to a Claris spokeswoman.

The audience for the authoring version will be commercial and corporate in-house programmers and multimedia developers,

See HyperCard, Page 9

NEWSPAPER SECOND CLASS

Front page from MacWeek, Coastal Associates Publishing, L.P.
Original size 10¾" x 13½". See Chapter 15.

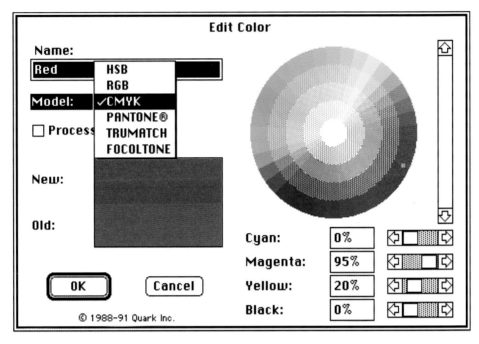

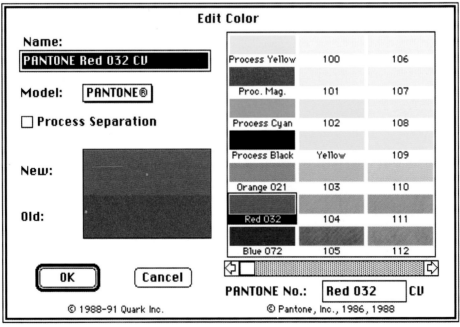

Edit Color dialog box with CMYK (top) and PANTONE (bottom) selected. See Chapter 13.

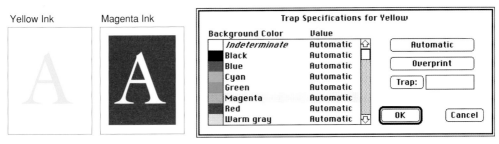

Trapping for Yellow in regards to Magenta specified as Automatic.

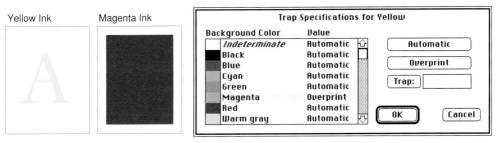

Trapping for Yellow in regards to Magenta specified as Overprint.

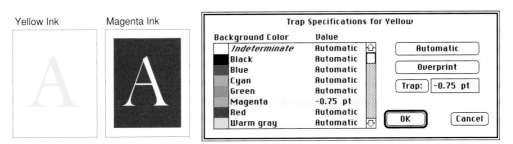

Trapping for Yellow in regards to Magenta specified to "choke" .75 pt.

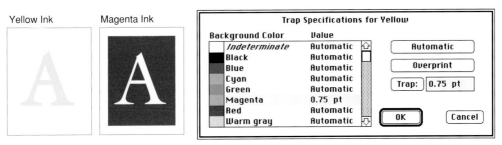

Trapping for Yellow in regards to Magenta specified to "spread" .75 pt. See Chapter 13.

JAPAN'S TRADITION COMES WEST

KIMONO WEST

DAVID SMITH / SAUSALITO, CA

JUST AS WAS ANTICIPATED BY VERY PROMINENT CLOTHING DESIGNERS SEVERAL MONTHS AGO, JAPAN'S TRADITIONAL ATTIRE IS COMING WEST WITH SOME VERY UNIQUE TEXTURES AND PATTERN

Lately Japan has been the forerunner in high technology. Here in the United States we are being constantly bombarded by so many Japanese techno-devices we fail to remember the tradition of such a country.

Some of the new Japanese devices now include Super Ultrasonic Washing Machines, Video Still Camera (film being replaced by a tiny 2.5-inch floppy disk) Ultrathin Wall-Mounted Television Sets, Vegetable Factories, and Moon Houses for habitation of people living on the moon.

This is a small list of a very innovative culture, but many people in Japan as well as in the United States and other countries around the World find this rapid leap into the future somewhat hard to handle.

This explains the most recent trend in the clothing design industry looking back At traditional images for modern day wear. Designers such as Yves St. Laurent and even Calvin Klein have introduced the Japanese Kimono in some of their new clothing lines for fall fashion.

There are Kimonos made of simple cotton to wear casually around the house, some silk designs that could be worn by both men and women, and a very interesting blend of cottons and silks to make a very elegant looking piece.

Some are long, some are short, worn as you would wear a short Jacket. Some of the most stylized Kimonos can be found in many small boutiques from San Francisco, Los Angeles, to New York. Los Angeles, especially has found a new craze to follow, for kimono-clad star-

Kimono West page layout designed by TechArt, San Francisco; illustration by David Smith, Sausalito, California. Original size 6⅛" x 10¼". See Introduction and Chapter 1.

increments: the LaserWriter, for example, only can print 1/300th of an inch (0.24 point).

Printer Fonts

Another major difference between printers is the number of fonts that are built in to the printer's ROM (read-only memory). You learned in Chapter 5 how to install *screen fonts* through the menus in QuarkXPress, but to print a document, the same fonts must also be available as *printer fonts*. Built-in printer fonts are installed by the manufacturer, and are always available for printing any document. They are always high-resolution fonts and are never jagged when printed out. Ideally, every font would be built in to the printer. Unfortunately, because fonts take up space in the printer's ROM, most printers have few or no built-in fonts.

If the printer font is not built in to the printer itself, then it must be available in the System folder when printing so it can be downloaded to the printer. The number of typefaces you can download at one time is limited by the amount of memory in the printer (as described later in this chapter) unless you are using fonts that are permanently downloaded to a hard disk attached to the printer. (See "Fonts Selection," under "Special Considerations in Printing," later in this chapter.)

Paper Size and Type

Most laser printers use ordinary paper stock; some special paper stocks are also available for these printers, including glossy paper, transparencies, waxable paper, adhesive labels, and so on. High-resolution imagesetters use rolls of photographic paper or clear film. Some color printers require thermo-sensitive papers.

The most common laser printers handle paper in letter or legal sizes. Some feeders let you load smaller sizes of paper, but you can't load paper wider than 8.5 inches. Other printer models accommodate a wider range of sizes, including letter, legal, 11" × 17", A3, A4, A5, B4, and B5. For example, the Linotronic series imagesetters are roll-fed printers that handle up to 12-inch-wide rolls, and you can print pages of any length. The Versatec Thermal Color Printer handles 8.5 × 11" or 11 × 17" paper. Another Versatec color printer handles pages up to 42 inches wide, of any length, and can print files that have been saved in EPS format and rasterized through Adobe's Encapsulated POWERSCRIPT workstation developed by Colossal Graphics, Inc.

All printers leave a margin of white space at the edge of the paper or roll—nothing will print in this area. The page outlines in the QuarkXPress document window represent the actual edges of the paper (if page size is the same as paper size), so you need to be familiar with your printer's margin limitations and make sure that your page designs do not include text or graphics in the nonprinting area at the edges of the page. On a LaserWriter, for example, you should leave at least .5-inch margins all around the page (or or at least .25 inches if you select Larger Print Area through the Print dialog box's Options for laser printers). On a Linotronic with a 12-inch-wide roll, the maximum print width is 11.7 inches. To effectively print bleeds, you need to print to a paper size that is larger than the page size.

Color

An increasing number of color printers and slide recorders are available for electronic publishing. There are electrophotographic, ink-jet, thermal, and thermojet color printers, which offer a range of resolutions (200 dots per inch and up) and color quality. Very often, they are used to print color *comps* (design ideas) or *proofs* (to check the final page layout), but they also offer opportunities for printing short-run color publications, color overhead transparencies, and slides. While most of these printers do not currently have the resolution to effectively output type, significant advances in this area are likely in the near future.

Meanwhile, color printers are impractical for making many color copies for distribution because:

- The color and typographic quality available on most color printers is not as good as offset lithography.
- Some color printers require special paper that cannot be printed on both sides (so you cannot produce two-sided color documents).
- Most color printers are extremely slow, requiring three minutes or more per full color page.

In QuarkXPress, color is most commonly used to produce color separations for printing on an offset press. The basics of creating and applying colors are described later in this chapter; Chapter 13 offers a detailed explanation of issues relating to color separations.

Printing from QuarkXPress

If you have more than one printer hooked up to your system through AppleTalk, you can select the Chooser command under the Apple menu to choose the target printer. Three commands from the File menu directly affect how a document will print: Document Setup, Page Setup, and Print. These commands are described under the next headings.

Choosing the Target Printer

In many cases you will go through the entire production sequence using the same printer for early proofs as for final masters. In fact, many installations have only one printer, or only one type, of printer even if they have more than one.

If your installation has more than one printer hooked up to your workstation through a network, then you can select the Chooser command under the Apple menu to change from one printer to another, either before starting a document or during production. To do this, the driver for each type of printer installed must be in your System folder when you boot the system.

When you select Apple ➤ Chooser, the Chooser dialog box (Figure 7-2) shows icons in the left side of the window that represent printer drivers that are in your System folder (as well as other types of resources installed in your system or network). Click on a printer driver icon to list the printers of that type currently installed on your AppleTalk network and for which the power is turned on.

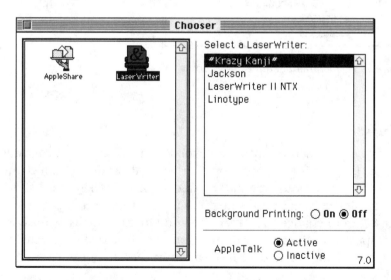

Figure 7-2 The Chooser command dialog box.

Switching a document from a PostScript printer to a non-PostScript printer, or vice versa, may cause unexpected changes to the way in which text prints. (When printing to a PostScript printer, it's best to set the

Character Widths to Fractional in the Typographic Preferences dialog box by selecting Edit → Preferences → Typographic; when printing to a non-PostScript printer, such as an ImageWriter, it's best to set Character Widths to Integral.)

Document Setup

You can select File → Document Setup (Figure 7-3) to change the page size that was originally set up for the document when it was started through File → New (⌘-N). You can change the page size at any time, and all of the elements on each page will keep their same position relative to the top left corner of the page. However, QuarkXPress will not allow you to change the page to a size that would force items currently on the page to move off the page.

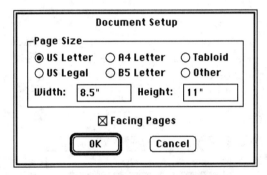

Figure 7-3 Document Setup dialog box.

Page Setup

The File → Page Setup command displays a dialog box that contains information for printing purposes only—these entries do not affect the document itself (page size, orientation, and so on). The keyboard shortcut for displaying the Page Setup dialog box is ⌘-Option-P. You can select File → Page Setup to change the Paper Size and Orientation, as well as other settings specific to the type of printer you have installed or selected through the Chooser command described earlier in this chapter.

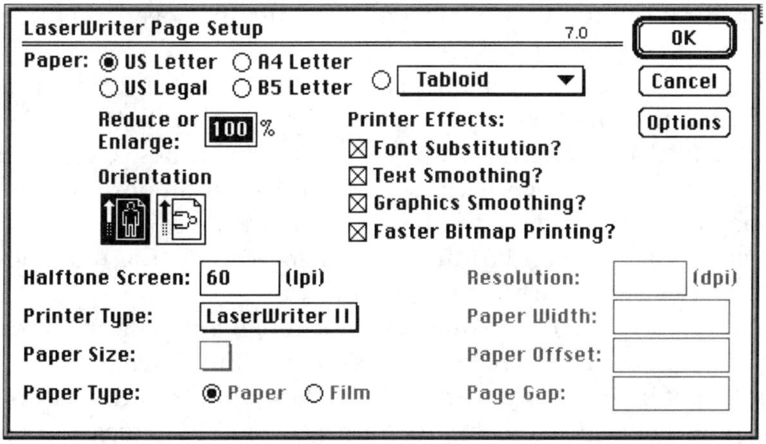

Figure 7-4 Page Setup dialog box for a LaserWriter printer.

The difference between Page Size (specified in the New or Document Setup dialog box) and Paper Size (specified through the Page Setup command) is that *page size* determines the dimensions of the pages shown on the screen display in QuarkXPress, and it is from these dimensions that margins and crop marks are measured. If the *paper size* is larger than the page size, the page will print in the upper left corner of the paper; if the paper size is smaller than the page size, the document must be printed Tiled (as described later under "The Print Command").

Portrait (tall) orientation is the default selection unless the Page Size defined in the New or Page Setup dialog box is wider than 8.5 inches, in which case default orientation changes to Landscape (wide).

Other options in this dialog box are specific to particular printer types.

LaserWriter and Other PostScript Printers

The Page Setup dialog box (Figure 7-4) for a LaserWriter or any PostScript printer lets you **Reduce** or **Enlarge** pages by any percentage from 25% to 400%. The top left corner of each page as shown on the screen remains the top left corner of the printed pages, and all enlarging or reducing is done to the right and down the page. The results of printing enlargements are easily predicted: If you scale a page to be larger than the printer paper, you will lose part of the page image from the right and bottom edges.

The results of printing reductions might not be what you'd expect. Only those elements that actually touch the page on the screen will appear on the printout. Elements that fall completely onto the Pasteboard will not be printed in a reduction. Elements that overlap both the page and the Pasteboard will be printed.

You can specify **Printer Effects**, including Font Substitution, to substitute printer fonts for three Macintosh system fonts that do not have printer font equivalents (New York becomes Times, Geneva becomes Helvetica, and Monaco becomes Courier); Text Smoothing, to smooth bitmap fonts; Graphics Smoothing to smooth the edges of bitmap graphics; and Faster Bitmap Printing, which speeds printing (but some documents will not print with this option).

You can also set a **Halftone Screen** through a pop-up menu or by typing any number between 15 and 400. The halftone screen is the number of lines per inch that will define the pattern of dots in the halftone when you print grayscale TIFF and RIFF images and PICT images. This setting also applies to shades—for backgrounds, frames, and text—created in QuarkXPress. The normal default, 60 lpi, is the most common setting for printing halftone pictures in newspapers. A 300 dpi printer cannot accurately reproduce screens finer than 75 lpi. The setting shown in this dialog box will apply to all such images unless you override this default for specific pictures using commands under the Style menu, as described in Chapter 6.

The **Printer Type** pop-up menu lets you choose from specific models of PostScript printers, corresponding to the Printer Description files that are contained in the program, or in the QuarkXPress folder or the System folder. Possibilities include LaserWriter or LaserWriter II; Linotype Linotronic 100, 300, and 500; Dataproducts LZR2665; TI OmniLaser 2115; Varityper VT-600, 600W, 4200B-P, and 4300P; Agfa Compugraphic P-400PS; Compugraphic 9000PS; Schlumberger 5232; Monotype; Business LaserPrinter; and QMS ColorScript.

The printer selection in the Page Setup dialog box should match the type of printer selected through the Chooser (described earlier in this chapter), or the document might not print as expected. The selection shown here need not match your printer type exactly, but it does affect the Paper Size list and other options in the Page Setup dialog box. If you are printing to a device that is not included in the list, simply choose LaserWriter to print to any PostScript printer.

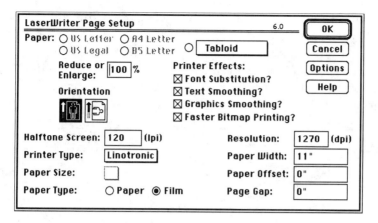

Figure 7-5 Page Setup dialog box for a Linotronic 300.

For some printers, a pop-up menu for **Paper Size** lists the range of paper sizes handled. Possibilities include letter, legal, ledger, and statement, as well as European sizes, such as A3 (11.7" × 16.5"), A4 (8.3" × 11.7"), and A5 (5.8" × 8.3"). The list shown in the pop-up menu corresponds to the sizes supported by the printer selected in the Printer Type field. When this field is available, the list of standard paper sizes selected through radio buttons is dimmed (that is, not available) at the top of the dialog box.

The next options are available only if you have selected a roll-fed photographic typesetter such as the Linotronic as the Printer Type. You can choose Paper or Film, to specify whether you are printing on opaque photographic paper or clear film. You can specify the **Resolution** here in dots per inch. You should enter a resolution that is supported by the specified printer, or you can enter your own preferred resolution between 72 and 5,000. (This setting affects QuarkXPress's smoothing algorithms and does not change the settings on the image-setter itself, but it should *match* the current setting on the imagesetter.)

For printers that can handle rolls of paper in different paper roll widths, you can specify the **Paper Width** here. You can also enter **Paper Offset** to shift the printing area to the right of its normal position (against the left edge of the paper). The **Page Gap** is the amount of space QuarkXPress will leave between pages on the roll-fed typesetter. When **Spreads** is checked in the Print dialog box (described later in this chapter), the value you enter in the Page Gap field is inserted between horizontal spreads, not between the pages in the spread itself.

The buttons at the top right of the Page Setup dialog box let you select a Help screen, or choose other **Options** applicable to PostScript printers.

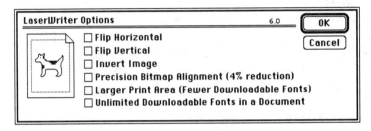

Figure 7-6 The Options dialog box shows various options for PostScript printers.

If you want to output negative film (right-reading, emulsion-side-down page art that reads correctly when the emulsion side of the film is facing down), check Flip Horizontal and Invert Image in this dialog box, and choose Film as the Paper Type in the Page Setup dialog box (described later in this chapter) when printing to a phototypesetter. The list of options may change depending on the LaserWriter driver version installed with your system.

ImageWriter and Other QuickDraw Printers

The Page Setup dialog box for an ImageWriter (Figure 7-7) and other QuickDraw printers lets you specify only one Special Effect: No Gaps Between Pages, which eliminates the unprinted area at the top and bottom of pages. (QuarkXPress presets optimized resolution for ImageWriters, and the Tall Adjusted and 50% Reduction options are not available.) You can also set Color Printing to Off or On for printing with the color ribbon on an ImageWriter II.

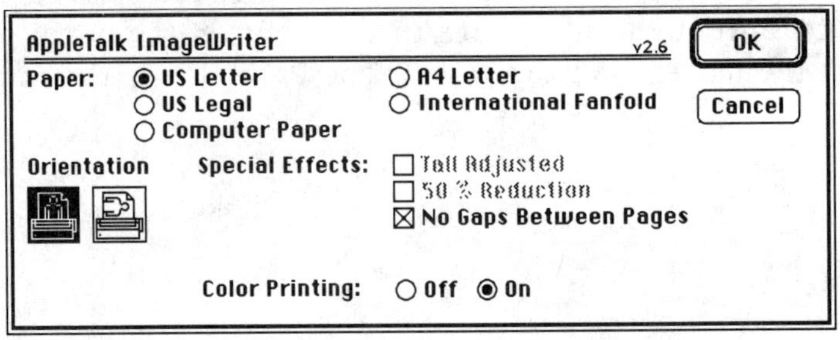

Figure 7-7 Page Setup dialog box for an ImageWriter printer.

The Print Command

Use the File → Print (⌘-P) command throughout the production process to print both preliminary drafts and final camera-ready copies of your document. *It is always a good idea to save your document immediately before using the Print command.*

The File → Print command results in a dialog box (Figure 7-8) through which you specify the number of copies and range of pages to be printed, as well as other special options described below.

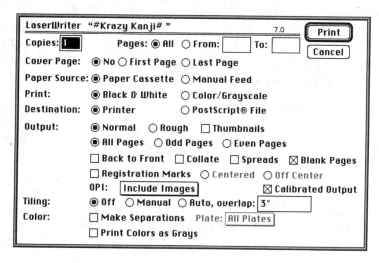

Figure 7-8 The Print command and dialog box.

Copies and Page Range

You can specify the number of Copies that you want to print of each page as well as the range of Pages (either All or starting From and going To the page numbers you specify).

The page range option is useful when you make changes that affect just a few pages, or when you want to print the finished parts of a document that is still in process. You can enter a user-defined section number, or you can enter the "absolute" location within the active document by preceding the number with a plus sign. For example, if the active document includes 10 pages beginning with page 11 and you want to print beginning with page 13, you can print From page 13 or you can print From page +3 (that is, start with the third page in this document). An absolute page sequence number represents a page's sequential location in a document, regardless of the automatic page numbers. In specifying an actual page number, if the document has more than one section, you must include any prefix that has been assigned as part of the page number through the Page → Section command.

Cover Page

If you are printing to a PostScript printer, you can print a Cover Page that shows the name of the document and the date and time printed. This is not counted as one of the numbered document pages. Having a cover page is handy when printing in a networked environment where several people use one printer or when printing more than one document at a time through a print spooler—it can help you separate documents printed from different locations or multiple documents printed from one location. You can specify that No cover page will be printed, or you can print it as the First Page or the Last Page.

Paper Source

The Paper Source option is most often used when printing to laser printers. If you specify the Paper Source as Paper Cassette, then the printer draws sheets of paper from the currently loaded cassette. If you specify Manual Feed, the printer pauses after printing each page and looks for a sheet through the manual feed slot. The manual feed option is used most commonly when you are printing using special stock that does not feed smoothly from the tray.

Color/Grayscale Versus Black and White

You can specify that QuarkXPress Print each page to a color printer using the full range of Color/Grayscale tones, or convert each page to Black and White.

Normal Versus Rough Output

On PostScript printers, Normal output can be changed to Rough (in which text is formatted but pictures are not printed and complex frames are simplified).

Printing Thumbnails

QuarkXPress allows you to print Thumbnails, in which each page is printed in miniature, with several pages on a sheet of paper. You can make Thumbnails larger or smaller, thus allowing more or less thumbnails to print per page, by entering a value in the Reduce or Enlarge field of the Page Setup dialog box. If you are printing to an ImageWriter, you can also choose Best quality or Draft quality (in which only text is printed and text formatting is eliminated).

Printing Only Odd or Even Pages

You can print All pages, or only the Odd Pages or the Even Pages in a document. These options enable you to print two-sided copies directly on the printer—by printing all the odd-numbered pages first, putting them in the paper feed tray, and printing all the even pages. These options are also useful when you are preparing a two-sided manuscript to be reproduced on the type of copier that prompts you to insert all odd or even pages first.

Collating Pages

You can print pages Back to Front (that is, in reverse order), which has the effect of collating a single copy in the correct order when you are printing to a laser printer that feeds printed sheets out faceup. If you are printing multiple copies, you can choose Collate to print one complete set of pages at a time. This means that when you go to pick up the document from the printer's tray, it will already be in the correct order for the readers. This can be handy if you want the first copy to be available for review while the other copies are printing, and it definitely saves you the time it would take to sort the copies manually, but it often requires significantly longer printing time than when multiple copies are not collated. When copies are not collated, the printer processes each page once only and prints multiple copies immediately from the same drum image. For collated copies, the printer must process each page for each copy—in other words, the drum image is reprocessed for each sheet of paper printed.

Printing Spreads

If you click Spreads, facing pages or pages arranged as horizontal spreads print contiguously (if the paper size can accommodate this)—side by side with no break between pages.

Printing Blank Pages

QuarkXPress 3.1 gives you the option of printing the blank pages in a document. A blank page is a page that contains no printable items. Empty, unframed boxes and items to which Suppress Printout (Item → Modify) has been applied are considered nonprinting items. When Blank Pages is unchecked, blank pages in the document are not printed.

Registration Marks

You can select the Registration Marks feature to generate automatically marks traditionally used to indicate where the pages would be cut when trimmed to their final size as well as registration marks for color separations. This option works when you are printing on a paper size at least one inch taller and wider than the page size specified for the document. You can also use this option when you are printing a reduced page size using the Scaling factor described later under this heading.

The registration marks can be Centered between the cut marks on each side of the document or printed Off Center so that the bottom and left registration marks are slightly off center (Figure 7-9). This is useful when you are printing color separations (described in Chapter 13).

Figure 7-9 A page printed with registration marks centered and off center.

Open Prepress Interface (OPI) Comments

This option lets you specify the way in which pictures and OPI comments are output. The Include Images option includes both high-resolution TIFF and EPS files in the output. Omit TIFF files includes comments about TIFF file (location, size, and so on), but not the high-resolution image itself; choose this option if high-resolution images will be substituted for TIFF images on the OPI prepress device. Omit TIFF and EPS includes the OPI comments, but not the high-resolution TIFF or EPS picture.

High-end output devices that have an OPI converter use PostScript files that are downloaded. These comments have an effect only when you print a file to disk as a PostScript file. See "Making a PostScript File Version of a Document" later in this chapter.

Calibrated Output

QuarkXPress' printer files include information that calibrates output to specific printers, including, in some cases, compensation for dot gain. This "intelligence" on the part of QuarkXPress is helpful, but if your page includes graphics created in other programs that do not have special calibration, the same colors from the two programs (QuarkXPress and some other program) may print slightly differently. This can occur especially with programs that create EPS files.

To ensure that QuarkXPress' output will match that from other applications, uncheck this box. The default is that the box is checked.

Printing Tiled Pages

You can select the Tiling option to print large pages in pieces on smaller paper. A common application of the Tiling feature is to print out draft versions of tabloid-size (11" × 17") or larger pages on 8.5" × 11" paper. The tiled papers can be assembled into one piece for reproduction, or they can be used as proof sheets only: You can print the final version of a tabloid page directly to a typesetter's 12-inch wide roll of photosensitive paper without using the Tiling option.

In Tiling, you can select the Auto option and specify by how much you want the images on each tile to overlap (from 0 to 6 inches). Normally, the top left corner of the page becomes the first tile and is positioned at the top left corner of the paper. The right margin of the page might be wider on the paper, depending on the page size, the paper size, and the amount of overlap specified. If you want the image on the left most and right most tiles to be equal sizes, precede the overlap value with a greater-than character (>).

Once you start printing a page with Auto Tiling selected, you cannot interrupt the printing process and restart where you left off. If you stop the printing process, when you restart QuarkXPress, printing will begin again at the top left corner of the page.

You can also select the Manual option and define the limits of each tile piece by moving the 0 on the ruler. For example, under the Manual Tiling option you would first print one "tile" with the zero point at the top left corner of the page, then you would move the zero point to mark the top left corner of the next tile and print again. (Remember from Chapter 2 that you move the zero point by choosing Show Rulers from the View menu, positioning the pointer over the box where the two rulers intersect, and dragging the pointer to the position on the page where you want the zero point to be.) See "Oversize Documents," later in this chapter, for more information about Tiling.

Printing Color Separations

If the pages include **Color**—whether imported as part of color graphics or applied using QuarkXPress commands—you can Make Separations or Print Colors as Grays. If you Print Colors as Grays, each color is printed at a shade of gray. If the color is set to print at a shade of 100%, it will print lighter when this option is selected in order to distinguish it from true blacks. Lighter shades of the same color appear correspondingly lighter on the printout. Otherwise, if you are printing to a black-and-white printer and you are not printing color separations, all colors set at 100% shade appear black on the printout.

If you select Make Separations, QuarkXPress prints each page color plate separately, as specified in the Plates field. This option is described briefly in a discussion of the issues involved in printing color documents, later in this chapter, and in more detail in Chapter 13.

Print Status

The Print Status dialog box displays valuable information about your job as it's printing. To display the Print Status dialog box, hold down the Shift key as you click the Print button in the Print dialog box (File ➔ Print).

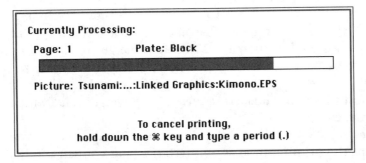

Currently Processing:

Page: 1   Plate: Black

Picture: Tsunami:...:Linked Graphics:Kimono.EPS

To cancel printing,
hold down the ⌘ key and type a period (.)

Figure 7-10 Hold down the Shift key as you click the Print button in the Print dialog box to display the Print Status dialog box.

The Print status dialog box displays the page number that is currently printing, the CMYK or spot color separation plate currently printing (if Make Separations was selected in the Print dialog box), and the path and file name of the picture that is currently printing. If you have selected the option for printing tiled pages, the number of the currently printing tile is displayed.

Printing Master Pages

You can print out the master pages in a document. To print a master page, simply display that page in the document window. All the commands in the Page Setup dialog box and in the Print dialog box are available, except From and To pages.

Making a PostScript File Version of a Document

You can create a PostScript version of a document, so that all of the printing information is stored as a disk file instead of being sent to the printer. This is useful for printing the document from other systems without installing QuarkXPress.

To create a PostScript version of a document or page, including the Laser Prep information, type ⌘-K immediately after clicking OK in the Print dialog box. This makes it possible to print the file from a non-Macintosh computer.

To create a PostScript version of a document or page, *excluding* the Laser Prep information, type ⌘-F immediately after clicking OK in the Print dialog box. This type of PostScript file can be printed from any Macintosh.

To create a PostScript version of a document, select these commands with All pages selected as the page range. To create a PostScript version of a single page, select only one page in the Print dialog box.

Stopping the Printing Process

You can stop the printing process by clicking Cancel in the Print dialog box before you start printing. Once you click OK in the Print dialog box, QuarkXPress begins preparing each page for printing, and displays a dialog box with a changing message about the current status of the printing process.

You can press ⌘-period to terminate the process while pages are printing or while they are being formatted for the print spooler if you have activated that resource in the Macintosh operating environment.

Turning the printer off is an emergency measure and is advisable only if you are the only person on the printer network, if the printer does not include downloaded fonts, and if the equipment allows midprocess termination (see the manual for your hardware).

Creating, Applying, and Printing Color

QuarkXPress lets you create colors and apply them to selected items on a page. Color pages can be printed on a color printer, but most often the final document is reproduced in color by an offset print shop. Because the offset printing process prints each color with a different printing plate, elements that are to be printed in different colors must be *separated* from each other in printing the camera-ready masters through QuarkXPress.

QuarkXPress offers the option of automatically separating colors through the Print command. QuarkXPress can print color separations of any elements that have been assigned colors through QuarkXPress commands, plus color separations of EPS pictures. Chapter 13 offers a detailed look at preparing files for color separation. The next sections describe how to create and apply colors to Quark pages.

Creating Colors

You can create new colors in QuarkXPress using the Edit Colors dialog box (Edit ► Color). This dialog box offers the same types of options as those offered in the Edit Style Sheets dialog box or the Edit H&Js dialog box. You can add to the preset default list of colors or append colors set up in another QuarkXPress document. The preset default list of colors includes black, blue, cyan, green, magenta, red, registration, white, and yellow. Only blue, green, and red can be deleted from the default list.

If you choose Edit ► Colors when no document is open, changes you make to the color palette are stored as part of the QuarkXPress program. If you choose Edit ► Colors when a document is open, changes you make to the color palette are stored as part of that document only.

The first dialog box displayed when you choose Edit ► Colors (Figure 7-11) shows the list of colors currently available and offers several options.

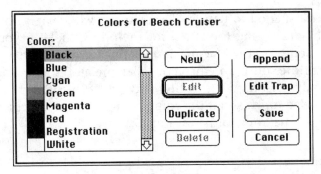

Figure 7-11 The Colors dialog box.

Click New to get the Colors dialog box and create a new color. Click on a color name and then click Edit (or press Return) to change the specifications set up for a current color, click Duplicate to create a new color based on an existing color, or click Delete to remove a color from the list. If you Edit a color, all of the elements in the document that have been assigned that color will change to reflect the changed color. If you delete a color, black is substituted wherever that color was applied. (You cannot edit or delete the primary colors used by QuarkXPress: cyan, magenta, yellow, black, or white.)

Click Append to import the color palette from another QuarkXPress document. Click Edit Trap to change the specifications in printing traps for a selected color. Click Save to save any changes that you make or Cancel to reverse any changes you made through this dialog box or its subsidiaries, described under the next headings.

The Edit Color Dialog Box

The Edit Color dialog box (Figure 7-12) is displayed when you choose New, Edit, or Duplicate from the Colors dialog box. You must enter a Name for a new color, or you can change the name shown in this field. The name you assign appears in the Color submenu and pop-up menus, and is listed in the Plate pop-up menu in the Print dialog box if Process Separation is set to Off. If you turn Process Separation on, the color is reproduced by printing cyan, magenta, yellow, and black plates.

You can create or edit any color using any of six color models: Hue, Saturation, and Brightness (HSB); Red, Green, and Blue (RGB); Cyan, Magenta, Yellow, and Black (CMYK); PANTONE colors; TRUMATCH colors; or FOCALTONE colors. These color models are described in detail in Chapter 13.

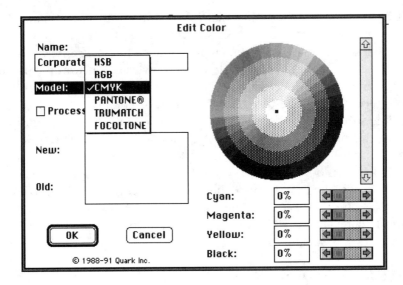

Figure 7-12 The Edit Color dialog box.

If you choose one of the first three color models, the upper right area of the dialog box displays a color wheel and the bottom right corner of the dialog box displays the scales on which a color can be adjusted. You can adjust a color in three ways: If you are working in HSB or RGB mode and you have a color monitor, you can drag the pointer around the color wheel and watch the New area of the dialog box to see what color you are choosing; otherwise, you can enter percentage values in the boxes next to each scale, or you can click or drag the scroll bars next to each scale. The Brightness Scroll Bar, available when RGB or HSB modes are selected, lets you adjust the brightness or amount of black in the color.

If you choose the PANTONE, TRUMATCH, or FOCALTONE color model, the upper right area of the dialog box displays part of the Color Selector for each (a catalog of colors that comes with QuarkXPress). You can use the scroll bars to see other parts of the catalog or type a number in the No. field below the catalog window (Figure 7-13).

For PANTONE colors, the CV that follows the PANTONE No. field indicates that the selected color is a computer video simulation of the actual PANTONE-identified number. You can create new colors based on existing PANTONE, TRUMATCH, or FOCALTONE colors, and you can change the name of PANTONE, TRUMATCH, or FOCALTONE colors that you add to the color palette.

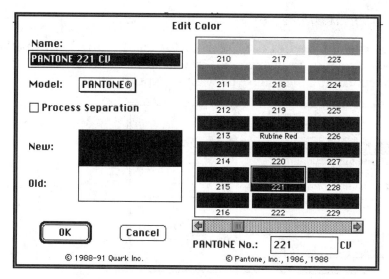

Figure 7-13 The Edit Color dialog box with the PANTONE option selected.

Regardless of how a color was initially created—using the HSB, RGB, CMYK, PANTONE, TRUMATCH, or FOCALTONE system—you can switch to any other system to edit the color further. Whichever method you choose, the color you create is automatically displayed in the New area of the dialog box, and the color wheel marker, percentage entries, and scroll bars all reflect your current changes. The Old area of the dialog box shows the color as defined when you chose Edit or Duplicate on the previous dialog box. You can click on the Old color to reset all values to the original color.

If Process Separation is On, then the color you are creating or editing broken into the four process colors when you print separations through the File → Print command. Otherwise, the color—including PANTONE colors—is separated onto a single separate color plate bearing the color's name (when separations are specified in the Print dialog box).

Click OK to end the editing process, and be sure to click Save in the Colors dialog box in order to save all of the colors you create or change for this document.

If the Colors palette is displayed (View → Show Colors), you can access the Edit Colors dialog box quickly by holding down the ⌘ key and clicking on the name of a color.

The Append Dialog Box

If you click Append in the Colors dialog box (Figure 7-14), QuarkXPress displays a directory dialog box through which you can select the document containing the colors you want to append.

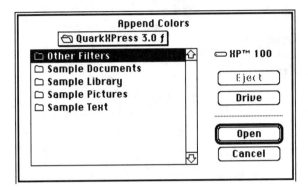

Figure 7-14 The Append colors dialog box.

Append imports all colors from the selected document except those that have the same names as colors already in the palette of the active document. You can define up to 128 colors in one palette.

The Edit Trap Dialog Box

The Edit Trap dialog box allows you to specify trapping relationships between colors in a QuarkXPress document. Trapping controls the way two colors print when they are adjacent to each other, by overprinting, knocking out, or overlapping slightly (spreading or choking).

You can also specify the Automatic trapping used by QuarkXPress in the Application Preferences dialog box (Edit ➤ Preferences ➤ Application), or you can specify trapping on an item-by-item basis using the Trap Information palette (View ➤ Show Trap Information). See Chapter 13 for a detailed discussion of all of QuarkXPress' trapping controls.

Applying Color

QuarkXPress comes with nine preset colors that are displayed on the Style ➤ Color submenu and on the pop-up menus in dialog boxes. You can apply color to text or text rules through the Style ➤ Character and Style ➤ Rules commands; the Style menu lets you apply color to selected lines drawn using QuarkXPress' tools, or an imported Black-and-White bitmap picture or TIFF/RIFF picture. (You cannot change the color of color pictures that have been imported into QuarkXPress, nor can you change the color of EPS or black-and-white PICT files.) You can specify color for a box background through the Item ➤ Modify command, or for a box frame through the Item ➤ Frame command. The fastest way to apply color, however, is using the Colors palette (View ➤ Show Colors), which lets you apply color to all of the above items (except rules in text).

Applying Color to Text, Rules, and Pictures

To apply a color to text or to an imported picture, first select the item with the Content tool (☞) and then choose the color from the Style ➤ Color submenu. For text, highlight the text you want to color, then select color from the Style ➤ Color submenu; or you can also apply color through the color pop-up menu in the Character Attributes dialog box (Figure 7-15).

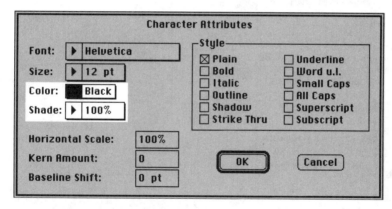

Figure 7-15 You can apply color to selected text through the Character Attributes dialog box, or make it part of a style sheet through the Edit ➤ Style Sheets command.

You can also apply color to text or pictures using the Colors palette (View ➤ Show Colors). For text, select text and click on the text icon, then click on a color in the list. For pictures, make sure the picture box is active and the Content tool is selected, then click on the icon for the content of the picture box and choose a color from the list.

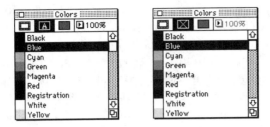

Figure 7-16 The Colors palette set to apply color to text (left) and to a picture (right).

The color and shade that you apply to an imported picture using the Style → Color submenu (Figure 7-17) or the Colors palette affect all areas of the image that would otherwise print as black or a shade of gray; white areas are not affected.

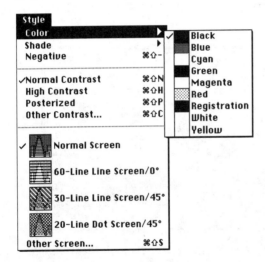

Figure 7-17 You can apply color to imported pictures through the Style → Color submenu.

To apply color to rules above or below paragraphs, select Style → Rules. You can then specify color in the Paragraph Rules dialog box (Figure 7–18).

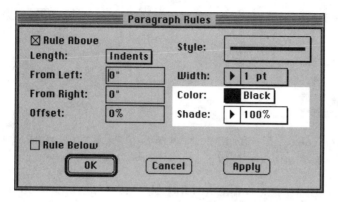

Figure 7-18 You can apply color to selected Paragraph rules through the Style ➤ Rules command.

Applying Color to Lines and Box Backgrounds

To apply color to a line or to the background of a box drawn using QuarkXPress tools, first select the item, then select the Item ➤ Modify command and choose a color from the Line Specifications dialog box, the Picture Box Specifications dialog box, the Text Box Specifications dialog box, or the Colors palette. To apply color to lines, you can also use the Style ➤ Color submenu.

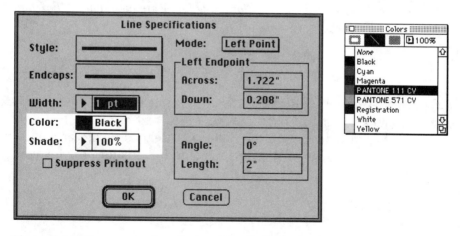

Figure 7-19 You can apply color to active lines through the Item ➤ Modify command (left) or by using the Colors palette (right).

When you apply color to a box, the box background appears behind text and in the white areas of an imported bitmap or TIFF or RIFF image. (Background color does not show through color TIFF, PICT, or EPS images.)

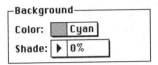

Figure 7-20 You can apply color to the background of an active picture box or an active text box through the Item ➤ Modify command.

To apply color to the frame around box, first select the item, then select the Item ➤ Frame command (Figure 7-21), or use the Colors palette.

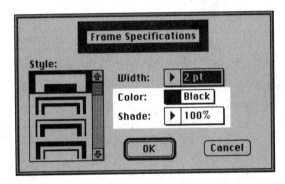

Figure 7-21 You can apply color to the frame around an active box through the Item ➤ Frame command.

Applying Two-color Blends

QuarkXPress 3.1 allows you to apply simple two-color blends to box backgrounds using the Colors palette. With a text or picture box active, select the background icon in the Colors palette, choose Linear Blend from the pop-up menu, then specify the color and shades of color you with to blend.

Step 1   With a picture or text box active, select the background icon in the Colors palette and choose Linear Blend from the pop-up menu.

Figure 7-22 Select Linear Blend from the pop-up menu in the Colors palette.

Step 2   Make sure the button for color #1 is selected, then choose the color and shade for the first color of the blend; click on the button for color #2 and choose the color and shade of the second color. Specify the angle of the blend.

Figure 7-23 Use the Colors palette to apply two-color blends to box backgrounds; select the color and shade of color #1 (left), then select the color and shade of color #2 (right).

Step 3   Click on the box with the Item tool selected, or deselect the box if the Content tool is selected to view the blend.

Figure 7-24 View the blend by selecting the box with the Item tool.

You can select two different colors to blend, or you can specify different shades of the same color. You can specify any angle from 0° to 360° in .001° increments.

Applying Registration "Color"

The Registration color is normally set to black, but you can change it to any color for on-screen display. You can apply the Registration color to any elements on a page. These elements then print on every separation plate—regardless of their on-screen color setting—when Make Separations is selected on the Print dialog box. You can select QuarkXPress's line tool to draw your own cut or fold marks, for instance, and print them on every plate.

Special Considerations in Printing

The next sections discuss some of the general considerations that can arise in printing documents, including font selection, imported picture types, system changes (including sending documents to a service bureau), and oversize documents.

Font Selection

To see a list of the fonts used in a document, select Utilities ➤ Font Usage, described in Chapter 4. You can also globally find and change fonts through the Font Usage dialog box (Figure 7-25), as described in Chapter 3.

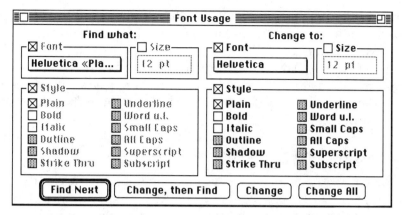

Figure 7-25 The Font Usage dialog box.

Downloading Fonts

If you are using only those fonts that are built in your printer, the printing process is straightforward: Simply select the Print command from the File menu. However, you can buy more fonts on disks from various sources. They are called "downloadable" fonts, because in order to use them you need to send—or download—them to the printer prior to printing the page or document. Downloadable fonts can be purchased from the printer manufacturer or from a software developer. Companies such as Adobe Systems and Bitstream are common sources for downloadable PostScript fonts.

Experiment a little with downloadable fonts before you design a large document that calls for them, and before you decide whether to download the fonts *before* you start printing or as part of the printing process.

The first step in using a downloadable font is to install the *screen* font on your system—using any of the methods described in Chapter 5. The second step is to copy the *printer* font files into the System folder or onto a hard disk attached to your printer. If these two conditions are met, you will be able to select the fonts, and when you print the document QuarkXPress automatically sends the fonts to the printer as needed by each page during the printing process. When QuarkXPress downloads a font, it is flushed out of the printer memory when the document is finished printing.

As an alternative, you can download fonts to the printer before you print, using such programs as Adobe's Font Downloader, which is included with every font you buy from Adobe. Pre-downloaded fonts remain in the printer's memory as each page is printed and until the printer is turned off. You can print publications more quickly this way, but the number of fonts downloaded limits the amount of memory remaining for processing each page.

If you have pre-downloaded any fonts at the beginning of the day, and you run into memory problems when printing pages with graphics that do not use those fonts, you can flush the fonts out of the printer's memory by turning it off.

Printing Without Downloading

If you have installed the screen font but do not have the equivalent printer font, you can choose the font from the QuarkXPress menus, but when you print the document to a PostScript printer either the font will printed as low-resolution bitmap characters (based on the screen font) or another font will be substituted.

Some service bureaus will give you their screen fonts on disk so you can use them in your documents. But the document will have to be printed by a service bureau that has the printer fonts, which are licensed only to the purchaser.

Limiting the Number of Fonts

If you are following the rules of good design, your pages probably use a limited number of different typefaces, styles, and sizes. There are at least two reasons other than good design for limiting the number of fonts you use in a document: time and space. The more fonts you use, the more space they require in your printer's memory (if they are downloaded fonts) and the more time it takes to print each page.

Remember, as you learned in Chapter 4, a font is a particular combination of typeface and style. You need to download four different fonts in order to use the entire "family" in the Palatino typeface, for example: normal, bold, italic, and bold italic. Different typefaces and styles take up different amounts of memory, and different types of graphics make different demands on memory as well. Before you design a long document with downloadable fonts, try printing one or two sample pages with representative graphics as well as text that uses all of the fonts called for in the design.

Working with Large Picture Files

Because EPS, TIFF, and RIFF images can be quite large, rather than incorporating them in the document, QuarkXPress stores and displays them in a low-resolution PICT format. QuarkXPress uses the larger, high-resolution image to print the document.

If you move or change the name of the high resolution picture file, or if you use another program to modify it, then when you print the document QuarkXPress displays a dialog box (Figure 7-26) that enables you to re-establish the link, to print anyway, or to cancel the print job.

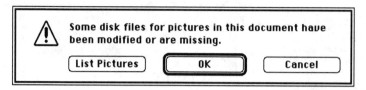

Figure 7-26 Alert box prompting for response to missing or modified picture condition.

Click List Pictures to view a list of all missing or modified pictures. The Missing/Modified Pictures dialog box is handled the same way as the Picture Usage dialog box, described below. Click OK to continue printing, using the low-resolution version of all missing pictures. Click Cancel to cancel the printing process.

If you want QuarkXPress automatically to reimport all pictures that have been modified since the document was last open, you can select Edit ➤ Preferences ➤ General to set Auto Import to On (as described in Chapter 3). Missing pictures will still result in a dialog box during the printing process.

If you want to resolve all of these issues before you print, select Utilities ➤ Picture Usage. EPS, TIFF, and RIFF files are listed in the Picture Usage dialog box (Figure 7-27), through which you can locate pictures for printing and determine their status. Status indicators include OK (QuarkXPress knows where the picture is and it has not been modified), modified (QuarkXPress knows where the picture but it has been modified), and missing (QuarkXPress does not know where the picture is).

Name	Page	Type	Status
Hard Disk :Cycle pictures :Cycle Race EPS	1	EPS	modified
Hard Disk :Cycle pictures :Sprockets TIFF	1	TIFF	OK
Hard Disk :Cycle pictures :Bicycle EPS	1	EPS	missing

Picture Usage

Update   Show Me

Figure 7-27 Picture Usage dialog box.

To locate a missing picture in the document, double-click on the picture name, or click once on the picture name and click Update. The Missing/Modified Picture dialog box is displayed (Figure 7-28), through which you can specify the new path to the picture or the new picture name.

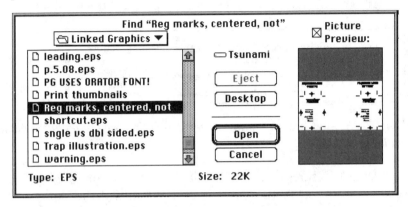

Figure 7-28 The Missing/Modified Picture dialog box.

To view the picture, click once on the picture name and click Show Me. QuarkXPress scrolls through the document and displays the page with the picture on it.

Printing at High Resolutions

Because of the way information is stored for grayscale TIFF and RIFF images, the amount of memory required to process the image increases the higher the resolution. For this reason, printing images takes longer at higher resolutions. You might run into memory overload or printing time-out errors when printing pages with grayscale TIFF and RIFF images at high resolutions—especially the high resolutions offered by imagesetters such as the Linotronic models. You can work around these problems by printing those pages at lower resolutions.

Changing Systems and Using Service Bureaus

If you take your QuarkXPress document from one system to another, you need to take the following files with you besides the document file itself:

- All high resolution picture files (EPS, TIFF, or RIFF) used in the document.

- Printer and screen fonts used in the document (or a list of fonts, so you can check that they are installed in the other system).

Since QuarkXPress 3.1 does not require the external file *XPress Data* to store hyphenation exceptions, or kerning or tracking table edits, you do not need to send any external files to your service bureau. Your service bureau should simply use the default settings in your file. In the meantime, you should always keep a backup of your files, especially when taking them from one machine or system to another.

Oversize Documents

QuarkXPress lets you specify page sizes up to 48 inches square. Unfortunately, no PostScript printers can handle paper this large. (The largest we know of is a Versatec printer that can print rasterized versions of QuarkXPress pages that have been saved as EPS files, and handles pages up to 42 inches wide, of any length.)

When you print a document with pages that are larger than the size of the paper in the printer, you must either print a reduced version of the pages or print them out in *tiled* sections.

Printing Reductions

As you learned earlier in this chapter, you can print reduced versions of pages by entering a value below 100% in the Reduce or Enlarge field of the Page Setup dialog box. Some standard reductions are shown in Figure 7-29.

Original Size (inches)	Percentage reduction needed to fit on 8.5" × 11" paper:
8.5" × 11" (letter)	100%
11" × 14" (legal)	77%
11" × 17" (tabloid)	64%
15.5" × 22.5" (newspaper)	48%
34" × 44"	25%

Figure 7-29 Reduction percentages required to fit oversize proofs on an 8.5" x 11" page.

Printing Tiled Sections

The Tiling option in the Print dialog box (Figure 7-30) lets you print large pages in sections on a PostScript printer. This feature was mentioned earlier in this chapter, but we will describe it in more detail here.

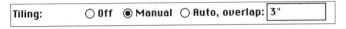

Figure 7-30 The Tiling options in the Print dialog box.

When you select Auto Tiling and specify the amount of overlap you want between tiles, QuarkXPress automatically divides the page into the number of tiles needed to print given the size of the page, the size of the paper, and the amount of overlap specified. QuarkXPress prints the tiles at the top of the page first, from left to right, and works down the page.

When you select Manual Tiling, you control the placement of the upper left corner of each tile by relocating zero point on the ruler. This is useful if you want to reprint one tile after you have printed all tiles automatically, or for printing the last few tiles of a page that was interrupted during printing.

Since moving the zero point on one page effectively moves it for all pages (if Item Coordinates is set to Page in the Edit ➤ Preferences ➤ General dialog box), you can print the currently specified tile for all pages in the document at once.

To help assemble tiles that are printed with the Auto option, QuarkXPress prints tile location information in the upper left corner of each tile, in the format "Page x (y, z)" where x is the page number, y is the column number, and z is the row number. QuarkXPress prints tick marks where each tile can be cut or trimmed for alignment, but if you have allowed overlap you might choose to trim tiles along column gutters or some other natural feature of the page. You do not get tick marks or tile location information when you select Manual Tiling.

Whether you select Auto or Manual Tiling, you generally need some overlap in order to achieve precise alignment between adjacent tiles when you paste them together. At minimum, the overlap needs to account for the nonprinting edges of the paper (that is, at least .5 inches on a laser printer, or at least .25 inches if you select Larger Print Area through the Print dialog box's Options for laser printers).

Figure 7-31 Newspaper page printed in four tiles on 8.5" by 11" paper, with overlap between pages (left), then assembled into full-page layout (right).

Summary

In this chapter you learned how print pages from QuarkXPress, and about special considerations in printing oversized pages or in using a service bureau to output your pages. This chapter also covered the basics of how to create and apply color to items in QuarkXPress.

This chapter completes Part I of this book, a description of all the commands, tools, and features of QuarkXPress. Part II presents some of the advanced techniques that can be used in building QuarkXPress documents.

P A R T

II

ADVANCED TECHNIQUES

8 *Templates and Design*

Whenever you start a new document, you must go through certain steps to set up the pages before you begin importing text and graphics from other programs. In traditional terms, you define the design specifications for the document. In QuarkXPress terms, you make selections in the New dialog box, set up guides and other elements on the master pages, define style sheets, and set other preferences and defaults before you begin adding elements to the first page. This chapter describes how to use QuarkXPress to generate design ideas and to create templates that embody the design specifications.

QuarkXPress can be used to sketch out rough ideas for designs that can be reviewed with the rest of the production team or the client; however, it goes a step further than the traditional pencil sketch in that it can implement the design by creating templates, including style sheets, that help ensure that all parts of a document will follow the same design specifications.

In practice, some of the steps described here might be done first on paper rather than on the computer. In fact, the designers on some teams might never actually touch the mouse. Whether you—as the designer—are simply drawing and writing out the design specifications or actually setting up the master template yourself, knowing how QuarkXPress works before you make your specifications will help.

For example, QuarkXPress generally defines a page in terms of the margins, the number of columns, and the space between columns. If you divide a text box into columns, you cannot enter the column widths directly. Your specifications must be in terms of the number of columns and space between, rather than the width of the columns themselves. This chapter shows you how to prepare your design specifications in terms of QuarkXPress' commands and capabilities.

Whenever you want to create a series of similar documents in QuarkXPress—documents with similar design specifications and page layouts—you can avoid repeating steps by initially capturing the design in a template, as described later in this chapter.

Creating Design Alternatives

You can use QuarkXPress to create a series of quick roughs of different designs for a document before deciding on the final design. The advantage of using QuarkXPress rather than pencil and ruler to sketch out your ideas is threefold:

- It is easy to copy and move elements on a page as you work on a design.
- It is efficient to make copies of the first design and modify it to create alternative designs.
- It is effective to show clients crisp text and graphic elements printed on a high-resolution printer. (We use the term "client" to include managing editors, publication department managers, end-user groups, or others with whom the designer must share decisions.)

Whereas in final documents you import the actual text and graphics that comprise the work, you need not know the exact text or contents of the document in order to rough out a design idea. You can use QuarkXPress' built-in text and graphics features to create representations of the basic elements in a document. For example, you can use *dummy text* to show the position and size of text on a page. You can use shaded boxes to show where graphics will be imported. You can use rules to enhance the design. Figure 8-1 shows how design ideas can be handled in QuarkXPress.

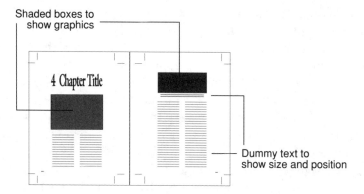

Figure 8-1 Rough page comps can be done by hand or using QuarkXPress.

Rather than create a different QuarkXPress document to represent each design idea, you can use one design document to create many variations, as shown in Figure 8-2.

Step 1 Create representations of all the basic design elements once and store them on the master page.

Step 2 Add a page for each design idea.

Step 3 Modify or rearrange the master page elements on each page to develop design variations.

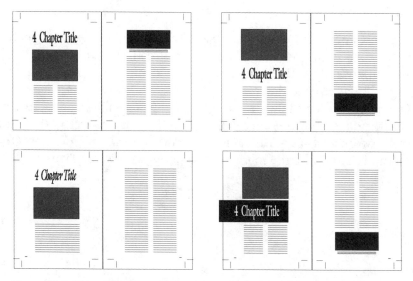

Figure 8-2 Example of variations on one design idea in a design document.

After reviewing different design ideas, the designer can translate those ideas into the specifications that will be applied in QuarkXPress and the other programs that will be used to construct the pieces of the document, such as a word processing program or graphics programs.

By printing documents as Thumbnails (File → Print), you can see several different design treatments or the overall layout for a longer document, such as a book (Figure 8-3). You can vary the number of thumbnail pages that will print on a sheet of paper by changing the percentage of enlargement or reduction in the Page Setup dialog box (File → Page Setup). Reduce the percentage to make each thumbnail page smaller, allowing more pages to print on each sheet of paper; enlarge the percentage to make each thumbnail page larger, with fewer pages shown on each sheet of paper.

Figure 8-3 Printing thumbnails lets you see how well a design carries throughout a document.

Create a Grid System

The best document designs are based on an underlying *grid* structure that is used to position elements throughout the document. Pages of Gutenberg's Bible show traces of the grid system he used to lay out his pages. A few decades later a book named *De Divina Proportione*, written by Fra Luca Pacioli and illustrated by Leonardo da Vinci, applied the rules of classic proportion to book design. Contemporary designers still study this masterwork and apply the same principles in new book designs. One such method of defining the margins for a book is shown in Figure 8-4.

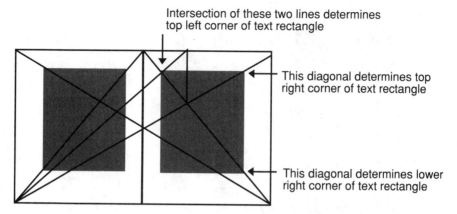

Figure 8-4 One method of determining the classic proportions for a book design.

In traditional production, a grid system is a series of vertical and horizontal lines drawn or printed in light-blue ink on the layout boards used to paste up galleys of typeset text and inked line art. The "nonrepro" blue lines are not picked up by the camera during the process of making plates for printing the final pages. The practical function of the blue lines is to help ensure that the galleys of type are laid straight on each page and that all pages have the same margins. Because every page is pasted up using the same grid of blue lines, the entire document has a fundamental consistency.

In QuarkXPress you can set up a grid of page and ruler guides on the master pages or document pages to make it easy to align elements consistently. These guides are visible on the screen but will not print. We normally think of a grid as simply the margin guides and column guides for a document. Of course, these are the basic elements of any grid system. Professional designers often use more elaborate grid systems than that, however. In QuarkXPress the grid can include up to 200 ruler guides as well as printed elements, such as rules between columns or frames around pages.

Simple grid structures that involve one, two, or three columns are relatively easy to work with, but complex grids usually offer more design possibilities. For example, a one-column grid structure can have only as much variety in the layout as can be achieved by varying the type specifications and paragraph indentations. A two-column grid structure offers the added possibility of making graphics and text expand to the full page width on selected pages if necessary or desired. A three-column grid offers at least three page variations, as shown in Figure 8-5.

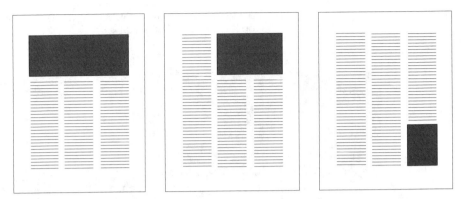

Figure 8-5 Examples of different layouts that are possible on a three-column grid.

The spacing between the columns is normally set to a default width of 0.167 inch, or 1 pica. You can make this wider if you will be dropping hairline rules between columns, but a good rule is to keep the space between columns under 2 picas.

What Is a Template?

A template is a QuarkXPress document that embodies the basic features of the design specifications (Figure 8-6). A template usually makes use of master pages, and may include some sort of grid system for laying out the pages (beginning with page size and margins), a system for applying type specifications (via style sheets or via text boxes from a Library), a source of standard symbols and graphics used in the document (stored on the Pasteboard, in a Library, or in external files to be imported), and standing items that are always printed in the same location on certain pages (such as a newsletter banner). A template is set up with all defaults tailored to match the design specifications for the document.

A template might consist of no more than a simple grid of margin guides and an automatic text box with column guides. For example, whenever you start a new document in QuarkXPress, you specify the basic parameters, such as the size of the page, the orientation of the printed image, and the text margins, before adding any text or graphics to the pages. By setting up these specifications in the template, you can be sure that all documents created from it have the same page size and orientation settings.

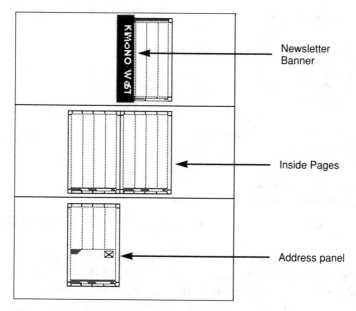

Newsletter
Banner

Inside Pages

Address panel

Figure 8-6 A template document.

A more complex template might include common text and graphic elements, such as headers and footers, headlines, rules, and other repeating symbols and graphic elements. A template can include style sheets for applying type specifications used throughout the publication. A template can also incorporate productivity aids, such as guides for aligning objects across facing pages and for positioning text and graphics. It can include common elements that will appear within the document in specific locations or at repeated intervals.

Once a template document is created, it can be used over and over to create a series of documents that follow the same design specifications. For instance, a long publication might have one template document that is used to create a series of sections or chapters that all follow the same design specifications. A short publication that is produced regularly—such as a newsletter—would have one template from which each issue is created.

As you learned in Chapter 2, the Save as dialog box in QuarkXPress lets you save a document as a template (Figure 8-7). A QuarkXPress template differs from a document in that when you use the Save command, a template always displays the Save as dialog box without a document name, so you cannot inadvertently overwrite the original.

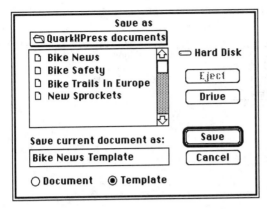

Figure 8-7 The Save as dialog box lets you save a document as a template.

You can easily distinguish between the two types of documents in the Open dialog box by choosing to display either Templates or Documents. If you check the Template Preview option in the Open dialog box, then a thumbnail preview of the first page of the template and the page size will display in the dialog box when you click once on the template file name, as shown in Figure 8-8.

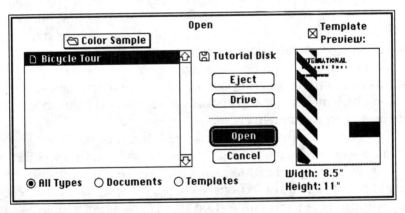

Figure 8-8 The Open dialog box lets you view a thumbnail preview of a template.

Benefits of Using Templates

The essential benefits of using a template system are that it saves repeated set-up steps, helps you to think ahead, embodies design, and helps enforce consistency.

Templates Save Repeated Set-up Steps

One major benefit of using a template system is that the decisions and actions described under the next headings are executed only once during the production cycle, rather than once for every new file that will be a part of the full publication. Templates save time in large production projects by capturing a few of the steps required to set up a new document, so the same steps do not have to be repeated every time a similar document is started. You can save hours or days over the life of a project by using a template system for large or periodical publications.

It is a good idea to develop a template system for any project that will require more than one QuarkXPress document file. Books, reports, manuals, newsletters, and magazines are candidates for template systems whereby a single template is used to create a separate document file for each chapter, section, or issue. Even if the number of pages required for a document is less than the maximum allowed by QuarkXPress, there are good reasons for dividing these publications into several documents, all built from the same template. Shorter documents such as price lists, menus, ads, and brochures are candidates for template systems if you will be producing more than one document with the same or similar layout.

Templates Help You to Think Ahead!

It's a good idea to think out the design of your document before making your initial page set-up. Never sit down at your computer to produce a report or newsletter without planning ahead. The first step in thinking out a production plan is to list the design specifications that will be applied throughout a publication. Wherever possible, design specifications should be captured in the template system. Even if the design specifications are already clearly written out on paper, the QuarkXPress menus and options can provide a structure for organizing them.

Templates Embody Design

Aside from the practical considerations of saving time and providing a disciplined approach to producing a document, a template system can ensure that design specifications are easy to apply. By incorporating as many of the design specifications as possible into a QuarkXPress template, the production group can better preserve the look intended by the designer.

Templates Help Enforce Consistency

It goes without saying that a good designer always applies the rule of consistency. This means that part of the designer's responsibility is to make sure that all elements have been considered, and that no one on the production team will need to invent design specifications for details that were not covered by the designer's original specifications.

In the past the designer enforced consistency by issuing lists of standards and having blue lines printed as grid guides on the final page-layout boards. In QuarkXPress you can enforce consistency by using templates and style sheets to enforce a grid system, apply type specifications, and set up specific line lengths and widths, box background colors, tab settings, paragraph alignment (flush left, justified,and so on), and indentations.

The designer also needs to specify standard spacing between figures and text as well as the spacing between headings and body copy. You can use the Item → Modify command to define the inset that will determine the distance between the contents of that box and adjacent boxes.

Creating a Template Document

The next sections describe the basic steps in creating a template document in QuarkXPress. This procedure is a very organized approach to developing a series of similar documents: Create a template that includes all of the elements that are common to all documents in the series, then use the template by adding text and graphics to create each final document in the series. Instead of creating a template per se, you might choose simply to create the first document completely, then copy that document and *delete* parts you don't need, then add new text and graphics to create the second and subsequent similar documents.

 Whichever approach you take, it is important to set up the elements described in the next sections carefully in the first document—whether it is a template or a finished document—so that subsequent documents based on it will match the design specifications. If you are careless in creating the first document, you might end up with a series of documents that all share the same *incorrect* specifications, and add hours of work in making the same corrections in every document individually.

Define the Page Size, Margins, and Columns

Whenever you open a new document you first define the page size, margins, and columns through the New dialog box (Figure 8-9). The values specified here for margins and columns will affect the first page of the document and the original Master Page A. You can change the page size at any time using the File ⭢ Document Setup command. You can change the margin and column guides for any given master page by choosing Page ⭢ Master Guides.

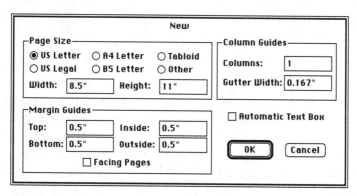

Figure 8-9 Page size and margins are set in the New dialog box when a new document is created.

Most publications use the same page size for all sections, but the orientation of the pages may vary from section to section. For instance, you might have a set of appendices that need to be printed wide to accommodate many columns of numbers in a financial report. These types of documents are easy to accommodate since QuarkXPress lets you have up to 127 different master pages.

Calculating the Width of the Automatic Text Box

In the New dialog box, you begin a new document by specifying (among other things) the width of the margins, and this determines the width of the automatic text box on the first master page. The automatic text box is especially useful for longer documents, such as books or reports, since text flows into the automatic text box on a document page when a new page is inserted.

If you know the margins and the page size, as specified in the New dialog box, you can calculate the width of the automatic text box using the following formula:

Automatic text box width = (page width) – (inside margin measure + outside margin measure) – (twice the text inset)

If you know the column widths for your document, you can use the following formula to calculate the widths of a text box based on column width. You can set up columns in the New dialog box or the Master Guides dialog box (for master pages) or in the Text Box Specifications dialog box (for any text box):

Text box width = (Column width × number of columns) + (gutter width × number of gutters)

If you are more accustomed to defining page layouts in terms of the width of the text area rather than the width of the margins, you can set the width of the automatic text box *after* you close the New dialog box by making the first master page active (or whatever master page you have set up with the automatic text box), selecting the automatic text box, and using the Item ➛ Modify command to set the width of the box. This procedure changes the width of the automatic text box on all pages based on that master page, but it does not change the margin guides on the screen.

If you want the width of the automatic text box to match the margin guides, you can convert your specifications for the automatic text box width into margin widths using a variation of the previous formula:

Total space available for inside and outside margins = page width – automatic text box width

For example, if you know you want the automatic text box to be 6 inches wide on an 8.5-inch-wide page, then the total amount of space available for both the inside and the outside margins is 2.5 inches (8.5 – 6).

Remember that the actual width of the *text* in the automatic text box will be the width of the text box *minus twice the text inset value.* QuarkXPress' default text inset value is 1 point, but you may want to change this to 0 for the automatic text box by changing the text inset value for the automatic text boxes on the master pages.

If you make your calculations before starting a new document, you can enter these values directly in the New dialog box. Otherwise, you can change the margins through the File ➛ Document Setup command or the Page ➛ Master Guides command after you have started a document.

Select a Unit of Measure and Display Rulers

If all of your design specifications are given in the same unit of measure, then you can set your preferences in the template document and the same unit of measure will apply to all files created from the template. Use the Edit ➤ Preferences ➤ General command (Figure 8-10).

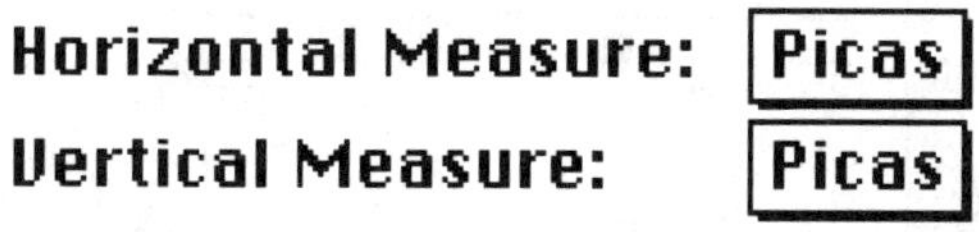

Horizontal Measure: | Picas |

Vertical Measure: | Picas |

Figure 8-10 Set the preferred unit of measure in the template document in the General Preferences dialog box.

If your specifications are given in two or more different measures—inches for margins and points for type, for instance—then select that unit of measure in which you prefer to view the rulers.

You will probably use View ➤ Display Rulers (⌘-R) to display the rulers during the design phase in order to help lay out your grid precisely. If you leave the rulers on in the template document, they will be displayed automatically in all documents that are created from the template.

Set Up the Master Pages

We have already suggested that a different master page might be appropriate for each unique page margin specification and for each different column setting, and you saw in the previous section how two master pages can be used to create four variations in facing-page layouts. In general, you should set up a different master page for each section of the document that requires different margins, columns, or page orientation (Figure 8-11).

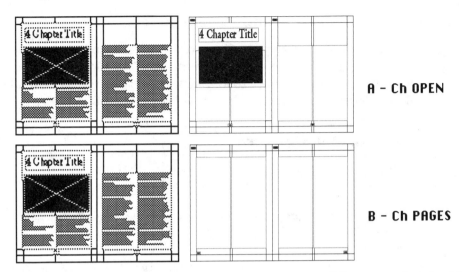

A – Ch OPEN

B – Ch PAGES

Figure 8-11 Each section of the document that requires different margins should have a different master page.

In addition, there may be other essential differences between sections of the document that can be handled efficiently through different master pages (Figure 8-12). For example, when the overall format specifies that the headers and footers change between major sections of a document, then multiple master pages are called for.

When you click on a master page icon in the Document Layout window (View ➤ Show Document Layout), the bar below the icons displays the name of the master page. You can change that name by selecting and retyping the text in the bar (though the icons will still be labeled A, B, C, and so on). By assigning names to master pages, you make it easy to select and apply the correct master page to document pages.

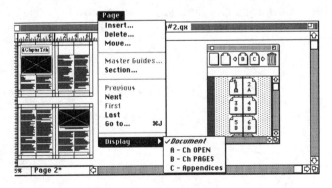

Figure 8-12 Pop-up menu of View ➤ Display command shows list of master pages by letter and name.

Master Page Elements

Elements that appear on every page in the same position belong on a master page. This includes graphic elements such as a logo that appears on every page, rules between columns, frames around pages, and other design elements.

Other elements that should be included on the master page are headers and footers. The headers and footers on the master pages of the template may be set up as placeholders only: They are set up in position with the correct type specs and alignment, but the text can change for each document that is created from the template. One of the first steps in using the template, then, would be to change the text of the header and/or footer (Figure 8-13).

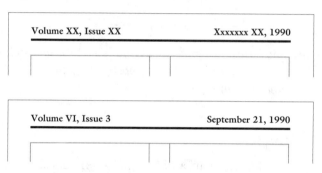

Figure 8-13 The headers and footers on the template document are placeholders only and must be updated each time the template is used.

Headers and footers have logical positions on a typical page. The most readily referenced part of any book is the outer edge of the page. Figure 8-14 shows some examples of how these four positions can be used to make page numbers and section names easy to find.

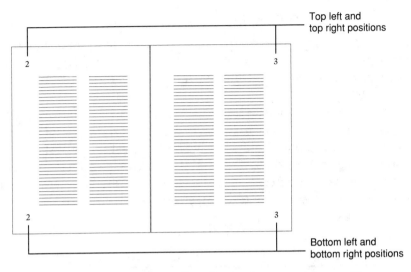

Top left and
top right positions

Bottom left and
bottom right positions

Figure 8-14 The four most easily referenced page number positions are: top left of even-numbered pages and top right of odd-numbered pages; bottom left of even-numbered pages and bottom right of odd-numbered pages.

Setting Up Multiple Master Pages

To set up multiple master pages in a document, consider how your text needs to flow throughout your document. For example, let's say you are creating a template for a book. The template file contains two master pages—one for the opening of each chapter and one for the following pages in the chapter.

The automatic text box that you specify in the New dialog box will appear on the first page of the document and on Master Page A (Figure 8-15). Display Master Page A to create the master page for the chapter opening, and format the automatic text box using Item → Modify and the various commands from the Style menu.

Subsequent master pages will not have an automatic text box. To link the second master page to the first, so that text flows from one to the next, first create a second master page by choosing View → Document Layout, and drag either a single-sided or double-sided master page icon into position to the right of Master Page A.

When you choose the Page → Display command, Master Page B will be listed. Display Master Page B; no text boxes will appear. Draw a text box on the page (or pages, if you are using a facing-pages master page) and format the box(es).

Finally, establish a link between the text box on new master pages and Master Page A by clicking on the Broken Chain icon in the upper left corner of the master page; a marquee is displayed around the icon. Next, click on the text box on the master page to establish it as an automatic text box, into which text will flow after it fills the automatic text box on Master Page A.

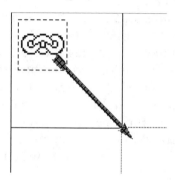

Figure 8-15 Creating an automatic text box on a master page.

Set Up Style Sheets

You can set the defaults for the normal body copy style sheet and any other standard text formats of the template document using Edit → Style Sheets as described in Chapters 5. All documents that are created from the template will have the same style sheets. See Chapter 10 for tips on creating more effective style sheets.

Identify Common Text and Graphic Elements

Most of the contents of the document will probably be imported from other programs. Some elements, however, will be repeated throughout the document. In a template, these repeated elements can be positioned on the master pages, on the Pasteboard, and on some document pages as described in this section. You can also set up a QuarkXPress library of commonly used elements, to go with the template for the publication.

Library Elements

In addition to the elements that belong on the master pages, certain other elements might be repeated throughout a document in an irregular pattern. These can be created once and stored in a library (Utilities ➤ Library), for use wherever they are needed. The Library palette stores all items reduced to fit in the same size rectangle. The Library palette can be moved anywhere on the screen and can be changed to display items horizontally (Figure 8-16) by clicking in the zoom box to expand the palette or by dragging the resize icon in the lower right-hand corner, similarly to the way all windows on a Macintosh can be resized and reshaped.

Libraries have many uses in setting up standards for a document. For example, if every story in a newsletter or magazine ends with a graphic symbol, you can store the symbol in a library and drag it onto the page whenever you reach the end of a story. Just as you created headers and footers on master pages, you can create standard dummy text blocks for pull quotes or captions within the document and store them in a library. If the document will include display ads in predetermined sizes, you can store boxes drawn to those sizes in a library. You can select multiple items on a page, such as a magazine banner made of several items, and drag them into a library as one object.

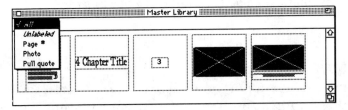

Figure 8-16 Common elements stored in a library.

You can add text boxes to the library. Any text formatting that you apply to these boxes will become the default formats when you type text in these boxes on document pages. For example, the pull quote text box in the library list shown in Figure 8-17 might be formatted with dummy text that has rules above and below, and the text box would be set up with the text inset appropriate for pull quotes. Whenever a pull quote is needed, you simply drag the pull quote text box from the library, copy or type the quote to replace the dummy text, and then resize and position the box on the page.

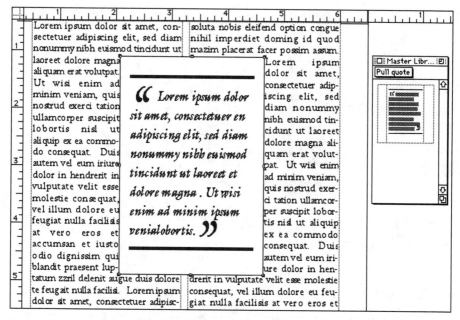

Figure 8-17 Pull quote box from the Library file with dummy text as a placeholder for the actual text that will be typed in.

Similarly, you can format a picture box with predefined settings for frame and background. Those settings will be retained when you drag the box from the library into the document. For example, you can create an empty picture box, give it a black frame and background, and store it in the library. Then drag the black box onto a document page whenever you want to make a placeholder for a photo that will be dropped in by the print shop.

When you place an item that contains a high-resolution image into a library, QuarkXPress saves the picture file's path (the volume and folder location of the picture). When you drag the item from the library onto a page, the path information is copied onto the page as well.

Standard Elements on Document Pages

Besides the elements that are positioned on the master pages or stored in the library, certain elements may appear on the document pages in predictable locations. For example, the template for a newsletter could include the banner on page 1 (Figure 8-18). If each issue of the newsletter is always the same number of pages, you might also be able to predict the positions of the subscription information and other standing features. You can also add placeholders for the text of headlines for feature articles that start on page 1.

Figure 8-18 Newsletter templates can include standing elements on document pages.

Design Specifications for Graphics Programs

In addition to providing the specifications for the QuarkXPress document, the designer should have a good idea of the number and source of graphic elements that will go into the document and provide the correct specifications to the production team. Knowing the capabilities and limitations of the available programs, the designer is responsible for specifying the treatment of each illustration. What are the size limitations or preferences for the figures? If you are following a grid system, you will want to make each figure's width match the increments allowed by the grid: a two-column grid allows only two figure widths (one column wide or the full page width), a three-column grid allows three different figure widths, a four-column grid allows four widths, and so on.

What fonts/styles/sizes will be used in illustrations and their captions? Will the figures be enlarged or reduced during page composition? Will photographs and other special illustrations be pasted up by hand or scanned into the computer? These specifications can be written down, or the programs that will be used to create the illustrations can be used to create "figure templates" just as QuarkXPress is used to create document templates.

Special Handling of Captions

One of the characteristics of any designed document is consistency of treatment, including the treatment of labels within figures as well as the figure titles or captions. This consistency can be difficult to achieve when you are bringing figures from other programs into QuarkXPress. The designer needs to specify how captions, figure titles, and figure labels will be handled in each different program that may be the source of illustrations for the document. Will the charting program be able to match the fonts used in figures from other drawing packages? Will the figure be scaled larger or smaller after it is in QuarkXPress?

You might decide that all figure titles and captions will be entered directly in QuarkXPress to ensure consistency, but you will still need to specify the preferred font for labels that fall within the figures. Furthermore, you may need to account for changes in the size of type that result when you shrink or enlarge a figure in QuarkXPress. As you learned in Chapter 6, when you change the size of a graphic imported from another program, you also change the size of the type used therein. If you know that you will be shrinking a figure by 50 percent, for instance, then the illustrator might need to make the type twice as large in the drawing program as it will be in the final document.

Instructions for Working with the Template

It's important that the same steps be followed each time a template is used. You may want to provide production notes for your own reference or for others who might use the template. Such notes are especially useful if you are working in a group where work on a series of documents is shared among several people. The notes can be a simple list of steps that serve primarily as reminders. For example:

Step 1 **Open the template and immediately save it under a new name.**

Step 2 **Change the headers and footers on the master pages.**

Step 3 **Change the volume/date information on page 1, below the newsletter banner.**

Step 4 **Drag the Table of Contents text box from the library, and retype the new issue's contents.**

Step 5 **Continue placing text and graphics as specified for the current issue.**

Test the Design and Template

Finally, it is a good idea to run a few sample pages of the document through the entire production process, starting with the various application programs used to create source files, including a word processing program and graphics programs, and finally using QuarkXPress. This will test all of the specifications before finalizing the design and the template. This dry run is more effective than any other review procedure in:

- flushing out any mismatches between the design specifications and the system capabilities,
- fine-tuning the template as needed, and
- identifying the detailed list of steps that should be followed for efficient production.

Unfortunately, we often skip this final test: It may seem like a luxury when working under the pressures of a short deadline. We tend to trust that our own knowledge of the system is sufficient to anticipate any problems. In fact, however, the test run can save time on a project by developing efficient procedures and thereby shortening the production cycle. Failing to anticipate major problems (such as discovering that your printer cannot handle the graphics from the sources specified in the design) can add many hours to a project.

Template File Management

Certain files should always be copied and used with any given template file, including the fonts used in the template. See Chapter 14 for a detailed discussion of this and other workgroup-related issues.

Summary

We hope the tips in this chapter have inspired you to use QuarkXPress as a design tool and to create a template for any group of documents that follow the same design specifications. The next chapters offer additional tips that can be applied to laying out individual document pages.

9 *Advanced Page Layout*

Chapters 2 and 3 described the basic steps and commands used in creating a document. This chapter goes beyond those basics, offering tips on choosing between alternative methods of storing and positioning commonly used items, aligning items on a page, changing the relationships between items, reformatting a document, and handling difficult page layouts.

Storing Commonly Used Items

Whenever you want to use the same item in several places, you can use one of three aids in QuarkXPress: You can put it in a QuarkXPress library, you can put a copy on the pasteboard and store it as part of the document so you can access it any time you want, or you can simply use the Copy and Paste commands to make duplicates through the Clipboard.

Using a Library

As described in Chapter 3, a library is a special QuarkXPress file for storing commonly used text and graphic items so that they can be accessed easily. Each library can contain up to 2,000 items, and you can create as many libraries as you like. A QuarkXPress library can store items in any format supported by QuarkXPress and retain the path information that is sometimes needed in printing. You can label, sort, and preview items in a library—making this a more flexible and convenient way of accessing items than simply copying from one document to another or using any of the storage methods described under the following headings.

Using the Pasteboard

The area surrounding the page in the document window serves as a pasteboard for storing text and graphics while you are working. You can use this area as an active storage area while you are building a master page or a document page, or you can use it as a permanent storage area for the document—an alternative to libraries.

To position an item on the document's pasteboard, you can drag it off a page (to remove it from a QuarkXPress page), you can paste it onto the pasteboard from another document or elsewhere in the active document, or you can use one of QuarkXPress' item creation tools to draw a box on the pasteboard and use the Get Text or Get Picture command to import other items into the box.

Items on the pasteboard remain next to the numbered page or master page where they are first positioned, so it's a good idea to store only those items that are related to individual pages. If you want to move an item from the pasteboard beside one page to another page, you can select the Zoom tool (Q) and click with the Option key down to get a reduced view of many pages at once, then drag the item across several pages without using the scroll bars.

Items stored on the pasteboard are saved as part of the document. It's a good idea to keep the pasteboard clear of extraneous items to minimize the document size. Use a library to store commonly used items that appear throughout a document.

Using a Scrapbook

The Scrapbook is a common desk accessory used on the Macintosh for storing items that can be copied from one document to another or from one application to another. A basic scrapbook desk accessory is part of the System that comes packaged with the Macintosh. You can buy other desk accessories that let you build and access more than one scrapbook or let you copy items from clip art libraries.

The disadvantage of using a scrapbook with QuarkXPress is that the *path* information normally stored by QuarkXPress is lost when an item goes into a Scrapbook.

Using the Clipboard for Repeated Copies

The Clipboard, a built-in feature of the Macintosh, is used to store selected items whenever the Cut or Copy command is used. It is common to use Cut or Copy to make copies of a selected item as part of normal editing.

It can also be efficient to use the Clipboard (rather than the pasteboard or a library) when you want to make many copies of an item and place them throughout a document. For example, let's say that you want to anchor a graphic logo within text throughout a document. For efficiency, go through the entire document pasting the graphic throughout the text from the Clipboard, as described in the next steps, rather than performing other edits on each page and then going back to a library or the pasteboard to copy the graphic again.

Step 1   In typing the text, include a text placeholder such as the word "LOGO" wherever you want the graphic to be positioned.

Step 2   Prepare a picture box with the logo scaled to the size that will fit in the text.

Step 3   Copy the picture box into the Clipboard with the Item tool selected.

Step 4   Select the Content tool (⌐⁷) and use the I-beam pointer to position the text insertion point at the beginning of the text.

Step 5   Use the Edit ➤ Find/Change command to locate the word LOGO. (Or scroll through the text to find all the places where you want the graphic logo.)

You cannot use the Find/Change command automatically to replace text with a graphic, so you still need to do the next step manually.

Step 6   Each time you find a place where the graphic should be anchored in the text, use the I-beam pointer to position the text insertion point, then use the Paste command to insert the logo.

Repeat steps 5 and 6 until all cases of the logo have been handled, then go on with other edits in the document.

The Clipboard can hold only one selection at a time, and its contents are replaced each time you use the Cut or Copy command. Its contents are deleted when you turn the computer off. You must use the Clear command, the Delete command, or the Delete or Backspace key to delete other text or graphics when you specifically do not want to replace the contents of the Clipboard. For this reason, it is better to use a library, a scrapbook, or the pasteboard for more permanent storage, as described under the previous headings.

Tips on Aligning Items

WYSIWYG (What You See Is What You Get) refers to what you see on the screen as compared with what prints out. Most desktop publishing systems and applications are not 100 percent WYSIWYG. Discrepancies occur because it is impossible to create an exact correlation between the 72 dpi screen resolution of most Macintosh computers and the 300 dpi resolution of most laser printers or the 2540 dpi resolution of high-resolution imagesetters. Besides, the fonts displayed on the low-resolution screen are shown as bitmaps, while high-resolution printers define the letters mathematically (in PostScript code) during the printing process.

Because no system is truly WYSIWYG, it is a good idea to use QuarkXPress' built-in features and commands for aligning items on a page, rather than to rely on your eye's judgment about whether items align vertically or horizontally. The next sections summarize the alignment aids that were first introduced in Chapters 1 through 6, offering more specific tips about when and how these aids can be used.

Using Commands for Aligning Text

Always use QuarkXPress' commands for aligning text, rather than doing it visually on the screen display. For example, if you want two lines of centered text, use the Style ➤ Alignment ➤ Centered command for both lines, rather than insert space at the beginning of each line until the two lines appear to be centered. Use the Item ➤ Modify command to align text relative to the top of a text box, rather than insert carriage returns to drop the text in the box.

Always use the Style ➤ Formats command to indent paragraphs or create hanging indents, rather than using spaces or tabs to indent lines.

Always use tabs rather than spaces to align tabular columns. If, for example, you want a title on the left side of a running head and a page number on the right side, use a right tab to align the page number where you want it rather than using spaces or moving a left-aligned block to the right. These last two techniques may yield results that appear correct on the screen, but might not print out the way you'd expect.

Using the Snap to Guides

Use the snap to feature of QuarkXPress' margin guides, column guides, and ruler guides to align objects. The edges of boxes and lines will "snap to" a guide when brought within 6 pixels of the guide. You can change the distance at which objects snap to guides in the General Preferences dialog box (Edit → Preferences→ General), as described in Chapter 3. Or you can turn snap to off by toggling the View → Snap to Guides command, as described in Chapter 2.

Using Column Guides as Spacing Guides

In positioning ruler guides on document pages, you can use the automatic column guide feature to divide automatically an area on the page into equal parts, using the next steps.

Creating a Vertical Grid

The most common way to create a vertical grid is to display a master page and choose Page → Master Guides. In the Master Guides dialog box, you can enter the number of columns you want to have on the page. If an automatic text box is on the master page, the text box will be divided into columns of equal width; if there is no text box on the page, gridlines will be positioned vertically on the page but they will not affect text. The minimum gutter allowance is .042 inch, or 3 points.

You can specify vertical gridlines without a text box on the page, and then draw a text box and specify a different number of columns by selecting the Item → Modify command, or by changing the number of columns for the text box in the Measurements palette.

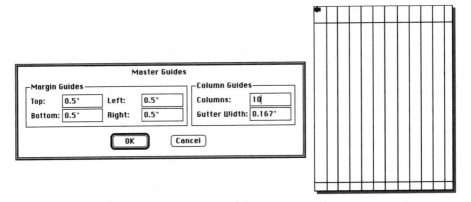

Figure 9-1 The Master Guides dialog box lets you specify a vertical grid.

Creating a Horizontal Grid

You could create a horizontal grid on a master page by selecting
Page ➤ Master Guides and specifying the number of columns with the nar-
rowest gutter possible (.042 inch). Then rotate the text box 90°, and drag
guides from the ruler to line up with the columns in the text box. The
page will then be divided equally between the top and bottom margins,
and you can delete the text box.

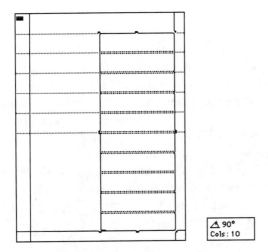

*Figure 9-2 Rotate the text box, then create a grid of equally spaced horizontal
ruler guides.*

Using the Space/Align Command

You can use the Item ➤ Space/Align command to align boxes and lines. If all the items are the same size, you can space the items apart by a specific measure between items, or you can distribute the items between the items themselves, left edges, centers, or right edges.

If the selected items are all different widths, you can make the space between items equal if you set the items to be distributed horizontally between *items*—that is, from the right edge of one item to the left edge of the adjacent item. Otherwise, the space between items will vary (Figure 9-3).

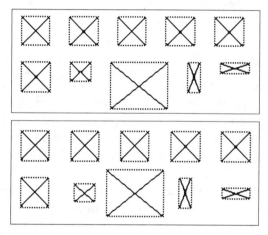

Figure 9-3 Items distributed horizontally between items (top) always have equal space between them; items distributed between centers can have different amounts of space between them (bottom).

Similarly, if the selected items are all different heights, you can make the space between items equal if you set the vertical space to be measured between items—that is, from the bottom edge of one item to the top edge of the adjacent item. Otherwise, the space between items can vary.

 The Space/Align command moves all items in the group—including locked items—except the rightmost item (in horizontal movement) and the topmost item (in vertical movement).

Creating Relationships Between Boxes

As you learned in Chapters 2 and 3, all text and some of the graphic items on a page are contained in boxes that are drawn using QuarkXPress' item creation tools. You can create relationships between these boxes in several ways.

- You can *link* text boxes to control a flow of text through a document.
- You can *anchor* boxes or lines within text so that they become part of the flowed text that moves when the text changes due to edits.
- You can *group* boxes or lines so that they can be multiple-selected with a single click.
- You can *constrain* a group of items to force them to remain within the boundaries of a constraining box.

The next headings offer some additional suggestions about when and how each of these relationships can be used.

Linking Boxes That Are Already Filled with Text

You can link two text boxes before they are filled with text, or you can link from a text-filled box to an *empty* text box, but you cannot link two boxes if they both already contain text. Normally, you either can import text into an automatic text box, so that a chain of linked boxes is created automatically, or you can link a filled text box to a series of empty boxes manually.

So what can you do when you have a series of unlinked boxes, all filled with text, and you decide you want them all to be linked? This condition might arise when you are composing a document from a series of boilerplate paragraphs that you have stored in a library, as is common in legal documents.

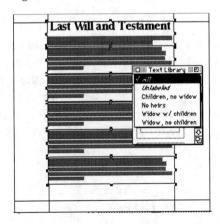

Figure 9-4 Legal document composed of a series of unlinked text boxes copied from a library.

You have to cut the text from each box and paste it at the end of the text in the previous box, but the obvious approach to this problem is not the most efficient.

The obvious solution is to start at the beginning—the first box in the series that you want to link. Select the Content tool (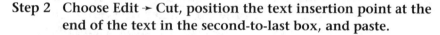), select all of the text in the *next* box in the sequence, choose Edit ➤ Cut, position the text insertion point at the end of the text in the first box, and paste. Now you can select the Linking tool (⊂⊐⊃) and link the first box to the (now-empty) second box. Select the Content tool (⟨ᵐ⟩) again and follow the same steps to empty the third box into the second, select the Linking tool again and link, and so on.

The less obvious solution offers one small economy in that you can stay with one tool at a time instead of switching between the Content tool and the Linking tool repeatedly:

Step 1   **Start at the *end* of the series of boxes. Select the Content tool (⟨ᵐ⟩), then select all of the text in the *last* box in the sequence.**

Step 2   **Choose Edit ➤ Cut, position the text insertion point at the end of the text in the second-to-last box, and paste.**

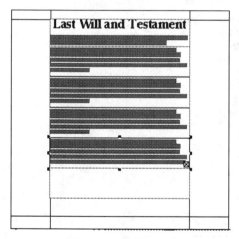

Figure 9-5 Text from last text box cut and pasted into second-to-last box.

Step 3   **Don't link the two boxes yet. Follow the same two steps to empty the second-to-last box into the third-to-the-last box, and so on.**

Figure 9-6 Text from all text boxes cut and pasted into the first box.

Step 4 **When all of the text has been pasted into the first box in the series and all other boxes are empty, select the Linking tool (⊞) while holding the Option key (to keep it selected) and link the boxes from the beginning to the end of the chain.**

Figure 9-7 All text boxes linked.

In this particular example where the entire page is composed of linked text boxes only, with no graphics or other items, you could delete all the empty text boxes after step 3 and enlarge the first text box, but the steps given here will work for any type of page layout.

Linking Text Boxes on Nonconsecutive Pages

Linked text boxes need not follow on consecutive pages. This feature is especially useful for creating newspaper or magazine layouts in which an article begins on one page and then jumps to another page in the document. QuarkXPress offers several ways of handling text jumps.

Method 1

If the page to which you want to link text is already part of the document, and the unlinked text box to which you want to jump the text is already in place, you can simply select the "jump from" box then select the Linking tool (⬛), click on the "jump from" box, scroll to the "jump to" page, and click the Linking pointer on the target text box.

Method 2

If the page to which you want to link text is already part of the document, and the unlinked text box to which you want to jump the text is *not* already in place, you must create the target text box before linking.

Step 1   Scroll to the "jump to" page and create the "jump to" text box.

Step 2   Return to the "jump from" page, and follow the procedure under the previous heading to link the boxes.

Depending on how far apart the two pages are, it might be quicker to create the "jump to" text box on the pasteboard next to the "jump from" page, link the two boxes, then *drag* the linked "jump to" text box to the "jump to" page (Figure 9-8). The farther apart the two pages, the less efficient it will be to drag the box down the pasteboard area.

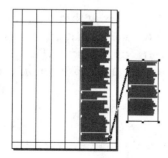

Figure 9-8 "Jump to" text box on pasteboard at first, then moved to appropriate page.

Method 3

If you are already working at the end of the document, and you want to jump the text ahead *past pages that have not yet been inserted*, the most efficient thing to do is insert the new "jump to" page immediately after the page you are working on, and insert the other pages between these two pages later (Figure 9-9).

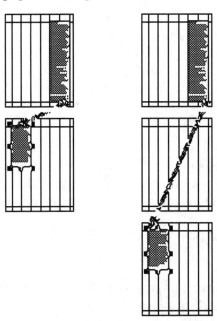

Figure 9-9 "Jump to" text box positioned on next page, with other pages to be inserted between the linked boxes later.

Working with Anchored Boxes

As you learned in Chapter 3, you can anchor a box within text. Anchored boxes can be either text boxes or picture boxes. You may find it useful to anchor an illustration to a figure caption, for example (Figure 9-10). Anchored items will flow with the text—and change position on the page if the text changes due to edits.

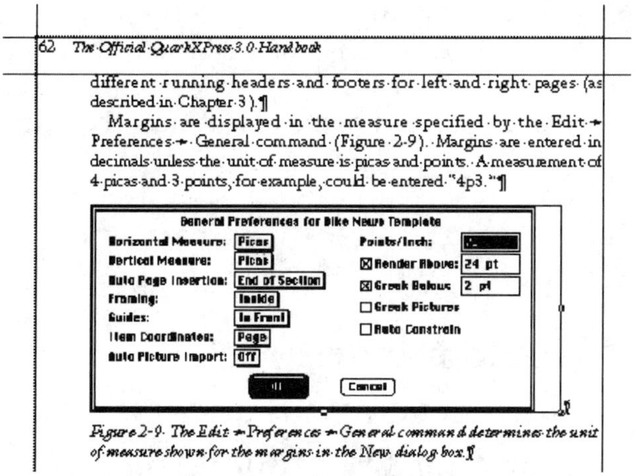

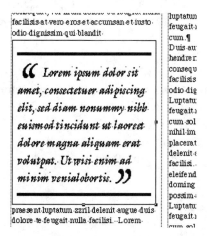

Figure 9-10 Anchored box contains an illustration related to a figure caption.

Anchored text boxes can be useful for anchoring pull quotes within an article. Another example of how you might use an anchored text box is to achieve a layout where single-column text is followed by two-column text; you could anchor a text box containing the two-column text withing the single-column text box.

Figure 9-11 Anchored text box containing a pull quote.

You can indent any paragraph using the Style ➤ Formats command, or you can hang an anchored box to the left of indented text by entering an Indent Here character (⌘-\) following the anchored box (Figure 9-12). Lines are indented from the position of the Indent Here character.

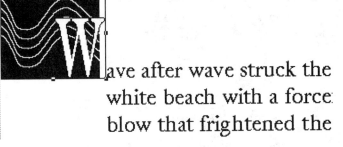

ve after wave struck the white beach with a force blow that frightened the

Figure 9-12 Anchored picture box followed by Indent Here character.

Working with Constrained Boxes

As you learned in Chapter 3, you can constrain boxes within other boxes. This creates a relationship that was called a "parent-child" relationship when it was the *only* way to work with boxes—in previous versions of QuarkXPress. Here we present some examples of when or why you would want to constrain or not constrain boxes.

Never group or constrain items that you want to anchor in text—grouped or constrained items cannot be anchored. If you attempt to anchor grouped items, a warning dialog will appear that says "The items currently on the Clipboard can't be anchored in text."

Do group and constrain a selection of items that together compose a table or figure, such as the one shown in Figure 9-13.

Option·Plans¶	
Plan·A⇥	$20,000¶
Plan·B⇥	$50,000¶
Plan·C⇥	$35,000¶

Figure 9-13 Tabular data composed as a constrained group. The vertical line cannot be drawn outside of the constrained group.

If you are working on a document with Auto Constrain set to off in the General Preferences dialog box, you can constrain specific items in the document by first grouping them and then choosing Item ➤ Constrain.

Tricky Page Designs

Even though you might be familiar with all of QuarkXPress' commands and tools, some page designs present challenges. Here are some tips for handling complex page layouts as well as simple problems that we have seen encountered by those who are new to document production.

Double-Sided Documents

QuarkXPress automatically handles most of the "tricky" issues in producing double-sided documents, but be aware of the points mentioned in the following sections.

Include Blank Pages

In preparing a document for double-sided printing, be sure to account for and print every page — including blank "left" pages that will be needed to force new sections or chapters to start on a right page (Figure 9-14). Having a numbered sheet for every page of the document will help in printing or copying the document. If you do not number blank pages, but want them to print so they are collated within other pages, be sure the Print Blank pages option is checked on in the Print dialog box.

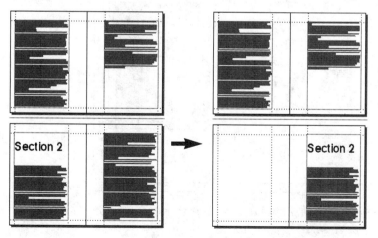

Figure 9-14 Blank page inserted to force new section onto a right-facing page.

Inserting an Odd Number of Pages

If you need to insert pages between existing pages in a document set up with Facing Pages, QuarkXPress will automatically shift the pages. If you add an even number of pages, of course, all left and right pages remain as left and right pages. If, however, you insert an odd number of pages, right pages must become left pages and vice versa. QuarkXPress will automatically "shuffle" the pages so that they take on the specifications of the appropriate left or right master.

Changing the First Page of a File

If you need to change the starting page number of a document (set up with Facing Pages) from an even-numbered page to an odd-numbered page, you can simply change the starting page number in the Section dialog box and QuarkXPress will shift the pages to the correct left and right master pages. However, to change an odd-numbered page to an even-numbered page, you need to follow certain steps to ensure that pages will shuffle correctly—so that pages formerly printed as right pages will shift to print on the left and vice versa.

For example, let's assume that you've set up a document as the second chapter of a report, beginning on an odd-numbered page, number 35 (set up in the Section dialog box by selecting Page ➤ Section). If you change the first page of the document to an even-numbered page, 36, only the first page shifts to a left page. The steps described next will shift all pages.

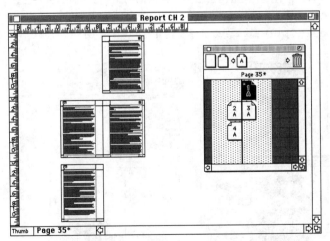

Figure 9-15 The first page of the file is set up as page 35 (Page ➤ Section) and needs to be changed to page 36.

Step 1 Insert a new document page BEFORE the first page of the file to force the pages in the document to take on the format of the new, correct left and right master pages.

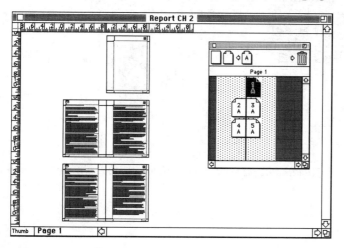

Figure 9-16 The Document Layout palette after inserting a new page before the first page of a file.

Step 2 Click on the Page 2 icon. Click on the label "Page 2" under the master page icons. The Section dialog box will appear; change the starting page number to 36.

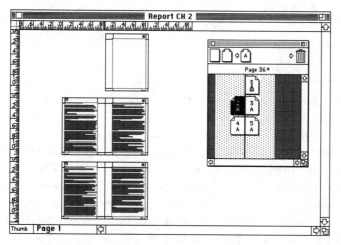

Figure 9-17 Change the starting page number to 36.

Step 3   Delete the blank first page.

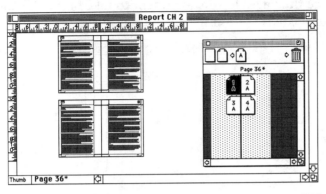

Figure 9-18 The document pages are renumbered with the correct master pages.

Creating Spreads

QuarkXPress lets you create multiple-page spreads, with the option of creating items that span the gutter between facing pages. Any pair of facing pages in a two-sided document is considered a spread, but you can also create spreads of more than two facing pages for multifold brochures or documents with fold-out pages (Figure 9-19).

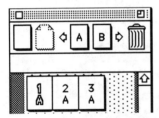

Figure 9-19 Fold-out panels in a two-fold brochure.

To create two-page or facing-page spreads (as is common in documents that will be printed double-sided), choose Facing Pages in the New dialog box or in the Document Setup dialog box, as explained in Chapter 2.

To create a multiple-page spread of any number of pages—or to create a facing-page fold-out panel in a single-sided document—drag page icons in the Document Layout palette into position beside each other. You can drag master page icons to create new pages or drag existing document pages to move current pages. Figure 9-20 shows various alternatives.

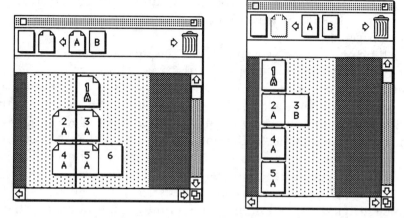

Figure 9-20 Normal double-sided document with a fold-out panel (left) and fold-out panel in a single-sided document (right).

Bleeding Text or Graphics

Items that run off one or more edges of a page onto another page are said to "bleed" off the page. Any text or graphic item can bleed off a page. A bleed is a commonly used effect that makes a layout more dynamic by giving the reader's eye a fluid line that does not end on the page (Figure 9-21).

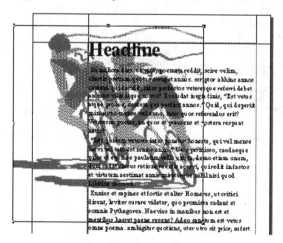

Figure 9-21 Image "bleeds" off left side of page.

Always print registration marks when printing pages with bleeds. When you print a document with Registration Marks selected in the Print dialog box, QuarkXPress increases the print area by .25 inches around document pages to accommodate items that bleed into the pasteboard area. To print bleeds effectively, you need to print on paper that is larger than the document page size.

All printers leave a margin of white space at the edge of the paper or roll—nothing will print in this area. The page outlines in the QuarkXPress document window represent the actual edges of the paper (if page size is the same as paper size), so you need to be familiar with your printer's margin limitations and make sure that your page designs do not include text or graphics in the nonprinting area at the edges of the page. You can determine the limits of the print margins on your printer by printing out a page that is covered by a solid black box.

Figure 9-22 shows an image that bleeds across two letter-size pages. The inside margins may be lost in the nonprinting edges of the paper, particularly if you are using a laser printer that does not handle ledger size paper.

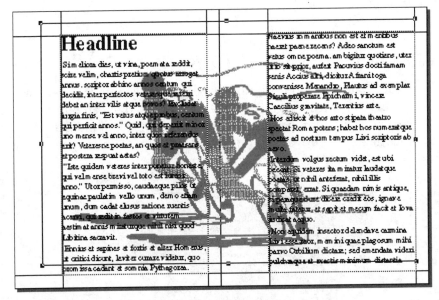

Figure 9-22 Image "bleeds" across two pages.

Controlling Text Runaround

As you learned in Chapter 3, you can make text flow around a box or line created with one of QuarkXPress' item creation tools by positioning the item on top of a text box and using use Item ⇥ Runaround to set runaround to a value other than None.

If you specify a runaround in the Runaround dialog box, you can enter the distance between the runaround text and the top, left, bottom, and right edges of a box. You cannot, however, specify text outset distances for lines. Here are some additional tips on how this feature can be used.

When you flow a single column of text around an item, the text will flow only on the side with the widest text area between the item and the edge of the text box (Figure 9-23).

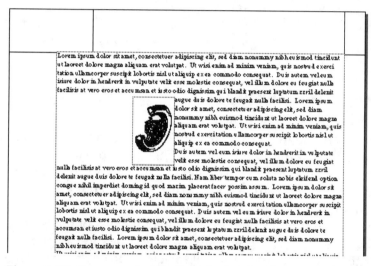

Figure 9-23 Runaround set to Item for box inside a one-column text box.

You can make a line or box any color and shade, or specify a color of none or a shade of 0 percent to make a transparent line or box. You can force text to runaround a transparent item by using the Item ⇥ Runaround command to specify Item mode (Figure 9-24). You can also use the Item ⇥ Modify command to suppress printout of the item and still have it affect text runaround.

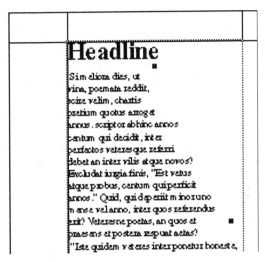

Figure 9-24 Slanted margin forced by a transparent line.

Auto and Manual Image Runaround

If you have a picture box filled with an imported picture and you use Item ➤ Runaround to set the Mode to Auto Image, QuarkXPress automatically runs text around the picture in the active picture box. This is the type of runaround produced with graphics in QuarkXPress 2.12.

If you set the Mode to Manual Image, QuarkXPress creates an *editable* runaround polygon around the picture in the active picture box. You can modify a runaround polygon by adding, removing, or repositioning handles and by repositioning segments, as described in Chapter 6. You can specify the Text Outset for Manual Image mode just as you can for Auto Image mode.

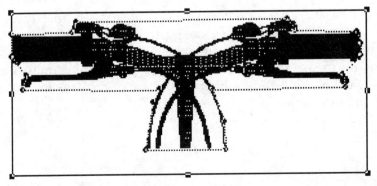

Figure 9-25 A runaround polygon created automatically around an imported image.

You can also select Invert to run the text *inside* a picture's manual image polygon. See Chapter 11 for tips on how to use this feature to flow text inside a shape.

You can use a picture to create a runaround polygon and then delete the picture but keep the polygon. Doing so is handy when you want to use a for-position-only scan of an image to create text wrap, so the lithographer can strip in the photographic halftone of the image manually. You would use the for-position-only scan to create the polygon, and keep it on the page for draft printouts and for a sample to show the printer how to scale and crop the stripped-in halftone. The scan could then be deleted from the final camera-ready pages that you print.

Another time-saving trick if you are paying a print shop to strip in halftones and you want to use a for-position-only scan to help shape text runaround is to scan an *outline* of the photographic image instead of scanning the image itself. The outline scan will scan more quickly, take up less disk space, redraw more quickly on the screen, and print more quickly for draft versions.

 You can disable screen redraw and save time in editing a runaround polygon by holding down the space bar as you edit. Release the space bar to redraw the screen and reflow text.

Creating Forms

You can use all of the alignment techniques described earlier in this chapter to create forms easily in QuarkXPress. Here we outline the steps used to create the sample form shown in Figure 9-32. You can adapt these steps to your specific needs, since the exact sequence of steps and the commands you use will vary depending on the content and design of the form you are creating. It's a good idea to start with some idea of what the final form will look like, even though you can, of course, add, delete, or rearrange fields in the process of creating the form in QuarkXPress.

Step 1   **Sketch the form and list the fields on a piece of paper before you start.**

Step 2   **In QuarkXPress, select the Text Box creation tool (Ⓐ) and create separate boxes for each distinct area on the form.**

Some forms require only one text box; others might add one or two text boxes *on top of* the full-page text box; others might be composed of separate *adjacent* text boxes (Figure 9-26).

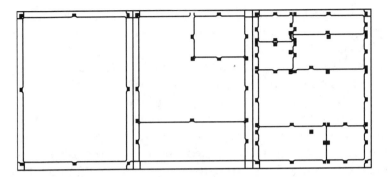

Figure 9-26 Some forms require only one text box (left); others might add one or two text boxes on top of the full-page text box (center); others might be composed of separate adjacent text boxes (right).

Step 3   Type and format the text in each text box. Set tabs to position text across a line.

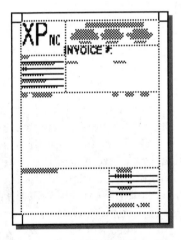

Figure 9-27 Form with text typed into boxes.

You can use flush-right tabs with underscore characters as leaders to create lines under fields that will be filled in.

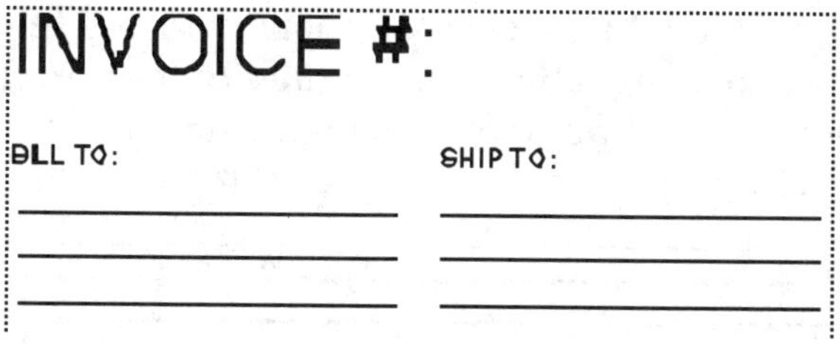

INVOICE #:

BILL TO: SHIP TO:

_____   _____
_____   _____
_____   _____

Figure 9-28 Tabs with underscore characters as leaders created the two sets of entry fields in this box.

You can use Style ➤ Rules to create lines above and below fields that extend the width of the box margins.

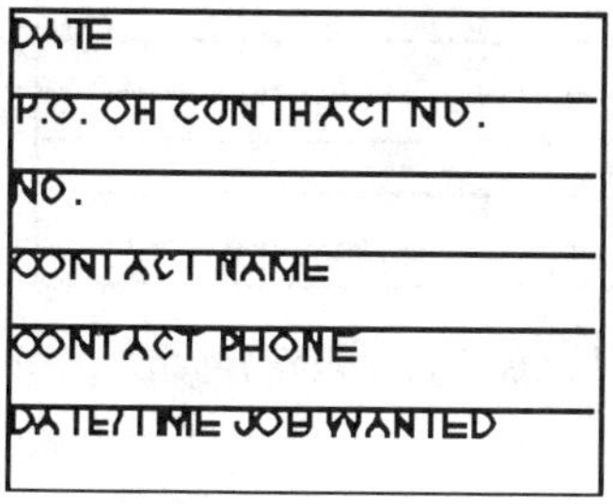

DATE

P.O. OR CONTRACT NO.

NO.

CONTACT NAME

CONTACT PHONE

DATE/TIME JOB WANTED

Figure 9-29 The lines in this box are created using Style ➤ Rules.

Step 4   Add frames around text boxes as appropriate.

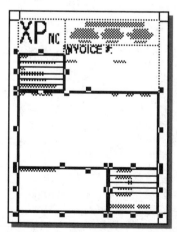

Figure 9-30 Four of the seven text boxes in this form have 1-point black frames.

Step 5   Select the Orthogonal Line creation tool (+) to add lines that were not created using tab leaders or rules that are part of the text. Use Item ➤ Step and Repeat to duplicate series of lines at equal intervals.

QTY	DESCRIPTION		HRS	RATE	TOTAL

Figure 9-31 The Step and Repeat command was used to create this series of parallel lines.

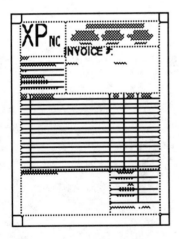

Figure 9-32 The final form.

Creating Forms for Typewriters

In creating a form that will be filled in using a typewriter, follow all the same steps as just outlined, but set the distance between lines on the form to equal a multiple of the distance between lines when typed on the typewriter.

You can determine this distance by typing a few lines on a blank sheet of paper at the intended setting—usually double-spaced or space and a half. Measure the distance between lines, and use this distance—or some multiple of it—as the leading value (in setting lines of text) or as the vertical offset value in using the Step and Repeat command.

If the form consists of more than one text box, set the Baseline Grid at the typewriter's interline spacing value, and make sure the text in each boxed is locked to the baseline grid.

If you will be adding horizontal lines with the Orthogonal Line creation tool (+), create horizontal ruler guides across the page at intervals that match the typewriter's interline spacing value, and use these guides in creating the first line, before using Step and Repeat to duplicate the line.

Summary

This chapter provided information on the pros and cons of various ways to store items—using a library, the pasteboard, or a scrapbook. We also provided tips on aligning items, linking text boxes, and anchoring boxes in text. Finally, we offered guidance for working with tricky page layouts, including creating spreads and bleeds, and tips for creating forms.

The next chapter discusses how to work with text from databases or mainframe computers.

10 *Working with Text from Databases and Mainframes*

Database publishing encompasses many kinds of documents, from financial reports to membership directories. The text, or data, which is generated by database programs has the unique characteristic of containing commas or tabs to separate information. Another characteristic of text from a database is that it is often published in a repetitive format. If you use QuarkXPress solely for the task of publishing text from database, we strongly urge you to consider some of the excellent QuarkXTensions that help streamline the process tremendously. One of the most popular programs for this purpose is Xdata by Em Software (see the appendix).

While publishing databases offers a unique set of challenges, another category of text that also has unique characteristics is text created on non-Macintosh computers, especially text created using text editors on mainframe computers, which often have little or no formatting capabilities. It would be nice if the entire computing world enjoyed the many benefits of using Macintosh computers, but since the reality is that they don't, it may be useful to know how to work with text you get from another type of computer. Especially bothersome can be the fact that sometimes unwanted characters, such as paragraph returns at the end of every line, are embedded in the text.

353

This chapter offers tips on how to work globally with invisible characters as an aid to both database publishing and in "cleaning up" text telecommunicated from other computers. This chapter also covers XPress Tags, special codes for formatting text that can be input on non-Macintosh computers and are recognized in QuarkXPress.

Finding and Changing Special Characters

As you learned in Chapter 4, QuarkXPress has a Find/Change command for searching and globally replacing words, phrases, or character attributes in text. You can search for special characters and hidden characters by holding down the ⌘ key and typing the key that you would normally use to insert the special character in the text, as shown in Figure 10-1.

Special Character	Find/Change Entry	Dialog Box Display
Space	Space	
Tab	⌘-Tab	\t
New Paragraph	⌘-Return	\p
New Line	⌘-Shift-Return	\n
New Column	⌘-Enter	\c
New Box	⌘-Shift-Enter	\b
Wild Card	⌘-?	\?

Figure 10-1 Searching for special characters.

The space, tab, and new paragraph characters are search parameters in the common conversions of imported ASCII text, described under the next headings.

Be sure to include spaces in the Change To field if you type them in Find What field. You need not type a space before and after a word in the Change To field—if you check Whole Words, QuarkXPress will find the word when it is framed by spaces or followed by punctuation.

Eliminating Unwanted Paragraph Returns

Text can be telecommunicated from one computer to another, either directly or through a mailbox facility. Mailbox transfers are convenient because the sender and receiver can access them at any time—you need not coordinate having a person available at each end of the phone lines at the same time. It is preferable to use a mailbox or transfer software that lets you preserve any formatting that was done, but most electronic mail services force you to transfer text in ASCII format (text only with no formatting).

If the transfer or conversion method forces paragraph returns (also called hard carriage returns) at the end of every line, it is a good idea to insert at least two carriage returns after every paragraph or intended line break in the text *before it is transferred.* You can quickly reformat this type of file in QuarkXPress without referring to a printed version of the text to find paragraph breaks, following the steps described next.

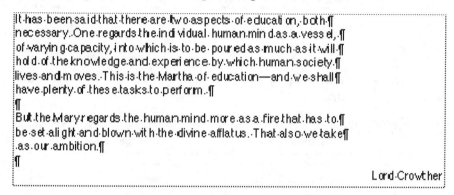

Figure 10-2 Telecommunicated text sometimes has unwanted returns at the end of every line.

Step 1   **Globally change all double carriage returns (which appear only at the end of each paragraph) to some unique character string that is not found elsewhere in the text, such as "xyz".**

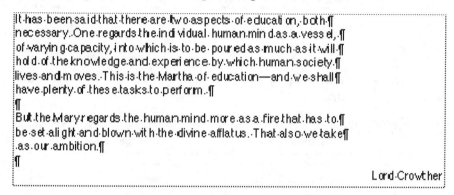

Figure 10-3 Type ⌘-Return in the Find/Change dialog box, which shows returns as \p.

Step 2 Globally change all single carriage returns to nothing or to a space (if the line-break returns replaced spaces in the conversion process).

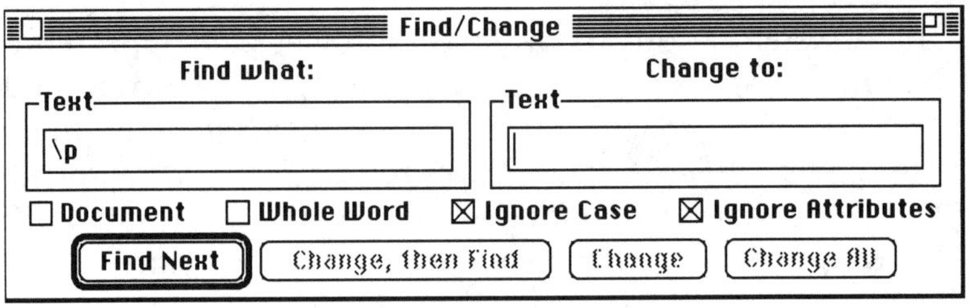

Figure 10-4 Find/Change dialog box shows a space as nothing.

Step 3 Globally change all occurrences of "xyz" to single carriage returns.

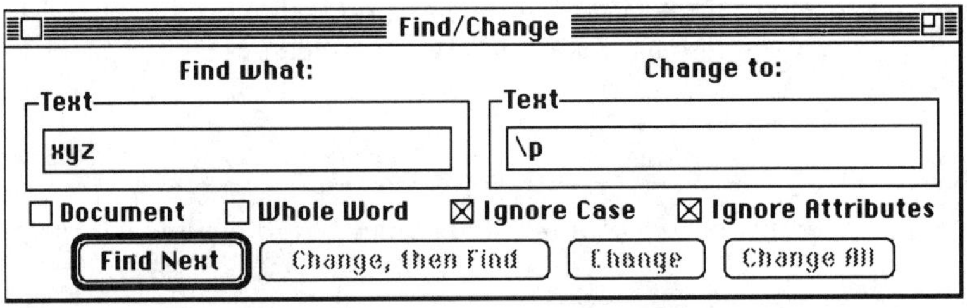

Figure 10-5 Change unique characters back to a paragraph return.

After following these steps, the file appears as you'd normally expect it to—with no paragraph returns *except* those at the end of each paragraph.

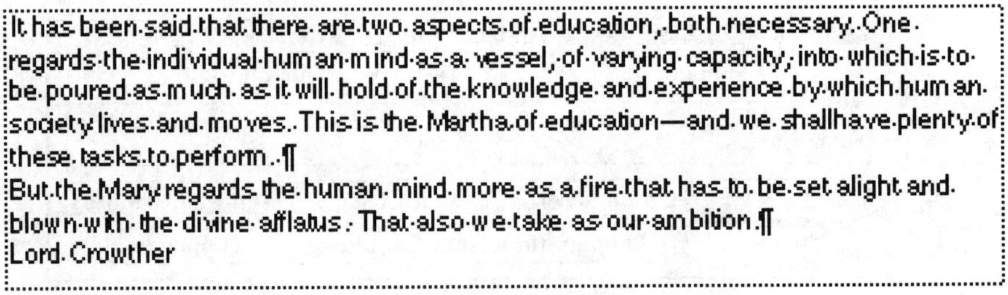
It has been said that there are two aspects of education, both necessary. One regards the individual human mind as a vessel, of varying capacity, into which is to be poured as much as it will hold of the knowledge and experience by which human society lives and moves. This is the Martha of education—and we shall have plenty of these tasks to perform.¶
But the Mary regards the human mind more as a fire that has to be set alight and blown with the divine afflatus. That also we take as our ambition.¶
Lord Crowther

Figure 10-6 Text in QuarkXPress after global changes.

Converting Data Files to Tabular Format

If the text fields exported from a spreadsheet or database are separated by the tab character, then you can set tabs in QuarkXPress and the data should fall into tabbed columns. However, if the program used commas or some other delimiter, you will need to convert these to tabs before the data can be arranged in columns.

Sometimes text-only files exported from a spreadsheet or database include quotation marks around fields that happened to use the field delimiter as part of the data. In either case, you can use QuarkXPress' Find/Change command globally to convert the field delimiters to tabs.

Step 1   **Export the data from the spreadsheet or database in ASCII text format, then use the Get Text command to import it into QuarkXPress.**

Kay,Atherton,Medi-Calls,"248 Texas Street, #9",San Francisco,CA,94107,626-8343
Hector,"Barrera, Jr.",Azteca,1521 Manor Drive,San Pablo,CA,94949,415/233-9239
David,Jewett,"CJS, Inc.",1920 Francisco,Berkeley,CA,94709,415/548-4762
Grace,Moore,TechArt,400 Pacific Avenue,San Francisco,CA,94133,415/362-1110

Figure 10-7 Text as originally imported.

Step 2   **To distinguish between a comma used as a delimiter and a comma that is part of a field entry, globally change all incidences of comma-space to some unique character string that is not found elsewhere in the text, such as "xyz."**

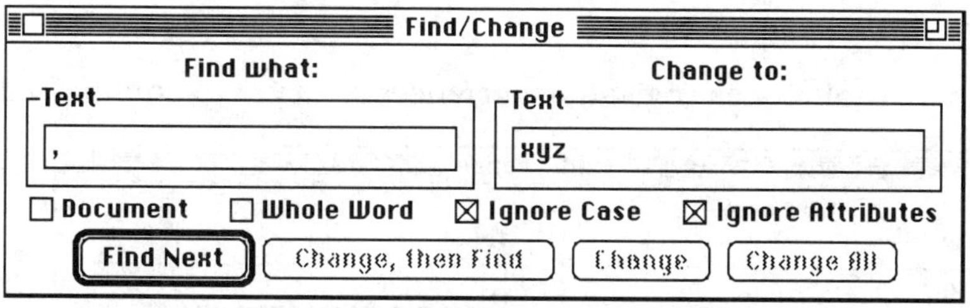

Figure 10-8 The Find/Change dialog box.

In order for the global searches suggested here to work, we have to assume that a comma that is part of a field entry will always be followed by a space, whereas a comma that is a delimiter will usually be followed by the contents of the next field or by another comma (if the field is empty). If a field entry in the spreadsheet or database actually starts with a space, then the delimiter in front of that field will not be converted to a tab with the searches suggested here. You should check the results of these replacements after you have set tab stops to format the text correctly.

Step 3   Globally change all commas to tabs.

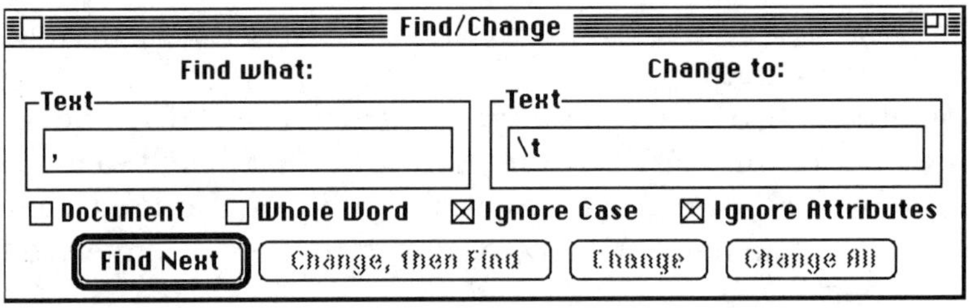

Figure 10-9   Type ⌘-Tab in the Find/Change dialog box, which shows tabs as \t.

Step 4   Globally change all quote marks to nothing. Examine your file to confirm whether these are actually inch or feet marks or true opening and closing quote marks.

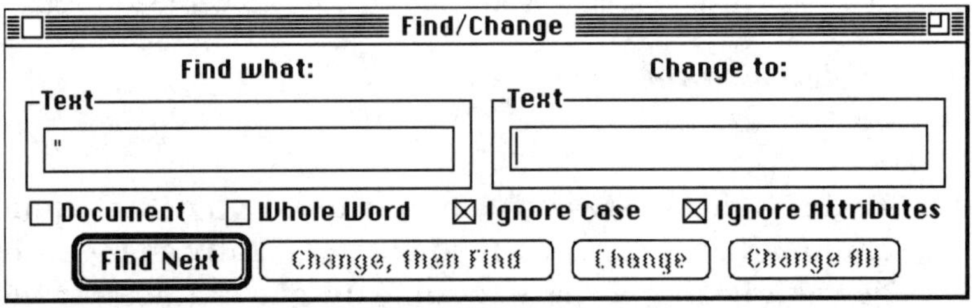

Figure 10-10   Change quote marks to nothing.

Step 5   Globally change all occurrences of "xyz" to comma-space.

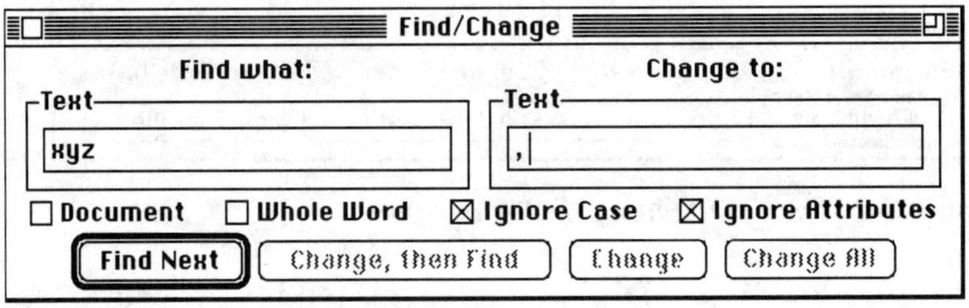

Figure 10-11   Change the unique characters back to comma-space.

Step 6   **Select all of the data and choose Style ➤ Formats. With the Paragraph Format dialog box displayed, set tab stops on the text ruler.**

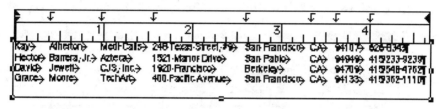

Figure 10-12 Text falls into place when tab stops are set in QuarkXPress.

In step 6, you can define a style sheet for the data lines and set tabs through the style sheet.

Converting Data Files to Nontabular Formats

Sometimes you will want to convert data from a spreadsheet or database to nontabular formats. A common example of this is converting a data file of names and addresses to a directory listing format.

One approach is to use the mail-merge feature of your word processing application to create a formatted text file directly from the data file. The alternative is to start the formatting processing in the spreadsheet or database and then finish the formatting in QuarkXPress using the Find/Change command. This second approach is described here.

Assume that the spreadsheet or database lists the entries for each record in the following order:

first name
last name
company
street address
city
state
zip code
phone number

What you want to end up with is a directory listing format:

first name last name
company
street address
city, state zip code
phone number

If you simply export the data in its current format, you will end up with commas or tabs between every field, and it will be nearly impossible to use global changes to change the format appropriately. You can save a lot of time and trouble by making a few changes to the data *before* you export it.

Figure 10-13 Data in a spreadsheet format.

Step 1   Insert unique search codes between certain fields in the data:

- Insert "xyz" in a new column or field between the first name field and the last name. This will be changed to a space in step 4.

- Insert the same code, "xyz", between the state field and the zip code.

- Insert a different code, such as "zzz", between the city field and the state. This will be changed to a comma in step 5.

In a spreadsheet, you can insert columns between fields and fill the columns with the search codes as shown in Figure 10-14. In a database, you could make the search codes part of the "report format" and output the data to disk as a report.

Figure 10-14 Data file with unique search codes entered between selected fields.

Step 2   Export the data from the spreadsheet or database as text and import it into QuarkXPress. Here we assume that the fields are separated by tabs in the export process. (See "Converting Data Files to Tabular Format," earlier in this chapter.)

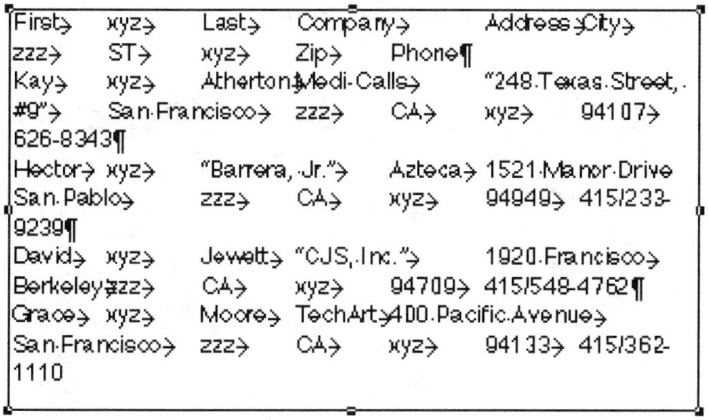

```
First→    xyz→     Last→    Company→        Address→City→
zzz→      ST→      xyz→     Zip→     Phone¶
Kay→      xyz→     Atherton→Medi-Calls→     "248.Texas.Street,.
#9"→      San·Francisco→   zzz→     CA→      xyz→     94107→
626-8343¶
Hector→ xyz→      "Barrera, ·Jr."→   Azteca→ 1521·Manor·Drive
San.Pablo→        zzz→     CA→      xyz→     94949→ 415/233-
9239¶
David→    xyz→     Jewett→  "CJS,·Inc."→     1920.Francisco→
Berkeley→zzz→     CA→      xyz→     94709→ 415/548-4762¶
Grace→    xyz→     Moore→   TechArt→400.Pacific.Avenue→
San·Francisco→    zzz→     CA→      xyz→     94133→ 415/362-
1110
```

Figure 10-15 Data file when exported from the spreadsheet or database as text and imported into QuarkXPress.

Step 3   Globally change all carriage returns to double carriage returns.

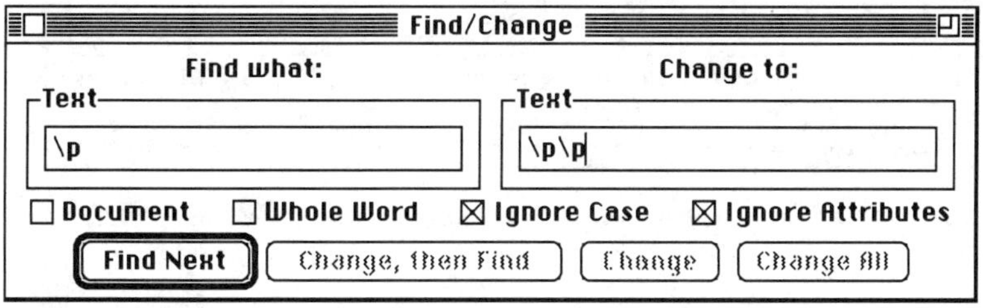

Figure 10-16 Type ⌘-Return in the Find/Change dialog box, which shows returns as \p.

Step 4   Globally change all occurrences of Tab-xyz-Tab to spaces.

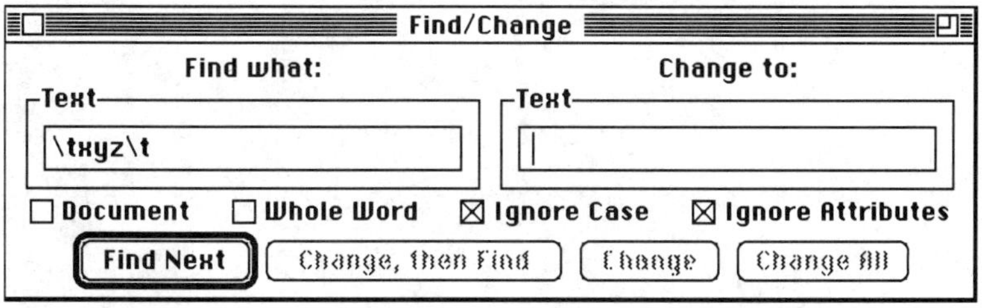

Figure 10-17 Type ⌘-Tab in the Find/Change dialog box, which shows tabs as \t.

Step 5 Globally change all occurrences of Tab-zzz-Tab to comma-space.

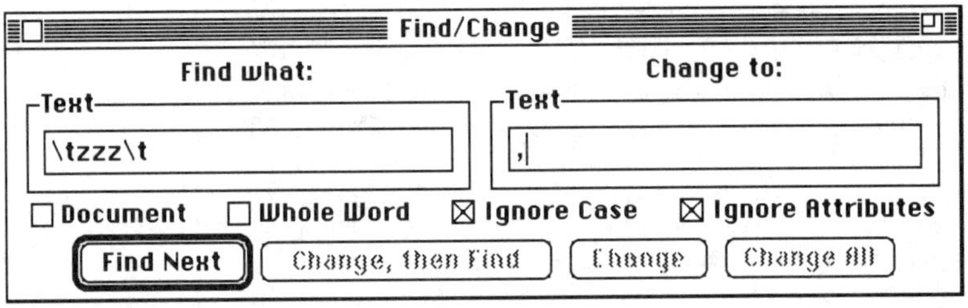

Figure 10-18 Find/Change dialog box.

Step 6 Globally change all remaining occurrences of Tab to Return.

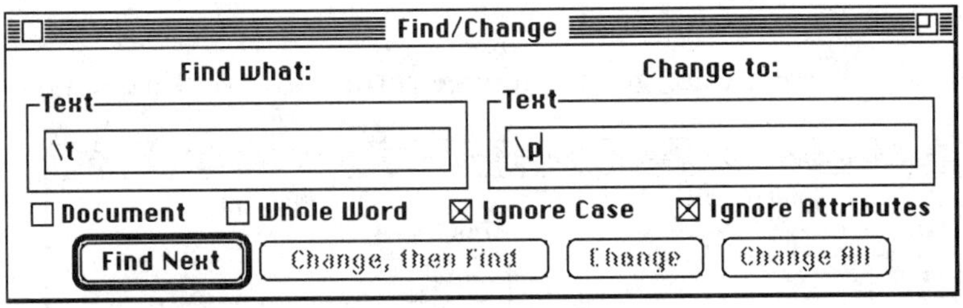

Figure 10-19 Find/Change dialog box shows tabs as \t and carriage returns as \p.

Step 7 If the spreadsheet or database added quotation marks around fields that contained a comma, globally change the quotation marks to nothing (strip them out). Examine your file to confirm whether these are actually inch or feet marks or true opening and closing quote marks.

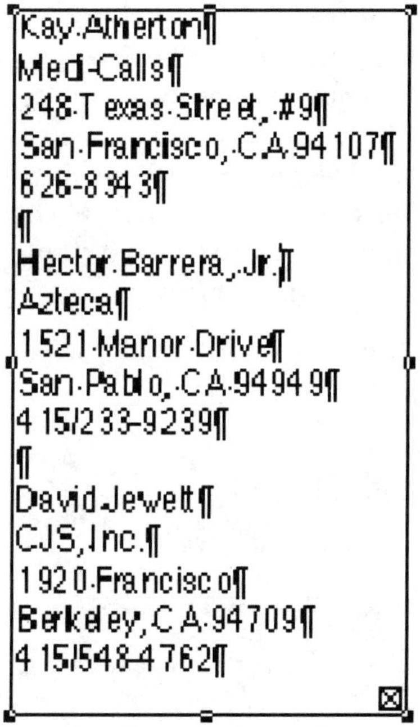

```
Kay Atherton¶
Medi-Calls¶
248 Texas Street, #9¶
San Francisco, CA 94107¶
626-8343¶
¶
Hector Barrera, Jr.¶
Azteca¶
1521 Manor Drive¶
San Pablo, CA 94949¶
415/233-9239¶
¶
David Jewett¶
CJS, Inc.¶
1920 Francisco¶
Berkeley, CA 94709¶
415/548-4762¶
```

Figure 10-20 Final text format.

Embedding Format Codes in Data Files

Sometimes you will want to convert data from a spreadsheet or database to nontabular formats where some fields have different character formats. A common example of this is converting a data file of names and addresses to a directory, similar to the previous example.

As you have seen earlier, you can use global searches to reformat data imported from a spreadsheet or database file. You can use the same techniques to embed QuarkXPress tag codes, discussed later in this chapter.

For example, let's say you want to convert the same data file of names and addresses to a directory listing format as described under the previous heading, but you want the different fields to have different character formats, such as:

first name last name
company
street address
city, state zip code
phone number

You can use the mail-merge feature of your word processing application to create a formatted text file directly from the data file, or format the text in QuarkXPress using the Find/Change command as described here.

Step 1 Insert unique search codes between certain fields in the data. This is the same as Step 1 in the previous example, with the addition of inserting a unique code between last name and company and between company and address:

- Insert “xyz” between the first name field and the last name.
- Insert “xyz” between the state field and the zip code.
- Insert “xxx” between last name and company.
- Insert “yyy” between company and address.
- Insert “zzz” between the city field and the state.

Address File

	A	B	C	D	E	F	G	H	I	J	K	L	M
1	First	xyz	Last	xxx	Company	yyy	Address	City	zzz	ST	xyz	Zip	Phone
2	Kay	xyz	Atherton	xxx	Medi-Calls	yyy	248 Texas Street, #9	San Francisc	zzz	CA	xyz	94107	626-8343
3	Hector	xyz	Barrera, Jr.	xxx	Azteca	yyy	1521 Manor Drive	San Pablo	zzz	CA	xyz	94949	415/233-9239
4	David	xyz	Jewett	xxx	CJS, Inc.	yyy	1920 Francisco	Berkeley	zzz	CA	xyz	94709	415/548-4762
5	Grace	xyz	Moore	xxx	TechArt	yyy	400 Pacific Avenue	San Francisc	zzz	CA	xyz	94133	415/362-1110

Figure 10-21 Data file with unique search codes entered between selected fields.

You can insert these codes using techniques described under step 1 under the previous heading.

Step 2 Export the data as text from the spreadsheet or database and import it into QuarkXPress as described under the previous heading.

```
First→    xyz→    Last→    xxx→    Company→        yyy→    Address→City→
zzz→      ST→     xyz→     Zip→    Phone¶
Kay→      xyz→    Atherton→xxx→    Medi-Calls→     yyy→    "248·Texas·
Street,·#9"→      San·Francisco→   zzz→    CA→     xyz→    94107→  626-
8343¶
Hector→   xyz→    "Barrera,·Jr."→  xxx→    Azteca→ yyy→    1521·Manor·
Drive→    San·Pablo→       zzz→    CA→     xyz→    94949→  415/233-9239¶
David→    xyz→    Jewett→  xxx→    "CJS,·Inc."→    yyy→    1920·Francisco→
Berkeley→zzz→     CA→      xyz→    94709→  415/548-4762¶
Grace→    xyz→    Moore→   xxx→    TechArt→yyy→    400·Pacific·Avenue→
San·Francisco→    zzz→     CA→     xyz→    94133→  415/362-1110
```

Figure 10-22 Data file when exported as text from the spreadsheet or database and imported into QuarkXPress.

(Opening the text in a word processing application and performing these global changes *before* importing the text into QuarkXPress is preferable; doing so eliminates step 10 in this sequence.)

Step 3 **Globally change all carriage returns to double carriage returns and the formatting code <B> (a QuarkXPress Tag that will make the name bold).**

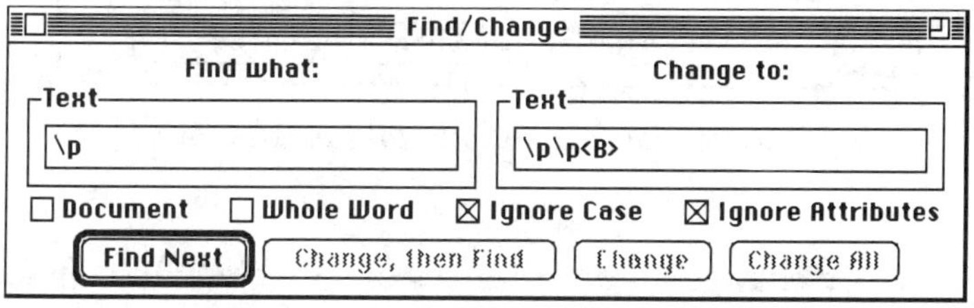

Figure 10-23 Change single paragraph returns to double paragraph returns followed by the code for bold.

Step 4 **Globally change all occurrences of Tab-xxx-Tab to <B>return<I> to turn bold off after the name, and start the company on a new line in italics.**

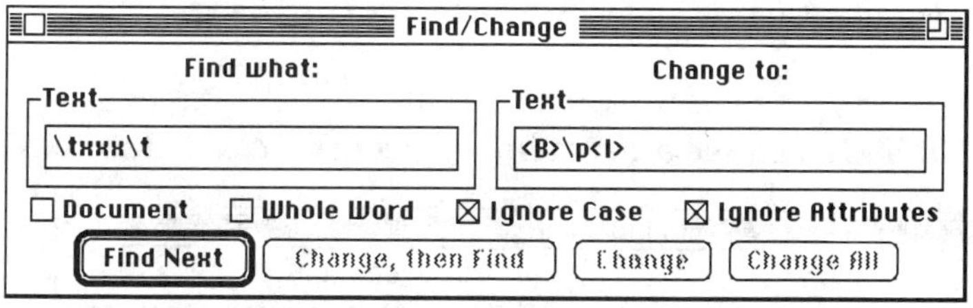

Figure 10-24 Find/Change dialog box shows tabs as \t.

Step 5 **Globally change all occurrences of Tab-yyy-Tab to <I>return to turn italics off and start the address on a new line.**

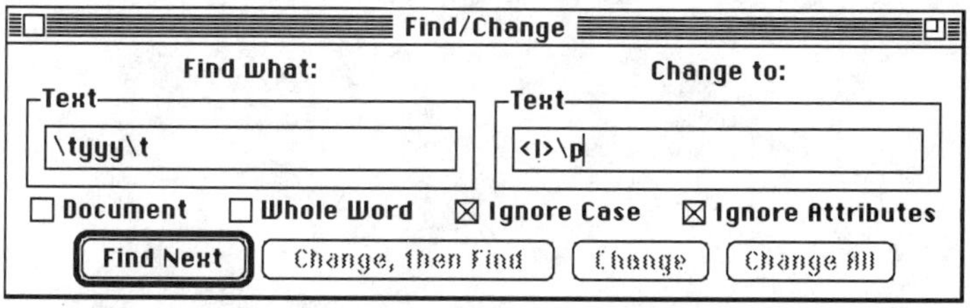

Figure 10-25 Find/Change dialog box.

Step 6   Globally change all occurrences of Tab-zzz-Tab to comma-space.

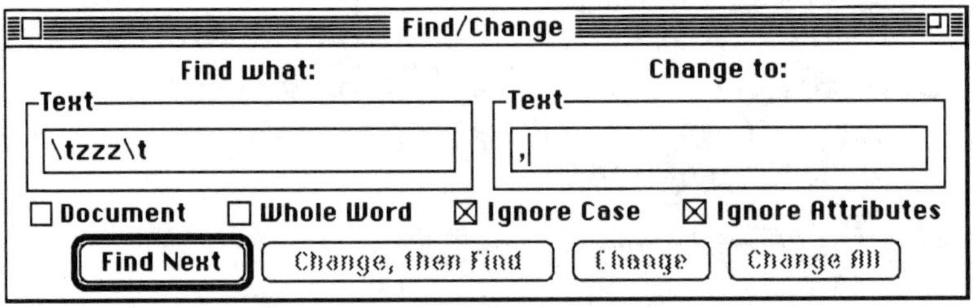

Figure 10-26 Find/Change dialog box shows tabs as \t.

Step 7   Globally change all occurrences of Tab-xyz-Tab to spaces.

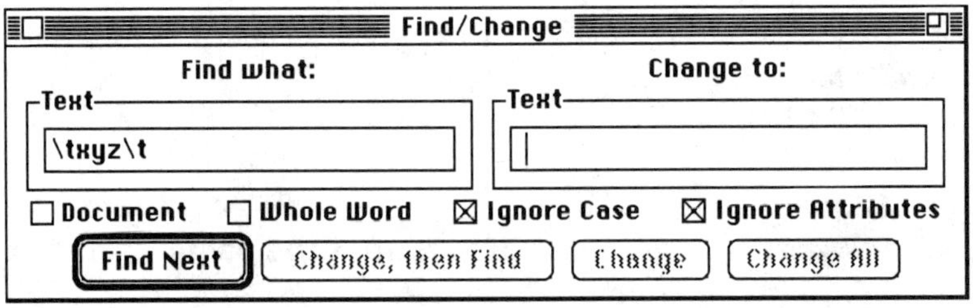

Figure 10-27 Find/Change dialog box shows tabs as \t.

Step 8   Globally change all remaining occurrences of Tab to Return.

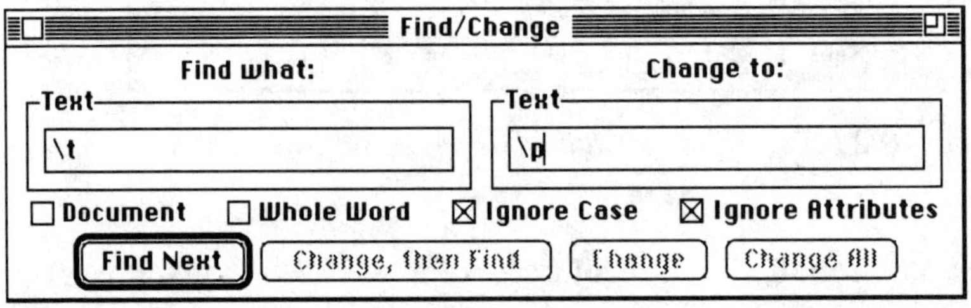

Figure 10-28 Convert remaining tabs to paragraph returns.

Step 9 **If the spreadsheet or database added quotation marks around fields that contained a comma, globally change the quotation marks to nothing (strip them out). Examine your file to confirm whether these are actually inch or foot marks or true opening and closing quote marks.**

If these above changes were done in a word processing application, the database text is ready to be imported into QuarkXPress (step 11). If you performed these steps in QuarkXPress, you'll need to export the text and reimport it, as described in step 10, so that the XPress tags will be converted to the correct formatting.

```
<B>Kay Atherton<B>
<I>Medi-Calls<I>
248 Texas Street, #9
San Francisco, CA 94107
626-8343

<B>Hector Barrera, Jr.<B>
<I>Azteca<I>
1521 Manor Drive
San Pablo, CA 94949
415/233-9239

<B>David Jewett<B>
<I>CJS, Inc.<I>
1920 Francisco
Berkeley, CA 94709
415/548-4762

<B>Grace Moore<B>
<I>TechArt<I>
400 Pacific Avenue
San Francisco, CA 94133
415/362-1110
```

Figure 10-29 Text format after global changes.

Step 10 If you performed these searches in QuarkXPress, then you need to save the text to disk in ASCII format.

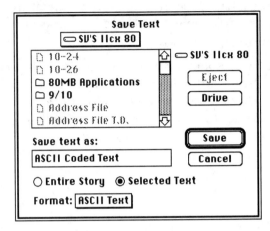

Figure 10-30 Save Text dialog box.

Step 11 Import the exported text and the embedded codes will be translated into the final formatting automatically.

Kay Atherton
Medi-Calls
248 Texas Street, #9
San Francisco, CA 94107
626-8343

Hector Barrera, Jr.
Azteca
1521 Manor Drive
San Pablo, CA 94949
415/233-9239

David Jewett
CJS, Inc.
1920 Francisco
Berkeley, CA 94709
415/548-4762

Grace Moore
TechArt
400 Pacific Avenue
San Francisco, CA 94133
415/362-1110

Figure 10-31 Final text format.

Using Wild Cards in Searches

You can use the wild card (⌘-?) to search for words that have been typed with different spellings. For example, if you wanted to change all occurrences of the word gray to shaded, and if the word gray also appeared as grey in some places in the text, you could search for gr\?y (Figure 10-32). (The backslash before the question mark is what appears in the dialog box when you type the wild card code, ⌘-?.)

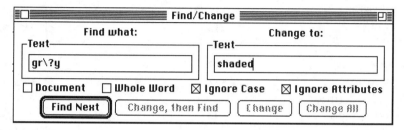

Figure 10-32 Changing all occurrences of gray or grey to shaded.

This procedure works because gray and grey are the only English words that fit the format gr\?y—griy, groy, and gruy are not valid words. You should use Find Next, Change, then Find rather than Change All so you can skip occurrences such as "Gray Line Tours," and manually change occurrences such as "shades of gray."

Inserting XPress Tags in ASCII Text

QuarkXPress lets you insert "tags" into any ASCII text so that the text will be formatted automatically when imported into a QuarkXPress document. This can be handy if you are preparing text using a word processor that is not directly supported by one of QuarkXPress' application-specific import filters—such as text from a dedicated word processing system or a mainframe text editor. XPress tags are also useful in preparing text in a spreadsheet or database format, as described later in this chapter.

The following table shows codes that you can type to format ASCII text. The initial attributes for text imported will be the same as the attributes where the insertion point is located when the File ➤ Get Text command is used. Current attributes remain in effect until they are explicitly changed by an embedded code.

You must check Include Style Sheets in the Get Text dialog box when importing, and the XPress Tags filter must be in the QuarkXPress program folder, or the XPress tags will come in as ASCII text. You cannot import text through two filters at the same time: XPress Tags inserted in formatted text imported from Microsoft Word, for instance, will not be interpreted as formatting codes. You must save coded text in ASCII format

Character Attributes

Description	Start Code	End Code
Plain	<P>	<P> or <$>
Bold	<B>	<B> or <$>
Italic	<I>	<I> or <$>
Outline	<O>	<O> or <$>
Shadow	<S>	<S> or <$>
Underline	<U>	<U> or <$>
Word Underline	<W>	<W> or <$>
Strikethrough	</>	</> or <$>
All Caps	<K>	<K> or <$>
Small Caps	<H>	<H> or <$>
Superscript	<+>	<+> or <$>
Subscript	<->	<-> or <$>
Superior	<V>	<V> or <$>
Current style sheet	<$>	

These codes can be combined within brackets. For example, you can type <BI> to set text to bold and italic.

In the next codes, italicized text indicates variables that you enter and *ddd.dd* represents any two-place decimal number. Names of fonts must always be framed in quotation marks.

Description	Start Code	End Code
Change font	<f"*font name*">	<f$>
Change size	<z*ddd.dd*>	<z$>
Shift Baseline	<b*ddd.dd*>	<b$>
Change shade %	<s*ddd.dd*>	<s$>
Scale horizontally %	<h*ddd.dd*>	<h$>
Kern @ *d*/200ths em	<k*ddd.dd*>	<k$>
Track @ *d*/200ths em	<t*ddd.dd*>	<t$>

Change color	<c"*color name*">	<c$>

You can enter abbreviations for primary colors:

Cyan	<cC>
Magenta	<cM>
Yellow	<cY>
Black	<cK>
White	<cW>

Paragraph Attributes

Description	Start Code
Align Left	<*L>
Center	<*C>
Align Right	<*R>
Justify	<*J>
Normal Style sheet	@$:
No style sheet	@:
Change style sheet	@*style sheet*:
Define new style sheet	@*style sheet=definition*

In the next codes, if you omit a parameter in a string, you must still include the comma that follows that parameter. Missing parameters will be set to match the current style sheet settings.

Description	Start Code	End Code
Set tabs	<*t(*dd.dd,T."character"*)>	<*t$>

with *ddd.dd* = tab position, *T* = tab type (L,R,C,D), and *"character"* = the leader character, framed in quotation marks.

Description	Start Code	End Code
Set paragraph format	<*p(*left indent,first line indent, right indent, leading,space before, space after, G/baseline grid*)>	<*p$>

where all values are entered in the form *ddd.dd* except the baseline grid.

Description	Start Code	End Code
Hyphenation & Justification	<*h"*hyphenation name*">	<*h$>
Rule above	<*ra(*rule width,line style ID, "color name",line shade, left indent or Tline length, right indent, rule position* or %*percentage*)>	<*ra$>

where *rule width* and *right indent* are entered in points in the format *ddd.dd*;

the *line style ID* is entered as *d* (counted by position down on the menu);

the *color name* can be entered as an abbreviation for one of the primary colors: C, M, Y, K, or W;

the *line shade* is entered as a percentage in the format *ddd.dd;*

the *left indent* can be entered in points in the format *ddd.dd* or the entry can be the *length of the line* if preceded by a T (T*ddd.dd*);

and the *rule position* can be entered in points or as a percentage if followed by a % (*ddd.dd*%).

Rule below	<*rb(*ddd.dd,d,"color name", ddd.dd,ddd.dd, ddd.dd,ddd.dd*)>	<*rb$>

where the parameters are as described for Rule Above.

Drop cap	<*d(*d,d*)>	<*d$>

where the parameters are character count, line count.

Keep with next	<*kn1>	<*kn$> or <*kn0>

where kn$ = use current style sheet, kn0 = do not keep with next.

Keep together	<*kt(A)> or <*kt(*d,d*)>	<*kt$>

where the A = all lines or *d,d* = start line, end line.

The current style sheet remains in effect until a new style sheet or no style sheet is applied using one of the @ codes shown in the table. Applying a new style sheet overrides all previous formatting codes.

In defining a style sheet, you can follow @*style sheet=* with any of the codes shown in the table. Style sheet names cannot include the special characters :, =, or @.

Style sheet names must be defined in the QuarkXPress document or in the ASCII file as an XPress tag code (using @*style sheet=*, as shown in next table) before the text is imported. Colors and H&J names must be defined in the QuarkXPress document before the text that references them is imported. If a color is not found, Black will be used. If an H&J is not found, the default H&J is used.

Figures 10-33 and 10-34 show an example of text with XPress tags before and after being imported into QuarkXPress.

```
@DropCapParagraphStyle=<*L*h"Standard"*kn0*kt0*ra0*rb0*d(1,3)*p(0,0,0,0,0,0,
g)*t(0,0," "):
Ps100t0h100z12k0b0c"Black"f"Times">
@DropCapParagraphStyle:<*L*h"Standard"*kn0*kt0*ra0*rb0*d(1,3)*p(0,0,0,0,0,0,
g)*t(0,0," "):
Ps100t0h100z12k0b0c"Black"f"Times">Si meliora dies, ut vina, poemata reddit,
scire velim, chartis pretium quotus arroget annus. scriptor abhinc annos cen-
tum qui decidit, inter perfectos veteresque referri debet an inter vilis
atque novos? Excludat iurgia finis, "Est vetus atque probus, cent<P>um qui
perficit annos." Quid, qui deperiit minor uno mense vel anno, inter quos ref-
erendus erit? Veteresne poetas, an quos et praesens et postera respuat aetas?
@BodyCopyStyle=<*L*h"Standard"*kn0*kt0*ra0*rb0*d0*p(0,12,0,0,0,0,g)*t(0,0,"
"):
Ps100t0h100z12k0b0c"Black"f"Times">
@BodyCopyStyle:<P>"Iste quidem veteres inter ponetur honeste, qui vel mense
brevi vel toto est iunior anno." Utor permisso, caudaeque pilos ut equinae
paulatim vello unum, demo etiam unum, dum cadat elusus ratione ruentis
acervi, qui redit in fastos et virtutem aestimat ann<P>is miraturque nihil
nisi quod Libitina sacravit.
<P>Ennius et sapines et fortis et alter Homerus, ut critici dicunt, leviter
curare videtur, quo promissa cadant et somnia Pythagorea. Naevius in manibus
non est et mentibus haeret paene recens? Adeo sanctum est vetus omne poema.
ambigitur quotiens, uter utro <P>sit prior, aufert Pacuvius docti famam senis
Accius alti, dicitur Afrani toga convenisse Menandro, Plautus ad exemplar
Siculi properare Epicharmi, vincere Caecilius gravitate, Terentius arte.
@FloatingSubStyle=<*L*h"Standard"*kn0*kt0*ra(24,0,"Blue",100,T0,0,-
4.97)*rb0*d0*p(0,0,0,0,12,0,g)*t(12,0," ",93,0," ",0,0," "):
PBs50t0h100z18k0b0c"Yellow"f"Times">
@FloatingSubStyle:        Subhead
@BodyCopyStyle:<P>Hos ediscit et hos arto stipata theatro spectat Roma
potens; habet hos numeratque poetas ad nostrum tempus Livi scriptoris ab
aevo.
<P>Interdum volgus rectum videt, est ubi peccat. Si veteres ita miratur lau-
datque poetas, ut nihil anteferat, nihil illis comparet, errat. Si quaedam
nimis antique, si peraque dure dicere credit eos, ignave multa fatetur, et
sapit et mecum facit et Iova iudic<P>at aequo.
<P>Non equidem insector delendave carmina Livi esse reor, memini quae plago-
sum mihi parvo Orbilium dictare; sed emendata videri pulchraque et exactis
minimum distantia miror. Inter quae verbum emicuit si forte decorum, et si
versus paulo concinnior unus et al<P>ter, iniuste totum ducit venditque poe-
ma.
```

Figure 10-33 ASCII text with XPress tags.

S i meliora dies, ut vina, poemata reddit, scire velim, chartis pretium quotus arroget annus. scriptor abhinc annos centum qui decidit, inter perfectos veteresque referri debet an inter vilis atque novos? Excludat iurgia finis, "Est vetus atque probus, centum qui perficit annos." Quid, qui deperiit minor uno mense vel anno, inter quos referendus erit? Veteresne poetas, an quos et praesens et postera respuat aetas?

"Iste quidem veteres inter ponetur honeste, qui vel mense brevi vel toto est iunior anno." Utor permisso, caudaeque pilos ut equinae paulatim vello unum, demo etiam unum, dum cadat elusus ratione ruentis acervi, qui redit in fastos et virtutem aestimat annis miraturque nihil nisi quod Libitina sacravit.

Ennius et sapines et fortis et alter Homerus, ut critici dicunt, leviter curare videtur, quo promissa cadant et somnia Pythagorea. Naevius in manibus non est et mentibus haeret paene recens? Adeo sanctum est vetus omne poema. ambigitur quotiens, uter utro sit prior, aufert Pacuvius docti famam senis Accius alti, dicitur Afrani toga convenisse Menandro, Plautus ad exemplar Siculi properare Epicharmi, vincere Caecilius gravitate, Terentius arte.

Subhead

Hos ediscit et hos arto stipata theatro spectat Roma potens; habet hos numeratque poetas ad nostrum tempus Livi scriptoris ab aevo.

Interdum volgus rectum videt, est ubi peccat. Si veteres ita miratur laudatque poetas, ut nihil anteferat, nihil illis comparet, errat. Si quaedam nimis antique, si peraque dure dicere credit eos, ignave multa fatetur, et sapit et mecum facit et Iova iudicat aequo.

Non equidem insector delendave carmina Livi esse reor, memini quae plagosum mihi parvo Orbilium dictare; sed emendata videri pulchraque et exactis minimum distantia miror. Inter quae verbum emicuit si forte decorum, et si versus paulo concinnior unus et alter, iniuste totum ducit venditque poema.

Figure 10-34 ASCII text with XPress tags after being imported into QuarkXPress.

Page Number Characters

Description	Code
Previous box's page	<\2>
Current box's page	<\3>
Next box's page	<\4>

Insert Special Characters

Description	Code
Return	<\n>
Discretionary New Line	<\d>
Indent here	<\i>
New column	<\c>
New box	<\b>
Discretionary hyphen	<\h>
Standard space	<\ ➤ or <\! ➤ for nonbreaking character
Figure space	<\f> or <\!f> for nonbreaking character
Punctuation space	<\p> or <\!p> for nonbreaking character
1/4 em space	<\4> or <\!4> for nonbreaking character
Hyphen	<\-> or <\!-> for nonbreaking character

Since @, <, and \ characters have a special meaning as XPress tag codes, you must use codes to enter these characters if you want them to print as part of the text:

Symbol	Code
@	<\@>
<	<\<>
\	<\\>

Summary

This chapter offered tips on how to work with text from databases and non-Macintosh computers, including how to use the Find/Change command to remove unwanted characters or to insert formatting codes. We also discussed how to insert XPress tags into text created on a non-Macintosh computer so that text will format automatically when imported into QuarkXPress. The next chapter offers special tips and techniques for using QuarkXPress' powerful typographic capabilities.

11 *Tips on Typography*

Many people fear that the Macintosh is partly responsible for causing typography to become a lost art. The Macintosh makes it so easy to print type that looks good at first glance that many Macintosh users with no design training have missed some of the traditional education regarding type aesthetics. This book does not aim at bridging that gap. We begin this chapter, however, with some advice about points a designer should consider about type when designing a document in QuarkXPress: why style sheets should be used, considerations to take into account in adjusting leading, and information on adjusting word and character spacing.

The chapter continues with some tips on how to create special typographic effects, including special drop caps, reverse type, and setting type within a shape.

Designing Type Specifications

If you are coming from a traditional typesetting background, you are probably familiar with most of the design guidelines offered in this section. On the other hand, if you are coming from an office environment in which all documents were previously printed on a letter-quality printer, then you may find the comparatively wide range of fonts offered by

QuarkXPress rather confusing. There are two ways of approaching the type specifications for a document.

The fastest way to acquire a sense of design and develop specifications is to study and imitate published works that are similar in structure to your document. Match your design specifications as closely as possible to the published documents; in other words, select fonts that are similar to those used for headings, body copy, and captions in the published document. You need not match the typefaces exactly, but try to substitute typefaces that are in the same category (serif or sans serif, roman, italic, or bold, and so on).

Second, study the underlying principles that designers and typographers follow. Some of these guidelines are listed here, but few documents can follow all of these guidelines without making exceptions to the rules. A good designer knows when and how to break the rules.

Match the Type Specifications to the System Capabilities

The first step in the process of creating type specifications is to list the different fonts *available* for use in your design specifications. The second step is to list the fonts that you will *use* in a particular document.

One factor in determining the number of fonts is the number of text elements used in the document. Elements that can require differentiation include:

- Chapter openings, section openings, or feature article headlines
- Different levels of headings or headlines
- Body copy
- Figure captions
- Labels within figures
- Footnotes
- Special sections such as sidebars, summaries, tables, and the like.

The type specification process, then, involves merging the two lists: a list of the fonts that are available, or that you wish to use, and a list of the different type elements within the document.

The design specifications should also include instructions for paragraph alignment (left, right, justified, centered) and spacing between paragraphs—for the body copy, the captions, and the figure titles.

Use Only One or Two Typefaces

Most designers mix two different fonts (or typefaces, in the traditional world of type) at most. For example, it's common to see a sans serif face, such as Helvetica or Avant Garde, used for headlines and a serif face, such as Times or Palatino, used for the body copy. Use variations in size and style to distinguish between different elements.

Documents that incorporate many changing formats—such as magazines and newsletters—might use more than four fonts throughout the document, though each page, feature, or ad uses only one or two.

Just as graphics are too often used simply because they are available, so too are fonts—simply because they're there. Too many fonts make the page confusing and uninviting.

Use Larger Point Sizes for Longer Text Line Lengths

There is a good reason why the text in magazines is run two and often three columns. It is very difficult for the eye to follow text, especially in small point sizes, from one edge to the other of an 8.5-inch-wide page.

If you must use a small point size to fit more text on a page, be sure to break the page into at least two columns. Even regular text—12 point—is easier to read if it runs in columns no wider than 4 to 5 inches. One rule of thumb is that optimum line length is between 45 and 60 characters per line.

Above all, the text should be easy to read. If the copy doesn't fit the space allotted, think about editing out some of the text rather than reducing the point size or the space between lines.

Don't Use Underscores

Use italics rather than underscores within body copy. (Underscored text was a convention developed for use in documents printed on typewriters or letter-quality printers.)

Use All Caps Judiciously

Capitalize whole words as a deliberate design strategy, rather than as a method for showing emphasis or differentiating heading levels. Use variations in size rather than all-caps text to differentiate headings. One common exception to this rule occurs when the list of available fonts is too limited to accommodate all heading levels; in this case, all caps can be used to distinguish between two heading levels that are otherwise the same font.

Differentiate Figure Captions from Body Text

Here we use the term "caption" to mean the descriptive lines of text that run below, beside, or above a photo or illustration. Some layout artists use the term "cutline" instead, reserving "caption" (or lead-in or catchline or kicker) to describe only the boldface words that lead in to the rest of the descriptive text. Whatever you call it, the caption is usually differentiated from the rest of the text by boldface or italics or a different typeface altogether.

Besides specifying the font to be used in captions, you should also specify the positioning of the caption text. The most natural position is below the illustration or photo, extending the same width as the graphic. Other variations include indenting 1 pica or more on each side or centering the catchline above justified text. Some variations are shown in Figure 11-1.

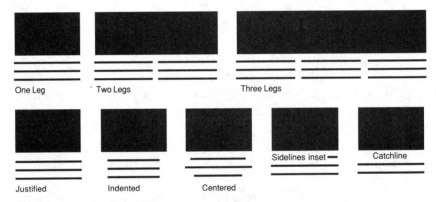

One Leg   Two Legs   Three Legs

Justified   Indented   Centered   Sidelines inset ━   Catchline

Figure 11-1 Variations in placing captions.

Tips on Using Style Sheets

The procedures for creating and applying style sheets were given in Chapter 4. Here specific tips and examples relating to style sheets follow a brief commentary on why style sheets are so useful. The advantages of using style sheets are similar to those outlined for using templates, described in Chapter 8.

Benefits of Using Style Sheets

Within one document or between documents, whether the production is executed by one person or many, style sheets are tremendous productivity tools. They reduce the number of steps required to format text, simplify the formatting process, embody "design," and enforce consistency. In addition, style sheets let you change your design easily.

Style Sheets Reduce the Number of Steps

The process of creating a new set of style sheets the first time might require, let's say, 40 individual steps, whereas the process of applying each style sheet requires only two steps. This savings is one of the first benefits of using style sheets. You can save hours or days over the life of a project by using style sheets.

Fast operators might complain that it takes too long to set up a set of style sheets—that they can format a document just as fast without one. For short documents and simple formats, it might be faster to format each paragraph independently, but there are other advantages to consider.

Style Sheets Simplify the Formatting Process

If a document has many different paragraph formats, and some are fairly complicated, then style sheets can simplify the formatting process by reducing the number of variables that you have to remember or look up. Was the leading 13 point or 14? Does the paragraph need extra space above or below? And what were the tab settings for a five-column table?

Even if the type specifications are already clearly written out on paper, it is a good idea to translate a designer's specifications into the commands you will use in QuarkXPress. When "captured" in style sheets, the list of commands is reduced to a simple list of style sheet names, and the process of marking up copy for formatting is simplified to writing the name of the style sheet assigned to each paragraph.

Style Sheets Embody Design and Enforce Consistency

Aside from the practical considerations of reducing steps and simplifying the process of formatting a document, a style sheet system can ensure that design specifications are correctly and consistently applied. By incorporating as many of the design specifications as possible into style sheets, the production group can better preserve the look intended by the designer.

Furthermore, once a set of style sheets is created, it can be used in many files that follow the same design specifications. For instance, a book or long proposal might be divided into several text files and worked on by several different editors. Once the style sheet set is created, it can be applied to each section or chapter—you don't have to re-create the style sheets for each new file.

A short document that is produced on a regular basis—such as a newsletter—would have one set of style sheets with which each issue is created. If you have ever worked on a newsletter only once a month or once a quarter, you know how hard it is to remember elaborate type specifications from one issue to the next. If the production team changes from month to month, the process of learning elaborate type specifications can add hours to each issue. With a style sheet system, a list of style sheet names is automatically displayed in a submenu in QuarkXPress and is easy to apply.

Style Sheets Let You Change Your Mind

In addition to ensuring consistency, style sheets offer a tremendous amount of flexibility in changing the design of a document. Have you ever gone through a long document meticulously formatting each paragraph and then decided that you really want a different paragraph indent, or all the body text to be on 13 point leading instead of 12? The change would be a nightmare without a style sheet. If you had used a style sheet from the beginning, you could change the font or paragraph formats for any element globally simply by changing the specifications for the style sheet. You could change the formatting of all the level-1 headings, for instance, by changing the style sheet attributes only.

This capability can be useful over the lifetime of a magazine that you want to modify to suit changing tastes in type, but it is especially handy during the initial design stages for a new document. You can test different design ideas by changing the specifications for each style sheet name and quickly print out the variations for review by your team or your client.

You can also make slight modifications in the spacing assigned for headings or body text to make the text for a newsletter fit exactly four pages, for instance. (See "Adjusting Text Spacing" later in this chapter.)

Tips for Creating and Applying Style Sheets

If you use style sheets, the following tips can help you save time in developing and applying them.

Specify the Normal Style Sheet First

When you are setting up style sheets, make the settings for Normal text in QuarkXPress match the specifications for your document's body text. Most documents tend to be primarily one set of specifications for the body text, with variations on that specification for headings, captions, tables, and the like.

Create a New Set of Style Sheets in an Unformatted Document

In applying style sheets to paragraphs in a document that has not yet been formatted, define the style for Normal text, then proceed through the document by moving to successive paragraphs and apply the style for heads, and so on.

If the paragraph format is a new one that you have not yet defined as a style sheet, you can create the style sheet by first formatting the text as needed. When you select Edit ➤ Style Sheets, and click New, the definition of the style will be that of the selected text. Simply name the style and Save it. Then use the keyboard shortcut or the Style ➤ Style Sheets submenu to apply it to subsequent paragraphs.

Assign and Use Keyboard Equivalents

You can assign a keyboard equivalent that you can later use to assign the style sheet instead of going through the Style ➤ Style Sheets submenu. You can press any keys on the numeric keyboard, along with ⌘, Option, Control, and Shift, or any of the function keys (F1, F2, and so on) on an extended keyboard. The keys you press when the cursor is in the Keyboard Equivalent field become the keyboard shortcut for assigning the style sheet.

Even though you are limited to using function keys and numeric keys on the numeric keypad, you can assign numbers in an organized way. For example, you could let the numbers correspond to headings levels:

- Heading level 1 would be assigned keypad 1 or F1 or some combination with the ⌘, Option, Control, or Shift keys.

- Heading level 2 would be assigned keypad 2 or F2 or the same combination with the ⌘, Option, Control, or Shift keys as used for heading 1.

- Normal text, figure captions, and other nonnumeric style sheets could use numeric or function keys that start above the highest number used by the headings.

Organize the Style Sheet Names

You can enter a style sheet name up to 64 characters long. The style sheet names will be displayed in the Style ➤ Style Sheets submenu in alphabetical order. It's a good idea to decide on the naming conventions you will use for style sheet names so you can locate style sheets in the list easily and know what they mean.

One helpful guideline is to name the different categories of text elements such that they appear in a logically grouped order when you view them alphabetically. For example, in the system shown in Figure 11-2, all the headings begin with the word "head" in the style sheet name, and all the list formats begin with the word "list."

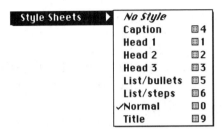

Figure 11-2 Logically grouped style sheet names, with keyboard equivalents displayed after style sheet name.

Another approach is to include the type specifications in the style sheet names. Figure 11-3 shows style sheet names that include font, size, and other information about the style sheet specification.

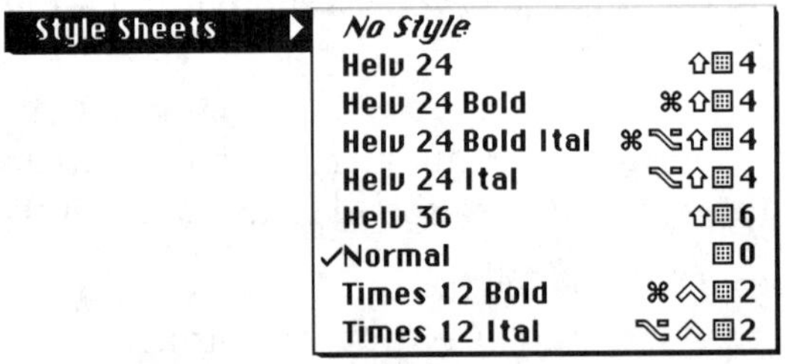

Figure 11-3 Type Specifications included in style sheet names.

As a learning aid, QuarkXPress displays the keyboard equivalents in the style sheet submenu. This way, you can use the keyboard equivalents when you remember them, or choose from the submenu while viewing a reminder of the keyboard equivalent that you might remember the next time. The numeric keypad is represented by the ⊞ icon, the Option key by the ⌥ icon, the Command key by the ⌘ icon, the Shift key by the ⇧ icon, and the Control key by the ⌃ icon.

Formatting Headings with a Style Sheet

A number of conventions in formatting headings can and should be captured in the style sheet specifications:

- Use Edit ➤ Style Sheets to display the Paragraph Formats dialog box and add Space Above and Space Below each heading level, rather than using leading or carriage returns to force the space around a heading. This way, you will achieve normal line spacing for headings that run more than one line long.

- Use Edit ➤ Style Sheets to display the Paragraph Formats dialog box and set all headings to Keep with Next ¶ and Keep Lines Together. This way, a multiline heading will never be broken across two pages or columns or separated from the first paragraph that follows it.

- Normally, headings are not hyphenated or justified. If you have not changed the Standard H&J, which is preset with hyphenation turned off, you need not apply any other H&J. If you have changed the Standard H&J to include hyphenation, use Edit ➤ H&Js to create an H&J file with hyphenation turned off, then apply the new H&J to the appropriate style sheets by changing the paragraph formats under Edit ➤ Style Sheets.

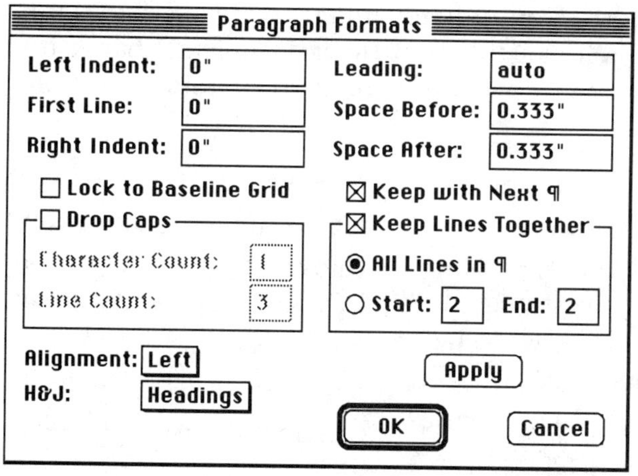

```
═══════════ Paragraph Formats ═══════════

Left Indent:    [0"]          Leading:       [auto]

First Line:     [0"]          Space Before:  [0.333"]

Right Indent:   [0"]          Space After:   [0.333"]

☐ Lock to Baseline Grid       ☒ Keep with Next ¶
☐ Drop Caps                   ☒ Keep Lines Together

Character Count:    [1]       ◉ All Lines in ¶

Line Count:         [3]       ○ Start: [2]   End: [2]


Alignment: [Left]                    ( Apply )

H&J:       [Headings]         (   OK   )     ( Cancel )
```

Figure 11-4 Example of the Paragraph Formats dialog box for a heading.

- Often, headings are kerned or tracked for tighter spacing than normal body copy. Use Edit ➤ Style Sheets to display the Character Attributes dialog box and activate tracking for each heading style sheet, and manually kern letters in individual headings as needed.

Another way to adjust the spacing between characters in headings is to use the Edit ➤ H&Js command to set optimum character and word spacing in a special H&J specification for headings, then use Edit ➤ Style Sheets to display the Paragraph Formats dialog box and select the special H&J specifications for the heading style sheets.

Adjusting Text Spacing

Text spacing may need to be adjusted for two reasons. One is aesthetic: The spacing between lines or letters might be adjusted to be typographically pleasing. The other is to fit a certain amount of text into a given amount of space. Adjusting spacing for this purpose is called *copyfitting*.

Adjusting the Leading (Line Spacing)

Whether you initially use QuarkXpress' Auto Leading feature or specify the exact leading (spacing between lines) yourself, you can always make fine adjustments in the leading in order to improve the appearance of text or to fit copy into a defined space. You can specify leading in increments of .001 point in the Paragraph Formats dialog box. You can change the leading for the entire document, for specific style sheets, for selected text, or for selected pages to make copy fit.

In adjusting the leading, be consistent: Change the leading on all of the body copy rather than on individual paragraphs. If you do not want to change the leading for an entire article or document, change it for facing pages and keep the leading the same across columns on a single page (Figure 11-5).

A powerful idea communicates some of its strength to him who challenges it.
    Marcel Proust

A powerful idea communicates some of its strength to him who challenges it.
    Marcel Proust

A powerful idea communicates some of its strength to him who challenges it.
    Marcel Proust

A powerful idea communicates some of its strength to him who challenges it.
    Marcel Proust

Figure 11-5 12-point Times with leading of 12, 14, 15, and Auto.

Changing the leading is a common and preferred method of fitting copy once the design specifications are finalized—rather than changing the specifications for typeface, size, or style.

Hyphenation and Justification

Hyphenated text can take up less space than text that is not hyphenated. Furthermore, justified text can take up less space than text that is not justified if the minimum word space (in the Edit Hyphenation & Justification dialog box) is set to less than 100 percent (Figure 11-6). The justification process can then reduce the space between words, whereas text that is not justified has standard spacing between words. Justification can also reduce the space between characters if you set the minimum character spacing to less than 0 percent.

I don't know Who—or what—put the question. I don't even know when it was put. I don't even remember answering. But at some moment I did answer *Yes* to Someone—or Something—and from that hour I was certain that existence is meaningful and that, therefore, my life in self-surrender, had a goal.

Dag Hammaraskjöld

I don't know Who—or what—put the question. I don't even know when it was put. I don't even remember answering. But at some moment I did answer *Yes* to Someone—or Something—and from that hour I was certain that existence is meaningful and that, therefore, my life in self-surrender, had a goal.

Dag Hammaraskjöld

Figure 11-6 Justified text can require less space than text that is not justified.

   Normally, QuarkXPress does not hyphenate text automatically unless you use the Edit ➤ H&J command to create a new H&J specification with hyphenation. The dialog box lets you turn Auto Hyphenation on or off and specify how many hyphens in a row will be allowed. You can enter a number including 0, or type the word "unlimited."

   In entering the number of hyphens allowed in a row, a value of 0 has the same effect as "unlimited." It does *not* mean that no hyphens are allowed.

Hyphenation On for Justified Text, Off for Headings

Justified text usually calls for hyphenation, especially when the columns are narrow. Justified text that is not hyphenated tends to have more "rivers"—wide areas of white space within the text caused by forced spacing between words.

   Normally, body copy is hyphenated but headings are not. For this reason, most documents need two H&J files: the Standard file that comes with QuarkXPress and is initially set up with hyphenation off, and one that you create that turns hyphenation on (Figures 11-7 and 11-8).

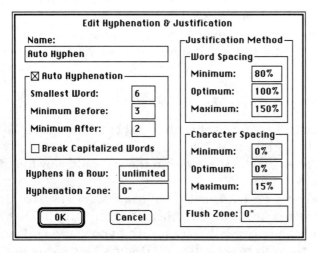

Figure 11-7 Standard H&J specifications, with hyphenation turned off, can be used for headlines.

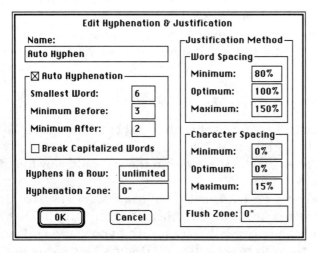

Figure 11-8 Hyphenation and Justification dialog box applied to body copy.

Adjusting the Hyphenation Zone

The Hyphenation Zone in the Edit ➤ Hyphenation and Justification dialog box applies to non-justified text only. If you enter a value of 0, QuarkXPress will break any words that start on a line but would cross the right margin if not hyphenated. You can enter a value higher than 0 to limit how far in from the right margin QuarkXPress will go to hyphenate a word—the previous word must end *before* the hyphenation zone and an acceptable hyphenation point must fall within the zone.

In hyphenating unjustified text, QuarkXPress follows this sequence of steps:

1. If a word cannot be hyphenated within the hyphenation zone, carry it to the next line (that is, do not hyphenate).

2. Otherwise, hyphenate.

In other words, you can control the minimum line length of unjustified text through this setting. The larger the hyphenation zone, the more ragged the right margin will appear (Figure 11-9).

Hyphenation zone = zero
...the usual modern collection. Wilson Steer, water in watercolour; Matthew Smith, victim of the crime in slaughtercolour; Utrillo, whitewashed wall in mortarcolour; Matisse, odalisque in scortacolour; Picasso, spatchcock horse in tortacolour...Roualt, perishing Saint in thoughtacolour; Epstein, Leah waiting for Jacob in squawtacolour.
                                        Joyce Cary

Hyphenation zone = 1inch
...the usual modern collection. Wilson Steer, water in watercolour; Matthew Smith, victim of the crime in slaughtercolour; Utrillo, whitewashed wall in mortarcolour; Matisse, odalisque in scortacolour; Picasso, spatchcock horse in tortacolour...Roualt, perishing Saint in thoughtacolour; Epstein, Leah waiting for Jacob in squawtacolour.
                                        Joyce Cary

Figure 11-9 A wide hyphenation zone results in a more ragged look and can increase the number of lines.

When hyphenation is turned off, the text can appear very ragged. Hyphenation is not only for justified text!

Adjusting the Number of Hyphens Allowed in a Row

The Edit Hyphenation & Justification dialog box also lets you specify how many hyphens in a row will be allowed, but changing this setting is unlikely to change the amount of space taken up by the copy unless the text invites heavy hyphenation (that is, is characterized by short line lengths and a lot of long words).

Adjusting Word and Character Spacing

When text is not justified, the amount of space between words and characters is determined by the font and by kerning tables. Justified text, on the other hand, is achieved by adding or subtracting infinitesimal increments of space between characters and words. The Edit ➤ H&Js (Hyphenation & Justification) command lets you control the amount of space added or deleted between words and characters as part of the justification process.

Most publishers are likely to accept QuarkXpress' defaults for these settings rather than change them. You can change the settings to force copy to fit a given space, however, and you might want to change these settings as a deliberate design strategy to achieve a custom look in certain documents.

The entries under the Justification Method area of the Edit Hyphenation & Justification dialog box (Figure 11-10) apply to justified text only—except Optimum values, which will be applied to nonjustified text as well. You can enter the Minimum (down to 0 percent between words, or –50 percent between characters), Optimum, and Maximum (up to 500 percent between words, or 100 percent between characters) Word Spacing (space between words) and Character Spacing (space between characters) that QuarkXPress will apply in adjusting horizontal space in order to justify a line of text. Values are normally entered as percentages of normal word space for space between words and as percentages of an en space between characters.

```
┌─────────────────────────────────────────────────────┐
│         Edit Hyphenation & Justification              │
│  Name:                     ┌Justification Method─┐    │
│  ┌──────────────────┐      ┌─Word Spacing────────┐    │
│  │ Standard         │      │ Minimum:   │ 100% │  │    │
│  └──────────────────┘      │                     │    │
│  ┌─☐ Auto Hyphenation──┐   │ Optimum:   │ 100% │  │    │
│  │ Smallest Word:  │ 6 │   │ Maximum:   │ 150% │  │    │
│  │ Minimum Before: │ 3 │   └─────────────────────┘    │
│  │ Minimum After:  │ 2 │   ┌─Character Spacing───┐     │
│  │ ☐ Break Capitalized Words│ Minimum:  │ 0% │   │     │
│  └────────────────────┘    │ Optimum:  │ 0% │   │     │
│  Hyphens in a Row: │unlimited│ Maximum: │ 15% │  │     │
│  Hyphenation Zone: │ 0" │   └─────────────────────┘    │
│  ┌──────┐  ┌────────┐       Flush Zone: │ 0" │         │
│  │  OK  │  │ Cancel │                                  │
│  └──────┘  └────────┘                                  │
└─────────────────────────────────────────────────────┘
```

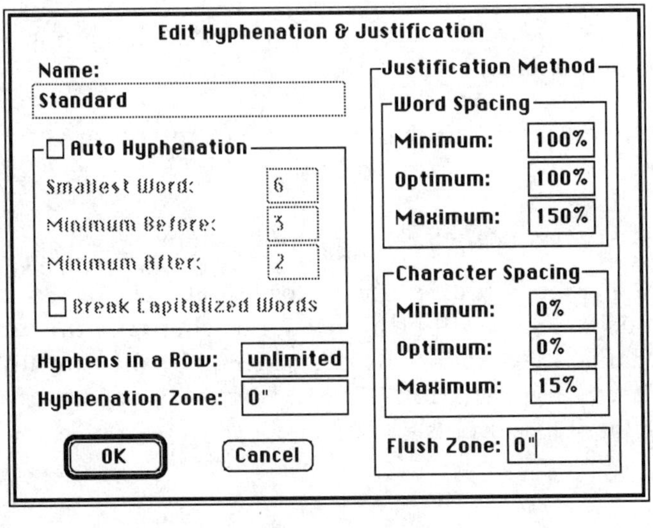

Figure 11-10 H&J dialog box.

QuarkXPress will start with the desired space between each word on the line, and expand or condense from there up to the limits specified as minimum and maximum for justified text. If condensing the space between words cannot make the line fit within the margins, QuarkXPress will hyphenate (if hyphenation is turned on, which is normal for justified text). If hyphenating and adjusting the space between words is not enough to make the line hit the margin, the space between letters will be adjusted (Figure 11-11).

Word Spacing
Minimum: 80%
He can be called a remarkable man who stands out from those around him by the resourcefulness of his mind, and who knows how to be restrained in the manifestations which proceed from his nature, at the same time conducting himself justly and tolerantly towards the weaknesses of others.
George Gurdjieff

Word Spacing
Minimum: 100%
He can be called a remarkable man who stands out from those around him by the resourcefulness of his mind, and who knows how to be restrained in the manifestations which proceed from his nature, at the same time conducting himself justly and tolerantly towards the weaknesses of others.
George Gurdjieff

Word Spacing
Minimum: 120%
He can be called a remarkable man who stands out from those around him by the resourcefulness of his mind, and who knows how to be restrained in the manifestations which proceed from his nature, at the same time conducting himself justly and tolerantly towards the weaknesses of others.
George Gurdjieff

Figure 11-11 Same paragraph justified with different spacing allowances.

For text that is not justified, the spacing set as Optimum will be used throughout.

If you think you can improve the appearance of your document by making the spacing between words smaller, consider the tradeoffs: with a wide allowance for spacing between words and letters, the "rivers" of white space may seem wide in justified text, but fewer words will be hyphenated. Text with a narrow allowance for space between characters and words is likely to have a high number of words hyphenated.

Special Typographic Effects

The next headings describe special effects that might be difficult to achieve using conventional typesetting technologies but are easy with QuarkXPress.

Making Drop Caps and Variations

QuarkXPress lets you create drop caps and other special effects for letters that start a paragraph. The automatic drop cap feature lets you set a large cap against two or more lines of text. The next headings describe this and other methods of setting large initial caps at the beginning of a paragraph.

Automatic Drop Caps

You can create automatic drop caps by clicking on the Drop Caps check box in the Paragraph Formats dialog box.

Step 1 Select the Content tool (☝) and position the text insertion point in the paragraph, then choose Style → Formats to display the Paragraph Formats dialog box.

Step 2 Click on the Drop Caps check box and enter the Character Count (number of drop cap letters at the start of the paragraph) and Line Count (number of lines of text to run beside the drop caps).

Step 3 Click on OK to close the dialog box and apply the drop cap specifications, or click on Apply to view the effects of the specifications before you accept them.

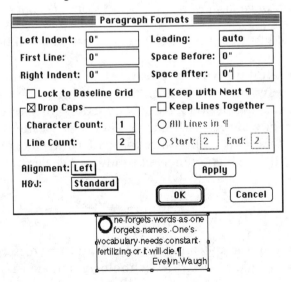

Figure 11-12 Paragraph Formats dialog box with Drop Caps selected and resulting drop cap.

QuarkXPress automatically adjusts the height of the first letter(s) of the paragraph to match the height of the number of lines specified in the dialog box. If the single initial drop cap is a lowercase letter, it will be adjusted to the full height of the lines specified as the line count; if the character count is greater than one and the drop caps include upper- and lowercase letters, the drop caps will retain appropriate relationships between the sizes of uppercase and lowercase letters. The maximum number of lines deep you can specify is 8. If you need to run the drop cap more than 8 lines deep, try creating a separate text box with the drop cap in it, instead of using the automatic drop caps command.

Manually Sized Drop Caps

You can change the size of the automatic drop cap (Figure 11-13) by selecting it and changing the value via the Measurements palette, the Character Formats dialog box, or the keyboard shortcuts (⌘-> and ⌘-<).

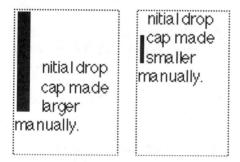

Figure 11-13 Drop caps can be sized manually after they have been created through the Paragraph Formats dialog box.

Notice that the Measurements palette and the Character Formats dialog box show the size of the drop cap as a percentage. You can enter a different percentage, but you *cannot* enter an absolute value by including the unit of measure as you can for normal characters.

You can make other adjustments to a drop cap character, including changes to the style, horizontal scaling, color and shade.

Large Initial Caps

The automatic drop caps feature creates large initial caps automatically, but it forces you to set the line count to at least two lines. If you want a large initial cap followed by only one line of text, you can scale the first character(s) of a paragraph manually using the Style ➤ Size command, the Style ➤ Character command, the ⌘-Shift> keyboard shortcut, or through the Measurements palette. If you have specified auto leading for the paragraph, the enlarged letters will affect the spacing between the first and second lines (Figure 11-14). Use absolute leading instead.

You can use Style ➤ Leading, Style ➤ Formats or the Measurements palette to change the leading manually. The Paragraph Formats dialog box displayed by the Style> Formats command offers the flexibility of viewing the effects of your leading entry (through the Apply button) before closing the dialog box. You can specify font size in inches for a large cap by typing an inch mark (") after the number in the size field.

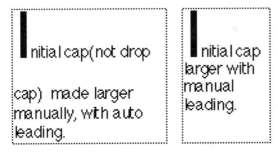

Figure 11-14 Use absolute leading for large initial caps to avoid uneven line spacing in the paragraph.

Creating Shadow Type

You can use shaded type to create your own custom shadow type.

Step 1   Type the text you want in a text box.

Step 2   Select Item ➤ Duplicate to create a second box. Select Item ➤ Modify to make the top box transparent (Background set to 0 percent), and set the text runaround (Item Runaround) to None.

Step 3   Offset the position of the two boxes slightly so the bottom type appears behind the top layer of type.

Step 4   Select the text in the top box and use Style ➤ Shade and/or Style ➤ Color to make the shade and/or color different from the text in the bottom box.

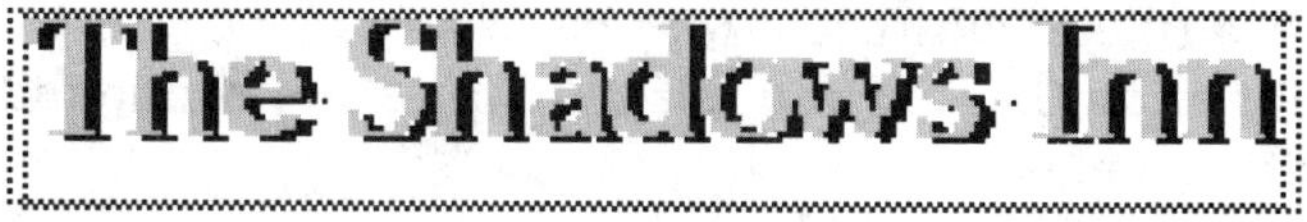

The Shadows Inn

Figure 11-15 Two text boxes overlapped.

Reversing Type on a Black Background

Reversed type, or dropout type, is the name applied to white type on a dark background. To create reversed type, you can use white or lightly shaded text (Style ➤ Shade and Style ➤ Color) on any dark background color or shade in the text box (Item ➤ Modify), as shown in Figure 11-16.

WEIGHT REVERSAL, INC.

Figure 11-16 Reverse type in a box with a dark background.

You can also create a line of reversed type on a dark background by using the Rules command. This is the preferred method of reversing elements that might be repeated throughout text that is not otherwise reversed—such as reversed headings with normal body copy. This method can be applied through a style sheet, making it easy to change the specifications globally.

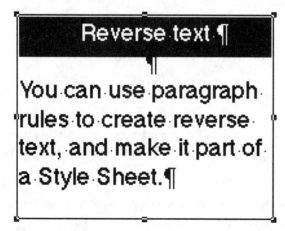

Figure 11-17 Reverse type on a dark ruled line.

Step 1   Apply a rule to white text (or text of any shade or color) by highlighting the text and selecting the Rules command from the Style menu.

Step 2   Choose the color, shade, length, and width (up to 503 points) of rule desired; then input a *negative* value in the Offset field. Since the default unit for Offset is in percent when you first open the dialog box, and you cannot enter a negative percentage here, you must enter a unit of measure after you type in a negative value. The rule must be a different color or shade from the text, and there must be a carriage return above (or below) the text in order for a rule above (or below) to appear.

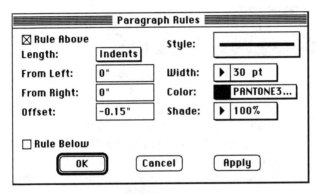

Figure 11-18 Rules dialog box for reversing type on a background.

Rotating Text Boxes in a Symmetrical Circular Pattern

Here's a simple technique for rotating text in a symmetrical, circular pattern:

Step 1   Type the *longest* text label in a text box, adjust the character attributes, paragraph format, and size of the box to fit the space allowed.

Step 2   Select Item ➤ Duplicate to make as many copies of the text box as there are elements in the circular design.

Step 3   To determine how many degrees to rotate each element, divide 360° by the number of elements to get the first angle of rotation.

Step 4 Let the first element remain horizontal (no rotation), but use the Measurements palette or the Item → Modify command to enter degrees of rotation and rotate the second element.

Figure 11-19 First of five elements remains horizontal, second element is rotated 72° (360/5).

Step 5 Increase each consecutive element's rotation by the amount of the first rotation.

Figure 11-20 Third element is rotated 144° (72°+72°), fourth is rotated 216° (144°+72°), and fifth is rotated 288° (216°+72°).

Step 6 Arrange the elements in a symmetrical, circular pattern and edit the text in each text box.

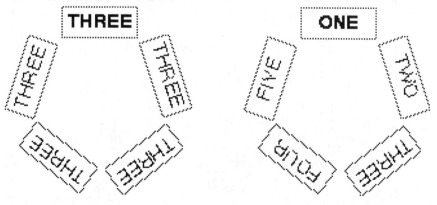

Figure 11-21 Final format.

Text Inside a Shape

QuarkXPress gives you the ability to format type inside a shape, including irregular shapes. No single command achieves this effect; rather you perform a series of steps to create both a picture and a text box. To flow text inside a shape:

Step 1   Create a text box, and type in or import the text you want flowed into a shape.

Step 2   Create a picture box (you can use any shape picture box, but the rectangle or polygon picture box works best). To create a runaround polygon, import a graphic, and then choose Item ➤ Runaround; use the pop-up menu and select Manual Image, and click the Invert check box. In this case, the runaround polygon will be in the shape of the graphic.

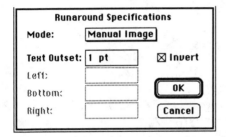

Figure 11-22 The Runaround dialog box set up for flowing text inside a shape.

Step 3   With the editing tool selected, delete the graphic by pressing the Delete key.

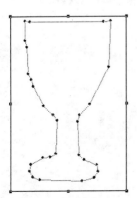

Figure 11-23 Runaround Polygon remains in a Picture Box after graphic is deleted.

Step 4   **Make sure the picture box is on top of the text box (select Item ➤ Bring to Front); when the space inside the polygon wrap is larger than the space available in the text box, the text will flow inside the runaround polygon shape.**

Lorem ipsum dolor sit amet, con-
sectetuer adipiscing elit, sed diam
nonummy nibh euismod tincidunt
ut laoreet dolore magna aliquam
erat volutpat. Ut wisi enim ad min-
im veniam, quis nostrud exerci
tation ullamcorper suscipit lobor-
tis nisl ut aliquip ex ea com-
modo consequat. Duis et al
autem vel eum iriure
dolor in hendrerit in
vulputate velit le
volut esse
molestie
conse-
quat, vel
i l l u m
d o l o r e
eu feugiat
nulla facilisis at verot et

Figure 11-24 Text flows inside the shape.

You can move the handles on the runaround polygon anywhere within the picture box. You can add handles to the runaround polygon by holding down the ⌘ key as you click on the polygon. To remove handles, hold down the ⌘ key as you click on a handle. To prevent screen redraw while you are adjusting the shape, hold down the space bar. When you release it, the screen will redraw.

Summary

This chapter offered tips and suggestions for creating design specifications for type and using QuarkXPress tools and commands to achieve special typographic effects. The next chapter offers a range of ideas for using special graphic techniques in QuarkXPress.

12 *Special Graphic Techniques*

In this chapter we present some special techniques related to graphics. The basic issues of creating and importing graphics in QuarkXPress were covered in Chapter 6. Special techniques presented in this chapter include how to create special effects such as drop shadows and custom rules, and how to draw perfect polygons (pentagons, hexagons, and the like). You will also learn how to create common graphic elements, such as bar charts and organization charts, using QuarkXPress' tools.

Working with Graphics

QuarkXPress is not a drawing package; it can in no way approach the capabilities of such programs as Adobe Illustrator or Aldus FreeHand, one or both of which should probably be part of your electronic "toolbox."

However, you should become familiar with the graphics tools that QuarkXPress does have to offer, for these built-in tools have much more capability than you might think. Understanding thoroughly how the picture box and line tools work will also make it easier for you to work with imported graphics, and will help you keep QuarkXPress' full design potential in mind.

Using Two Sets of Defaults for Picture Boxes

If you always want the same inset or border or background for your picture boxes, you can use Edit ➤ Preferences ➤ Tools, as described in Chapter 3, to change the defaults for the item tools. Sometimes, however, you might want two sets of defaults. For example, you might repeatedly add picture boxes for imported graphics plus black-background boxes that are placeholders for photographic halftones that will be stripped in at the print shop.

With normal defaults, you would need to use Item ➤ Modify to set the background shade to 100 percent black every time you draw a box that is a placeholder for a photograph. The following method can save you from opening the Picture Box Specifications dialog box repeatedly, and save time in producing a document with a lot of placeholders:

Step 1   Use Edit ➤ Preferences ➤ Tools to set the defaults for a rectangular box to match what you want for boxes that will hold imported pictures.

Step 2   Use Edit ➤ Preferences ➤ Tools to set the defaults for the Rounded-corner Rectangle Picture Box tool (⊠) to match what you want for boxes that will serve as placeholders for photographs. Set the Corner Radius to 0 (to make the Rounded-corner Rectangle Picture Box tool draw rectangles as the default), and set the background to 100 percent black (Figure 12-1).

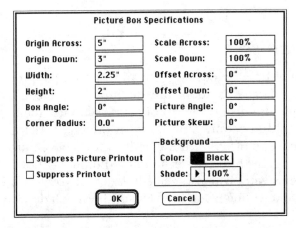

Figure 12-1 Picture Box Specifications dialog box set up for black-box placeholders shows corner radius is set to 0 for the Rounded-corner Rectangle Picture Box tool.

Now every time you use the Rectangle Picture Box tool (⊠), you will draw a box with the default specifications for imported pictures, and every time you use the Rounded-corner Rectangle Picture Box tool (⊗), you will draw a black box as a placeholder for a halftone to be stripped in later (Figure 12-2).

Figure 12-2 Rectangles drawn with the Rectangle Picture Box tool (left) and with the Rounded-Corner Picture Box tool (right).

You can use variations on this tip to create any two sets of specifications. The key is that you are actually turning the Rounded-corner Rectangle Picture Box tool into a Rectangular Picture Box tool by setting the corner radius to zero.

Creating Drop Shadows

The simplest method of creating a three-dimensional effect is to create a "shadow" of a box by placing a copy of the box behind it, offset slightly and assigned a dark fill pattern. The effect is commonly referred to as a drop shadow. This technique is frequently used to add dimension or visual interest to conceptual illustrations such as bar charts and organization charts. You can add special effects to any page using this technique on boxes or lines.

Step 1 **Draw a box with one of QuarkXPress' item tools. Use the Text Box tool (Ⓐ) if you will be filling the drop-shadowed box with text. Use one of the picture box tools if you will be filling the box with an imported picture. Or use one of the line tools if you want to create a drop-shadowed line.**

Figure 12-3 Box drawn with the Text Box tool.

Step 2   Use Item ➤ Modify to assign a 100 percent black fill or any shade or color other than white or transparent (0 percent).

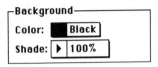

Figure 12-4 Box Specifications dialog box.

Step 3   Use Item ➤ Duplicate to create a second box, and position the copy on top of the first box, offset slightly. Or make the second box a picture box, since picture boxes store less information in them than text boxes.

Step 4   Use Item ➤ Modify to assign a 100 percent white fill (or any shade or color other than what you used on the first box).

Step 5   Use Item ➤ Frame to assign a frame to the top box.

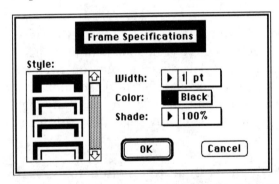

Figure 12-5 Frame Specifications dialog box.

Step 6   Fill the top box with text or graphics.

Figure 12-6 Finished drop shadow box.

Step 7   If you want to make duplicates of the drop-shadowed box, select both boxes and group them.

Figure 12-7 Grouped boxes show boundary box when selected.

Layering Lines for Special Effects

Sometimes you might want to draw lines that appear to have a center that is different from the the outer edge of the line—such as a white line with black edges. QuarkXPress offers several line styles with this effect, but what if you want specific control over the width of each part of the line, or you want the center to be shaded instead of white? You can align copies of straight lines next to each other, but here is a simpler method.

Step 1   **First, draw the line and set the color and width. Figure 12-8 shows a black line, 5 points wide.**

Figure 12-8 A wide black line.

Step 2   **Select Item ➤ Duplicate to create a second on top of the first, slightly offset. Position the second line on top of the first (you don't have to position it precisely). Set the second line's attributes — Figure 12-9 shows a white, 3-point line. (The second line must be thinner than the first.)**

Step 3   **Select both lines and use the Space/Align command to align the centers horizontally and vertically (if you want the outer edges to appear equal), then use the Group command to keep them together when you move them.**

Figure 12-9 A wide black line overlaid by a thinner white line.

You can use this technique to create lines composed of several shades or colors, or experiment with more complex lines composed of three or more layers. If the second line is dashed, you can create the look used in maps to represent roads or railways (Figure 12-10).

Figure 12-10 More variations of layered lines.

Drawing Polygons

Equal-sided polygons—such as 3-, 5-, 6-, or 8-sided boxes—are difficult to draw visually on the screen with the Polygon Picture Box tool (⊗). Here are two techniques that will help you draw polygons with equal sides. Use the first technique to create polygons with an even number of sides; use the second technique to create polygons with an odd number of sides.

Creating Polygons with an Even Number of Sides

Step 1   Select the Orthogonal Line tool (+) and draw a straight line.

Step 2   Select Item ➤ Duplicate to make as many copies of the line as needed. If the polygon is to have an even number of sides, you want the number of lines to total half the number of sides.

Figure 12-11 For a six-sided polygon, you want to create three identical lines.

Step 3   Select the lines one by one and rotate them in multiples of the number of degrees yielded by the formula:

360° divided by the number of lines

For a six-sided figure, create three lines. Because 360° divided by 3 equals 120°, rotate the first line 0°, rotate the second line 120°, and rotate the third line 240° (Figure 12-12).

Figure 12-12 Three lines rotated in multiples of 120° for a six-sided polygon.

Step 4   Select all of the lines and use the Item ➤ Space/Align command to align the centers vertically and horizontally.

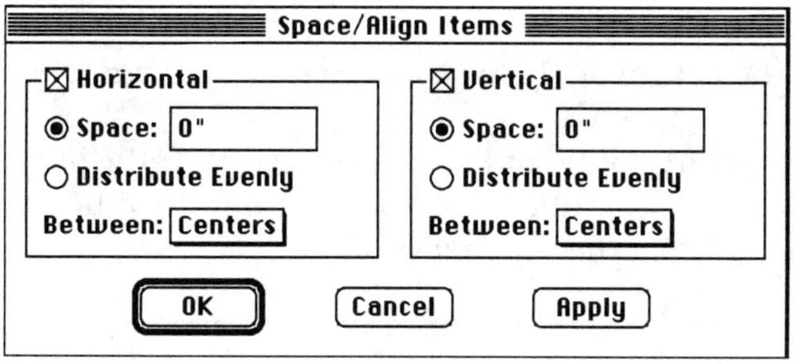

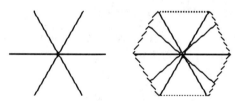

Figure 12-13 Space/Align dialog box.

Step 5   Select the Polygon Picture Box tool (⊠) and draw a polygon by clicking on the end points of the lines.

Figure 12-14 Three rotated and aligned lines create six end points. Use end points as guides in creating the polygon with the Polygon picture box tool.

Step 6 Delete the three lines that you used as guides.

Figure 12-15 The final six-sided polygon.

Creating Polygons with an Odd Number of Sides

Step 1 Select the Orthogonal Line tool (+) to draw a straight line.

Step 2 Make as many copies of the line as needed. If the polygon is to have an odd number of sides, you want the total number of lines to equal the number of sides.

Figure 12-16 For a five-sided polygon, you want to create five identical lines.

Step 3 Select the lines one by one and rotate them in multiples of the number of degrees yielded by the formula:

360° divided by the number of lines

For a five-sided figure, create five lines. Because 360° divided by 5 equals 72°, rotate the lines at 0°, 72°, 144°, 216°, and 288° (Figure 12-17).

Figure 12-17 Five lines rotated in multiples of 72° for a five-sided polygon.

Step 4 Select all of the lines and use the Item ➤ Space/Align command to align the centers vertically and horizontally.

Step 5 Select the Polygon Picture Box tool (⊗) and draw a polygon by clicking on the end points of the lines, *skipping every other point.*

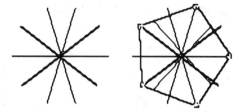

Figure 12-18 Five rotated and aligned lines create 10 end points. Skip every other point in drawing the polygon.

Step 6 **Delete the five lines that you used as guides.**

Figure 12-19 The final five-sided polygon.

Drawing Cartoon Balloons and Other Special Shapes

Unusual shapes such as cartoon balloons can be created by converting ovals to polygons and dragging a handle. Here are the steps in creating a cartoon balloon.

Step 1 **Select the Oval Picture Box tool (⊗) and draw an ellipse.**

Figure 12-20 An ellipse created with the Oval Picture Box tool.

Step 2 **Choose Item → Picture Box Shape and select the polygon from the pop-up menu.**

Step 3   Choose Item ➤ Reshape Polygon to display handles all around the ellipse.

Figure 12-21 Handles display all around the ellipse when you choose Reshape Polygon.

Step 4   Drag one of the handles to create a pointed extension from the ellipse.

Figure 12-22 Drag a handle to create a pointed extension.

Step 5   Select the Text Box tool (⒜) and create a text box on top of the balloon. Use the Style ➤ Alignment command to center the text horizontally and the Item ➤ Modify command to set the background to None and to center the text vertically.

Figure 12-23 Text added in a text box.

You can use this technique to create other shapes that can stand alone as graphic design elements on a page or that can be used to crop imported pictures in unusual ways or force unusual text wraps.

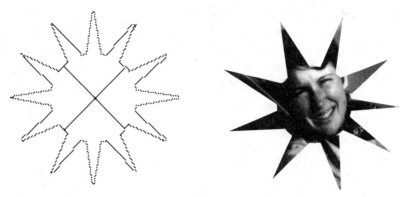

Figure 12-24 Reshaped polygon creates unusual crop.

 When creating anchored picture boxes, regardless of the shape of the box you copy into the Clipboard, the picture box will become a rectangular picture box; it will not maintain its original shape.

Creating Business Graphics with QuarkXPress

Using QuarkXPress' built-in graphics tools, you can build simple bar charts, organization charts, and other basic diagrams.

Creating Bar Charts

Bar charts are very common business graphics. You can generate bar charts using a charting or spreadsheet application and then import the chart into QuarkXPress to create a business proposal or report. If you don't have a charting package, or if your artists don't want to learn how to use a spreadsheet package simply to generate bar charts, you can use the technique described here to generate roughly accurate bar charts using QuarkXPress.

Step 1   Select the Orthogonal Line tool (+) and draw a horizontal line the width you want for the bar chart. Draw a vertical line the height you want for the chart. Draw a short horizontal tick mark near the bottom of the vertical axis.

Step 2 Select the Text Box tool (A) and create a text box to the left of the tick mark, making it wide enough to hold the longest tick mark label. Type the longest label in the box (you will change the labels later), and use the Style menu commands to choose the Font and Size you want and set Alignment to Right.

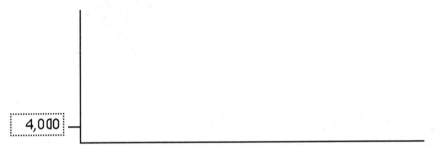

Figure 12-25 Two axes and the first tick mark on the vertical axis are created with the Orthogonal Line tool. Text box initially shows the longest label.

Step 3 Select the Item tool (✥) and select both the tick mark and the text box. Optionally, you can group these items.

Step 4 Use the Step and Repeat command to make as many copies of the tick mark and text box as you want along the vertical axis.

Step and Repeat

Repeat Count:	4
Horizontal Offset:	0"
Vertical Offset:	-0.25"

[OK]   [Cancel]

Figure 12-26 Step and Repeat dialog box.

In the Step and Repeat dialog box (Figure 12-26), the repeat count is one less than the number of tick marks you want on the vertical axis (since you have already created one). The Horizontal Offset should be specified as 0. The Vertical Offset is the distance between tick marks, which you can calculate by dividing the number of tick marks into the length of the vertical axis.

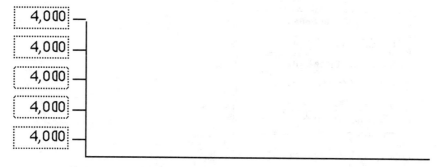

Figure 12-27 Chart shows labels on vertical axis.

Step 5 **Edit each text label for the tick marks.**

Step 6 **Select the Rectangle Picture Box tool (⊠) and create a rectangle the width of one bar. Position it on the horizontal axis near the origin of the two axes.**

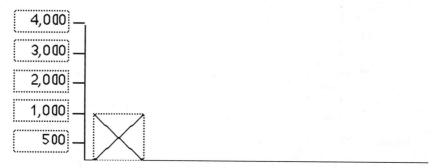

Figure 12-28 Chart shows a bar of the desired width, set to any height, in the first position.

The width you choose should be based on the length of the horizontal axis of the chart and the number of bars. For example, if the axis is 6 inches and your chart has 5 bars, you might make each bar 1 inch wide and distribute the extra inch for the space between bars. This first bar can be any height—you will adjust the height of each bar later.

Step 7 **Use the Step and Repeat command to make as many copies of this basic unit as you need bars and arrange them along the horizontal axis.**

```
┌─────────────────────────────────┐
│  ╔═══════════════════════════╗  │
│  ║      Step and Repeat      ║  │
│  ║                           ║  │
│  ║  Repeat Count:    ┌────┐  ║  │
│  ║                   │ 4  │  ║  │
│  ║  Horizontal Offset:│0.6"│ ║  │
│  ║                           ║  │
│  ║  Vertical Offset: │ 0" │  ║  │
│  ║                           ║  │
│  ║  ╭────────╮   ╭──────────╮║  │
│  ║  │   OK   │   │  Cancel  │║  │
│  ║  ╰────────╯   ╰──────────╯║  │
│  ╚═══════════════════════════╝  │
└─────────────────────────────────┘
```

Figure 12-29 Step and Repeat dialog box.

In the Step and Repeat dialog box (Figure 12-29), the repeat count is one less than the number of bars in the chart (since you have already created one bar). The Horizontal Offset is the distance between bars. Make it equal to the bar width if you want the bars to touch each other, wider if you want space between them.

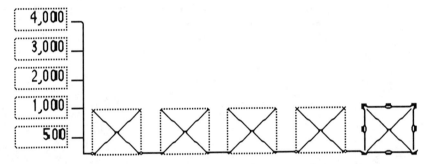

Figure 12-30 Duplicated boxes.

Step 8   Select the Item tool (✥) and scale each bar vertically by dragging the handle at the center of the top of the box up or down to align with the appropriate value along the vertical axis.

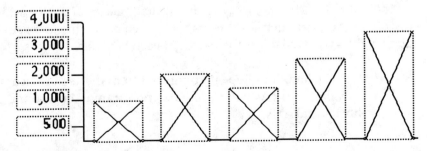

Figure 12-31 Scaled boxes.

Step 9 To add text boxes to label each bar in the chart, you can create one text box that runs the length of the horizontal axis
and set tabs to position each label.

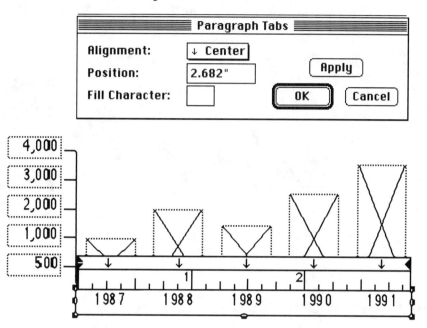

Figure 12-32 Set tabs in text box that runs below bars.

If you create each bar using the Text Box tool (☐) in step 6, you can
type text labels directly into each bar. Use the Style ➤ Alignment command to align the text Left, Right, or Centered in the bar. Use the
Item ➤ Modify command to set the Vertical Alignment of the text to the
top, center, or bottom of the bar.

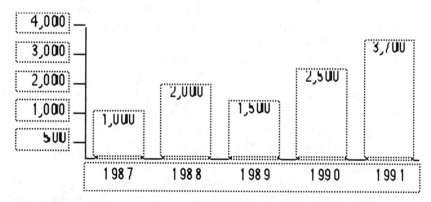

Figure 12-33 Bars created with the Text Box tool can contain labels.

Step 10 Finish the chart by adding a title and caption. You can use the techniques described in steps 6 to 8 to create a second set of bars that overlay the first. You can set different background colors or shades for the two sets of boxes, and add a legend to differentiate the two sets.

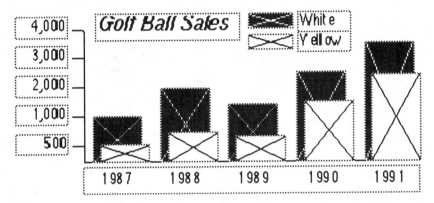

Figure 12-34 Chart with second set of bars and a legend.

Using the Space/Align Command

Chapter 3 described the basic features of the Space/Align command. Here we offer a few more tips about using that command to align objects when at least one item is already positioned such that you do not want the Space/Align command to move it.

Normally, when you use the Space/Align command to align objects horizontally, the item in the leftmost position of the group will remain in place and items to the right of it will be moved to meet the specifications in the Space/Align dialog box. Similarly, when aligning objects vertically, the item in the topmost position of the group will remain in place and items below it will be moved.

If you have already positioned an item on the page and you do not want to move it, you can use the Lock command to prevent inadvertent movements with the Item tool. However, the Lock command does not prevent an item from being moved through a dialog box entry. The Space/Align command will cause *locked* items to move if they are not in the leftmost position for a horizontal move and the topmost position for a vertical move.

 When aligning a group of items relative to one item that you do not want moved, position all other items to the right of the fixed item when moving along the horizontal and below the fixed item when moving along the vertical.

For example, if you have created a bar chart using QuarkXPress' tools and you want to align text labels below each bar, you can use the Space/Align command:

Step 1   Create the bar chart (as described earlier in this chapter).

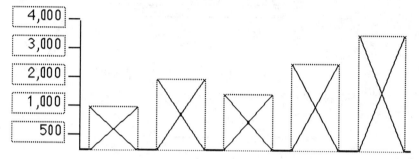

Figure 12-35 Bar chart before labels are added to bars.

Step 2   Type the first bar's labels in a text box and position it any-where to the right of and below the first bar. Use the Style ➤ Alignment command to center the text in the box.

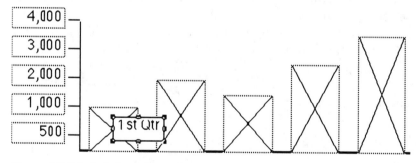

Figure 12-36 Label positioned to the right of the first bar.

Step 3   Use the Space/Align command to center the label 3 picas below the bar.

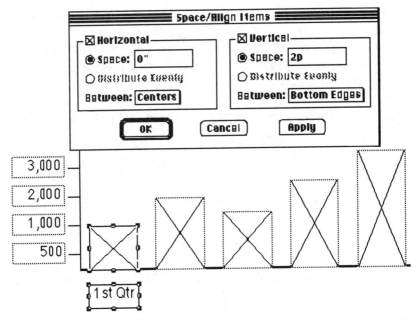

Figure 12-37 Space/Align dialog box shows Horizontal spacing set to 0, with Centers aligned. Vertical spacing is set to 2 picas with Bottom Edges aligned.

If you want to center the label *above* the bar, you can use the Space/Align command to align the centers horizontally, but you must select the Item tool (✥) to drag the label into position above the bar. You cannot use the Space/Align command to position the label above the bar without starting with the label above the bar, in which case the Space/Align command would move the bar.

See "Creating Bar Charts" for a full description of creating this chart and alternatives for labeling the bars.

Organization Charts

Organization charts are a very common form of business graphic. Here is a technique for quickly producing an organization chart in QuarkXPress. We assume that you have already sketched the chart roughly on paper before you start building it in QuarkXPress.

Step 1   Select the Text Box tool (Ⓐ) and create a small text box of the most common size to be used in the chart.

Make this text box large enough to fit any entry in the chart by typing the text of the longest name and title or department that will appear in the organization chart, and using commands in the Style menu to set up the type specifications that you will use throughout the chart. Then scale the text box so it is just large enough to fit each line of the entry.

Step 2   Use the Item → Modify command to make the box opaque (not transparent). Use the Item → Frame command to add a visible border around the box and special effects (such as rotation or skewing). Drop shadows can be added later, if desired.

Figure 12-38 Longest name, title, and department are typed in the first box.

This item will be the basic unit used throughout the chart. The text typed in this first box need not reflect reality—the person's name you type need not hold that title or be in that department.

Step 3   Working in Fit in Window view (⌘-0), make as many copies of this basic item as you need to fill the chart. Roughly drag the copies into the positions they would take to fit on the page.

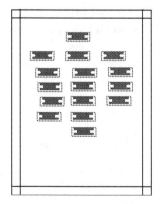

Figure 12-39 Initial layout can be rough.

Step 4   Select the items in each column or along each vertical division or department line in the chart and use the Space/Align command to align them precisely with Horizontal spacing set to 0, aligning the centers, and even Vertical spacing set to any amount larger than the height of each box.

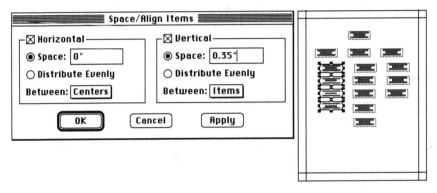

Figure 12-40 Space/Align dialog box and results.

Select and align each column of boxes in the chart using the same vertical spacing.

Step 5   Optionally, you can add drop shadows to all the boxes by selecting all the text boxes in the chart: Use the Item → Duplicate command to copy them. Use the Item → Modify command to give the copies a dark background. Use the Group command to group them. Move them into position slightly offset from the first set of boxes. Use the Item → Send to Back command to send the shadows behind the chart.

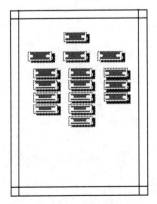

Figure 12-41 Chart items with drop shadows.

Step 6 Select the Orthogonal Line tool (✛) and draw lines to mark the chart organization.

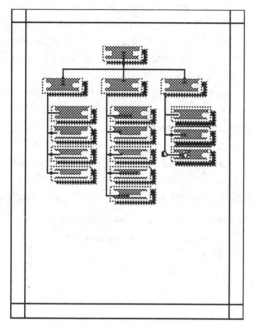

Figure 12-42 Chart items with lines overlaid.

Step 7 Group all of the lines and use the Item ➤ Send to Back command to send them behind the text boxes.

Step 8 Finally, return to Actual Size view and edit the text in each box to reflect the appropriate name and affiliations.

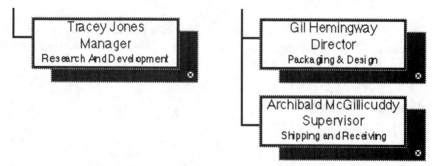

Figure 12-43 Edit text in boxes in Actual Size view.

Using the Frame Editor

As you learned in Part I, you can assign a frame (border) around a text box or a picture box using the Item ➤ Frame command. Frames listed in the pop-up menu of the dialog box include the basic frames that come with QuarkXPress, plus any that you have added using the Frame Editor—a separate program that comes with QuarkXPress.

Any changes or additions you make to frames through the Frame Editor are stored as part of the *XPress Preferences* file. Once you use frames created in the Frame Editor in a document, the frame information is also stored in that document. If you then use the Frame Editor to change or delete frames that have been used in a document, when you next open that document, a dialog box appears that lets you choose to use the information in *Xpress Preferences* or to keep the information as it is in the document.

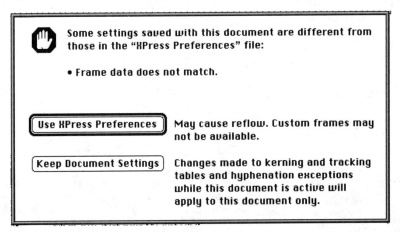

Figure 12-44 If you edit frames used in a document in the Frame Editor, a warning appears when you next open the document.

If you choose "Use XPress Preferences", the frames may not print correctly. Choose "Keep Document Settings" if you want to be sure that custom frames print correctly.

Creating a New Frame

To create a new frame:

Step 1   Double-click on the Frame Editor application icon on the desktop to start it.

Step 2 Choose New Style from the File menu.

Step 3 Enter the width of the new frame in pixels in the dialog box.

```
Enter new size: [12|        ]
    ( OK )    [ Cancel ]
```

Figure 12-45 Enter the width of the new frame in the first dialog box displayed.

When you click on OK, the Frame Editor displays the Element Selection window.

Step 4 In the Element Selection window, click on the button representing the side or corner element you want to create.

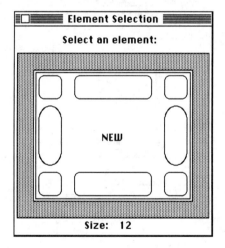

Figure 12-46 Eight buttons represent side and corner elements.

When you click on an element, the Frame Editor displays a dialog box for entering height and width—this time, of the element only.

Step 5 Enter the pixel height and/or width (depending on which element you've selected) of the frame element in the dialog box.

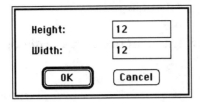

Figure 12-47 Enter the height and width of the frame element in the dialog box.

When you click on OK, the Frame Editor displays the Frame Edit dialog box.

Step 6   In the Frame Edit dialog box, use the mouse to add or delete pixels in the window at the left in the dialog box.

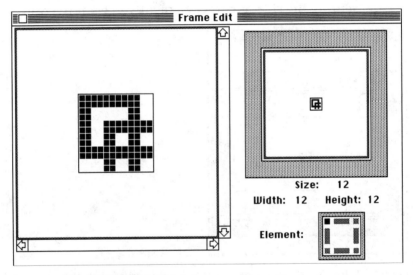

Figure 12-48 Frame Edit dialog box.

You add and delete pixels in the Frame edit dialog box just as you would when working in Fatbits in MacPaint. When you click on a white pixel, it changes to black, and vice versa. The right side of the dialog box shows what element you are working on and gives the frame measurements in pixels as you entered them.

When you click on the close box in the Frame Editor dialog box, the Element Selection window is displayed. When you create the first corner or a side in the new frame, QuarkXPress automatically copies that element to the other three corners or sides. If you modify a corner or side of an existing frame, you can copy the modified element to the other corners or sides as described in the next steps:

Step 7 **After you've modified an element, to copy it to other sides of the frame, choose Copy Elements from the Element menu to display the Copy Elements dialog box.**

Step 8 **Click on the button in the top part of the dialog box that represents the element you want to copy.**

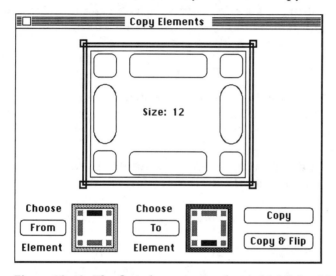

Figure 12-49 The first element you select is highlighted in the From area at the bottom of the Copy Elements dialog box.

Step 9 **Click on the To button in the Copy Elements dialog box, then click on the button representing the element you want to copy.**

Step 10 **Click on Copy if you want the two elements to be identical. Click on Copy and Flip if you want the copy to be a mirror image of the first element.**

You cannot copy a corner element to a side element or vice versa.

Step 11 **Click the close box in the Copy Elements dialog box to return to the Element Selection dialog box and continue editing elements.**

Step 12 Click the close box in the Element Selection dialog box when you are finished creating a frame. A dialog box appears asking if you want to save changes.

Step 13 Click Yes in the warning box to save your changes—up to this point, no changes have been made to the *XPress Preferences* file.

Step 14 When the Style Selection window is displayed, you can continue editing or creating frames or you can choose the File → Quit command to exit the Frame Editor.

Editing Frames

You can change a frame that you have created. (You cannot change the frames that come with QuarkXPress, but you can copy them and change the copies as described in the next section).

Step 1 Double-click on the Frame Editor application icon on the desktop to display the Style Selection window.

Step 2 Double-click on the frame you want to edit.

Step 3 Choose the size you want to edit, or choose New Size from the File menu. (See "Changing the Size of a Frame," later in this chapter).

Step 4 Follow steps 4 to 14 from "Creating a New Frame."

Copying and Changing Frames

You can make a copy of a frame that you have created or of any of the frames that come with QuarkXPress, and make changes to the copy to create a new frame.

Step 1 Double-click on the Frame Editor application icon on the desktop to display the Style Selection window.

Step 2 Click once on the frame you wish to copy.

Step 3 Choose Duplicate from the File menu to display the new copy at the top of the Style Selection window.

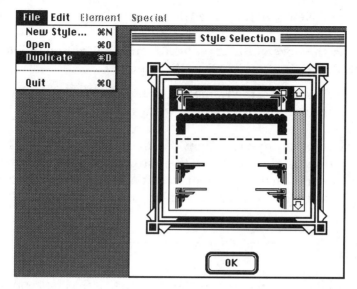

Figure 12-50 Choose Duplicate to make a copy of an existing frame you want to edit.

Step 4 Double-click on the new frame copy.

Step 5 Choose the size you wish to edit, or choose New Size from the File menu (described under the next heading).

Step 6 Follow steps 4 to 14 from "Creating a New Frame."

Changing the Size of a Frame

The width of a frame can be scaled using the Item ➤ Frame command when a box to which it is applied is active, but a decorative bitmap frame will print best in the widths that have been specified for it. To make a new size for a frame:

Step 1 Double-click on the Frame Editor application icon on the desktop to display the Style Selection window.

Step 2 Double-click on the frame you want to edit.

This can be a frame that you have created or a *copy* of one of the frames that came with QuarkXPress.

Step 3 Choose New Size from the File menu.

Step 4 Enter the new width in points (or enter the abbreviation for another unit of measure) in the dialog box.

When you click on OK, the Frame Editor displays the Element Selection window with the frame scaled to the new size.

Step 5 If you notice any distortions due to the scaling in the Element Selection window, click on the button representing the side or corner element you want to edit and proceed as described in "Creating a New Frame," earlier in this chapter.

Summary

This chapter included specific tips about using QuarkXPress commands and features for special graphic effects. The next chapter offers tips on how to create color separations using QuarkXPress.

13 *Printing Color Separations*

One of the most exciting aspects of desktop publishing today is the ability to create high-quality color separations directly from the Macintosh. Over the last two years, the Macintosh has made significant inroads into the world of color prepress. This has been possible due to a variety of technological advances, including capabilities offered by QuarkXPress. Since the release of QuarkXPress 3.0, QuarkXPress users have had the option of producing color separations of pages, including those containing Encapsulated PostScript (EPS) illustrations created by Adobe Illustrator, Aldus FreeHand, and other programs, and, with the help of other programs, pages containing continuous-tone color images (that is, color photographs).

In Chapter 7 you learned the basics of how to create new colors and how to apply colors to items in QuarkXPress. In this chapter we discuss how to use QuarkXPress to create color separations.

General Considerations

In order to take advantage of QuarkXPress' excellent capabilities for printing color separations, it's important to understand the basics of color printing. With the Macintosh, for the first time, designers have been given technology that allows them directly to control the entire prepress process. Whether or not you as a designer choose to take advantage of these capabilities is a matter of individual choice.

The Macintosh can be part of the production of final film for printing at various levels. For example, many times pages are created in QuarkXPress and output to film, with traditional process color separations stripped in manually. Another commonly used alternative is to create pages in QuarkXPress, including low-resolution images, and send the pages to a high end system, such as a Scitex, where high-resolution images are substituted for the low-resolution images. In this case, all film is output on the high end system. Finally, it is becoming more and more practical to include all elements on a page, including high-resolution images, and output them directly from QuarkXPress to a PostScript imagesetter.

No matter which alternative you choose, it is imperative that you talk to your printer before preparing any job that involves printing in color. The best method will often be dictated by the financial or time economics of a specific job.

If you've worked with creating color separations on the Macintosh, you know that there are many variables that come into play in getting the results you're looking for. One key challenge is calibrating the color definition on display and output devices. This allows you to achieve the most predictable results possible. There are a variety of solutions for monitor calibration, ranging from simple, no-cost solutions to hardware and software solutions that cost thousands of dollars.

There are some common-sense steps you can take to ensure consistency in the colors that appear on your monitor. For example, keep the lighting conditions stable in the room where you're working, which usually means using artificial light that has the same brightness at all times of day. A simple INIT, called Gamma, lets you adjust the gamma, or the rate at which colors get dark or light on a monitor. This INIT is available from Adobe Systems (and ships with the program Photoshop).

Several manufacturers have developed devices that read values from your monitor and attempt to adjust the monitor to accurately simulate colors. Manufacturers of monitor calibration instruments include Barco, Radius, SuperMac, and RasterOps.

Another important calibration that needs to be made for working with color separations is the adjustment of the imagesetter that will be used to output film. It's important to adjust the gray screens printed on the imagesetter to match those used by a software program. A key piece of equipment, called a densitometer, is necessary to measure the actual screen percentages printed by an imagesetter.

Regardless of how carefully you calibrate your monitor or imagesetter, it's important to obtain a quality color proof of your work. In the simplest case, this might be a printout on a 300- or 400-dpi color printer, or, in the case of pages containing color photographs, a proof made from the actual film, such as a proof created on a Matchprint or Chromalin system, is necessary.

A number of vendors are working on solutions that will eliminate or greatly reduce the discrepancy between color on computer monitors and color printed on a press. For example, Adobe's PostScript Level 2 has the capability to use a color model, called the CIE (Commission Internationale de l'Eclairage) color model, that has the promise of providing device-independent color in the future.

Spot Color vs. Process Color

There are generally two ways to prepare film for color printing jobs. One is to create separate plates for printing with spot colors, the other is to create separate plates for each of the four process colors—cyan, magenta, yellow and black. Spot color separations, often used for drawn illustrations and solid-color graphics, usually involve preparing film that will be used by a printer when premixed inks will be used in the printing process. PANTONE colors are one of the most common systems for premixing inks. Film prepared for a spot color printing job includes a layer of film output for each premixed ink.

Process color, usually used for continuous tone images, like photographs, is made up of four inks—the three subtractive primaries, yellow, cyan, and magenta, plus black—printed one on top of the other in a pattern of halftone dots. Both spot color and process color require separation of color elements, and QuarkXPress lets you specify either type of separations for any color you create.

Offset printing presses produce spot color by filling each ink well(s) of the press with one premixed color. If the press has only one ink well, the job would be run through once with one color, then the pages would be allowed to dry, the press would be cleaned and filled with a second color, and the dry pages would be run through a second time for the second color. Many print shops have presses that can print two or more colors in one run, but in any case each individual color requires a separate plate, or color separation.

On the other hand, to understand process color, think about a pointillist painting. The painting actually consists of many minute dots of paint, but the eye blends the dots into solid tones. Similarly, in four-color process printing adjacent dots of ink printed in different colors—usually cyan, magenta, yellow, and black—will be interpreted as a single color by the eye. For example, in areas where yellow and cyan are printed together the eye will perceive green. Each of the four colors requires a different plate, or color separation.

Screen Angles

As mentioned earlier, the film that must be generated to produce plates for four-color process printing consists of a pattern of halftone dots for each color—cyan, magenta, yellow, and black. Traditional halftone screens are generated by photographing an image through a screen that actually contains dots of various sizes (Figure 13-1). Lighter areas of an image are made up of smaller dots, darker areas are created by larger dots. The spacing of the lines of dots is called the screen frequency, or screen lines per inch (lpi).

Figure 13-1 A traditional halftone screen enlarged.

If cyan, magenta, yellow, and black were printed directly on top of each other, the result would be muddy and inexact colors. So in traditional color printing, each color is printed at an angle; the combined angles, when printed together, form tiny rosettes of color, which simulate a particular hue. The algorithms for the angle of rotation necessary, called *irrational* angles, were developed by Dr. -Ing. Rudolph Hell GmbH., the parent company of Hell Graphics Systems, now Linotype-Hell Co., and all prepress systems have licensed these screen angles for use on their equipment. The traditional screen angles rotate cyan at 105°, magenta at 75°, yellow at 0° or 90°, and black at 45°.

To understand some of the potential problems of printing color separations to PostScript imagesetters, it's important to understand how PostScript devices simulate halftone screens. Imagesetters cannot physically create dots of various sizes; a pixel is either on or off. In order to create halftone dots, an imagesetter prints pixels that are grouped in cells, with each cell corresponding to a halftone dot, thus simulating the traditional halftone dot. On an imagesetter, the only line frequencies possible are those that divide evenly into the resolution of the imagesetter, since it cannot print half of a pixel. As a result, color separations printed on PostScript imagesetters cannot always accurately reproduce irrational screens. Sometimes they produce moiré patterns in color images.

Since producing irrational screens requires tremendous computational power, Adobe has licensed Linotype-Hell's *rational tangent* screening (RT screening) algorithm, which approximates the ideal values. RT screening, however, limits the variety of screen angles and frequencies that can be achieved and varies the screen frequency from plate to plate, producing unsatisfactory results, especially moirés, with some images. Most PostScript imagesetters manufactured before 1991 use RT screening. Newer imagesetters, however, are employing improved screening methods.

High Quality Screening (HQS)

The merger of Hell Graphics and the Linotype Company has led to the incorporation of some of Hell's irrational screen technology in Linotype's PostScript RIP 30 and RIP 40. High Quality Screening (HQS) algorithms approximate traditional screen angles by modifying the traditional angles only slightly (Figure 13-2). For an image set to print with a line frequency of 133 lpi, each plate printed using HQS angles varies from the traditional angles somewhat, but the variance from plate to plate is much less than RT angles.

Process Color	Traditional Angle/Screen	RT Screening Angle/Screen	HQS Screening Angle/Screen
Cyan	15°/133 lpi	18.435°/133.871 lpi	15.0037°/138.142 lpi
Magenta	75°/133 lpi	71.565°/133.871 lpi	74.9987°/138.142 lpi
Yellow	0°/133 lpi	0°/127 lpi	0°/138.545 lpi
Black	45°/133 lpi	45°/119.737 lpi	45°/138.158 lpi

Figure 13-2 Traditional irrational screening vs. RT screening vs. HQS screening.

Adobe Accurate Screens

Accurate Screens is a technology for optimizing the results of process printing that has been developed by Adobe Systems Incorporated. Accurate Screening uses a rational algorithm that attempts to eliminate the need for the heavy computational power required by irrational screening algorithms.

Accurate Screen first examines the difference between the desired screen and the achievable screen. When the program determines that the optimum screen and angle would require printing half a pixel, it builds a "supercell" and distributes the error over that supercell. For example, if a cell measuring 14.5 pixels is required, Accurate Screens builds a supercell of 29 pixels representing the same dot size that would have previously been represented by 14.5 pixels. By using memory more efficiently, more cells are possible than before.

Separating QuarkXPress Items

QuarkXPress can separate pages that contain items created only in QuarkXPress—text and simple graphics—as well as pages containing graphics created in other programs. This section discusses separating pages that do not contain elements created in other programs. For information on separating pages that contain graphics created in other programs, see "Separating Files Created in Other Programs" later in this chapter.

In order to print separations, colors must be set up correctly for spot or process separation. Once your file is set up with the desired colors and is set to produce spot or process separations properly, check Registration Marks and Make Separations in the Print dialog box (File → Print). The Plate pop-up menu lists all the colors in the document that were created using the Edit → Colors command. If you choose to print a plate for all the colors in a document, QuarkXPress only prints plates for colors that actually have been applied to items in the document, plus the black plate for all pages.

Color Models in QuarkXPress

As discussed in Chapter 7, colors are created in QuarkXPress by selecting the Edit → Colors command and defining a color in the Edit Color dialog box. A pop-up menu (Figure 13-3) offers six different color models to choose from to create a color: Hue, Saturation, and Brightness (HSB); Red, Green, and Blue (RGB); Cyan, Magenta, Yellow, and Black (CMYK); PANTONE, TRUMATCH, and FOCOLTONE.

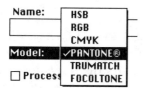

Figure 13-3 Six color models are available for defining new colors.

The most commonly used color models for preparing colors for separation for offset printing are CMYK, PANTONE, TRUMATCH, or FOCOLTONE. CMYK and PANTONE colors may be designated as either spot colors or process color, by turning Process Separation on or off in the Edit Colors dialog box. TRUMATCH and FOCOLTONE colors were designed to be used to designate process color printing only.

HSB Color Model

Hue, Saturation, and Brightness (HSB) is the common system for identifying the way in which artists' paints are mixed. *Hue* is the quality that gives a color its name, such as red, orange, yellow, green, blue, and violet. *Saturation* is a measure of the tint, or purity of a color. *Brightness* is a measure of the amount of light reflected from a color; black reflects almost no light and white reflects almost all light.

To create a color, enter a percentage value in the fields for Hue, Saturation, and Brightness, or use the scroll bars adjacent to each to indicate values. You can also click in the color wheel to indicate Hue and Saturation, and use the scroll bar to indicate Brightness. The color created is displayed in the dialog box. This color is a simulation only; you can expect some variation from the color displayed on the monitor and the final printed color.

RGB Color Model

Red, Green, and Blue (RGB) are the colors used to display color on computer monitors. To create a color, enter a percentage value in the fields for Red, Green, and Blue, or use the scroll bars adjacent to each to indicate values. You can also click in the color wheel to indicate color. The color created is displayed in the dialog box. This color is a simulation only; you can expect some variation from the color displayed on the monitor and the final printed color.

CMYK Color Model

When you choose the cyan, magenta, yellow, and black (CMYK) color model, QuarkXPress displays a color wheel similar to the Apple System color wheel (Figure 13-4). The wheel represents the hue and saturation, and the scroll bar represents the value, or the lightness and darkness of a color.

To create a color, first type in a name, then specify the percentages of CMYK desired by typing a value in the field adjacent to each color, or by using the scroll bars. The color you specify is displayed in the dialog box. Bear in mind this is a simulation only. You can expect some variation from the color displayed on the monitor and the final printed color. You can specify CMYK colors to print spot color or process color separations.

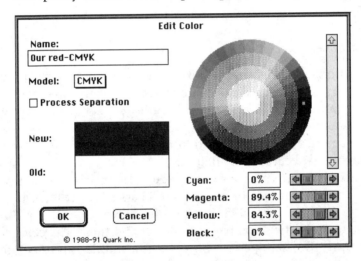

Figure 13-4 The Edit Colors dialog box when the CMYK color model is selected.

Color Swatchbooks

For spot color printing, you must specify precisely what color you want the offset print shop to use. There are a number of different ways of doing this. You can, for example, give the printer a sample of the color you want—it can be a piece of paper, a piece of material, anything—and that it be duplicated as closely as possible.

A more precise way of specifying color is to use a color matching system, such as the PANTONE Matching System (PMS). PMS ink swatchbooks can be purchased at any graphic arts supply store. Printers can usually get most of these types of inks, or they will mix the inks they have to match your swatch. You can create a color in QuarkXPress by specifying PAN-

TONE color numbers in the Edit Colors dialog box (as described later in this section).

Even though you can see colors used on QuarkXPress pages if you have a color monitor, it is a good idea to have an ink swatchbook available for reference. Color monitors can give you only an approximation of what the final printed color will really look like. Also, you can create colors on a monochrome monitor by applying specifications shown in the swatchbook. Ink swatchbooks generally give you a sample of a wide range of different inks, printed on both coated and uncoated paper. Paper type is very important; the appearance of the ink varies a great deal depending on the type of paper on which it is printed. In general, inks appear more brilliant on coated papers, softer and duller on uncoated papers. Finally, the swatchbook is a good reference when specifying spot colors at the print shop.

PANTONE Color Model

The PANTONE MATCHING SYSTEM is one of the most widely used systems for identifying ink colors. The system is based on nine basic PANTONE colors plus black and white. When mixed in various percentages, these colors yield the more than 700 colors in the system. PANTONE colors are cataloged in a swatchbook; choosing a color from this system ensures accurate color reproduction on a press.

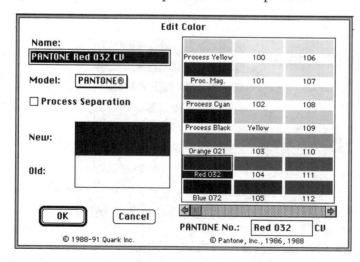

Figure 13-5 The Edit Colors dialog box when the PANTONE color model is selected.

To select a color from the PANTONE system, either type in the full name in the Name field, or enter a number in the PANTONE No. field underneath the display of colors (Figure 13-5). You can also scroll through the display of colors and click on a color. The color you specify is displayed in the dialog box.

This color is a simulation of the PANTONE color. Like CMYK colors, you can specify that PANTONE colors be printed as spot colors or process colors. Greatest accuracy will be achieved if you choose a spot color separation and let your printer mix the ink according to the color shown in the PANTONE swatchbook. QuarkXPress separates the PANTONE color to its process color equivalent, but some colors may vary from the original PANTONE color when finally printed by this method.

TRUMATCH Color Model

The TRUMATCH system was developed for achieving optimum results in printing process color separations using PostScript output devices. The TRUMATCH system is based on 50 different hues, with value graduations or tints of each color, totaling some 2,000 colors. It is essential to use the TRUMATCH swatchbook, called the TRUMATCH Colorfinder, when creating colors using this system, since your monitor can only approximate the color on the screen.

To select a color from the TRUMATCH system, either type in the full name in the Name field, or enter a number in the TRUMATCH No. field underneath the display of colors (Figure 13-6).

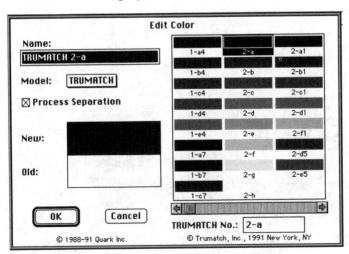

Figure 13-6 The Edit Colors dialog box when the TRUMATCH color model is selected.

You can also scroll through the display of colors and click on a color. Since the TRUMATCH colors were designed for process colors, click on Process Separation for best results.

FOCOLTONE Color Model

Like the TRUMATCH color system, the FOCOLTONE system was created to facilitate the selection of accurate process colors. The basic 763 FOCOLTONE colors consist of combinations of cyan, magenta, yellow, and black in varying percentages from 5 to 85 percent, in 5 percent increments. Additionally, 13 variations on each color are created by eliminating one, two, or three of the process colors. For example, color #1000, a light brown, contains 15 percent cyan, 30 percent magenta, 50 percent yellow, and 25 percent black. Variation number 1, color #1001, contains 15 percent cyan, 30 percent magenta, 50 percent yellow, and 0 percent black.

To select a color from the FOCOLTONE system, either type in the full name in the Name field, or enter a number in the FOCOLTONE No. field underneath the display of colors (Figure 13-7). You can also scroll through the display of colors and click on a color. Since the FOCOLTONE colors were designed for process colors, click on Process Separation for best results.

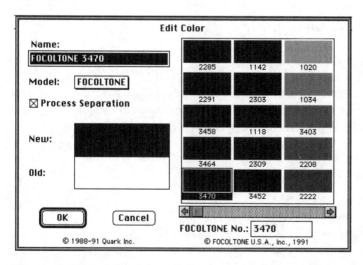

Figure 13-7 The Edit Colors dialog box when the FOCOLTONE color model is selected.

Working with Trapping

If your printing job uses more than one color, but elements of different colors do not touch each other directly, then printing is fairly simple. But if elements do touch—for example, if you have yellow type in the middle of a magenta box—then these elements meet precisely, and problems can occur on the printing press. If the elements are even a hairline out of register, you will see it in the printed piece (either as a dark line where they overlap or as a white line where they don't overlap). In color printing, these registration problems are controlled with trapping, generally by causing one color to overprint another very slightly.

You can avoid trapping problems by "designing" out colors that will be problematic when printing. One common way to do this is to ensure that all the colors you use share a common process color. You could, for example, add 5 percent black to all colors, and avoid any serious trapping problems.

When you can't avoid problem colors that need to be trapped, you'll find that QuarkXPress 3.1 greatly improves the trapping controls offered by version 3.0. In addition to specifying trapping relationships between colors on a document-wide basis, QuarkXPress 3.1 also lets you define automatic trapping and allows you to specify trapping on an item-by-item basis.

Setting Automatic Trapping

The default method that QuarkXPress uses to trap colors can be defined in the Application Preferences dialog box (Edit ➤ Preferences ➤ Application) shown in Figure 13-8. The default method of trapping is referred to as Automatic trapping, and it is based on the relative value (lightness or darkness) of object and background colors.

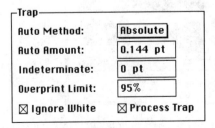

Figure 13-8 Trapping options in the Application Preferences dialog box.

In the Application Preferences dialog box, the settings that can be adjusted are as follows:

- **Auto Method** may be specified from a pop-up menu as Absolute or Proportional. If you select Absolute, Automatic trapping occurs at the absolute value specified in the Auto Amount field. If you specify Proportional, QuarkXPress uses a fraction of the value specified in the Auto Amount based on the difference between the luminance of the object and background color. The formula used is (value of Auto Amount) × (object darkness – background darkness). If the object color is lighter than the background color, it will be spread against the background color; if it is darker, it will be choked.

- **Auto Amount** is the value used by QuarkXPress for Automatic trapping values. You can enter a value between 0 and 36 points in .001-point increments. You can also type in the word "overprint," which causes all colors to overprint their backgrounds with no trapping.

- **Indeterminate** specifies the trapping relationship between an object color item and a background consisting of more than one color. If the object color has conflicting trapping relationships with background colors—that is, if it chokes with some and spreads with others—it will trap to the value specified here.

- **Overprint Limit** specifies the shade at which a color overprints its background color. For example, if the value entered in this field is 95 percent (the preset default), and an object color was shaded 90 percent, it would not overprint, even if that was the setting defined for that color. Rather, it would knock out the color underneath with the spread or choke specified by the Auto Amount.

- If **Ignore White** is checked (the preset default), QuarkXPress will not take background items that have the color white applied into consideration when determining trapping for an object color over multiple background colors.

- **Process Trap** specifies how QuarkXPress handles trapping of process colors. When Process Trap is checked, each process plate is handled individually; for example, on the cyan plate, the darkness of cyan of an object color is compared against the darkness of cyan in the background color, and trapped accordingly. When Process Trap is unchecked, QuarkXPress traps all process colors equally using the trapping value of the object color against the background color.

Trapping Colors

Normally, QuarkXPress controls trap conditions automatically. However, if you click Edit Trap in the Colors dialog box, QuarkXPress displays the Trap Specifications dialog box (Figure 13-9) through which you can control the trapping relationship between color pairs. You specify trapping in terms of the way an object color traps against its background color. Object color refers to the color applied to characters or to an item that is in front of another color, and background color is the color applied to the item that is behind another color item.

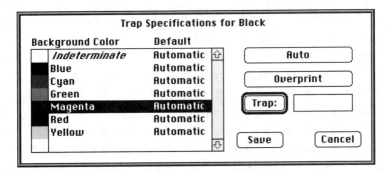

Figure 13-9 The Trap Specifications dialog box.

First, select Edit ➤ Colors; the Colors dialog box appears. In the Colors dialog box, choose the object color for which you want to specify trapping values. Click on Edit Trap to display the Trap Specifications dialog box. The scroll list displayed in the dialog box lists the trapping values specified for the the object color (shown in the dialog box title) relative to each of the colors in the Background color column. The Value column lists the trapping value specified for each background color. These values can be specified in one of three ways:

- **Automatic** lets QuarkXPress handle the trapping—the object color traps relative to the background color. Automatic utilizes the settings in the Application Preferences dialog box (Edit ➤ Preferences ➤ Application) to determine how much to spread (increase) the object color or choke (reduce) the background color. Automatic is the default setting.

- **Overprint** causes the object color to be printed without "knocking out" the background color when you are printing color separation plates—so the object color prints on top of the background color on the press. If you choose Overprint, the object color overprints the selected background color if its shade is greater than or equal to the Overprint Limit value in the Application Preferences dialog box (Edit ➤ Preferences ➤ Application).

- **Trap** value lets you enter a custom value for the trapping or overlap between the object color and the background color. You can enter a value between –36 points and +36 points, in .001-point increments. After you enter a value, click Trap to save the changes you make. A negative value chokes (reduces) the knockout area of the background color, a positive value spreads (increases) the size of the object against the background color. If you enter a value of zero, no choking or spreading occurs when the object is knocked out from the background.

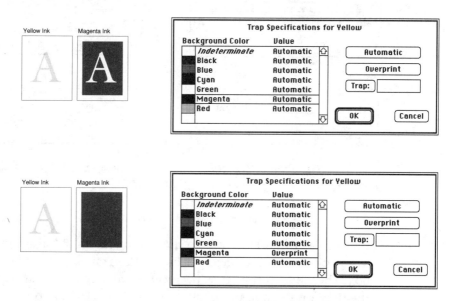

Figure 13-10 Effects of different trapping specifications.

When an object is in front of more than one color, in front of certain color pictures, or if QuarkXPress is unable to identify the background color, the program checks the relationship between the object color and each of the background colors. If there is no conflict, then QuarkXPress traps to the minimum value. If there is a conflict—that is, if the object color would spread into some items and choke others—the item traps to the setting for Indeterminate color.

Trapping Items

In addition to allowing you to set trapping relationships between colors in a document, QuarkXPress 3.1 allows you to set trapping relationships between individual items via the Trap Information palette (View ➤ Show Trap Information).

First, display the Trap Information palette if it is not already displayed by selecting View ➤ Show Trap Information. The palette shows the trapping information for the active item that has been selected. The pop-up menus allow you to control the trapping of box backgrounds, lines, text, pictures, and frames against their background color(s). The appearance of the palette changes based on the active item.

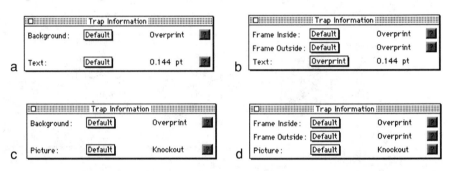

Picture 13-11 The Trap Information palette icons when a text box is selected (a), a framed text box (b), a picture box (c), a line (d).

Trapping values can be specified in one of six ways:

- Choose the **Default** setting on the pop-up menu if you simply want to use the trapping values specified in the Trap Specifications dialog box. The value in the Trap Specifications dialog box is displayed to the right on the pop-up menu on the palette. To obtain more information about the values, click on the question mark to the right of the value and hold down the mouse button. A small window containing information is displayed. If Automatic is the setting in the Trap Specifications dialog box, trapping is determined by the settings in the Application Preferences dialog box (Edit ➤ Preferences ➤ Application).

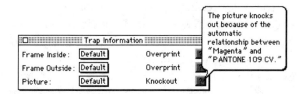

Figure 13-12 Click on the question mark to obtain more information about Default trapping specifications.

- Choose **Overprint** if you do not want the object color to knock out or trap the background color. Choosing this option overrides the Overprint Limit value specified in the Application Preferences dialog box.

- Specifying **Knockout** causes the object color to knock out the background color with no trapping. This type of trapping is sometimes called "butt" registration.

- **Auto Amount (+)** causes the object color to spread by the amount entered in the Auto Amount field in the Application Preferences dialog box.

- **Auto Amount (–)** causes the background color to choke the object color by the amount entered in the Auto Amount field in the Application Preferences dialog box.

- **Custom** lets you set a trapping value other than that specified for Auto Amount in the Application Preferences dialog box. Enter a value from –36pt to 36pt in increments as fine as .001 point. Enter a negative value to cause the background color to choke the object color; enter a positive value to cause the object color to spread.

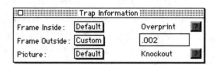

Figure 13-13 Choose Custom to specify trapping values other than the amount specified by Auto Amount in the Application Preferences dialog box.

Text always traps as the object color against the color of the background of the text box. If the text box background is specified with a color of None, and the text is positioned over another item of a single color, the text traps against the color of the item behind it.

If a transparent text box or other item is positioned over items of more than one color, the trapping relationship varies depending on the colors of the background items. If the text or other item of the object color is specified to spread against all the colors of the background items, the object color item spreads by the smallest amount specified. If the object color item is specified to be choked by all the background colors, the object color item is choked by the smallest value specified. If the object color item is specified to spread against some color and be choked by others, or if Knockout is specified, the object color item traps to the value specified for Indeterminate in the Application Preferences dialog box.

Separating Files Created in Other Programs

In addition to providing powerful controls for accurate separation of items created in QuarkXPress, the program also separates graphics created by other applications. The most commonly used applications for preparing graphics to be separated by QuarkXPress are Adobe Illustrator and Aldus FreeHand for illustrations, and Adobe Photoshop for continuous tone images.

Separating Files Created in PostScript Drawing Programs

In order to separate graphics created by Adobe Illustrator or Aldus FreeHand, the first step, of course, is to import the graphic. As discussed in Chapter 6, both Illustrator and FreeHand files must be saved with a screen preview, that is., in Encapsulated PostScript format (EPS). In Adobe Illustrator, these options are selected in the Save As dialog box (Figure 13-14); in FreeHand, you must select the Export command from the File menu to save the artwork in EPS format.

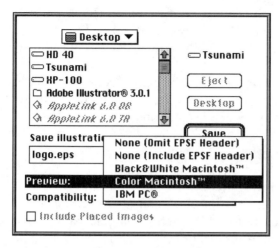

Figure 13-14 Save Illustrator files with a screen preview.

QuarkXPress' trapping controls have no direct effect on the Illustrator or FreeHand artwork itself, and trapping issues must be addressed "manually" in the drawing programs. When a color QuarkXPress item is placed over an imported color graphic, the item traps to according to the relationship specified between the item color and *Indeterminate* background color.

Custom and PANTONE colors created in Adobe Illustrator and imported into QuarkXPress are converted to their CMYK equivalents. In order for these colors to separate as spot colors, you must create the color in QuarkXPress by selecting the Edit ➤ Colors command, and specify that color with Process Separation *off*. This causes QuarkXPress to separate each custom or PANTONE color on its own plate. In the case of custom colors, it's important to name the color in QuarkXPress with the exact name of the color in Illustrator, including upper- and lowercase letters and spaces. Colors created in Illustrator using CMYK values entered in the Paint Style dialog box and TRUMATCH and FOCOLTONE colors are all treated as process colors and separated as CMYK plates.

Colors are created in FreeHand a little differently than in Illustrator. In FreeHand, you specify whether a color is to be separated as a spot color or a process color. When FreeHand colors are specified as spot colors, FreeHand graphics imported into QuarkXPress separate as Illustrator graphics do. If simply imported, spot colors in the graphic separate as process color; if the same color is created in QuarkXPress using the Edit ➤ Colors command and specified with Process Separation off, it separates as a spot color.

If colors are specified in FreeHand to be process colors, you cannot separate them as spot colors from QuarkXPress, even if you create the color in QuarkXPress and specify Process Separation off.

Separating Color Photographs

QuarkXPress can, with the aid of other programs and Xtensions, provide high-quality separations of color photographic images. Pages containing color images can be output to a PostScript imagesetter or sent to a high-end system where separations can be stripped into the page digitally.

Scanning

There's an old saying about computers, "garbage in, garbage out," and this is true when it comes to scanning color images. Regardless of the sophistication of QuarkXPress and any output device, if the quality of the original scan is poor, the image will not be of high quality when finally printed on a press.

High-end drum scanners made by companies such as Linotype-Hell, Scitex, Dai Nippon Screen, and others can be used to scan images that will ultimately end up on the Macintosh as part of a QuarkXPress page. These scanners help yield the best results. They do not merely digitize an image, but also have sophisticated controls for color correction and sharpening images.

Many of the manufacturers of high-end, traditional prepress systems have recently announced scanners that are less expensive than their top-of-the-line models and that can produce excellent results. They are still not intended to be part of an individual's desktop system; Scitex' Smart Scanner retails at around $100,000. Midrange scanners are also becoming more widely available.

Desktop scanners designed for individual use, priced at $10,000 and less, can produce acceptable results for low-quality printing, such as that found in newspapers, but generally are not considered viable sources for digitizing images for high-quality printing.

Regardless of the scanner used, it's a good idea to scan an image in at a size close to the final printed size, or slightly larger. If an image has to be made larger once it has been digitized, the software used for resizing the image essentially has to add information about the color of new pixels that are added in making the picture larger, and the final result may be a poorly reproduced image.

Another rule of thumb to use in scanning images is to scan them in at the number of pixels per inch (ppi) that is roughly equal to twice the line screen at which the image will be printed. For example, if your final page will be output at 150 lines per inch, the image should be scanned at around 300 pixels per inch.

Most high-end scanners have sharpening filters that help to further enhance the clarity of detail in an image after it's been scanned. Sharpening algorithms usually include commands for Sharp and Unsharp Masking. Unsharp Mask is a misleading name: It actually works by blurring the contrast of an image, then subtracting the blurred image from the original, thus brightening and sharpening pixels.

Preparing Files in Photoshop

One of the most common ways that continuous-tone color images are output from QuarkXPress is by preparing the image for color separation using Adobe Photoshop before importing the image into QuarkXPress. This technique puts the burden of the quality of the separations largely on Photoshop, which does an excellent job under the right input (scan)/output(imagesetter) conditions.

The first step is to use Photoshop to manipulate the image as necessary, make color corrections, and if not done already by the scanner, apply an unsharp mask to the image. Then, save the file in Desktop Color Separation (DCS) format. The DCS format was developed by Quark, Inc., and adopted by Adobe Systems for facilitating the output of separations for continuous-tone images. Instead of saving an image to one file, DCS images are broken down into five files: four files containing the image's components of cyan, magenta, yellow, and black, plus a fifth file containing a PICT image for preview on screen (Figure 13-15) and path information. Once the image is ready to be prepared for separations, DCS files can be prepared as follows:

Lizard final   Lizard final.C   Lizard final.M

Lizard final.Y   Lizard final.K

Figure 13-15 Saving Photoshop files in DCS format creates five files.

1.   Adjust the line screen to be used for printing the image by selecting the File ➤ Page Setup command. Click on the Auto button and set the resolution of the output device and the desired line frequency.

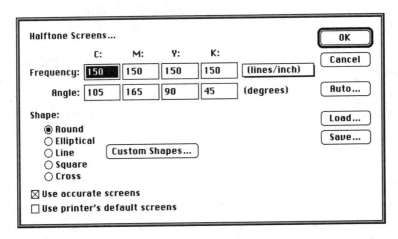

Figure 13-16 Set the line screen in Photoshop by selecting the Screens option in the File ➤ Page Setup command.

2.   If the file is not already in CMYK mode, convert it by selecting the Mode ➤ CMYK command.

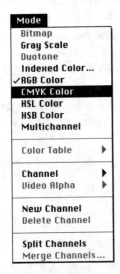

Figure 13-17 Convert the Photoshop image to CMYK.

3.   Save the file in EPS format (File ➤ Save As). Click the Okay button; the EPS options dialog box will appear. Check the settings as illustrated in Figure 13-18.

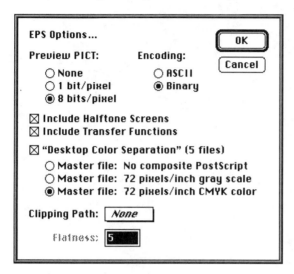

Figure 13-18 Settings for saving the file for Desktop Color Separations.

    Once you have imported the PICT preview file into a QuarkXPress file, it's important not to move the DCS files to any other folder. If you move the CMYK files, QuarkXPress will not be able to locate them for printing and will use the 72-dpi image instead of the high-resolution files.

By setting the line screen and transfer functions in Photoshop, they will not be affected by any settings you make for line screen in QuarkXPress.

Summary

This chapter outlined some of the basic considerations involved with printing color separations from QuarkXPress. Some of the techniques for printing separations were discussed, along with instructions for using QuarkXPress for separation of pages containing graphics created in other programs.

The next chapters cover issues related to publishing in workgroups.

14 *Managing Documents*

More than almost any other business or activity, publishing is ruled by deadlines. You can't send June's news out in July, and when the publication is part of a larger product package, it is likely that the marketing or distribution group will want the documents finished as soon as the product is ready for shipment. One way or another, the publication department is always pushed to complete everything as quickly as possible. Tips in this chapter will help you organize your projects so that they run as smoothly as possible—whether you are the only one in the production group or you are running a large department in a networked workgroup environment.

Organizing Your Disk Files

It's a good idea to organize your disk files before you start building a document in QuarkXPress. A few basic guidelines can save you a lot of trouble in the long run, especially if the document you are building is very large or uses a lot of different source files.

If two or more people are involved in the production process, the disk organization and file-naming conventions should be determined by the production manager and announced to the production crew. File organization and naming conventions might be incorporated into the list of standards and review items as guidelines for moving or renaming files as they move through the production process.

If possible, assemble all source files—the text and picture files as well as the QuarkXPress libraries, templates, and document files—onto one primary hard disk. This can be your internal hard disk if your computer will be the primary workstation for page layout activities, or it can be a file server if you are on a network and several people will be involved in the final document production. It could be a separate hard disk or a removable hard disk if you will need to carry the files from one station to another.

The key folders containing files that affect each document include the QuarkXPress program folder, the System folder, and the project folder (Figure 14-1). Each of these is described under the next headings.

Figure 14-1 Quark-related folders on the desktop.

The QuarkXPress Program Folder

The *QuarkXPress Program Folder* (Figure 14-2) is where the QuarkXPress program is stored. The folder can have any name, but whatever folder contains the QuarkXPress program, three other files must be present for the program to be fully functional. These are: *XPress Preferences, XPress Dictionary*, and *XPress Help*. These files should reside in the program folder or in the System folder. If you want to edit kerning or tracking tables, you must have the *Kern/Track Editor* Xtension in the folder. Your program folder may also contain QuarkXPress import/export filters. Each of these is described under the next headings.

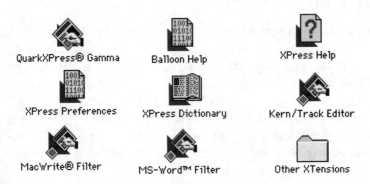

Figure 14-2 Contents of the QuarkXPress Program folder.

XPress Dictionary is used for spell checking. *XPress Help* needs to be available if you want access to on-line help through QuarkXPress. Both of these files are used optionally.

XPress Preferences File

The *XPress Preferences* file replaces the *Xpress Data* file used in QuarkXPress 3.0 and earlier versions. The *XPress Preferences* file contains:

- the Preference settings that will apply to any new document, including any changes you have made to the defaults by using the commands available when QuarkXPress is active but no document is open (as described in Chapter 2),

- the default style sheets, colors, and H&Js,

- hyphenation exceptions (if exceptions have been specified for any document),

- kerning table values (if you have edited any kerning tables),

- tracking edit values, and

- frame definitions, including the standard set that comes with QuarkXPress plus any you have created using the Frame Editor.

XPress Preferences

Figure 14-3 XPress Preferences file.

If you make changes to any of these items when no document is open, they are stored in the *Preferences* file. If you change settings when a document is open, the information is saved in *XPress Preferences* and the document file, or in the document file only. Since these settings are stored with each document, it is no longer necessary to have *XPress Preferences* or any other file available to keep these settings in document.

If a document is opened on a system containing different settings from those in the *Preferences* file, a prompt appears that asks if you want to use *XPress Preferences* only or to keep the settings in the document. If you want to keep the document as is, click on the document settings button.

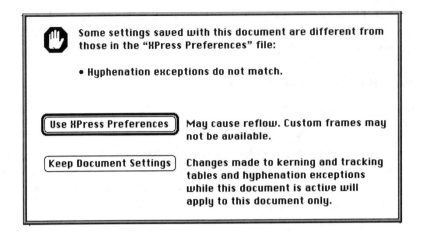

Figure 14-4 The Non-matching Preferences dialog box.

Import/Export Filter Files

In order for the formatting from word processing applications to be preserved when text is imported into QuarkXPress, you must copy the specific
import/export filter files (Figure 14-5) that come with QuarkXPress into
the same folder as the QuarkXPress program on your system.

MS-Word™ Filter   MacWrite® Filter   XPress Tags Filter   Kern/Track Editor

Figure 14-5 Import/export filter files.

Because storing import/export filters in the same folder as the
QuarkXPress program consumes System memory, it is a good idea to move
only those filters you need into the XPress Program folder.

Printer Information

QuarkXPress comes with a built-in capability of handling commonly used
printers without requiring separate Printer Description Files. When you
use File ➤ Printer, the Printer Type pop-up menu in the dialog box lets you
choose from specific models of printers, corresponding to the built-in list.
If you are printing to a PostScript device that is not included in the list,
simply choose LaserWriter.

As of this writing, the list includes LaserWriter or LaserWriter II;
Linotype Linotronic 100, 300, and 500; Dataproducts LZR2665; TI

OmniLaser 2115; Varityper VT-600, 600W, 4200B-P, and 4300P; Agfa Compugraphic P-400PS; Compugraphic 9000PS; Schlumberger 5232; Monotype; Business LaserPrinter; or QMS ColorScript.

The System Folder

Files in the System folder (Figure 14-6) that affect the printing capabilities of QuarkXPress (as well as all other applications) are printer drivers and fonts. Chapter 4 describes how to install screen fonts; Chapter 7 describes how to install printer fonts.

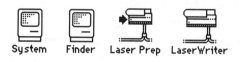

Figure 14-6 LaserWriter and Laser Prep Printer driver files (for System 6.0x, above, or System 7, below) must be in your System folder.

Other files in the System folder that can affect the performance of QuarkXPress (as well as all other applications) are initializers (INITs). INITs use up memory that might otherwise be available for applications, and QuarkXPress tends to run slower with more INITs in the System folder. INITS are loaded into the memory of your computer when you restart your system.

INITs are files that initialize the system to recognize peripheral devices such as CD-ROM drives, removable hard disk drives, and scanners. Some desk accessories are installed in the Apple menu through an INIT rather than through the Font/DA Mover. INITs include any documents in the System folder that are identified by type as a Startup document (Figure 14–7).

▯ Capture	3K	Startup document
▯ Easy Access	4K	Startup document
▯ RegisterName™ 8	2K	Startup document
▯ SFScrollInit	2K	Startup document
▯ SFVol INIT 1.5	5K	Startup document
▯ Suitcase™ II	40K	Startup document

Figure 14-7 Startup documents (INITs) consume memory.

To run QuarkXPress or any application with the maximum amount of memory, remove INITs for devices or accessories that you are not currently using from the System folder, or keep them in a subfolder within the System folder.

The Publication Folder

Before beginning the page layout process in an electronic publishing project, it is a good idea to set up a single folder on the hard disk for each document or publication, and move all of the text and graphic files into that folder. If there are very many files involved, then divide the main document folder into subfolders. Some publishers like to keep text sources in one folder and graphics elements in another. Another way of dividing the files is to put the text and graphics files related to a single chapter together in a folder, so you end up with one folder per chapter (Figure 14-8).

The publication-specific folder can also include a folder of the fonts used in the publication. Copies of these fonts can be stored in the System folder; however, if you keep a set in the publication folder, it will be easy to remember to take copies with you when you move the publication to another system to be printed.

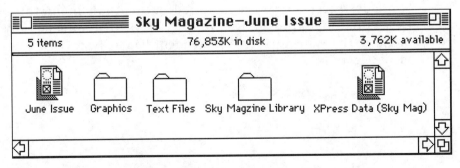

Figure 14-8 A sample project folder.

File Naming Standards

No matter how you organize your files, it is a good idea to develop logical naming conventions for them. Decide on the naming conventions you will use for all new files created during the project. The first goal is to be able to find documents easily and know what they contain. One helpful guideline is to name the different parts of the document so they appear sequentially when you view them alphabetically. For example, a chapter document might be named Chapter 1 or CH1 or 1 (Figure 14-9), but you don't want a set of documents related to one book to use different naming standards—Chapter 1, CH2, 3, 04, and so on.

Another goal is to keep the names short enough so that you can differentiate between files when you view a list in a dialog box that does not show the full file name. For example, XP01 Text can be distinguished easily from XP02 Text in the Get Text dialog box, but if you are running under System 6.0x, you won't be able to see the end of names longer than 27 characters, such as *Bantam/QuarkXPress Chapter 1* and *Bantam/QuarkXPress Chapter 2*. If you are *really* organized, you will apply naming conventions to *all* files in the project—text, graphics, and final page layouts.

To differentiate between types of files from the Desktop, you can include an indication of the file type as part of the name. If you are following the previous suggestion about making names sort alphabetically, it is a good idea to put the file type at the *end* of the file name. File type indicators might include TEMPLATE (for QuarkXPress template documents), LIBRARY (for QuarkXPress libraries), TEXT or ASCII (for imported or exported text files), or PICT, TIFF, EPS, PAINT, and the like (for imported picture files).

☐ CH 02	6K	document
☐ CH 03	5K	document
☐ CH 04	51K	document
☐ CH 05	5K	document

Figure 14-9 File naming systems.

Moving Files

If you move your QuarkXPress document from one system to another, you need to take the following additional files besides the document file itself:

- All high-resolution picture files (EPS, TIFF, and RIFF) used in the document.

- Screen fonts *and* printer fonts used in the document (or a list of fonts, so you can check that they are installed on the other system or on the hard disk drive connected to the printer). If the screen fonts are not available, the text might be reflowed when you open the document. If the printer fonts are not available, the printer might substitute other fonts when printing.

Backup Procedures

Keep a backup version of all files and back up changed files regularly. The backup system might simply be a collection of floppy disks. If you are using scanned images or very complicated illustrations, some files will probably be too big to fit on a floppy, so you will need to have a second hard disk (or a removable hard disk) in addition to the primary working hard disk.

Optimum File Size

A QuarkXPress document can be up to 2,000 pages or two gigabytes long (whichever limit is reached first), but it is more efficient to work with smaller files; long files have slower response time when redrawing pages or making text edits that carry over to subsequent pages. It's a good idea to divide a long document into individual files—divided by sections or chapters—because it is faster to work with smaller files.

If you want to be able to back your documents up onto floppy disks for storage and for transport, another important consideration in deciding how many pages a single file should have is the predicted size of the final document in bytes. You might want to keep your files under 800K for double-sided, double-density disks or under 1.4MB for high-density drives.

Build your files efficiently. Clear the Pasteboard area when you are finished using the elements on it, or when you save the final version of the document.

Organizing Libraries

QuarkXPress' library feature can be a tremendous production tool if the libraries are organized efficiently. Even though a library can contain up to 2,000 elements, it is a good idea to limit the number and keep the library file under 800K so you can copy it onto a diskette and easily move it to other systems if you are working in a geographically dispersed group.

One organization method is to create one library for each client, department, or periodical. This is a good way of distinguishing between libraries when you work on a wide variety of publications that have different design specifications and different standard graphics.

It's a good idea to assign labels to the elements in a library, using well-thought-out naming standards (since you can sort labels alphabetically, or selectively display entries with the same label, as described in Chapter 2).

Workgroup Scenario

Up to this point we have presented some general rules and guidelines for organizing disk files in a large project. The next sections present a scenario of how these ideas might be applied in workgroups.

A networked workgroup is a group of Macintosh computers, each with its own local hard disk, hooked up to a common file server through which they can share files. Network software through which Macintosh computers can share files include AppleShare, 3 COM, and Novell. Many large publications around the world have replaced their dedicated publishing systems with Macintosh computers and QuarkXPress. Many use commercially available or custom QuarkXTensions to use QuarkXPress in conjunction with dedicated publishing systems.

Quark, Inc. has announced its own workgroup products, CopyDesk and Dispatch. CopyDesk is an editing program that can be used in conjunction with QuarkXPress, and includes document management features. Dispatch is a server-based XTension that provides management and tracking capabilities for a variety of applications, including, but not limited to, QuarkXPress. You can expect to see more on these products in the 1992-1993 time frame.

The File Server

The file server in a network is a computer with a hard disk. Depending on the size of the hard disk, the file server stores the following types of files.

- The master files for the project. This includes everything described under the "Publication Folder" section earlier in this chapter. Some projects might be so large that the file server's entire hard disk is devoted to the project files.

- Other files shared among workstations, such as clip art and QuarkXPress Libraries that are not project specific.

- Printer fonts and screen fonts must be stored on the file server if printing will be spooled through the server. If printing is not spooled through the server, then each workstation must have the printer and screen fonts. In a production environment that uses many fonts, the ideal is to keep *all* printer and screen fonts on the file server and let local workstations copy only those fonts that are in use on active projects.

Quark and many other software manufacturers require that you purchase a separate software package for each workstation if you want more than one person to work with the application at a time. QuarkXPress is network-sensitive; when you start the program from any station on a network, QuarkXPress checks to see that a program with the same serial number is not already running on another station.

Individual Workstations

Individual workstations in a network often have the following types of files stored on their local hard disks.

- The project files currently in progress on that workstation. These files are copied from the file server, worked on at the local workstation, then copied back to the file server (see "Backup Procedures" described under the next section).

- Printer fonts and screen fonts that are in use on active projects. Never use the Suitcase desk accessory to load a font directly from the file server to a local workstation. Always copy fonts to the local workstation's hard disk and load the screen fonts from there, using Suitcase or Font/DA Mover.

- Applications and desk accessories that are commonly or currently used. Each station that uses QuarkXPress will also have copies of other QuarkXPress files as described earlier in this chapter.

If your workgroup shares one room, or if the project is well managed and there is good communication between group members, you should not need to take extra precautions that two people might start working on copies of the same file at once. If procedures are followed correctly and a project coordinator monitors the status of each file as work progresses, it is unlikely that someone will start working on a file that is not the latest version of that file.

However, if the group is widely dispersed in a building, if recommended procedures aren't followed, if the project is too large and the pace is too fast, if chaos reigns, then accidents can happen. By far the most efficient method of tracking the master copy of a document is through the careful attention of a project coordinator. The coordinator should maintain and post a log of each document's status, such as the one shown in Figure 14–10.

Disk File Name	Master File Start date	WIP Station ID	Date	Back to Master Date	Station #ID	WIP Date
CH01	4/1	SV	4/3	4/5	DB	4/8
CH02	4/1	SV	4/6	4/8		
CH03	4/1					

Figure 14-10 Example of a log of disk files.

Backup Procedures

The master files—or the most recently printed files that are still works in progress—are stored on the file server. When a file is to be modified, it is copied to a local workstation. Under this system, the file server is the back-up for whatever files are actively being worked on at local workstations. When the work is finished, the file is copied from the local workstation back to the file server.

If the work in progress on each workstation is going to require more than a day, then you might want each workstation to copy its works in progress back to the file server at the end of each day, to serve as interim backups. Be sure to maintain a copy of the most recently *printed* version of the documents; do not copy the work-in-progress files over the most recently printed "master" file on the file server. Instead, copy the interim versions into a separate folder, or add a suffix such as WIP (work in progress) to the file names.

When the entire project is finished, copy all files from the file server only onto diskettes or removable hard disks for storage. It is a good idea to keep copies of all disk files at least until the final document has been mass-produced and distributed. You can erase the disk files later if storage space is limited. If you are producing a newsletter or a magazine, for example, you can erase the disk files after each issue is printed.

At the end of each project, it is a good idea to collect parts of the document that can be re-used and store them as part of the template or a QuarkXPress library for use in later documents.

Summary

This chapter concludes Part II of this book, addressing advanced techniques in using QuarkXPress. Part III follows with case studies of documents created using QuarkXPress.

CASE
STUDIES

15 *Magazines and Newspapers*

This chapter begins our case studies. In this section of the book, we present several examples of companies that are using QuarkXPress to design and produce various products, some of which you see and use every day.

Many of these case studies take a look at documents that were produced using earlier versions of QuarkXPress, since most of this book was written before QuarkXPress 3.1 was released. However, the value of these case studies is not strictly to learn about commands or features of the program, but rather to look at the overall process of QuarkXPress in a publishing environment. It is hoped that these case studies will help you think about your own publishing environment in a more objective and creative way.

In this chapter we take a look at the use of QuarkXPress at two magazines, *Entertainment Weekly* and the news magazine *MacWEEK*. We also see how Tribune Media Services uses a QuarkXTension product to produce daily and weekly TV listings in the *Chicago Tribune* newspaper.

Some of the distinguishing characteristics of magazine and newspaper documents are that:

- The document is often multicolumnar, and the number of columns can change on a single page.
- The text can skip from one page to a point several pages later.
- The documents are usually produced as a series; that is, a document of the same basic format and length is produced at regular intervals.

- The documents often call for special layouts that may involve kerning headlines, wrapping text around graphics, or pasting display ads from one QuarkXPress document into another.

The following case studies explain and illustrate characteristics of documents that present their own special design and production problems and practices.

Magazine: Entertainment Weekly

Entertainment Weekly is Time Inc.'s newest offering in its internationally recognized family of magazines. Of Time Inc.'s magazine publications, which include *TIME*, *People*, and *Sports Illustrated*, *Entertainment Weekly* is the first publication to be produced completely from the desktop. (See color plate.)

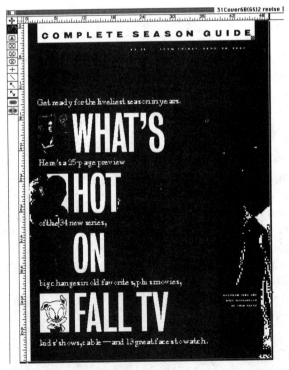

Figure 15-1 A cover for Entertainment Weekly *in QuarkXPress—the scan is for position only.*

Description

Entertainment Weekly is a standard magazine format, bound and trimmed to 8-by-10.75 inches. Basic grid structures within its pages include 4-column, 3-column, 2-column, and 2-column plus a column for captioned photos.

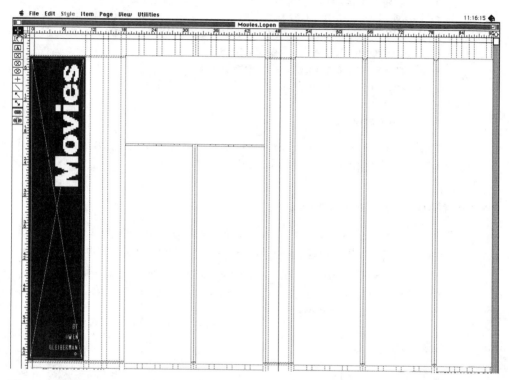

Figure 15-2 Basic grid structures are each created in documents used as templates.

Software

- QuarkXPress
- Microsoft Word
- Aldus FreeHand
- Adobe Illustrator
- Letraset ColorStudio
- Adobe, Bitstream, Monotype, and custom-made fonts

Equipment

Entertainment Weekly started its operation with complete systems for the entire staff, including:

- 70 Macintosh IIcx models with 80MB hard disks
- 14 LaserWriter II NTX printers
- 1 QMS Colorscript 100 printer
- 2 QMS PS-2200 Laser printers (handles tabloid size-paper)
- 2 Linotronic 300 with PostScript RIP 3
- Sharp color scanner (for opaque color)
- Nikon color scanner (for 35 mm slides)
- Apple Scanner
- 3Com Network

The total cost of *Entertainment Weekly's* system, including software and training, was approximately $1.3 million.

Production Steps and Tricks

Entertainment Weekly, as its name suggests, is published on a weekly basis. Briefly, steps in the design and production of each issue are as follows.

1. The text of articles can be written before or after a layout design is finished. Style Sheets are applied to the copy in Microsoft Word and in QuarkXPress.

No Style	
Capsule Grade	⇧F8
Capsule Head	⇧F6
Capsule Text	⇧F7
Capsule Title	⇧F5
Caption	F12
Caption Follow	⇧F12
Credit	F13
Credit Big	⇧F13
header	
Normal	
Notes Head	F10
R-Artist	F2
R-Genre	F3
R-Grade	F7
R-Info	F4
R-Signer	F8
R-Text Lead	⇧F2
R-Text Lead Small Caps	⇧F3
R-Text Lead Title	⇧F1
✓R-Title	F1
R-Top Initial	F5
Text	F6
Text Small Caps	⌘F6
xtra 1	⌥F1
xtra 2	⌥F2
xtra 3	⌥F3
xtra 4	⌥F4
xtra 5	⌥F5
xtra 6	⌥F6

Figure 15-3 A typical set of style sheets set up for the magazine.

2. Editing to fit is done in QuarkXPress. A template file with several different master pages is used.

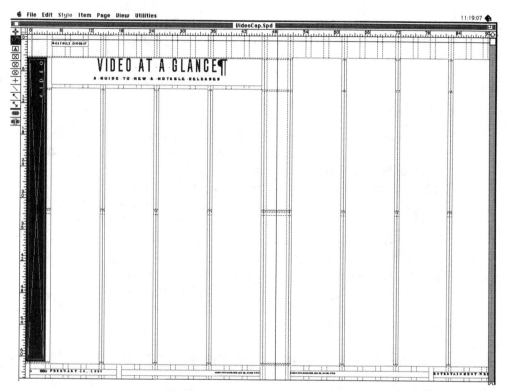

Figure 15-4 A standard document used for a regularly appearing section in the magazine.

3. Graphics are scanned in at 72 dpi and are used, in all cases, for position only. Virtually none of the final artwork, including line art, is actually produced on the Macintosh.

4. Final proofs are generated on the Linotronic 300s.

5. Once completed, the QuarkXPress files are sent to an engraver, where the artwork is removed, and the files are printed to disk as PostScript files (holding the keys ⌘-F while printing causes any Macintosh file to be printed to disk as a PostScript file). The PostScript files are then run through a Scitex VIP (Visionary Interpreter of PostScript) RIP. Photographs are scanned in high resolution on a Scitex system and electronically merged with text from the QuarkXPress files.

There are several interesting issues with this procedure. First of all, it works! Every week, *Entertainment Weekly* appears on newsstands around the country. The system used offers design director Michael Grossman far more flexibility in modifying the design than traditional systems might offer.

At least ten pages of the magazine are closed every day of the week in order to meet the weekly deadline for printing. The following headings describe just two of the many issues that arise in the successful design and production of a weekly magazine.

File Management

Since QuarkXPress does not offer the type of file management and copy-routing tools offered by high-end publishing systems, *Entertainment Weekly* had to come up with a manual system of its own.

For each story in the magazine, there is a manila file folder (the type you can buy in a stationery store); only the person who has that folder is allowed to change the file. *Entertainment Weekly* calls this manual system "conch control." (The name comes from the William Golding novel *Lord of the Flies*, in which a conch shell is used to establish protocol at meetings; only the person holding the conch shell can speak.)

Future plans include installation of P.INK Press, a publishing system that includes an SQL dataserver and a text editor front end to QuarkXPress.

Figure 15-5 A typical spread created in QuarkXPress.

Tabloid Newspaper: MacWEEK

MacWEEK is one of the prominent magazines of computer publishing giant Ziff Communications. It is one of the most successful publications devoted exclusively to news and information related to the Apple Macintosh computer and is a pioneer in publishing from the desktop. (See color plate.)

Description

MacWEEK is a weekly publication that combines a typical newspaper layout with a bound magazine format printed on glossy paper and trimmed to 10.75-by-13.5 inches. The most commonly used grid is 4 columns, though 5- and 3-column grids are also used.

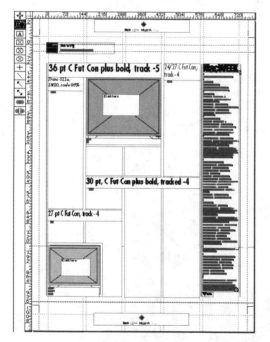

Figure 15-6 A 5-column template used to produce MacWEEK.

Software

- QuarkXPress
- Microsoft Word
- Adobe Illustrator
- Adobe Photoshop
- Fractal Design Painter
- Adobe and custom-made fonts

Equipment

MacWEEK uses the Macintosh computer throughout its operations, including sales and marketing. The magazine has approximately 70 systems installed, networked on Ethernet and local talk. The following equipment is used in the editorial, art, and production departments only.

- 35 Macintosh computers:IIse, IIcx, and IIfx models with varying storage and memory configurations from 40MB through 330MB hard disks, and 4MB RAM through 20MB RAM
- 7 Syquest removable hard drives in art and production departments
- 2 QMS colorscript 11 × 17 tabloid color printers
- 2 Linotronic imagesetters: one 300 RIP 30, one 330 RIP 40
- Kodak 520 film processor
- Leaf 45 multi-format scanner
- AVS 3000 CL Plus flatbed color scanner

Figure 15-7 A final layout of MacWEEK *done in QuarkXPress.*

Production Steps and Tricks

MacWEEK is published on a weekly basis. Briefly, steps in the design and production of each issue are as follows.

1. Advertising closes each Thursday evening. The weeks issue is dummied or laid out based on editorial percentage of the advertising total. Final page counts per section or department, such as News, Reviews, will be finalized each Friday.

2. All articles are received electronically, via diskette, modem, or in the case of staff writers, via network. Section editors read and edit according to the weekly plan. The story is formatted using a courier style that allows for accurate count of lines per article. Photographic or illustrative art is usually assigned at the beginning of the story assignment, but charts and infographics are completed on a daily deadline basis.

3. Section editors drop their section copy via network to their section teammate on the copy desk. The copy desk performs a dual role at MacWEEK; that of copy editor as well as editorial paginator.

4. Copy Desk may create the layout on the fly using QuarkXPress templates as in News, Gateways, and GA News; or build pages in QuarkXPress based on layouts designed in the art department again using the stylized templates whenever possible, as in Reviews, Product Watch, Business Watch, and special supplements. The copy desk then flows the Microsoft word stories onto the appropriate QuarkXPress template. MacWEEK is designed using an 11-point grid, and stores a body of approximately fifteen templates.

5. Art for the newspaper is digital as well, and comes to the magazine via modem, on diskette, cartridge or is scanned at the publication from 35mm, transparency, or reflectives. Art at MacWEEK could be digital screen dumps (PICT files), sample files, illustrations, photography, infographics.

6. The copy and the art once proofed by section editors, artists, etc. are dropped via network in the production art department's library at the tech stations in art/production.

7. The art will be separated, manipulated, proofed, and electronically stripped into the electronic page appropriate by the production prepress techs.

8. Once the page is electronically stripped a digital color proof will be generated. Once approved, the page is electronically sent to the Linotype imagesetters, which print negative film.

9. MacWEEK's film specs are: 2,540 resolution, 133 line screen, EDRR, with a d-max of 4.25. Film and chemistry are Kodak HNU laser film with ultratech chemistry. Film is pressed on Kodak 520 processor. A Multiple layer proof is made at MacWEEK for all full tab editorial pages (e-down) and proofed by editorial and art staff. MacWEEK uses Dupont Chromacheck proofing material.

10. All full tab editorial pages (E-down pages) and their film proofs as well as tabloid advertising and their single-layer proofs are shipped directly to the printer in Baraboo, Wisconsin. Any editorial corrections are modemed directly to press.

11. All combination editorial and advertising (pages which have edit and ads) are sent to a prep house where the ad is stripped into the e-up film produced at MacWEEK. The multiple layer proof is then made at the prep house and messengered to MacWEEK for editorial and ad approval.

Monday	*Tuesday*	*Wednesday*	*Thursday*	*Friday*
Issue produced, film shipped to printer Wed.–Fri. AM in signatures formation				Issue dummy
			Ad close	mfg. specs complete

Figure 15-8 A typical cycle for production of the magazine.

TV Paginator *for Television Schedule*

One of the most common layouts in newspapers—the typical daily television schedule—could take hours to prepare each day without the help of a special QuarkXtensions product available through Tribune Media Services, called *TV Paginator*. Newspapers that use this product to produce their television listings include the *LA Times* and the *Chicago Tribune*. The standard format for these listings as they appear in QuarkXPress is shown in Figure 15-9. This case study looks at the *Chicago Tribune*'s production of its TV listings magazine, *TV Week*.

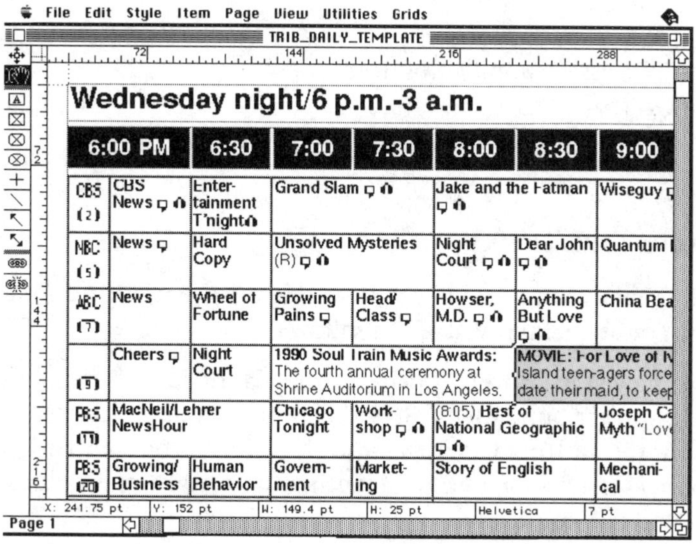

Figure 15-9 Television Schedule in the TV Paginator.

Description

The *TV Paginator*, like any XTension, is made active by simply placing it in the same folder with the QuarkXPress program. *TV Paginator* adds a Grids menu to the menu bar, which contains all the commands necessary to edit the TV listings. Television Program data from the Tribune Media Services wire is downloaded and positioned in a template using the Grids → Import Data command.

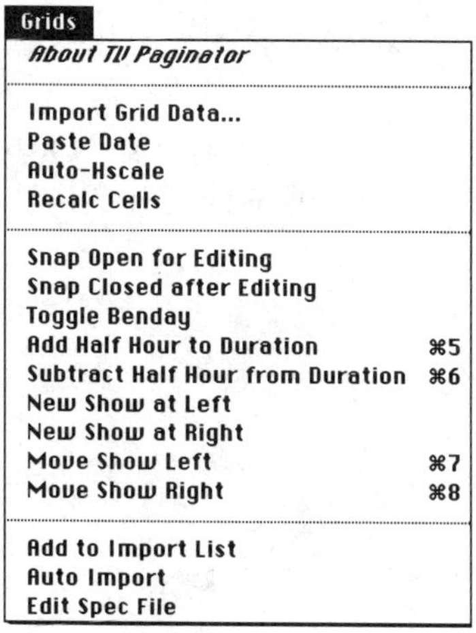

Figure 15-10 TV Paginator *adds a Grids menu to the menu bar.*

Software

- Word Processing application (optional)
- QuarkXPress
- *TV Paginator* XTension product

Production Steps and Tricks

Tribune Media Services provides a template for use with the *TV Paginator* XTension. The steps involved are as follows.

1. The television listings editor downloads the local listing information from Tribune Media Services. Imported data that has been coded for formatting will automatically fall into the standard grid set up in *TV Paginator,* and the length and position of each box is calculated automatically.

```
WEDNESDAY 3-14-90 CHICAGO DAILY
{3,10,10,20,20,20,10,20,20,10,20,30}{^CBS NEWS@ " \s}{^ENTER- TAINMENT
T'NIGHT@\s}{^GRAND SLAM@ " \s}{^JAKE AND THE FATMAN@ " \s}{^WISEGUY@ "
\s}{^NEWS@ \s}{^THE PAT SAJAK SHOW:@ COMEDIAN NORM MACDONALD. \s}{^ARSENIO
HALL:@ FARRAH FAWCETT; PHIL DONAHUE. (R) \s}{^NEWS@ (R) \s}{^NIGHT HEAT@
(R) \s}{(2:05) ^NIGHTWATCH@ \s\2 (4:00)  }<
{3,10,10,20,10,10,20,10,20,20,10,10,10,10,21}{^NEWS@ " }{^HARD COPY@
}{^UNSOLVED MYSTERIES@ (R) " \s}{^NIGHT COURT@ " \s}{^DEAR JOHN@  "
\s}{^QUANTUM LEAP@ " \s}{^NEWS@ " }{^THE TONIGHT SHOW:@ RANDY TRAVIS;
JONATHAN WINTERS. \s}{^LATE NIGHT:@ OREL HERSHISER; ALLYCE BEASLEY. (R)
\s}{^LATER W/BOB@ (R)}{^NEWS@ (R) }{^FAMILY FEUD@ }{^THE JUDGE@ }{^MOVIE:
SMASH-UP ('47)@ +++ SUSAN HAYWARD. \2 (4:30)}<
```

Figure 15-11 The television listings before they are imported into QuarkXPress.

2. Throughout the week, the updates to the listings are downloaded and edited as needed. A local service bureau outputs the final on a Linotronic 300 to positive film.

Menu selections in the *TV Paginator* let you change the length of time allotted for each program, and the length of the box and adjacent boxes adjusts automatically to any changes.

Wednesday night/6 p.m.-3 a.m.

6:00 PM	6:30	7:00	7:30	8:00	8:30
CBS (2)	CBS News ⌑ ⟰	Enter-tainment T'night⟰	Grand Slam ⌑ ⟰		Jake and the Fatman ⌑ ⟰	
NBC (5)	News ⌑	Hard Copy	Unsolved Mysteries (R) ⌑ ⟰		Night Court ⌑ ⟰	Dear John ⌑ ⟰

Wednesday night/6 p.m.-3 a.m.

6:00 PM	6:30	7:00	7:30	8:00	8:30
CBS (2)	CBS News ⌑ ⟰	Enter- tainment T'night⟰		Grand Slam ⌑ ⟰	Jake and the Fatman ⌑ ⟰	
NBC (5)	News ⌑	Hard Copy	Unsolved Mysteries (R) ⌑ ⟰		Night Court ⌑ ⟰	Dear John ⌑ ⟰

Figure 15-12 Program lengths can be adjusted by using commands such as Add Half Hour to Duration *or* Subtract Half Hour from Duration—*as was done with the program "Entertainment Tonight" in this example.*

Menu commands also let you set the box background to gray (as is commonly done to highlight movies) and set the height of boxes to accommodate multiple-line entries.

The production schedule for these listings is as follows: On Thursday, subscribing newspapers get a list of all movies from Tribune Media Services. On Friday, they get the grid information as ASCII text that has been coded for formatting through *TV Paginator*. On Monday, they get the rolling log listing (the longer program descriptions that supplement the grid summary). Between Monday and Wednesday, Tribune Media Services sends out updates to all listings. Additionally, the local stations or the networks may notify local newspaper editors of any changes. The magazine goes to the printer every Wednesday, around 7PM.

The Chicago Tribune also produces the TV listings that appear in the daily section called *Tempo*, which is printed 48 hours ahead of the day of printing the rest of the daily paper. So for example, at the end of the day Monday, the film for the Wednesday listings is sent to the printer.

Currently, black boxes are used as placeholders for ads and photos that will be stripped in at the printing company. In the future the *Chicago Tribune* plans to scan in the black-and-white photos.

Summary

The list of publications that use QuarkXPress is a long one, and we've looked at just a few. Many national publications as well as smaller, regional magazines and newspapers are finding that desktop publishing is not merely a fad, but is in fact the most efficient way to get the job done. Cost effectiveness and the ability to meet tight deadlines are only two of the reasons these publications are changing to desktop systems.

16 *Advertising, Packaging, and Corporate Identity*

Our case studies continue in this chapter, where we take a look at a different segment of the publishing world where QuarkXPress is used. We'll see how a small advertising agency in Denver, Croce Advertising, uses QuarkXPress as an integral part of its business. This chapter also examines toy manufacturing giant Mattel—we'll follow the design and production of a blister card package for *Hot Wheels* toy cars. Finally, we describe one of the many corporate identity manuals that Landor Associates created using the Macintosh and QuarkXPress.

As we mentioned in the previous chapter, the documents in the case studies reviewed were actually produced using earlier versions of QuarkXPress, since most of this book was written before QuarkXPress 3.1 was released. The value of these case studies is not strictly to learn about commands or features of the program, but rather to look at other companies that are making creative use of QuarkXPress.

Brochure by Croce Advertising

Croce Advertising, Inc., established in 1983 by Diane Croce, is a full-service marketing, advertising, and public relations firm headquartered in Denver, Colorado. Its range of services includes providing market research, direct mail campaigns, packaging, and corporate communications.

The works of Croce Advertising have been awarded several Alfie awards as well as many honors by various design and marketing associations, including the Society for Marketing Professionals, Financial Institutions Marketing Association (FIMA), and the Art Directors Club of Denver.

Croce Advertising uses QuarkXPress to produce brochures, ads, and presentations for many of its clients. In this case study we take a look at a sales brochure produced by Croce Advertising for a client in the financial industry, Alexander Management Capital Group.

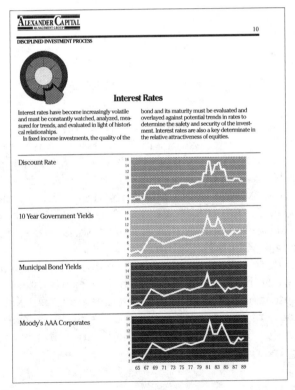

Figure 16-1 Sales brochure for Alexander Management Capital Group.

This brochure is published in 8.5-by-11-inch format, convenient for mailing in standard business envelopes, but it incorporates several design elements that require special handling—a luxury that is easily affordable when the document is short. Generally speaking, this is one of the characteristics of brochures, regardless of their size, that distinguishes them from longer documents: the importance of design as a major tool in creating an impact on the audience takes precedence over the goals of "convenience" or "efficiency" that can discourage certain design choices for longer documents.

Description

The brochure uses the same basic grid throughout, with one master page layout and a simple style sheet. The master page includes two text boxes, one for page-wide headings and one for two-column body copy. Text on each page is typed directly into the text boxes set up in QuarkXPress and edited to fit the space allowed. The Automatic Text Box option is turned off, and the text boxes are not linked on the master pages.

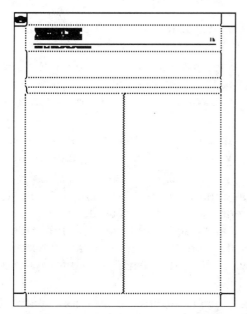

Figure 16-2 Master page elements for brochure by Croce Advertising.

Two text boxes on the master page are required in order to be able to position one-column headings over two-column body copy.

Croce Advertising reuses various parts of this piece. For example, the cover icons are now stored in a library and appear on all of Alexander Capital Management Group's publications, and the format of this brochure has been set up as a template and used for other types of documents designed for the same client.

Software

- QuarkXPress
- Adobe Illustrator
- Aldus Persuasion
- Microsoft Excel
- OmniPage

Equipment

- 1 Macintosh IIci with 80 MB hard disk
- 1 LaserWriter II NTX laser printer
- Hewlett Packard Scanjet Plus

Production Steps and Tricks

1. A QuarkXPress file was created with the default page for this document.

2. The logo for Alexander Capital Management Group in the upper lefthand corner of each page was scanned in and used for position only—it and the one or two color photos were stripped in by the printing company.

3. The pie chart–type icon in the upper lefthand corner was created in Adobe Illustrator '88, as were all the charts and graphs in this brochure.

4. All word processing was done in QuarkXPress, and a simple style sheet, with three different style sheets, was used. Other variations in text formats are handled as *No Style* and formatted through the Style menu commands. The length of the two-column text box from the master page was adjusted on each page to force the two columns to be equal length.

5. First proofs were printed on a LaserWriter printer for black-and-white proofs. Once the client reviewed the pages and changes were made, final proofs were printed on a QMS color printer.

```
┌─────────────────────────────────────────────────┐
│            Colors for Croce brochure-6-2-89       │
│ Color:                                            │
│   Black          ⇧     ┌─────────┐  ┌──────────┐ │
│   Blue                 │   New   │  │  Append  │ │
│   brochure blue        └─────────┘  └──────────┘ │
│   brochure green       ┌─────────┐  ┌──────────┐ │
│   BROCHURE RED         │   Edit  │  │ Edit Trap│ │
│   Cyan                 └─────────┘  └──────────┘ │
│   Green                ┌─────────┐  ┌──────────┐ │
│   Magenta        ⇩     │Duplicate│  │   Save   │ │
│                        └─────────┘  └──────────┘ │
│                        ┌─────────┐  ┌──────────┐ │
│                        │  Delete │  │  Cancel  │ │
│                        └─────────┘  └──────────┘ │
└─────────────────────────────────────────────────┘
```

Figure 16-3 Colors set up for the brochure.

6. The file was printed to film on a Linotronic 300 as spot color separations. The printing company said the separations were among the best they had ever seen.

Croce is one of many companies in the advertising and marketing industries around the world that has made QuarkXPress an integral part of their business.

Packaging by Mattel Toys

Mattel Toys is well known by children and adults around the world. Mattel uses QuarkXPress extensively to create a number of packages for their toys. This case study focuses on the Hot Wheels Package, which is a blister card designed by Luis Solorzano (see description below).

Figure 16-4 Blister card for Hot Wheels.

The steps described for the Hot Wheels Package are similar to those applied to other package designs by Mattel.

Description

A blister card is a standard form of packaging in which the product is mounted on a cardboard backing and shrink-wrapped. In Figure 16-4, the white boxes indicate where the Hot Wheels cars are positioned.

Software

- QuarkXPress
- Adobe Illustrator
- Aldus Freehand

Equipment

- 50 Macintosh CPUs
- 15 Mac IIfx with 19-inch color monitors,
- 5 Mac IIci
- 20 Mac SEs
- 1 QMS ColorScript printer
- 1 VT 600 B&W laser printer
- 3 LaserWriter laser printers
- 1 Howtek Scanmaster (for color transparencies)
- 1 Datacopy Flatbed 300 dpi grayscale scanner
- AppleShare file server running on LocalTalk
- Adobe fonts

Production Steps and Tricks

1. The art director prepares a rough comp by hand using markers and other traditional tools.
2. The exact specs for the size of the box are received from engineering.
3. The text that will go on the box is prepared by copy writers and stored on the file server.
4. Graphic production people review the specifications with the art director.

5. Special logos and artwork are done using Illustrator. If type on a path is required, Freehand is used.

6. The basic XPress file is created and the the text is brought in off the file server.

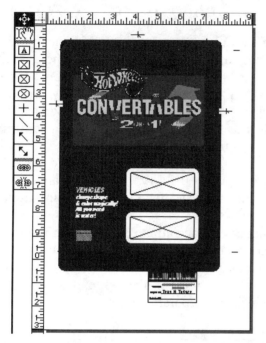

Figure 16-5 Graphic elements are brought together in QuarkXPress.

7. Proofs are created on the QMS and approved by the marketing department and art director, including color adjustments.

NOTE: Illustrator creates default line screens of 65. By using Quark's print dialog box to change the screens to 85, colors are smoother on the QMS. If there are graduated colors, banding still occurs on the QMS proof, but it is significantly reduced when the color separations are printed on a high-resolution imagesetter.

8. Final color separations are printed on film on a Linotronic 300; the printing company strips in color photographs. Alternatively, Mattel sometimes uses a Solotaire transparency maker at a service bureau that creates 16-bit color 4-x-5-inch transparencies of the full-color pages. Then the printing company makes color separations from these. These transparencies are better than film from the Linotronic imagesetter because Mattel uses printers from around the world and

each printing company can make separations optimized for its printing presses (especially overseas).

Corporate Identity Manual by Landor Associates

Landor Associates, founded by Walter Landor in 1941, is one of the largest corporate identity consulting firms in the world. Landor offices are located in 15 countries. Headquartered in San Francisco, the company has regional headquarters in New York, Tokyo, Hong Kong, Mexico City, and London. Landor Associates has developed the corporate identity programs for companies such as General Electric, Hilton International, and Japan Airlines. It developed the brand identity for many of the products we all see or use every day, including Coca-Cola, Marlboro Cigarettes (and other Phillip Morris products), Del Monte, and Pillsbury. Landor has also developed retail identities for companies such as Shell Oil, Chase Manhattan Bank, and Nissan Motors.

The CSR identity project and its accompanying manual, the subject of this case study, was created in the San Francisco office. This corporate identity manual was part of a project done by Landor Associates for the CSR Corporation of Australia. CSR hired Landor Associates to completely revamp the conglomerate's entire corporate look.

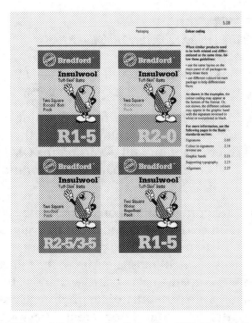

Figure 16-6 A page from the CSR Corporate Identity Manual.

Description

The CSR Corporate Identity manual was designed for the Australian standard A4 page size (8.268 by 11.693 inches), with final pages punched with four holes and inserted in a standard A4 binder (see color plate). Final pages were printed on a six-color press to accommodate full-color illustrations and photographs as well as a gray spot color ink printed as the solid background color for each page (instead of using a gray *shade* to produce a similar effect). The manual uses the same basic grid throughout, with three different master page layouts.

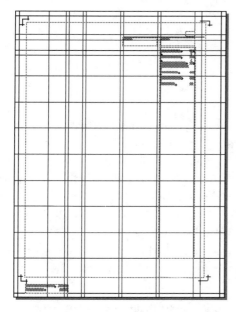

Figure 16-7 One of three different master pages used in the CSR Corporate Identity Manual.

Software

The company uses a wide variety of software packages, with the nature of each project dictating the specific software. Software used in this manual includes:

- Microsoft Word
- Adobe Illustrator
- Smart Art
- QuarkXPress

Equipment

Companywide, Landor Associates has over 300 Macintosh CPUs; each regional headquarters office has both color scanners and printers, so any job can literally be moved around the world. The San Francisco office is not only the company headquarters but is also the company's R & D center. The San Francisco office has approximately the following equipment configuration:

- 140 Macintosh CPUs
- 15 LaserWriter II NTX printers
- 7 QMS ColorScript 100 printers
- 5 color scanners
- Novell network

Production Steps and Tricks

1. The initial presentations of logo and other identity elements were created by hand. Once the client had agreed on a general direction, however, the entire project was done electronically. The first part of the project involved presenting to the client how the new identity would be handled on specific products such as packaging, stationery, vehicles, 35 mm slides, and so on. These exhibits were prepared for the client using Adobe Illustrator.

2. As the exhibits became finalized, production on the identity manual itself was begun. Text for the manual was written in Microsoft Word.

3. In QuarkXPress, a template file with different master pages was created. Each page was set up as an 11- x-17-inch page, providing room to create bleeds, crop marks, and registration marks outside the A4 (8.268-by-11.693 inches) trim size of the page.

4. The Microsoft Word text was flowed into QuarkXPress, where styles were applied. The massive collection of Illustrator files that had been used for the exhibits was assembled and named using a convention of the page number followed by the position of the page (for example, 3.5/1 or 3.5/2). This naming convention was possible because of the design of the manual, which had all graphics running essentially in a column down the left side of each page.

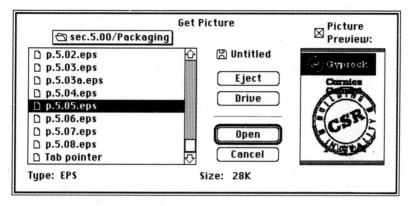

Figure 16-8 Filenaming convention for graphics files.

5. Once the manual was approved by the client, the project coordinator took the disk files to Australia, where the final film was generated using the Macintosh (except for full-color photographs, which were generated on a Scitex system) and the printing was done.

Summary

This chapter presented case studies from creative firms engaged in advertising, packaging, and corporate identity. The next chapter presents *The Official QuarkXPress 3.1 Handbook* as our final case study.

17 *How This Book Was Developed*

As our final sample document, we describe how this book was developed. You can apply the techniques used for this book to any long document, including books, manuals, and long reports. Whether you are producing a 300-page textbook, a 30-page business proposal, or a 3-page list of illustrated steps for a procedures manual, these publications share many characteristics.

For example, these publications are usually longer than the documents in the other categories presented in Chapters 15 and 16. The full publication is normally composed of several QuarkXPress files, so these types of documents are good candidates for template systems. Even though QuarkXPress can handle very large documents as a single file, dividing the material into several files still makes good sense in many cases. Chapter 14 offered tips on when and why to divide a document into several files.

The publications in this category have similar formats. These documents usually have a one-column format, although some have a second column for headings, captions, and figures. Traditionally, most business reports are single-sided documents, and manuals and books are usually double-sided documents.

Another common characteristic is size. Most business reports and many manuals are published in 8.5-by-11-inch format. Books frequently have smaller dimensions. This means you can print drafts of full pages on 8.5-

by-11-inch paper without tiling the pages (as might be required for newspaper and magazine pages).

This chapter focuses on the specific steps used in producing this book. You can apply the same production tips to any publication in this general category: long publications composed of several sections or chapters.

Description

The basic physical characteristics of this book should be obvious, in that you are presumably holding the book in your hands right now. The trim size is one of the commonly used sizes for books in the United States, and the page layout and typography were designed in part to be consistent with other books published by Bantam in this category.

The inside, black-and-white text pages of the book were produced using QuarkXPress and the supporting applications listed below. Final pages were printed as negatives on film from a Linotronic 300 typesetter. Some of the color plates were printed from color separations produced by QuarkXPress. Some of the color sample documents include pages that combined QuarkXPress page layouts with traditional photographic color separations, and the color separations for these were produced using traditional photographic methods. The cover of the book was also produced traditionally—though it could have been produced using QuarkXPress.

Software

In addition to the software listed for document samples in Chapters 15 and 16, this book was produced using:

- QuarkXPress
- Microsoft Word (for first drafts of manuscript)
- Capture (a utility for converting selected parts of a screen image into a MacPaint image in the Clipboard)
- DeskPaint (a desk accessory that lets us edit the captured screen images immediately and save them in MacPaint, TIFF, or PICT format)
- Adobe Illustrator
- Stone Serif font from Adobe

Equipment

The final production of pages for this book was handled by TechArt, Inc., in San Francisco—a typesetting and graphic design house that uses many Macintosh computers, laser printers, scanners, and a Linotronic typesetter in producing pages for a diverse range of clients. Equipment used in producing this book specifically included:

- Macintosh IIcx computers with 80MB hard disk
- LaserWriter II NTX printer for printing drafts
- QMS Colorscript 100 printer for printing proofs of color plates
- Linotronic 300 with PostScript RIP 3
- Hewlett-Packard ScanJet scanner
- AppleShare Network

File Organization

All files related to this book project were stored in a single folder on a file server, identified with a job name and number. Within that folder, the final QuarkXPress page layouts were stored in one folder, and linked TIFF and EPS files were stored in a separate folder. This organization was accommodated by the fact that the files did not need to be moved to another system for final printing as negatives. Otherwise, individual chapter folders might have been created that included the QuarkXPress file plus the linked graphics for each chapter.

One folder contained files related to the special font used throughout this book that shows small icons for the QuarkXPress tools and pointers. This font was created by Quark, Inc. The folder includes the printer font, the screen font, and references pages that show the font and the keys used for each symbol.

The Template & Library folder included the template (described next) and a library with the three icons that appear as graphics in the left margins of the pages of this book (a 3.1 icon, a shortcut icon, and an alert icon).

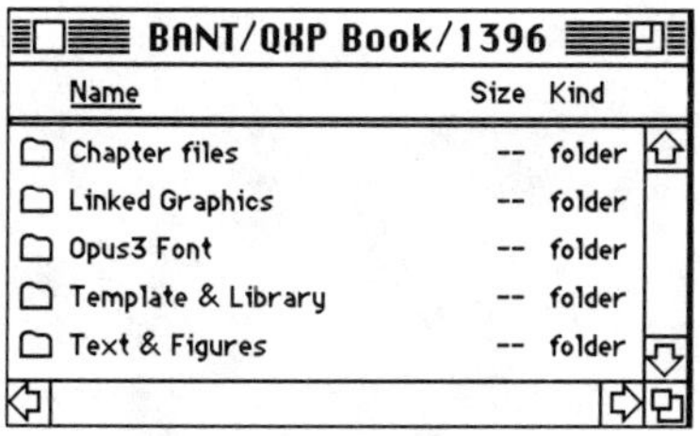

Figure 17-1 File organization for this book.

Last in the alphabetical list of folders (but first in the scheme of things) is the Text & Figures supplied by the authors. The text was originally typed in Microsoft Word, and the figures included some screen images that were cleaned up or revised before being copied to the Linked Graphics folder.

The Template, Master Pages, and Style Sheet

After the authors finished the first draft of the text and prepared a first round of figures, a chapter was created in QuarkXPress by first opening a template that had been created in QuarkXPress. The template included two master pages and two document pages: one for the opening page of the chapter (with a header line at the top of the page) and one for regular pages (with a footer line at the bottom of the page).

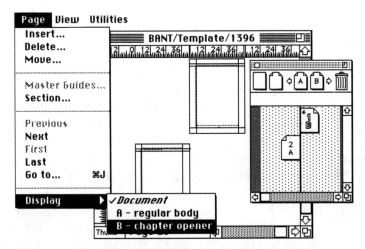

Figure 17-2 Template included two master pages and two document pages.

The style sheets were initially applied in Microsoft Word, where the drafts of the manuscript were printed in Times font. When the text was imported into the QuarkXPress template, where the same style sheet names were used, the text was converted to Stone Serif automatically.

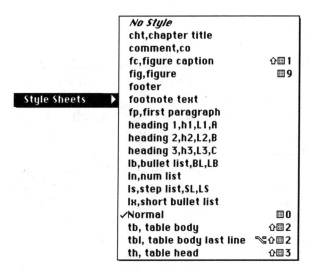

Figure 17-3 List of style sheets.

Production Steps and Tricks

Briefly, steps in the production of each chapter were as follows.

1. The text of articles was written in Microsoft Word. Styles were applied in Microsoft Word.

One trick worth noting here has to do with figure numbers in the figure captions. The figures were numbered automatically in Microsoft Word using the footnote feature. This way, if figures were added or moved during the editing cycles, the figures would be renumbered automatically. In-text references to the figure numbers were updated manually as a last step in Microsoft Word.

When a Microsoft Word file with footnotes is imported into QuarkXPress, the footnotes are renumbered to start with zero (instead of starting with one, as they did in the Word file). The workaround for this was to *add a dummy footnote at the beginning of the Word file* at the last minute, after updating all in-text references to the figures but before importing the text into QuarkXPress. Then, when the text is imported and the footnotes are changed to start with zero, the first footnote is deleted in QuarkXPress and the subsequent figure numbers are correct.

2. Figures were created using Capture and DeskPaint to create images of the screens displayed in QuarkXPress. Other figures were created using Adobe Illustrator. The authors arranged the figures in

sequential order in a QuarkXPress document that would be referenced by the production person in step 10.

Two tricks in producing the figure document are worth noting. First, the figure list, which was the same as the footnote list in Word, was copied from Word and pasted into QuarkXPress. This was done by opening the footnote window in Word, selecting and copying all of the footnotes (which showed the text of the figure captions), then opening a new QuarkXPress document and pasting the text into an automatic text box. (The footnote list per se does not come into the QuarkXPress document when you import text from Word—only the in-text figure *references*.)

The second trick was to create a picture box and use the Item ➤ Modify command to set the picture reduction to 60 percent. This picture box was then copied and pasted above each figure caption, *before* importing any figures. This way, imported images of menus and dialog boxes were uniformly reduced 60 percent, and other figures were adjusted as desired for clarity or as needed to fit the page width.

3. Text was imported into the template file in QuarkXPress.

4. The chapter title in the header and footer of the master pages was edited to match the current chapter. If the chapter number was a two-digit number, the style for the chapter title on page one was edited to change it from a one-character to a two-character drop cap. The number was selected and changed from italic to plain text, and space was added after the number by adjusting the kerning. The dummy footnote number at the beginning of the file was deleted.

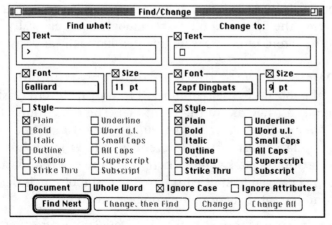

Figure 17-4 Find/Change dialog box for converting ">" to ➤.

5. A global search was performed to change the ">" character used by the authors in referencing Menu ➤ Commands to the ➤ character that you see throughout this book (Figure 17-4).

6. A global search was performed to change the word "Command" to the ⌘ character that represents the command key.

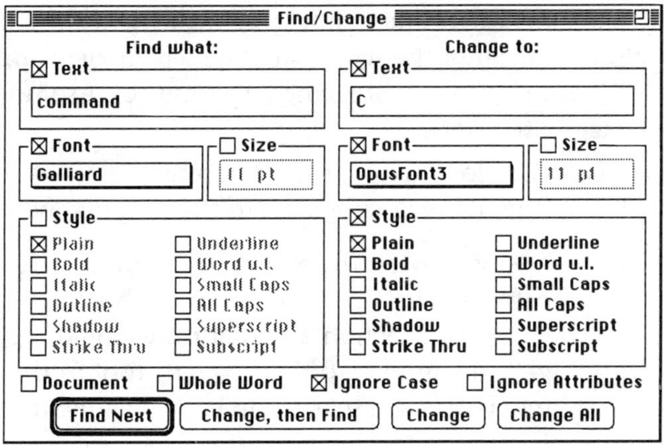

Figure 17-5 Find/Change dialog box for converting "Command" to ⌘.

7. A global search was performed to change the word "symbol" (used by the authors in referencing tool and pointer icons) to the appropriate characters.

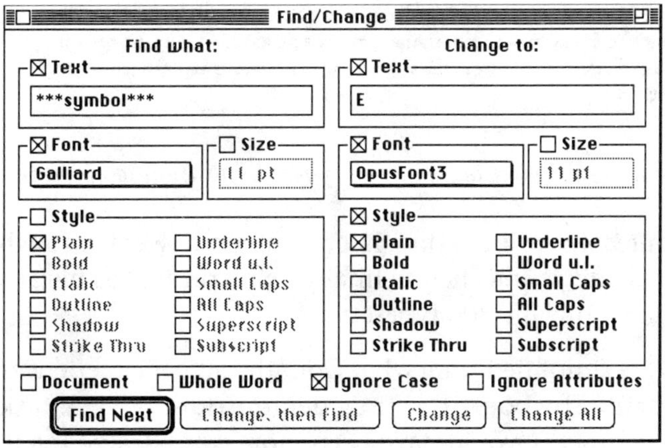

Figure 17-6 Find/Change dialog box for converting "symbol" to a special character; in this case the Content tool symbol, which is the Opus Font equivalent of the letter "E" from the keyboard.

8. The figure file supplied by the authors was opened as a second QuarkXPress document, and the two windows were arranged side by side. The library of three icons was opened and positioned at the right of the screen.

9. Starting at the beginning of the chapter, the production person used the Option-↓ keyboard shortcut to jump through the document one paragraph at a time to implement the next steps. By using Option-↓ instead of the scroll bars, the screen view jumped automatically from left to right facing pages as the cursor moved from one page to the next.

10. When the text called for a figure, the appropriate figure was copied and pasted from the figure document into the chapter document.

Copy/Paste commands were used instead of dragging the figure from one document to the other so the figure could be anchored in the text, above the caption. The toolbox selection automatically would toggle from the Item tool in the figure document to the Content tool in the chapter document, once these two tools were selected in each document.

11. When the text called for an icon in the left margin (such as the shortcut icon next to the previous paragraph), the appropriate icon was dragged from the library onto the page and the comment line in the text, calling for the icon, was deleted.

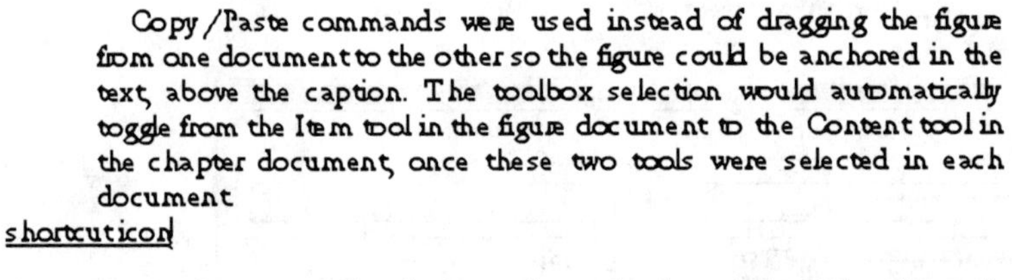

> Copy/Paste commands were used instead of dragging the figure from one document to the other so the figure could be anchored in the text, above the caption. The toolbox selection would automatically toggle from the Item tool in the figure document to the Content tool in the chapter document, once these two tools were selected in each document.
> shortcut icon

Figure 17-7 Comment line in text showed where to position icons in the margin.

12. The chapter was printed on a laser printer and went through several additional edit rounds before finally being printed as negatives on film on a Linotronic 300 typesetter.

These steps are simplified somewhat from the actual experiences of writing and producing the book, but they demonstrate the key tasks in the production. The process would have been more complicated if a file server was not available or if the files were to be transported to another system for final output. (See Chapter 14 for tips on file organization.)

Summary

Part III of of this book has presented a series of documents that demonstrate QuarkXPress' wide range of uses and helpful features for producing professional documents. No matter what equipment you may be using for final output—laser printer or typesetter—QuarkXPress guarantees high-quality output. Whether your publishing projects are large or small, QuarkXPress has the capabilities to produce high-quality published documents that just a few years ago could be produced only by professional designers and typesetters.

With QuarkXPress, professional quality is available to individuals, businesses and nonprofit, educational, and government organizations. We hope that the examples in this section of the book will get you started toward making QuarkXPress a true publishing tool.

Appendix A
Summary of Our
Favorite Tips

T hroughout this book we have offered a number of tips and shortcuts that will help you use QuarkXPress more efficiently. In this appendix, we list those tips that we feel are most important—the shortcuts we use most often. This is not an exhaustive listing of every tip and shortcut, just our favorites. Feel free to photocopy these pages and distribute them to other QuarkXPress users in your office.

General Tips

The following set-up tips relate to use of the program interface.

- Clicking through layers: if one item is covered by another, you can activate the item on the bottom by holding down the Shift-⌘-Option keys and clicking on the top item; this allows you to click through layers to the items below.

- Live dragging, rotating, resizing and cropping: if you wish to view an item and its contents as you are moving it, rotating it, resizing it, or cropping it, hold down the mouse button and pause one-half second before proceeding.

- Keyboard shortcuts for Item tool: if the Content tool is the currently selected tool, and you need to change to the Item tool in order to move an item, hold down the ⌘-key; the pointer temporarily changes to the Item tool (✛). When you release the ⌘-key, the pointer returns to the Content tool.
- Keyboard shortcuts for Zoom tool: if you need to temporarily select the Zoom tool, hold down the Control key; the pointer temporarily changes to the Zoom tool (🔍). Hold down the Option-Control keys to Zoom out (🔍)

Text Tips

The following shortcuts relate to formatting text and using typographic controls.

- Changing the font of one character: if you wish to type one character in Zapf Dingbats, hold down ⌘-Shift-Z; the next character you type will be in Zapf Dingbats. Hold down ⌘-Shift-Q to make the next character you type appear in the Symbol font.
- Keyboard shortcuts for changing text size: select the text you wish to change in size, and use the keyboard shortcuts that follow.

Style Menu Command	Measurements Palette	Keyboard Shortcut
Size	Yes	⌘-Shift-\ to specify a size
		⌘-Shift-> to enlarge selected type
		⌘-Option-Shift-> to enlarge selected type in one point increments
		⌘-Shift-< to reduce selected type
		⌘-Option-Shift-< to reduce selected type in one point increments

- Keyboard shortcuts for changing font style: use the shortcuts that follow to change the style of selected text.

Style Menu Command	Measurements Palette	Keyboard Shortcut
Type Style	Yes	various: ⌘-Shift-B = Bold ⌘-Shift-H = Small Caps ⌘-Shift-I = Italic ⌘-Shift-K = All Caps ⌘-Shift-O = Outline ⌘-Shift-P = Plain ⌘-Shift-S = Shadow ⌘-Shift-U = Underline ⌘-Shift-W = Word Underline ⌘-Shift-+ = Superscript ⌘-Shift-Hyphen = Subscript ⌘-Shift-/ = Strike Through ⌘-Shift-V = Superior

- Keyboard shortcuts for tracking and kerning: to kern two letters, if you wish to tighten the space between two letters, click once between them, and hold down the ⌘-Shift-{ keys to tighten spacing in $^{10}/_{200}$th-em increments; hold down the .⌘-Option-Shift-{ keys to tighten spacing in $^{1}/_{200}$th-em increments. To increase the space between letters, hold down the ⌘-Shift-} keys to increase spacing in $^{10}/_{200}$th-em increments; hold down the .⌘-Option-Shift-} keys to increase spacing in $^{1}/_{200}$th-em increments. Select a group of letters to change tracking values.

Graphics Tips

The following tips relate to working with graphics created in other programs and imported into QuarkXPress.

- Fitting graphics in a picture box: if you wish to scale a graphic to fit into a picture box and maintain its proportions, select the graphic with the Content tool, then press down the ⌘-Shift-Option-F keys.

- Keyboard shortcuts for scaling graphics: you can scale a graphic in 5% increments by selecting the graphic with the Content tool, then press ⌘-Shift-< to reduce the graphic in 5% increments; press ⌘-Shift-> to enlarge the graphic in 5% increments.

Appendix B
International Versions of
QuarkXPress

QuarkXPress is a truly international product. The program is available in 13 different international versions, listed below.

German

Available from

- **Prisma Computertechnologie Handelsgesellschaft mbH.**
Wandsbeker Zollstraße 87-89, D-2000 Hamburg 70, Germany

- **SWIP Handels AG**
Bahnhofstraße 9, CH-8153 Rümlang, Zürich, Switzerland
Fax: 41-1817-1120, Tel.: 41-1817-0717, Applelink: CH0117

- **Hard &Soft,**
Zirkusgasse 13, A-1020 Wien, Austria
Fax: 43-222-216-0793, Tel: 43-222-216-0790, Applelink: AU0002

Operating System required: German, Swiss German System 6.05
or higher
Operating System available from: Apple Computer Germany, Switzerland
QuarkXPress version 3.0; features German hyphenation

French

Available from:
- **P. Ingénierie**
  19-21 Rue de 8 Mai 1945, F-94117 Arcueil Cedex, France
  Fax: 33-1-47-40-81-72, Tel: 33-1-47-40-40-00, Applelink:X1230.

- **Softkey Benelux**
  Santvoortbeeklaan 21-23, B-2100 Antwerp, Belgium
  Fax: 32-3-360-0466, Tel: 32-3-360-0460, Applelink: BEL0077

- **SWIP Handels AG**
  Bahnhofstraße 9, CH-8153 Rümlang, Zürich, Switzerland
  Fax: 41-1817-1120, Tel.: 41-1817-0717, Applelink: CH0117

Operating System required: French, Swiss French System 6.05 or higher
Operating System available from: Apple Computer France, Switzerland
QuarkXPress version 3.0; features French hyphenation

Dutch

Available from:
- **Softkey Ltd.**
  Gedempte Gracht 6, Postbus 705, NL-7400 AS Deventer, Holland
  Fax: 31-5700-44-388, Tel. 31-5700-48-666, Applelink: HOL0123

- **Softkey Benelux**
  Santvoortbeeklaan 21-23, B-2100 Antwerp, Belgium
  Fax: 32-3-360-0466, Tel: 32-3-360-0460, Applelink: BEL0077

Operating System required: Dutch System 6.05 or higher
Operating System available from: Apple Computer Holland
QuarkXPress version 3.0; features Dutch hyphenation

Danish

Available from:
- **InterMac Distribution a/s**
  Egebaekvej 98, DK-2850 Naerum, Denmark
  Fax: 454-280-0645, Tel.: 454-280-0422, Applelink: DK0009

Operating System required: Danish System 6.05 or higher
Operating System available from: Apple Computer Denmark
QuarkXPress version 3.0; features Danish hyphenation

Norwegian

Available from:

- **Software Plus A/S**
  Nydalen Park, Gjerdrums vei 10D., N-0486 Oslo 4, Norway
  Fax: 47-2-18-37-16, Tel. 47-2-39-46-96, Applelink: NOR0029

Operating System required: Norwegian System 6.05 or higher
Operating System available from: Apple Computer Norway
QuarkXPress version 3.0; features Norwegian hyphenation

Swedish

Available from:

- **Software Plus AB**
  Lindovagen 65, S-60002 Norrköping, Sweden
  Fax: 46-11-12-71-50, Tel. 46-11-18-12-70, Applelink: SW0059

Operating System required: Swedish System 6.05 or higher
Operating System available from: Apple Computer Sweden
QuarkXPress version 3.0; features Swedish hyphenation

Finnish

Available from:

- **Acom Oy**
  Hannuksentle 1, SF-02270 Espoo, Finland
  Fax: 358-0-804-1660, Tel. 358-0-804-1600, Applelink: SF0005

Operating System required: Finnish System 6.05 or higher
Operating System available from: Apple Computer
QuarkXPress version 3.0

Spanish

Available from:

- **P. Ingenierie España S.A**
  Castello, 82 6o Izquierda, E-28006 Madrid, Spain   ·
  Fax: 341-411-7567, Tel. 341-5645-694, Applelink: SPA0076

Operating System required: Spanish System 6.05 or higher
Operating System available from: Apple Computer Spain
QuarkXPress version 3.0; features Spanish hyphenation

Italian

Available from:

- **Delta s.r.l.**
  Viale Aguggiari 77, I-21100 Varese, Italy
  Fax: 39-332-239-873, Tel. 39-332-236-336, Applelink: ITA0058

Operating System required: Italian System 6.05 or higher
Operating System available from: Apple Computer Italy
QuarkXPress version 3.0; features Italian hyphenation

Greek

Available from:

- **S.G. Zarganes ('Telesis')**
  44 Mitropoleos St., H-54623 Thessaloniki, Greece
  Fax: 303-1-281249, Tel. 303-1-263165

Operating System required: Greek
Operating System available from: Apple Computer
QuarkXPress version 3.0; features Greek hyphenation

Korean

Available from:

- **Elex Computer Inc**
  27-2 Yoido Dong, Youngdeungpo-ku, Seoul, South Korea
  Fax: 822-785-4838, Tel. 822-783-0401, Applelink: IT0103.

Operating System required: Korean
Operating System available from: Apple Computer
QuarkXPress version 3.0

Japanese

Available from:

- **SystemSoft Corp**
  3-10-30 Soft Building, Tenjin, Chuo-ku, Fukuoka 810, Japan.
  Fax: 81-92-752-3902, Tel. 81-92-732-1547, Applelink: X1276

Operating System required: KanjiTalk 6.03
Operating System available from: Apple Computer Japan
Version of QuarkXPress: 3.1J (available Q2, 1992); features input and output of double-byte Kanji characters, Katakana, Hiragana, and Romanji characters, vertical text handling

International English

Available from:

- **Computers Unlimited**
  2, The Business Centre, Colindeep Lane,
  London NW9 6DU, England, U.K.
  Fax: 01-200-3788, Tel. 01-200-8282, Applelink UK0018.

- **Laser Peripherals(NSW) Pty.**
  P.O. Box 105, Roseville NSW 2069, Australia
  Fax: 61-2-406-4383, Tel. 61-2-406-0344, Applelink: AUST0237.

International English is also sold in all other countries Quark ships to.

Operating System required: International English
Operating System available from: Apple Computer
QuarkXPress version 3.1; features European defaults

Appendix C
Quark XTensions

QuarkXTensions is a programmer's toolkit for creating customized modules for extending the capabilities of the QuarkXPress program. Extensions are produced using THINK's LightspeedC development environment. *Inside QuarkXPress*, the official Quark guide to programming extensions, shows programmers how to create software code that extends the capabilities of QuarkXPress.

Once the extension code has been developed, it is simply placed inside the same folder as the QuarkXPress program. When the program is opened, the extensions are automatically integrated and can be used as part of the program itself.

More than 200 different developers around the world are working with Quark to develop custom applications. The following is a partial list of available QuarkXTension products. Please note that all prices listed are U.S. dollars.

For additional information on XTention products, please contact Quark, Inc. in Denver, or contact Quark's authorized XTension distributor, XChange, at (800) 788-7557.

Agfa-Compugraphic GS/BIS

Prod. Mgr. Focus Scanners
80 Industrial Way
Wilmington, MA 01887 USA
(508) 658-5600

Agfa-Gevaert N.V. EPS/BIS
Prod. Mgr. Focus Scanners
SepteStraat 27
B-2640 Mortsel Belgium
(32) 3-444-3936

- Agfa XPressScan
  Agfa XPressScan is a scanner XTension that allows scanning with the
  Agfa ACS 100 and Focus scanners from inside QuarkXPress.
  Suggested Retail Price: $550

Baseview Products Inc.

P.O. Box 368
Dexter, MI 48130
(313) 426-5751
Fax (313) 426-0240

- ClassManager
  This Xtension is a full-featured classified-ad package that includes
  ad-taking, administration, and accounts receivable functions.
  Suggested Retail Price: one user, $2,495; each additional user, $495
- CommLink
  CommLink is a communications package that lets Macs accept text
  files from remote computers without operator intervention.
  Suggested Retail Price: $250
- NewsEdit
  NewsEdit is a multi-user editing and copy management XTension for
  newspapers.
  Suggested Retail Price: $349
- QSpool
  QSpool is a typesetter spooler.
  Suggested Retail Price: $495
- WireManager
  WireManager adds a wire capture function for newspapers.
  Suggested Retail Price: $1,895

Compumation, Inc.

820 N. University Dr.
State College, PA 16803
(814) 238-2120
(814) 234-6864 fax

- BureauExpress
  BureauExpress is FreeWare which eliminates the problems with file
  creation and modem transmission to the local service bureau.
  Suggested Retail Price: FREE from most BBSs and service bureaus

Computer Friends, Inc.

14250 NW Science Pk. Dr.
Portland, OR 97229
(503) 626-2291
(503) 643-5379 fax
AppleLink D0438

- ColorSnap 32+
  The ColorSnap 32+ XTension allows you to import high quality col-
  or images directly into your QuarkXPress documents from video
  cameras, VCRs, laser disks, television monitors (CNN shots, for
  example), or the new still video cameras and players from Canon,
  Sony and others.
  Suggested Retail Price: $995

DKA Inc.

1010 Turquoise Street, Suite 310
San Diego, CA 92109
(619) 488-8118
(619) 488-4021 fax
AppleLink D2018

- PALOS
  PALOS is a QuarkXPress workgroup publishing system for automat-
  ing the layout of magazines and catalogs.
  Suggested Retail Price: one user, $6,500; each additional user,
  $4,500; site license available

Em Software, Inc.

P.O. Box 402
Westbrook, CT 06498
(203) 399-8472

- Xdata
  Xdata is a sophisticated database publishing facility for QuarkXPress 3.0 that automates the production of catalogues, mailing lists, form letters, labels, or any repetitive publishing task. Supports the major Macintosh database and spreadsheet export formats.
  Suggested Retail Price: $149.95

- Xtable
  Xtable is a powerful, intuitive, fully integrated table editing facility for QuarkXPress 3.0 that automates the most tedious aspects of table creation and editing. Supports the major Macintosh database and spreadsheet export formats.
  Suggested Retail Price: $169.95

- Xstyle
  Xstyle adds to the power of QuarkXPress style sheets and text properties.
  Suggested Retail Price: $39

K. Erf Associates

28 Duck Pond Rd.
Weare, NH 03281
(603) 529-2512

- Autopage
  Autopage provides professional quality automated page makeup capabilities; it supports pagination for books, manuals, textbooks, technical documentation, and technical journals. Autopage also aids in placement of art, table, and footnotes.
  Suggested Retail Price: $5,000 for pagination application; $100 per workstation for the XTension

John Juliano Computer Services Co.

570 Fidelity National Bank Building
Decatur, GA 30030
(404) 373-8411
Fax (404) 633-9720

- Atan EXPRESS
Atan EXPRESS imports stories which have been prepared using Atex front-end system, allowing the user to see a WYSIWYG version of the Atex story. All Atex formats, variables, events and conditionals supported. Atan EXPRESS will also export any QuarkXPress story into ATEX markup.
Suggested Retail Price: $20,000 site license

- TMS EXPRESS
TMS Express imports stories which have been prepared on TMS-11 and EMS-11 systems. TMS markup is executed in the course of importing the story to QuarkXPress. TMS EXPRESS will also export any QuarkXPress story into TMS-11 markup.
Suggested Retail Price: $23,000 site license

David King & Associates

1010 Turquoise St., Suite 200
San Diego, CA 92109
(619) 488-8118

- Palos
Palos (Photo ad layout system) functions as an automated picture publishing database.
Suggested Retail Price: one user, $6,500; each additional user, $4,500

Liberty Engraving Co.

1112 S. Wabash Ave.
Chicago, IL 60605
(312) 786-0600
(312) 786-0621 fax
AppleLink V0617

- Grids&Guides
Grids&Guides offers a simple, precise, and versatile solution to these
and other guideline related problems. Two Utility menu additions
give you dialog box access to various guideline data.
Suggested Retail Price: $49.95

a lowly apprentice production

2504 Navarra Drive, Suite 201
La Costa, CA 92008

- Default Settings
Default Settings is Shareware Tension that allows you to customize
your version of Quark XPress to your liking, allowing you to control
the appearance of your windows, palettes, and dialog boxes as well
as guide colors. You can also customize the way QuarkXPress handles the display of TIFF images on screen—control the resolution, as
well as the number of levels of gray displayed.
Suggested Retail Price: $20

Managing Editor Software Inc.

8208 Brookside Road
Elkins Park, PA 19117
(215) 635-5074

- Page Director
  This XTension dummies a publication, controls configurations for color press setup, and generates reports.
  Suggested Retail Price: $895

- Ad Director
  Ad Director provides an automated advertising control and dummying system.

Mycro-Tek, Inc.

9229 E. 37th Street North
Wichita, KS 67226
(316) 636-5000
Fax: (316) 636-5007

- Mycro-Comp PAGE
  Mycro-Comp PAGE improves the speed of layout and design for editorial and classified sections. Among its capabilities: automatically inserts formattable jump text, maintains a list of unresolved jumps, handles automatic square-offs of multiple columns of text and paginates classified pages front-to-back or back-to-front with repeated auto-headers.
  Suggested Retail Price: $4,595

Nocturnal Creations

CompuServe 72717,2122
America Online Dave Batton

- Sounds
  Sounds is a program that adds sound to a variety of QuarkXPress functions, such as Startup, Quit, New Document, and Print.
  Suggested Retail Price: Free

North Atlantic Publishing Systems Inc.

P.O. Box 682
Carlisle, MA 01741
(508) 250-8080
Fax (508) 250-8179

- CopyFlow 2.3
  CopyFlow gives QuarkXPress the capability of automatic batch import and export of text and graphic files.
  Suggested Retail Price: $395

- CopyBridge
  This accessory to CopyFlow (see below) allows QuarkXPress import, export, and translate XyWrite files, communicating typographic and fit information between systems.
  Suggested Retail Price: $1,500

- CopyFlow Reports
  This accessory to CopyFlow (see above) generates reports on the status of files included in a QuarkXPress document, aiding in project management.
  Suggested Retail Price: $225

- Overset
  This XTension creates temporary text boxes to allow the user to view overset copy.
  Suggested Retail Price: $69

P.INK Software

Time & Life Building
1271 Sixth Avenue, 21st floor
New York, NY 10020
(212) 522-PINK
(212) 522-0414 fax

- P.INK Press
  P.INK Press adds workgroup management and tracking features to QuarkXPress and includes applications for administration, statistics, word processing and advertising management.

Press Computer Systems

James House
Rookery St., Wednesfield
Wolverhampton
England WV11 1UP
(902) 727 272
Fax (902) 734 563

- AdLinker
- EdLinker
- ClassLinker
These three XTensions provide a link between PCS's DEC-based Press 11/1100 advertisement booking system and its Mac-based pagination system running QuarkXPress. AdLinker handles display advertisements; EdLinker works with page layout; and ClassLinker manages classified ads.

Pre-Press Technologies Inc.

2443 Impala Drive
Carlsbad, CA 92008
(619) 931-2695

- SpectreSeps QX
SpectreSeps QX does continuous-tone color separations of XPress documents.
Suggested Retail Price: $295
- SpectreScan QX
This XTension allows direct imaging scanning from within QuarkXPress.
Suggested Retail Price: $295

Professional Computer

23 Summit Square
Langhorne, PA 19047
(215) 860-5200
(215) 860-2646 fax
AppleLink M526

- A Step and Repeat software XTension
  A Step and Repeat software XTension designed specifically for
  Flexography Printers. Professional PrePress Center, a division of PSTI,
  Inc., designs, sells, and supports prepress system for printers. This
  software is designed for Label, Tag, and Flexo printers and has fea-
  tured only in high-end dedicated platforms.
  Suggested Retail Price: $1,499

Publishing Technologies Nederland bv

P.O. Box 61
3700 AB Zeist
The Netherlands
(31) 3404-60044
Fax (31) 3404-58420

- The Puzzler
  The Puzzler XTension is a tool for designing crossword puzzles inter-
  actively.

- Word Perfect Xtension

- Word Perfect 5.0 Xtension

- Wang WP/PC Xtension
  With these three filter XTensions it is possible to import directly the
  MS-DOS versions of the documents into QuarkXPress. All of the fil-
  ters automatically convert the European and extended character set.
  It is also possible to include tags directly in your word processor doc-
  ument.

Reseaux

Porte de l'Arénas—Hall C
455, Promenade des Anglais
06300—Nice, France
(33) 93 18 73 33
(33) 93 83 35 51 fax
AppleLink RESEAUX

- ALIAS
ALIAS is a customizable typographic correction tool which adds multiple "search and replace" capabilities to QuarkXPress.
Suggested Retail Price: $65

- INFO
INFO compiles a whole set of otherwise unavailable (or too lengthy to attain) information about text boxes, picture boxes, document styles, HJs, and colors.
Suggested Retail Price: $65

- VideoCode
The VideoCode XTension—and its companion Postscript font—allows easy entry of "2/5 interlaced" code bar data to program video recorders.
Suggested Retail Price: $110

Software Consulting Services

3162 Bath Pike
Nazareth, PA 18064
(215) 837-8484

- SCS/LinX
This XTension is a link to Software Consulting Services' editorial and dummying systems; SCS/LinX allows QuarkXPress to read page dummies created by Layout-8000 and to import copy from the SCS-8000 editorial system.
Suggested Retail Price: $2,750

Synaptic Electronic Publishing

215 South St.
Excelsior Springs, MO 64024
(816) 637-7233

- NewsLink
  NewsLink allows QuarkXPress to import copy from Synaptic's PC-based editorial program for newspapers.
  Suggested Retail Price: $500

- ClassAdLink
  ClassAdLink enables QuarkXPress to import copy from Synaptic's PC-based classified ad program for newspapers.
  Suggested Retail Price: $500

- PhotoLink
  This XTension allows QuarkXPress to import data from Synaptic's PC-based wire Teknavia photo management program for newspapers.
  Suggested Retail Price: $500

- AdLink
  AdLink lets QuarkXPress to import data from Synaptic's PC-based ad scheduling program for newspapers.
  Suggested Retail Price: $500

- ArtBoard Pro
  This XTension is used for display ad makeup.
  Suggested Retail Price: $795

Virginia Systems, Inc.

5509 West Bay Court
Midlothian, VA 23112
(804) 739-3200

- Sonar Professional
  Sonar Professional is a high-speed text retrieval system with advanced text analysis, indexing capabilities, and search speeds over 10,000 pages per second.
  Suggested Retail Price: $795

- Sonar Bookends
  With Sonar Bookends one can easily make a professional index and table of contents for QuarkXPress documents in a matter of minutes. Words and/or phrases are automatically indexed and formatting is flexible.
  Suggested Retail Price: $129.95

Index

A

About QuarkXPress, 31–32
absolute leading, 205
absolute page sequence, 122–123
Accurate Blends option, 142
Accurate Screens, Adobe, 433
Actual Size, 67
Adobe Accurate Screens, 433
Adobe's Font Downloader, 293
Adobe Illustrator, 241, 243–245
    color separating, 446–451
Adobe Photoshop, 241, 430,
    449–451
    color separating, 446–451
Adobe Type Manager, 141, 198
advertising, 481–491
Aldus FreeHand, 241–245
    color separating, 446–451
alias icon, 30
alignment
    bar charts, 416–417
    icons, 166–167
    items, 95
    keyboard shortcuts, 166–167
    organization charts, 418–421
    paragraph, 166–167
    Space/Align command, 331
    tips, 328–331
    vertical, 208
Align On tab characters, 171
all caps, 379
anchored boxes, 336–338
anchored items, 35
    deleting, 101
    moving, 101
anchored picture, Measurements
    palette, 101
Anchored Picture Specifications
    dialog box, 100–101
anchored text, Measurements
    palette, 101
anchoring text and graphics,
    99–101

Anchored Text Specifications
    dialog box, 100
angle, box, 78–79
apostrophes, converting , 153
Append Colors dialog box, 286
Append H&Js dialog box, 215
Append Style Sheets dialog box,
    181
Apple menu, 27
Apple>Chooser, 268–269
AppleShare, 461–463
AppleTalk, 268
Application Preferences dialog box,
    132–136, 445
    trapping, 440–441
ascent height, 199
    relative to baseline, 206–207
ASCII text import, 156
    from databases and
        mainframes, 353–375
    tag codes, 84, 363–375
ATM—see Adobe Type Manager
Auto Constrain option, 103, 143
auto hyphenation, 212
auto image, text runaround mode,
    91–92
Auto Kern Above preferences, 201
auto leading formula, 200
Auto Library Save option, 136
automatic runaround, 345–347
automatic text box, 35, 57–58, 64,
    71, 97–99, 114
    adding pages, 121–123
    creating, 116
    multiple master pages, 318–319
    page size changes, 60
    removing, 115
    width calculation, 313–314
automatic text chain, 97–99
automatic trapping, 440–441
Auto Page Insertion, 85, 96–99,
    121–123, 138

Auto Picture Import option,
    139–140
Auxiliary Dictionary dialog box,
    190–192

B

background color, 256, 442–443
Backspace key—see Delete key
back slash, search, 184
backup procedures, 460
    workgroups, 463
backward, moving in layers, 95
balloon help, 31–32
balloons, cartooning, 409–411
banding, on screen, 142
bar charts, 411–416
based on style sheet, 178
baseline
    first, 206–207
    superscript/subscript, 199
baseline grid, 200, 207–208
    viewing, 68–69
Baseline Shift command and dialog
    box, 209
    anchored items, 100
    keyboard shortcuts, 209
binding edge, 62
bitmap graphics, 86, 241–242
bitmap printing, faster, 272
black boxes, 402–403
blank pages, 45, 339–342
    printing, 277
bleed, 63, 343–344
blending colors, 290–292
    on screen display, 142
blister card, 485–488
blue lines, 307
book, case study, 493–501
border—see frame
bounding box, polygon, 234